Palgrave Studies in Economic History

Series Editor
Kent Deng, London School of Economics, London, UK

Palgrave Studies in Economic History is designed to illuminate and enrich our understanding of economies and economic phenomena of the past. The series covers a vast range of topics including financial history, labour history, development economics, commercialisation, urbanisation, industrialisation, modernisation, globalisation, and changes in world economic orders.

Charles Read

Calming the Storms

The Carry Trade, the Banking School and British Financial Crises Since 1825

palgrave
macmillan

Charles Read
University of Cambridge
Cambridge, UK

ISSN 2662-6497 ISSN 2662-6500 (electronic)
Palgrave Studies in Economic History
ISBN 978-3-031-11913-2 ISBN 978-3-031-11914-9 (eBook)
https://doi.org/10.1007/978-3-031-11914-9

Cover credit: Princeton University Library/Charles Read

This Palgrave Macmillan imprint is published by the registered company Springer Nature Switzerland AG
The registered company address is: Gewerbestrasse 11, 6330 Cham, Switzerland

Frontispiece: The Overstone Cycle of Trade from The Money Bag, 1858 vol., between p. 112 and p. 113, fold out. The cartoon gives the Banking School's point of view and is actually a criticism of the Currency School (Princeton University Library)

Acknowledgements

The research presented in this book would not have been possible without the help of a large number of individuals and institutions, to whom I am extremely grateful. First of all, I would like to thank the British Academy for the award of a post-doctoral fellowship (PF2\180089), which funded the research in this book as part of a larger project entitled 'The causes and consequences of financial crises in the United Kingdom of Great Britain and Ireland, c.1801–1922'. Their support of my academic career through its post-Ph.D. stage has been invaluable.

My introduction to the crises of 1847 occurred during my doctoral research completed at the University of Cambridge for a thesis entitled 'British Economic Policy and Ireland, c.1841–1853' (2016). I would like to thank the Arts and Humanities Research Council of the United Kingdom for funding my doctoral work and to Eugenio Biagini and Martin Daunton for supervising it. The thesis reassessed the short-term causes and consequences of the financial crises in the City of London in 1847 and the impact they had on Ireland during its Great Famine, which was little understood in the academic literature up to that point. It was as I was finishing off my Ph.D. project that I realised the insights I drew about the crises of 1847 could also be applied more widely over the past 200 years of British financial history, sparking the genesis of this project.

I would like to acknowledge those institutions that have hosted my post-doctoral research and that allowed me to develop my ideas about the causes of financial crises in the United Kingdom. In particular, I would like to thank Roy Foster and the Principal and Fellows of Hertford College, Oxford, for electing me to the Irish Government Senior Scholarship there; the Master and Fellows of Fitzwilliam College, Cambridge, for electing me for a year as a bye-fellow; and the Master and Fellows of Corpus Christi College, Cambridge, for electing me to a fellowship and college lectureship in history. I wrote and redrafted substantial sections of this book living in Corpus during the lockdowns resulting from the covid-19 pandemic and I would like to thank those colleagues who kept my spirits up during that period, in person or online, particularly: Christopher Andrew, Marina Frasca-Spada, Andrew Harvey, John Hatcher, Philippa Hoskin, Shruti Kapila, Christopher Kelly, Peter Martland, Amar Sohal, Emma Spary, Michael Sutherland and Samuel Zeitlin. I would also like to thank my early-career comrades-in-arms for their moral support during the research and writing phases of this book, including but not limited to: Robin Adams, Eriko Padron-Regalado, Brian Varian and Lewis Willcocks.

I would like to thank all those who have helped with the research, writing and publication of this book, too numerous in number to mention all by name. Nevertheless, I would especially like to thank Kent Deng and my editors at Palgrave for including this volume in the Palgrave Studies in Economic History series. I would also like to thank those who attended papers I gave based on earlier versions of this research for their generous and useful feedback at the 'State, economy and society' conference at Churchill College, Cambridge in 2016, the Oxford Irish History Seminar at Hertford College, a workshop on the Bubble Act hosted by D'Maris Coffman and Helen Paul, and several Economic History Society annual conferences. My immense appreciation goes to Eugenio and Martin for reading many draft sections of this project over the past few years and to Rui Esteves, Aaron Graham, Sara Horrell, Harold James, Doug Kanter, Eoin McLaughlin, Duncan Needham, Kevin O'Rourke, Robin Pearson, George Peden, William Quinn, Sabine Schneider, Peter Solar and Solomos Solomou for useful support, feedback and research leads at critical moments in this project's gestation. All remaining errors nonetheless remain my own.

Finally, but most of all, I would like to thank my parents, Simon and Karin Read, for all their love and support, and without whom this project would never have seen the light of day. This book is dedicated to them.

Corpus Christi College, Cambridge

May 2022 Charles Read

Contents

Abbreviations

B.L.	London: British Library
CUP	Cambridge University Press
N.A.	Kew: National Archives
OUP	Oxford University Press
PP	Parliamentary Paper
UL	University Library
UP	University Press

List of Figures

List of Tables

CHAPTER 1

Introduction

> But this long run is a misleading guide to current affairs. In the long run we are all dead. Economists set themselves too easy, too useless a task if in tempestuous seasons they can only tell us that when the storm is past the ocean is flat again.
>
> —J. M. Keynes, 'A Tract on Monetary Reform' in *Collected Writings of John Maynard Keynes*, IV (Cambridge: CUP, 2013) p. 65.[1]

The quotation from John Maynard Keynes' *A Tract on Monetary Reform* (1923), that 'in the long run we are all dead', is probably the most misunderstood in economics. It is often naively assumed to be a *carpe diem* defence of Keynesian deficit financing during a downturn. That is, 'care about the recession we're in now, rather than about the long-term cost of borrowing'; or 'recklessly enjoy the present and let the future go hang'.[2]

However, here Keynes was not referring to deficit financing, discussion of which was to come later in another book, *The General Theory of Employment, Interest and Money* (1936).[3] Instead he was commenting upon the limitations of the quantity theory of money, the abstract idea that the general price level in an economy is directly proportional to either the amount of money in existence or circulation. Keynes was arguing that while this may be theoretically true in the long run, other factors might interfere with it in the short run, meaning that the long run either takes a very long time to arrive or may not occur at all. He was

C. Read, *Calming the Storms*, Palgrave Studies in Economic History,
https://doi.org/10.1007/978-3-031-11914-9_1

thinking of the huge increase in the world's money supply in 1900–1914 as a result of South African gold mining, which had virtually no impact on the general price level of the world, because central banks hoarded in their vaults the extra gold bullion being produced.[4]

Keynes was not the first economist to argue that the quantity theory of money ignores the short run. Adam Smith in the *Wealth of Nations* (1776) pointed out that it took at least twenty years after the discovery of the silver mines in Potosí in South America for the consequent increase in money supply to affect England's price level.[5] Likewise, Thomas Tooke and John Fullarton of the Banking School, a Victorian group of economists in the mid-nineteenth century, argued that bullion drains (which reduce the money supply) may not reduce a country's general price level in the short run.[6] Their intellectual opponents, the Currency School, who were strict believers in the quantity theory of money, thought that they did; bullion drains and crises would eventually resolve themselves when prices fell and exports increased. The Banking School saw this as *blasé* and argued that disequilibrium in the short run was possible and could have catastrophic effects. In particular, they saw investment flows that were part of what is now called the Carry Trade—a trading strategy involving borrowing at a low interest rate in one country or place to invest in another at a higher rate—as the prime factor behind crises.

The Carry Trade has not seemed worth consideration by academic economists in the past because in the long-term it cannot create overall wealth; the winners are cancelled out by the losers. Only one full-length book has been written in recent times critically analysing its effects on financial stability and the wider economy; this one is the second.[7] Nevertheless, as market participants and commentators increasingly observe, the lack of net profits for investors overall in the long run does not stop many individuals trying to make money from the trade in the short run. The tragedy is that attempts to profit from the Carry Trade have had important negative consequences for economies by helping to cause financial crises. Worse, those financial crises have had adverse effects on economic growth, equality and stability.

The contention of this book is that the Carry Trade—always a short-term phenomenon that only appears under certain circumstances—is also critical for an understanding of long-run British financial history over the past 200 years. The rise, fall and return of the Carry Trade should play an important role in the explanation for why there were regular financial crises between 1825 and 1866, then, outside the world wars, no major systemically important ones until 1973, before two massive ones in 1973–1975 and 2007–2009.

If crises are to be mitigated by 'Calming the Storms' in the future as successfully as the Banking School did at the end of the nineteenth century, the short-term processes that cause crises have to be understood. When Keynes quipped 'in the long run we are all dead', he was pointing out that the consideration of economic systems in the long term alone made it too easy to set aside the awkward and inconvenient factors that had produced short-run periods of instability and disruption over the previous century.

1.1 The Carry Trade and the Banking School

The Carry Trade has increasingly been connected with financial crises in recent decades. An investment strategy mainly known to professional traders, it is a method of making a profit with virtually no capital. Funds are borrowed or sourced in an area or country with low interest rates and invested in an area of high interest rates or returns.[8] Traders generally accept that interest rates in different countries will eventually move together according to the interest-rate parity theory on the basis of arbitrage caused by the flow of funds following the Carry Trade or for other reasons. However, the equalisation of rates may take as long as five years and until then a profit can be made on the difference between the rates, as viewed from the country from which the investor operates.[9] The risk involved includes the security of investments in the higher interest-rate regime, the fluctuations in currency exchange rates which may occur during the period of investment, and fluctuations in the comparative interest rates. The risk of exchange-rate variation can be countered by investors, to some extent, by hedging against future changes and the inevitable risk that high and low interest rates will move together has been avoided by careful monitoring of financial data and withdrawing funds or stopping investment before that event. Yet for all those who make a profit from the Carry Trade, many make big losses from it because of 'carry corrections' or 'carry crashes', or episodes when the Carry Trade suddenly unwinds, and the above hedging strategy does not work.[10]

It is that very change in investment flows, the unwinding of an investment position, that has been linked to financial crises. The subject of the investment will suddenly be deprived of investment and liquidity.[11]

Whether the target of the Carry Trade is a long-term infrastructure project or highly liquid securities such as publicly listed shares and bonds, the collapse of flows can cause instability both in the place that received the investment flows and the place that sent them. In addition, investors that left the withdrawal of their funds too late suffer big losses in asset values. Examples include the global financial crisis of 2007–2009, and there are some signs that the same situation has been developing in the aftermath of the covid-19 crisis.

Yet the Carry Trade and its consequences are not just a phenomenon that has come to worry economists and investors at the start of the twenty-first century. The roots of the trade go right back to the nineteenth century and the financial crises of that era. The worries of economists and bankers about the damage the trade could cause first emerged in that same era. This book traces and exposes those roots, which are embedded in the Banking School's opposition to the monetary theory and banking policy of the Currency School. It was the Currency School's ideas that substantially became embedded into British law in the Bank Charter Act of 1844.

The Banking School, traditionally seen as led by Thomas Tooke, and including the 'Free Banking School' championed by James Wilson, was a term used to describe a group of bankers, economists, businessmen and politicians who opposed the 1844 Act with a heterodox variety of opinions. Generally, they pointed to the financial crises between 1847 and 1866 as the product of the 1844 Bank Charter Act and defects in the currency and banking system that it had established. The question of whether this piece of legislation increased or decreased financial stability in the United Kingdom should be regarded as one of the most important questions in modern British history. Three severe crises—in 1847, 1857–1858 and 1866—followed the passing of that Act. However, after the collapse of Overend, Gurney & Co. in 1866, there were no major systemically important banking crises in the United Kingdom until the secondary banking crisis of the 1970s and the global financial crisis of 2007–2009. (The panic of 1914 is usually excluded from this assessment as it was caused by war not speculation; policymakers also managed to resolve both that and the sterling crisis of 1931 without any bank runs or systemically important banking collapses at home.)

This book uncovers the contribution of ideas generated by the economic thinkers of the Banking School to the development of this stability in late Victorian Britain. The conclusion of the book is that the disappearance of systemically important banking crises was in part because the Bank of England adopted many of the Banking School's prescriptions about how to manage what would now be called the Carry Trade. In short, while the Currency School won the battle in 1844, the Banking School won the war later that century in terms of its influence over the Bank of England's policies on interest rates and the management of its bullion reserves. However, no victory in history lasts forever. This book goes on to argue that the re-emergence of severe financial crises in 1973 and 2007–2009 was the result of the Bank of England forgetting the lessons the Banking School had taught it in the nineteenth century about how to manage the Carry Trade.

1.2 A British Bank Is Run with Precision?

Such a long record of having no major systemic banking crises is almost without precedent in the modern history of the world's major economies, many of which suffered regular banking crises over that same period. Perhaps the starkest international contrast can be found in the interwar years: in the depths of America's Great Depression, in 1933, only 13,500 of the 30,000 banks that had existed in 1920 still survived.[12] By contrast, in Britain, there were hardly any banking failures at all during the entire interwar period, in spite of the world depression, and none that caused severe systemic problems.

Since the end of the Bretton Woods exchange-rate agreement, which was in force between 1944 and 1971, a period in which financial crises almost disappeared across the world, serious banking crises have become more frequent.[13] The United Kingdom's spell without crises ended in the 1970s. The secondary banking crisis of 1973–1975, although systemically important, had a very limited impact on ordinary Britons, thanks to rescue efforts organised by the Bank of England and the larger clearing banks. Yet it was the global financial crisis, in 2007–2009, which was truly in scale and importance a return to the more serious events of the 1840s, 1850s and 1860s. In these Victorian crises, there were fears the Bank of England might run out of bullion or notes and the whole British banking system might have to shut down. In 2008 there were again fears of a sector-wide collapse of banks and the payments system, though this time as the result of Royal Bank of Scotland's problems. In a survey of 800 years of crises published in 2009, Carmen Reinhart and Kenneth Rogoff blamed a 'this time is different syndrome' (when little had changed in reality) for the fact that the crisis was for the most part not anticipated.[14] However, whereas many economists and policymakers have been caught by surprise by the return of severe banking crises in Britain, the global financial crisis would have looked rather familiar to many of their Victorian forebears.

Since the global financial crisis, scholars and policymakers, in Britain as well as around the world, have been looking to the past in order to find lessons to prevent crises in the future. As severe financial crises in the United Kingdom disappeared after 1866 for more than a century, can the same lessons learnt be applied again in the post-financial crash era in the early twenty-first century? What did the Banking School have to say about their experience of banking instability in Victorian Britain?

The focus of recent studies has been substantially microeconomic in nature. In many of these studies the root causes of financial crises have been identified as asset-price boom and busts caused by investor mania and irrationality that still needs to be controlled by regulation of bankers' activities. Their focus, therefore, has been substantially on microeconomic issues such as the incentive structures for bankers, corporate governance and the design of banking regulation rather than the effect of governments and central bankers in creating an unstable macroeconomic environment for the financial sector.

In 2014 John Turner wrote about how what he saw as a relatively stable banking system between the 1860s and the late twentieth century was due to an appropriate passing of risk to shareholders, which was frustrated in modern times by the withering away of the remaining liability that bank shareholders still possessed in Victorian times.[15] In 2015 Adair Turner, a regulator and a chairman of Britain's Financial Services Authority after the global financial crisis, drew attention to a number of interventionist proposals to manage the growth and allocation of credit creation: to diluting tax credit as a form of economic pollution, to boosting the capital of banks, and to the control of lending on real estate.[16] Nicholas Dimsdale and Anthony Hotson's useful collection of essays on crises in Britain suggests that the dismantling of credit controls which started during the 1970s is at the root of the problem with the inference that this was a reflection of railway mania in the 1840s.[17]

Ranald Michie's interesting study of the City of London over the period of the rise and fall of banking instability in Britain suggests that changing cultural attitudes towards the attractiveness of maturity transformation—in other words whether financial institutions should use short-term lending to make long-term loans and then sell them on—may have played a key role.[18] The lesson from the nineteenth century was that banks making long-term investments should avoid short-term wholesale markets as the source for lending rather than long-term deposits; the exact lesson Northern Rock forgot, resulting in a bank run in September 2007 that was the first high-profile bank run on any British financial institution since the crisis of 1866.[19] Michie commented that 'The lessons learnt over the space of 150 years had been undone in ten'.[20]

More recently still, in a book published in 2020, based substantially on episodes in British financial history, William Quinn and Turner conceived of bubbles as requiring a triangle of three factors: marketability, speculation and cheap credit.[21] A bubble requires an asset that can be bought and sold, cheap credit to fuel the buying of the asset and investors (often amateur or novice ones) willing to speculate on its future appreciation in value.[22] As the underlying assets that are the subject of bubbles can be used as the underlying collateral for loans, the financial system can be vulnerable to when the bubbles pop. The collapse of many such bubbles, which begin when one side of the triangle of causes suddenly disappears, can trigger banking crises, such as the role the implosion of the housing bubble in parts of America and Europe had at the start of the global financial crisis of 2007–2009.[23]

Yet although the rise and fall of banking stability in Britain is often discussed in terms of the structure of the financial sector or the incentives that bankers are given by regulators or by corporate governance structures, macroeconomic policy matters for two of the three sides of the triangle: for cheap credit and speculation. Both are not always naturally occurring and can be the result of policy decisions. Cheap credit conditions can be created by governments implementing financial repression to cut the cost of servicing a huge national debt and by the Bank of England cutting interest rates. That, in turn, can fuel speculation. As Quinn and Turner themselves note, paraphrasing Walter Bagehot, the great chronicler of Victorian financial markets, 'investors would often rather invest in something ridiculous than accept a low interest rate on a safe asset'—a desire fuelled when policymakers keep rates too low.[24] The idea that policymakers often have a role in creating the credit booms and busts that led to crises is one of the great insights provided by the Banking School, an angle that this book explores in detail over the past two centuries of British financial history.

A lot has been written about the Bank of England, by official historians and other scholars. However, this literature has often shied away from criticising many of the Bank's actions during previous crises—something which may not be entirely a surprise seeing that much of it has been written by current or former employees of the Bank itself.[25] For instance, it has rarely been noted that the Bank of England contributed to the crises of 1847 and 1857–1858 by keeping interest rates too low for too long in attempts to boost its market share in the discount market, and in doing so imperilled wider financial stability; nor that its actions in 1866 also conveniently disposed of its main rival in the discount market, Overend, Gurney & Co. This has produced a bias, which has not been fully or explicitly justified, in some of the more recent literature in favour of the ideas of the Currency School, whose adherents in the nineteenth century tended to campaign in support of the Bank's privileges.[26] Interest in the ideas of the Banking School has been relatively neglected in recent decades, with the notable exception of Matthew Smith's work that has excavated the monetary thought of Thomas Tooke.[27] Scholars have yet to fully piece together the Banking School's ideas on what would now be called the Carry Trade, how this type of speculation contributed to financial crises in the nineteenth century, and how managing the Carry Trade better could prevent similar policy errors and crises in the future. These are the three tasks this book sets out to achieve.

The Banking School's ideas have partly been obscured by the slow progress of economic historians in uncovering the history of how the macroeconomic weather in Victorian Britain affected the financial sector. That is, how policies made by government and decisions made by central bankers may have affected the incentives of the financial community, and whether this fuelled boom and busts that triggered the banking crises that scar the economic history of this period. Both economists and historians have tended to avoid this subject. Some 'standard' scholarly literature on the financial crises of 1847 and 1857–1858 was written as long ago as the 1950s and was influenced by the ideological preoccupations of the time about the merits of the gold standard.[28] A notable exception was Mac (H. M.) Boot's analysis of the 1847 crisis dating from 1984 which correctly identified the macroeconomic effects of the Irish famine and 'large speculative flows of bullion' between London and New York as throwing the Bank of England's currency system 'off course'.[29] It is my reassessment of the causes of the crises of 1847, published as *The Great Famine in Ireland and Britain's Financial Crisis* (2022), that provided the inspiration and first case study for the reassessment in this book of 200 years of British financial history.[30]

The reason for the lack of interest in this topic may be because of the growing disciplinary divide between economists and historians. Studies of British financial history using a historical-institutional approach have fallen out of favour in university economics departments since the 1960s, as Alec Cairncross has described, in favour of 'much more rigorous mathematical models, though ones which tend to assume a given and constant institutional background and whose underlying assumptions often hardly bear detailed scrutiny'.[31] Books seeking to put the Bank of England's policies in their historical and institutional context, such as Sir Ralph Hawtrey's *The Art of Central Banking* (1932) and *A Century of Bank Rate* (1938) or Richard Sayers's *Central Banking* (1957), are no longer produced by economists in university departments, even though, since these publications, a plethora of new archives and data has appeared for economists to work on.[32] Neither have economists found that the Banking School's ideas render themselves readily accessible to econometric analysis of long-term series. Meanwhile, most historians feel that they cannot add to the discussion without complex statistical computations, which most do not have the skills to undertake. To do real justice to the subject requires a historian's experience in digging in the archives combined with an economist's rigour when it comes to econometric analysis of the available economic and financial data. It is from this methodological starting point that this book springs.

1.3 Current Research in Economic History

Economic historians of Victorian Britain have instead turned their attention to three other macroeconomic areas of inquiry. The first is the debate over the speed and nature of the British industrial revolution at its zenith. The second is the debate over the reasons and the extent to which the growth performance of the British economy declined compared to those of its principal competitors later in the nineteenth century. These two subjects have swallowed up a lot of research time among British economic historians based in university economics departments, as well as reams of undergraduate essays. The third, which is a particular focus of scholars in history departments, is the provenance of sound finance (or 'Gladstonian finance') and the unilateral free-trade policies pursued after the repeal of the Corn Laws in 1846.

All three questions ultimately concern long-term economic growth and development. However, what has been neglected in these three areas of investigation is how short-term events, such as banking or financial crises, although short-lived, can dramatically affect the long run.

Since the global financial crisis of 2007–2009, the thrust of recent research in economic history, in general, has been to place more importance on the consequences of crises. It has been realised that economic growth in the long run is not all directly about long-run growth, as it were, elegantly presented with long-run growth models developed in the economics textbooks of the last half-century or so. Economic slumps, recessions and crises diminish growth, can permanently affect the development of an economy, and therefore need to be at the centre of historical narratives, even those about the long run. As many people who have lived through the global financial crisis can attest, such events and their consequences, including the austerity measures that often follow in their wake, can affect lived experiences, change lives, end lives and permanently blight the future for an individual or an entire economy. That applies to the nineteenth century as much as it does the twenty-first. For instance, the financial crises of 1847 in London made it harder to raise loans for Irish relief during the Great Famine, triggering cuts in spending that probably raised excess mortality by hundreds of thousands of lives and permanently reduced Ireland's population.[33] Consequent accusations by Irish nationalists that the British response to the famine was inadequate fuelled separatism that eventually resulted in the independence of the Irish Free State from the United Kingdom in 1922. The panics that triggered the 1847 crises were particularly short-lived, but British and Irish people still live with its long-term consequences today, 175 years on.[34]

The impact of short-term crises on the long term is increasingly recognised by economic historians. Most notably, Reinhart and Rogoff, in their book mockingly entitled *This Time is Different* (2009), argued that banking crises have longer term effects that other downturns do not.[35] Financial crises cause much longer and slower recovery paths than ordinary recessions in which there are no banking collapses. More recently still a series of papers by Stephen Broadberry and John Wallis have undermined the idea that long-term economic growth should be about growth at all. They have taken data for 18 countries in Europe and the New World, some from as far back as the thirteenth century. To their surprise, they found that growth during years of economic expansion has fallen in the recent era—from 3.88% between 1820 and 1870 to 3.06%

since 1950—even though average growth across all years in those two periods increased from 1.4% to 2.55%.[36] The solution to this apparent contradiction turned out to be that it was shorter and shallower slumps that were leading to rising long-term growth. Output fell in a third of years between 1820 and 1870 but in only 12% of those since 1950. The average rate of decline per recession year has fallen too, from 3% to 1.2%. In short, to really understand the nature of economic growth and the direction in which economies develop, it is necessary to understand the crises and downturns—perhaps even more so—than expansionary periods themselves.

There has also been a growing amount of research into the downturns that accompany banking crises. Generally, these are more serious than those caused by the normal fluctuations in business conditions. Research pioneered by Ben Bernanke suggests that this is because banking crises hinder the ability of banks to recycle savings into investment to help the economy grow. Increased costs of credit intermediation after banking failures reduce lending and raise the interest rate at which surviving banks are willing to lend at, to cover the higher perceived credit risk of new clients.[37] Financial crises also have more severe political effects than other types of downturn. In a paper originally published in 2015, Manuel Funke, Moritz Schularick and Christoph Trebesch looked at data for 20 countries over 140 years and found that in the aftermath of a financial crisis, the vote share for the extreme right increases by 30% on average, due to rising anger about slow growth and recovery in their aftermath.[38] In slumps without banking crises, however, there is less appreciable change in the political spectrum.

1.4 The Monetary Thought of the Non-conformist Conscience

Many of those associated with the Banking School were well aware of the threat to economic and political stability that extremists posed in the wake of financial crises. Notably, Marxist views on the inherent contradictions of capital accumulation and the crisis of capitalism were inspired by Karl Marx's writings on the crises of 1847.[39] In this context, it is important to acknowledge that the Banking School did not simply have economic or financial goals. Many scholars have dismissed its advocates too easily as simply making up arguments to further their own personal financial or business interests. They also had clear moral and political goals, namely, about how to avoid crises and the threat from extremism that such events imposed upon the emerging liberal societies of their era.

Another possible reason for the lack of academic attention to investment flows may have been driven by self-interest and the potential profits for bankers from the Carry Trade. This has been an accusation made by some followers of the Banking School from early on. In 1829 Thomas Attwood described those journals who supported Currency School views as 'stock-jobbers', only interested in their own profit.[40] The reputation of the Bank of England's directors was cast in a reactionary light in the 1830s when several appeared in the list of those receiving compensation for slave owners, published in a Parliamentary paper at the request of Daniel O'Connell.[41]

In 1847, after the Bank Charter Act of 1844 had become law, Thomas Wakley accused the reforms, inspired by Lord Overstone's campaigning as the intellectual leader of the Currency School, of favouring the wealthy.[42] *The Money Bag*, a financial and literary newspaper, took up this theme and in a cartoon attacking the Currency School made their character 'the hard calculator' resemble Overstone. The 'hard calculator' was a notorious reference to a City article in *The Times* which had complained that the 'hard calculator' could not make his 'deserved' profit from being 'prudent' because the Bank of England was refusing to raise interest rates to 12% or 15% during the crisis of 1857–1858—a rate so high it would have made many sound businesses go bust.[43] The article would have been authored by Sampson, the City correspondent who was himself later revealed as a 'stock jobber', taking money for promoting stocks. All these circumstances did not leave the Currency School's protagonists with a favourable reputation, so it was not surprising that *The Economist* in 1855 lectured the new breed of banks on morality, comparing them favourably against the old Bank of England and its supporters.[44]

There was indeed a philosophical divide between the Banking School, which was vehemently opposed to slavery and was much more inspired by Wesleyan and Gurneyite Quaker ideals of improving the world in general, and the lot of the poor in particular, and the Currency School, which tolerated and even at times supported slavery and was inspired by a much more severe form of Calvinism. In contrast, the Banking School took much inspiration from the ideas of Henry Thornton, the second most important abolitionist in the evangelical Clapham Sect after William Wilberforce, and the financial brains behind the eventually successful campaign to ban the slave trade in the British empire. This cast a long shadow over British debates about banking. Indeed, *The Economist's* continuing support for Overend, Gurney & Co. until its spectacular collapse during the crisis of 1866 was because of Overend's Gurneyite Quaker tradition and its anti-slavery attitude (*The Economist*'s founder, James Wilson, was also a Gurneyite Quaker and an abolitionist). This distinguished Overend's from the Bank of England, where slavery had been more tolerated and which was more conformist to the traditions of the Church of England.[45] This did not end well for the Banking School's reputation in the long term, however, when Overend's failed in 1866.

1.5 Re-introducing the Banking School

In short, recent research has shown that financial crises are much more important in the history of the long run than many historians or economists have previously appreciated. Yet, in spite of that importance, economists still feel ill-equipped to deal with the next crisis. Gertjan Vlieghe, an economist and Bank of England policymaker, has admitted to British MPs that they are probably not going to be able to predict the passage of the next crisis or recession: 'Our models are just not that good'.[46]

The aim of this study is to excavate from the archives the Banking School's critique of Overstone's description of how financial crisis occur, a description lampooned in the Banking-School cartoon on the front of this book. This book also investigates the available evidence indicating how far the Banking School's ideas can be applied to the financial crises that have occurred in the United Kingdom since 1825. Overstone considered financial crises as spontaneous occurrences, a small price to pay for the price stability induced by his policies. Meanwhile, the Banking School saw a mechanism entirely separate from prices as the fundamental cause of crises, one which could be exacerbated rather than curtailed by the Currency School's ideas and policies. Instead, the Banking School tended to emphasise the role of international flows of capital, triggered by a search for higher rates of return on investments, as the cause behind episodes of financial instability in Britain. The Banking School believed that excessively low interest rates demanded by a government concerned about the cost of financing its debt, inevitably kick-started foreign bullion flows and the financial crises that followed when they halted. As Tooke explained in his *History of Prices* in 1840:

> The probability is that [if] the market rate of interest in this country would, by...an operation of the Bank, be depressed below its ordinary rate relatively to other countries, there would be every inducement to the individuals who thus had their capitals disengaged to seek investment in securities abroad... the capitals to be transmitted abroad for such investments would be remitted in bullion.[47]

Disparities of interest rates between countries were therefore considered a factor in whether a crisis would arise. When nominal rates from home and foreign investments subsequently converged there would then be what would now be termed a 'carry crash' and a crisis would occur. In contrast, the Currency School's theories offered no explanation for crises based on interest rates in different countries. This study will examine in detail the Banking-School explanations for the phenomenon of nominal interest rates moving together during crises and will apply them to the past two centuries of British financial history.

By 1844 both Schools believed that at least a significant proportion of issued bank notes should be backed by a reserve of gold held by the issuing bank. This was so that the notes could be convertible into gold on demand and would therefore hold their value in the metal: there would be enough gold to exchange for notes if the holders wanted it. The Currency School is sometimes said to have evolved from the 'Bullionists' who campaigned for notes to be convertible to gold early in the 1800s, but the link is not exact because some of its protagonists, such as Robert Torrens, were originally 'Anti-bullionists'. The Bank Charter Act of 1844 began the statutory limitation of banknote issue of the Bank of England. The legislation specified a reserve of bullion that had to be held by the Bank in proportion to the notes issued (less a 'fiduciary' amount), but that the bullion could be owned by the bank or any of its depositing customers. This enabled the system to be set up with existing stocks of gold without the need for the Bank to purchase a large new bullion reserve.

The problem with this arrangement was that the bullion flowed in and out of the Bank's reserve independently of the Bank's wishes. It could 'drain' away internally or be swept away to other countries along with a general flow of bullion leaving the United Kingdom. Bullion flowed out of the Bank's reserve for a variety of reasons. It certainly left to make payments in foreign countries for goods imported to Britain, but the Banking School emphasised that some left to make profitable investments abroad. It was also sold as merchandise, in its own right, in articles such as jewellery and, at times, the main banks in different countries would lend each other gold in order to assist in periods of crisis. A banking crisis would potentially occur when the Bank of England's bullion reserves fell to a low level because this meant that the number of banknotes it could issue also had to be restricted.

Before 1844 there were a number of note-issuing banks in England that kept their own gold reserves. After 1844 note issue was restricted to the Bank of England and its gold bullion reserve became the most important. Under the Bank Charter Act of 1844, the Bank had to publish (i) the level of its notes issued and in reserve, and (ii) its bullion reserve, each week, and balance the two. The Banking School believed that when diminishing bullion reserves were published, they provoked a scramble for liquidity in the form of notes or credit as note issue would be restricted, resulting in damage to commerce and the value of assets that banks had loaned money against.

The important difference between the Banking and Currency Schools was that they had different theories about what caused bullion flows and what the response of the Bank of England should be in order to ensure that gold and silver returned to the country and to banking reserves. The attitude of the Currency School was built on the price-specie flow mechanism described by David Hume in the mid-eighteenth century. Adherents believed that the amount of bullion in different countries would be self-balancing because as gold left the country, prices would drop, which would encourage the export of goods and would bring back gold in return. This relied on the theory that the quantity of money affected commodity prices and that bullion flows were mainly to pay for trade. Notes had to be restricted in a crisis to lower prices and bring back bullion.

In contrast, the Banking School preferred to follow Adam Smith's metaphor of a lake fed by and emptied by rivers. Those included under this heading believed commerce should be supplied with the notes and credit they legitimately required and that the system would be self-balancing provided this money was backed by 'real bills', loans made on physical goods of value, even if they were not secured with gold. A similar argument was used by some 'Anti-bullionists', who did not see the convertibility of notes into gold as necessary, but the Banking School is not an exact continuation of that group and noted the stabilising effects of gold.

The Currency School did not recognise short-term flows of gold seeking investment at first, but the Banking School did, and saw them as a potential disturbance to self-balancing systems. However, they were also useful, the Banking School believed, because bullion could be brought back to Britain quickly by raising interest rates. The Currency School also came to accept that high interest rates were essential to bring back bullion in crises in the 1850s, borrowing the idea from the Banking School, but they preferred to think of them as also reinforcing restrictions on the quantity of money.[48]

Nonetheless, the importance of this split within classical economics between adherents of the Currency School and those of the Banking School has often been downplayed in both popular and scholarly discussions of economic ideology. Yet their intellectual descendants—monetarists and Keynesians—still disagree on fundamental points in economics. Under the influence of those scholars who like to emphasise the importance of the appearance of Marxist thinking in Victorian Britain, both schools have been lumped together as 'classical economics' or 'political economy'. However, the real ideological battle which mattered for policymakers in Victorian economic thought was that between the Currency School and the Banking School.

The Governors and Directors of the Bank of England included individuals from both Schools over the nineteenth century and as a group they never explicitly explained the reasoning behind their attempts to control gold flows by influencing interest rates. It is probable their reasons for raising or lowering the Bank Rate differed from individual to individual but resulted in the same action. It came to be accepted that drains of gold would result in the need for Bank Rate increases to attract it back.

Of course, if the link between the total number of notes which could be in circulation, including the note reserve, and the bullion in the Bank's reserve was suddenly broken, this was an instant solution to resolve a liquidity crunch. This is why the 1844 Act was 'suspended' at the peaks of the systemic crises in 1847, 1857–1858 and 1866, when the reserves of notes held by the Bank ran down to near zero. The advice of *The Economist*, later published in a book by Bagehot, an editor of the newspaper, for the Bank of England was to carry on lending to sound organisations in a crisis at high rates on the basis of good security, a practice that has become well-known as 'Bagehot's dictum'.[49] It combined both Currency School and Banking School theories by restricting credit with a high rate of interest while guaranteeing available credit to good quality risks and thus keeping commerce going. After the 1860s, the Bank became so confident in its use of interest rates to control its bullion reserve, using the Banking School's ideas, that it did not have to run down its note reserves to keep commerce flowing within reasonable levels in a crisis.

The modern incarnation of the Currency School is monetarism which also is based around the quantity theory of money and looks at international money flows in terms of the prices of commodities. Banking School attitudes tend to have been forgotten because they have been associated with post-Keynesian policies of the expansion of public spending in a crisis which came to be discredited in the 1970s and 1980s in an era of stagflation. Yet they need to be appreciated to fully understand and reconstruct how historic crises were viewed by those who lived through them.

This book re-examines the debate between the Currency School and the Banking School and suggests how the latter's ideas can be applied to the financial crises that have occurred in the United Kingdom since 1825. It does so by analysing both qualitative and quantitative evidence mined from financial newspapers and the Bank of England's archives. In particular, it uses the Bank of England's data on bullion flows, which were not publicly available for the Banking School's theorists to prove their ideas at the time, and a new series of short-term American interest rates collected from market reports in newspapers.[50]

The second chapter examines the intentions behind Sir Robert Peel's economic-policy regime change that established the macroeconomic backdrop for the set of severe crises that took place in mid-nineteenth century Britain. The third chapter explains how these reforms ignited a fierce debate between the Banking School and the Currency School in the 1840s, as well as how the Banking School's theories can be quantitatively used to analyse Britain's economy in the nineteenth century. The fourth to eighth chapters examine the most serious financial crises of the Victorian period—1825, 1837–1839, 1847, 1857–1858 and 1866—and trace how the Banking School's ideas developed as a result of them and eventually helped the Bank of England prevent the Carry Trade from triggering further systemic banking crises. The ninth chapter suggests how their ideas can be applied to the twentieth and twenty-first centuries, particularly in light of the increasingly prevalent Carry Trade.

Notes

1. J. M. Keynes, 'A Tract on Monetary Reform', in *Collected Writings of John Maynard Keynes* IV (Cambridge: CUP, 2013) p. 65.
2. See https://www.simontaylorsblog.com/2013/05/05/the-true-meaning-of-in-the-long-run-we-are-all-dead/ [accessed 28 May 2022].
3. J. M. Keynes, 'The General Theory of Employment, Interest and Money', in *Collected Writings of John Maynard Keynes* VII (Cambridge: CUP, 2013) e.g. pp. 220–221; see also idem., XVII, pp. 279, 352–354.
4. Keynes, 'A Tract on Monetary Reform', pp. 65–66.
5. Wood to Peel, 26 September 1849, Graham papers, B.L., Add. MS. 79713 f. 36.
6. T. Tooke, *On the Bank Charter Act of 1844* (London: Longman, 1856) pp. 85–87; J. Fullarton, *On the Regulation of Currencies* (London: John Murray, 1844) pp. 4, 58, 64, 81, 137, 142; *Committee…*, PP 1840 (602) IV.1, p. 298.
7. T. Lee, J. Lee, K. Coldiron, *The Rise of Carry: The Dangerous Consequences of Volatility Suppression and the New Financial Order of Decaying Growth and Recurring Crisis* (New York: McGraw-Hill, 2020). I have excluded 'how to-guides' and other non-scholarly books from this statement, which was correct at the time of writing.
8. Idem., p. 2.
9. Idem., pp. 47–48.
10. Idem., p. 4.
11. Idem., p. 128.
12. J. S. Olson, *Historical dictionary of the Great Depression 1929–1940* (United Kingdom: Greenwood Press, 2001) p. 26.
13. C. M. Reinhart, K. S. Rogoff, *This Time Is Different* (Princeton: Princeton UP, 2009) Figure 10.1, p. 156.
14. Reinhart, Rogoff, *This Time Is Different*, p. 208.
15. J. D. Turner, *Banking in Crisis* (Cambridge: CUP, 2014).
16. A. Turner, *Between Debt and the Devil* (Princeton: Princeton UP, 2015).
17. N. Dimsdale, A. Hotson, *Financial Crises since 1825* (Oxford: OUP, 2014).
18. R. C. Michie, *Guilty Money* (Abingdon: Routledge, 2009).
19. Ranald Michie has pointed out that there was a small run by savers on London and County Securities in December 1973 during the secondary banking crisis, but though episode was little reported upon the press and thus it does not count as a 'major' or 'high-profile' bank run in most British financial histories. See F. H. Capie, *The Bank of England: 1950s–1979* (Cambridge: CUP, 2010) pp. 525–585, cited in R. C. Michie, *British Banking: Continuity and Change from 1694 to the Present* (Oxford: OUP, 2016) p. 187.

20. Michie, *British Banking*, p. 270.
21. W. Quinn, J. D. Turner, *Boom and Bust: A Global History of Financial Bubbles* (Cambridge: CUP, 2020) pp. 4–10.
22. Idem., pp. 4–7.
23. Idem., pp. 2–5.
24. W. Bagehot, 'Investments', *Inquirer*, 31 July 1852, cited in Quinn, Turner, *Boom and Bust*, pp. 6–7.
25. See, for instance, R. Sowerbutts, M. Schneebalg, F. Hubert, 'The Demise of Overend Gurney', *Bank of England Quarterly Bulletin 2016 Q2* (2016) pp. 94–106, for a particularly hagiographical account of the Bank of England's actions during the crisis of 1866.
26. See, for instance, *The Economist's* recent special report on central banking, which follows the Currency School's old line that price stability alone should be the prime target for central bankers, even at the cost of other objectives: *The Economist*, 23 April 2022.
27. M. Smith, *Thomas Tooke and the Monetary Thought of Classical Economics* (Abingdon: Routledge, 2011).
28. For example: C. N. Ward-Perkins, 'The Commercial Crisis of 1847', *Oxford Economic Papers* NS2 (1950) 75–94; J. R. T. Hughes, 'The Commercial Crisis of 1857', *Oxford Economic Papers*, NS8 (1956).
29. H. M. Boot, *The Commercial Crisis of 1847* (Hull: Hull UP, 1984) p. 50.
30. See C. Read, *The Great Famine in Ireland and Britain's Financial Crisis* (Woodbridge: The Boydell Press, 2022) Chapters 3 and 4, also C. Read, 'Laissez-Faire, the Irish famine, and British Financial Crisis', *Economic History Review* 69 (2016) pp. 411–434.
31. For the full story see A. Cairncross and C. A. E. Goodhart, 'Richard Sidney Sayers (1908–1989)', in R. A. Cord (ed.), *The Palgrave Companion to LSE Economics* (London: Palgrave Macmillan, 2018) pp. 533–554.
32. R. G. Hawtrey, *A Century of Bank Rate* (London: Frank Cass & Co., 1968); R. G. Hawtrey, *The Art of Central Banking* (London: Frank Cass & Co, 1962); R. S. Sayers, *Modern Banking* (Oxford: OUP, 1938).
33. Read, 'Laissez-faire, the Irish famine, and British financial crisis', pp. 411–434.
34. For a longer discussion of this theme see Read, *The Great Famine in Ireland and Britain's Financial Crisis*, pp. 4–8.
35. C. M. Reinhart, K. S. Rogoff, *This Time is Different* (Princeton NJ, Princeton UP, 2009).
36. S. Broadberry, J. Wallis, 'Growing, Shrinking and Long Run Economic Performance: Historical Perspectives on Economic Development', *Working Paper Series*, 323 (CAGE, 2017).
37. B. N. Bernanke, 'Non-Monetary Effects of the Financial Crisis in the Propagation of the Great Depression', *NBER Working Paper*, 1054 (1983).

38. M. Funke, M. Schularick, C. Trebesch, 'Going to Extremes: Politics after Financial Crises, 1870–2014', *CEPR Discussion Paper*, DP10884 (2015).
39. J. Cohen et al. (eds.), *Karl Marx, Frederick Engels: Collected Works* X (London: Lawrence & Wishart, 2010) pp. 52, 695.
40. T. Attwood, *Distressed State of the Country* (Birmingham: Beilby, Knott and Beilby, 1829) p. 15.
41. *List of those who received compensation as slave owners* PP 1837–1838 (215) XLVIII.331.
42. *Hansard*, 15 December 1847, XCV, cc. 1148–1149.
43. *The Times*, 24 November 1857, p. 5.
44. *The Economist*, 23 June 1855, p. 671.
45. Bank of England, *Statement in relation to the Bank's historical links to the slave trade*, 19 June 2020, https://www.bankofengland.co.uk/news/2020/june/statement-in-relation-to-the-banks-historical-links-to-the-slave-trade [accessed 27 July 2021].
46. Parliament Treasury Committee, *Bank of England Inflation Report*, 10.38 a.m., 21 February 2017.
47. T. Tooke, *History of Prices* [1840] III (London: P. S. King & Son., 1928) p. 274.
48. D. P. O'Brien, J. R. McCulloch (ed.), *The Correspondence of Lord Overstone* (Cambridge: CUP, 1971) pp. 126, 140; 1972; Lord Overstone, *Tracts and Other Publications on Metallic and Paper Currency* [1857], (London, Clifton, NJ: Augustus Kelley, 1972) p. 355.
49. W. Bagehot, *Lombard Street: A Description of the Money Market* [1873] (Westport: Hyperion Press, 1962) pp. 27–28.
50. Bullion flows: Bank of England daily account books (recorded gold and silver imports and exports from 1852), Bank of England archive; American interest rates: *New York Daily Tribune*, 'Commercial and Money Matters' column.

CHAPTER 2

Peel's Economic-Policy Regime Change in Britain During the Early Nineteenth Century

> Sir Robert has *an immense scheme in view*; he thinks he shall be able to remove the contest [over repeal of the Corn Laws] entirely from the dangerous ground upon which it has got—that of a war between the manufacturers, the hungry and the poor against the landed proprietors, the aristocracy, which can only end in the ruin of the latter; he will not bring forward a measure upon the Corn Laws, but a much more comprehensive one. He will deal with the whole commercial system of the country. He will adopt the principle of the League, *that of removing all protection and abolishing all monopoly*, but not in favour of one class and as a triumph over another, but to the benefit of the nation, farmers as well as manufacturers.
>
> —Memorandum, Prince Albert, 25 December 1845.[1]

Sir Robert Peel is known by historians for many things: for the establishment of the Metropolitan Police in London (England's first modern constabulary), for enacting Catholic Emancipation (which granted them full civil rights for the first time since the seventeenth century), his family's controversial role in the abolition of the slave trade in the British empire and for being Britain's most recent prime minister for whom no photograph survives. Yet there is perhaps no moment of his career which is more controversial than the repeal of the Corn Laws, or duties on grain imports, in 1846.

Political historians remember this moment as one which permanently changed the British party system. Peel's loyal frontbenchers, who

C. Read, *Calming the Storms*, Palgrave Studies in Economic History,
https://doi.org/10.1007/978-3-031-11914-9_2

supported repeal, became known as the Peelites or the Liberal Conservatives and evolved after many mergers with other parties into today's Liberal Democrats. Peel's backbenchers, who opposed repeal, formed a new grouping that evolved into the modern Conservative Party. Debate still rages between his biographers over whether he should best be remembered as the founder of the modern Conservative Party or the progenitor of Gladstonian Liberalism. His legacy is still lionised today by modern Conservative MPs as well as among Liberal Democrats; a bust of him is still proudly displayed at the National Liberal Club in London.

Economic historians also remember 1846 as an important moment, but on the basis that it was the start of a new free-trade epoch in British history. Yet these debates all, if anything, understate the importance of Peel's reforms on British economic policy in the nineteenth century. As chairman of the Currency Commission in 1819 and then prime minister in the 1830s and 1840s, Peel set out a new policy regime of trade, currency, banking and fiscal policies that remained remarkably unaltered until the economic crisis of 1931. As Prince Albert noted privately in 1845, Peel's intention was not just to introduce 'a measure upon the Corn Laws', but a much more 'immense scheme' to 'deal with the whole commercial system of the country'. It was this 'immense scheme' that set up the institutional backdrop to the rise and fall of banking instability in nineteenth-century Britain.

This chapter describes how his set of reforms were intended to form a coherent plan. They were based on Peel's idiosyncratic understanding of political economy, more shaped by his desire to achieve a certain outcome than a dogmatic attachment to a particular method of doing so. His goals were to stabilise food prices, which would benefit society as a whole and diffuse class tensions, as well as construct a stable platform upon which economic growth could be built. In particular, the Bank Charter Act of 1844 was intended to prevent future banking crises on the scale seen in 1825 and 1837. Even so, as the next chapter goes on to explain, his reforms in the 1840s widened a bitter intellectual battle between the ideas of the Currency School and those of the Banking School on the causes and nature of banking crises.

2.1 Peel's Policies

There are three main strands to Peel's economic reforms between the 1820s and the 1840s. His policies can be summarised under three headings as follows:

(i) Opening up trade: following Peel's decision to allow the free movement of bullion in 1819, lower tariffs and the removal of prohibitions on trade in food and raw materials should be pursued to ensure low and stable prices.[2]

(ii) Currency: the value of British currency should be firmly fixed to a gold standard, with the pound freely convertible by the Bank of England. This implied a stable exchange rate with currencies that followed a similar policy. There should be a limited banknote supply, based on a multiple of gold reserves, to protect the principle of convertibility and prevent the inflation of commodity prices, particularly for foodstuffs.[3]

(iii) Interest rates: these should be kept low, by running a balanced government budget to prevent the cost of servicing the national debt becoming unaffordable. Government expenditure should be minimised and the national debt, which had greatly increased during the Napoleonic wars, should be reduced. Tax revenues lost by lowering tariffs should be replaced by direct taxes targeted at those most able to pay (such as by Peel's re-introduced income tax of 1842).[4]

Politicians and scholars alike have tended to refer to this group of policies as 'Gladstonian finance'. The orthodox interpretation sees William Gladstone, and to a lesser extent Benjamin Disraeli, who were both chancellors of the exchequer and prime ministers later in the century, as playing an important part in Britain's shift towards balanced budgets, the transfer of the tax burden from indirect to direct levies, and the movement towards unilateral free trade in the mid-nineteenth century. Indeed, as Ernest Bevin, a Labour politician, is said to have joked in 1940, 'they say that Gladstone was at the Treasury from 1860 to 1930'.[5] Colin Matthew in a seminal article published in the *Historical Journal* in 1979 argued that a 'fiscal compromise' was established in the age of Gladstone and Disraeli, who (except for a three-year interlude) between them totally occupied the chancellorship of the exchequer from 1852 to

1868.[6] However, although Gladstone, in particular, played an important role in solidifying this policy consensus, he did not originally establish it. As Martin Daunton has touched upon in *Trusting Leviathan*, the historiographical veneration of Gladstone has downplayed the role of Peel who played a much more important role in developing economic policy in the first half of the nineteenth century than is sometimes appreciated.[7]

Of the three main areas his policies affected, trade has been the most widely discussed by historians and economists. Peel intended his legacy to be treated in this way, drawing attention away from the Bank Charter Act of 1844, which was widely criticised at the time by those associated with the Banking School. Edward Cardwell, who had been Peel's Financial Secretary to the Treasury, informed him how unpopular it was during the election campaign of 1847.[8] While Cardwell was seeking election that year for the constituency of Liverpool, talking with commercial interests in that city he noted 'the strange prejudice they have taken up against the Bill of 1844'.[9]

The 'prejudice' was a complaint that the Act had caused an unstable commercial environment of widely fluctuating interest rates.[10] When the Bank of England bullion reserves were filling, rates were too low for ordinary firms; when the reserve was emptying, the rate was too high. Cardwell wrote to Peel, after the April 1847 financial crisis, that he had been 'told the Country Bankers could at any moment have gone to the Bank of England and brought it to a dead lock'.[11] When Peel wrote his address to electors in Tamworth for the 1847 election, he concentrated on the religious question of fair treatment of Catholics and on the commercial question of free trade, sidestepping the issue of the 1844 Act.[12] Cardwell based Peel's *Memoirs* on this election address and the 1844 Act received only a brief mention, while his famous 'U-turns' by which he wanted to be known by posterity, on Catholic Emancipation and on the Corn Laws, were discussed in considerable detail.[13]

More important for any analysis of nineteenth-century crises has been the impact of his policies on the two areas other than freer trade: banking regulation and interest rates. These, which have been downplayed by many scholars of Victorian economic policy, will be given full and equal consideration in this chapter. Peel's guiding principle was always to produce stable, low food prices, to keep the labouring population content, the manufacturers in business and to spare the nobility from civil unrest. This practical aim was more important than any particular fashionable liberal or *laissez faire* ideology. On the contrary, his adoption of restrictive Currency-School ideas became a greater ideology the more they were questioned after 1844, and their influence in British economic policy far outlived his untimely death six years later in 1850.

2.2 Opening up Trade

Peel was not the first prime minister in the nineteenth century interested in the maintenance of economic and political stability. The aims of Lord Liverpool, prime minister 1812–1827, were similar to Peel's: reverse the trend of worsening conditions for the ordinary people and maintain stability. However, Liverpool focused on the demand side of the economy and employment, rather than the supply side which pre-occupied Peel. In 1815 Liverpool's President of the Board of Trade, Frederick Robinson, introduced the 'Corn Laws'—a protectionist tariff on imported grain—in Parliament. (Ironically, under Peel's premiership on 25 May 1846, Robinson, by then raised to the peerage as the first Earl of Ripon, moved the abolition of the same 'Corn Laws' in the House of Lords.)

Yet the reasons for both the creation and "repeal" of the Corn Laws were remarkably similar: the preservation of stability. Liverpool was unwilling to implement a system of unrestricted trade without the consequences being fully considered and understood lest economic and political chaos resulted. Liverpool as prime minister told Parliament in 1820:

> It is utterly impossible, with our debt and taxation, even if they were but half the existing amount, that we can suddenly adopt the system of free trade. To do so would unhinge the whole property of the country; to make a change in the value of every man's possessions, and in none more so than in those of the agriculturist—the very basis of our opulence and power.[14]

In a pamphlet, which is believed to have been composed by Liverpool as it has written notes by 'the author' in his own hand, he suggests that a better way of helping the poor was to ensure that there was sufficient employment for them rather than bearing down on the prices of their food.[15]

Even so, as it turned out, the general working population did not feel much benefit from the Corn Laws. The new laws may have ensured that home-grown grain was retained in the country, and may have bolstered agricultural employment. However, they also appeared to push up prices as the tariffs were paid as a form of indirect taxation by everyone who bought bread. In addition, the high tariffs did not boost aggregate demand overall as much as Liverpool expected, which adversely affected employment in manufacturing and diminished the overall pool of wealth. Such outcomes caused political and civil unrest. Demands for Parliamentary reform and an end to favouring the influence of the rich through rotten boroughs increased throughout the summer of 1819. They culminated in Manchester with an attack by the yeomanry on a demonstration, killing at least 11 and wounding more, an event which came to be known as the Peterloo Massacre. A further crackdown was followed by the Cato Street Conspiracy in 1820 which threatened the lives of Liverpool and his cabinet. Liverpool responded with a draconian series of laws called the 'Six Acts'. Other repressive legislation followed for Ireland in 1822. However, Liverpool did encourage younger talented politicians such as Peel, Robinson and Huskisson, and gradually they began to change the focus of policy to a supply-side one designed to assist the working classes by means of lower and stable prices.[16]

Huskisson and Robinson concentrated on negotiating trade deals rather than pressing for unilateral abandonment of import taxes. The economy did improve and Robinson became known as 'Prosperity Robinson' because of the economic recovery that took place while he was chancellor of the exchequer (1823–1827), in spite of the banking crisis of 1825 under his watch.[17] However when he became prime minister, for five months in 1827–1828, his intended liberal economic policies and policies designed to benefit Ireland did not find general support in Parliament. In January 1828 he ended up as one of the last prime ministers in British history to be dismissed by a monarch. In general, Robinson favoured specific policies geographically focussed on Ireland that would have boosted its economy—the sort now often called 'place-based policies'—rather than overall macroeconomic policies which cost less and were intended to have a widespread beneficial effect. The outcomes of the macroeconomic policies were less certain, as they relied on particular assumptions about the behaviour of markets which, in retrospect, were little understood by politicians or economists in this period. They also suffered from the same problem in political economy that free-trade policies have always faced throughout the ages. Although they may be beneficial in net terms, the losses are more concentrated and visible, and so objections against them gain more political traction, while the greater amount of gains are more widely diffused and therefore less visible to voters.

Peel, nonetheless, increasingly came to favour overall macroeconomic policies over place-based ones. The clearest example of this is his policy agenda towards Ireland when he became prime minister again in 1841. Whereas his viceroy of Ireland, the 2nd Earl de Grey (Robinson's elder brother) favoured place-based policies to help Ireland, Peel and his ministers in Ireland preferred a focus on commercial policies that they thought would benefit the United Kingdom as a whole.[18] Before the budget of 1842, James Graham, Peel's Home Secretary, confided to De Grey, who was pressing for local legislation to boost Ireland's economy and had sent Lord Eliot over to London with a pile of draft bills, that 'while corn and finance are pending Ireland will be forgotten'.[19] Commercial policy for the United Kingdom overall, in contrast, was 'the cardinal point on which our Fortunes turn', Graham stated.[20]

The historical literature to date on why Peel sought to pursue these types of reforms has tended to concentrate on the choice of policy tool rather than the economic effect desired. In particular, it has focused on free trade as a policy aim in its own right, rather than the ways in which Peel thought it could affect the economy. These included avoiding the price effects of indirect taxation, as highlighted by David Ricardo; bringing down the prices of food and other goods and increasing productive efficiency, both described by Adam Smith; promoting international peace and helping the manufacturing interest, as championed by Richard Cobden, a free-trade campaigner; or a combination of these.[21]

A few historians, however, have recognised that Peel had wider aims. Martin Daunton, in considering the history of tax policy, has seen the lowering of tariffs and introduction of an income tax in Peel's 1842 budget as aimed at 'integrating classes and defusing social unrest'.[22] Douglas Irwin has convincingly argued that Peel was not dominated by political economy but noted his 'long' concern with 'the welfare of labour'.[23]

Yet it is Peel's religious and moral background which gives his economic agenda most clarity. Peel was an Anglican but one that came from a family that had great respect for Wesleyan Methodists: his grandfather had given the land for Tamworth's first Wesleyan chapel and used to employ only Methodists as foremen in his cotton mills and calico printworks.[24] John Wesley, the founder of Methodism, had made clear throughout many sermons, tracts and pamphlets that concern for the poor—irrespective of electoral calculation—was the moral imperative that should lie behind public policy.

Specifically, in *Thoughts on the Present Scarcity of Provisions*, published in 1773, Wesley outlined what he believed to be the moral responsibility of the rich and of government for ensuring that the poor had enough food in times of dearth. This was a view that challenged Malthusian-style political economy before Malthus. In the tract Wesley also outlines an idiosyncratic theory of economic growth: that falling food prices cause economic growth by leaving households with more income to spend on other items, which would boost employment and output in other sectors of the economy. To do this Wesley deployed a philosophically inconsistent (on the face of it) range of examples of policy actions that could be taken, including government intervention in some areas, the use of the free market to attack 'monopoly' in others and the use of extreme austerity to reduce taxes, fight what was later termed 'Old Corruption' and halve the national debt. Peel's specific policy prescriptions differed from Wesley's. Nevertheless, the theologian's outlook on dearth and economic ideas on food prices—that the government had a moral duty to combat famine and that it should use all means and policies at its disposal to lower food prices to do this—were clearly mirrored in Peel's thinking eight decades later in the 1840s.[25]

Peel's concern for the labouring poor can be seen clearly in his writings and speeches throughout his career. Peel was Home Secretary when Herries produced his report supporting lower tariffs and the resulting Importation of Corn Act 1828 replaced a fixed duty on corn with a sliding scale.[26] Peel's first serious policy initiative on free trade, with Herries and Goulburn, was trying to remove the tax on beer and reduce the duties on hops and sugar while replacing the government receipts using a property tax. It was stated as aimed at reducing the weight of indirect taxes, and therefore prices, placed 'on the shoulders of the middling and labouring classes'.[27] In 1834, when he spoke against free-trade proposals, he considered the Corn Laws protected 'moral and social interests of the whole community' because high commodity prices helped to generate the profits by which landowners paid their Poor Law contributions.[28]

Again in 1839, when he still spoke supposedly in support of the Corn Laws, the same concern for the poor showed through:

> Unless the existence of the Corn Law can be shown to be consistent not only with the prosperity of agriculture and the maintenance of the landlord's interest but also with the protection and the maintenance of the

> general interest of this country and especially with the improvement of the condition of the labouring classes, the Corn Law is practically at an end.[29]

In 1839 his practical hope was for a better Corn Bill that would help the working classes. Later, in 1842, describing his plans for reducing a range of tariffs that year, Peel was more focused: 'the great object...is the welfare and benefit of the great body of people'.[30] With regard to 1846, in his *Memoirs*, before presenting a case based on famine, Peel cited the interests of 'the whole community' and his 'serious doubts whether ...cheapness and plenty are not ensured for the future' better by free trade than protection.[31] His emphasis in his *Memoirs* on the role of the famine in his decision-making may well have been because the wider aim of low prices seemed weak and unsubstantiated, by comparison. Yet, even in 1850, he argued that the 'condition of the working classes' was still 'the test by which the merits of the question [commercial policy] must be decided'.[32]

Peel's views were strengthened by a fear of revolution, one which was common among politicians of his generation. David Eastwood has highlighted Peel's belief in 1842 'that if prices and unemployment continued at the current levels the security of property would be imperilled'.[33] Cobden claimed that Peel, on hearing of the overthrow of the French government in the 1848 revolution, had said:

> ...this comes of trying to govern the country through a narrow representation in Parliament, without regarding the wishes of those outside. It is what this party behind me [the protectionist Conservatives] wanted me to do in the matter of the Corn Laws [in 1846], and I would not do it.[34]

Both the working classes and middle-class industrialists were included in his reference to 'those outside' Parliament, but Peel's enquiries for evidence were focused on the working classes, particularly those living in industrial areas in the midlands and north of England.[35] These enquiries led Peel to believe lower food prices tended to benefit the working classes and would not necessarily lower industrial or agricultural wages.

Although Hilton has pointed out 'the "danger of civil war" argument' was mainly highlighted 'by those historians who wish to label Peel first and foremost as a pragmatist', a less extreme version of this concern also fits into his long-term aim, as Stewart has put it, of pre-empting the demands of the mob and taking care not to 'excite the feelings and inflame the passions of the people'.[36] Peter Ghosh has emphasised that Peel's 'oddity' in attending to the needs of the impoverished addressed 'a serious danger to the aristocracy'; this interest may have also been triggered by Peel's apprehension of attempts at electoral reform in the 1830s and 1840s.[37]

Therefore, Peel's attitude to the policy of free trade varied according to whether he believed it would produce the outcome he understood the masses wanted. He had defined their demand in his Tamworth Manifesto of 1841. In that election speech he sympathised with 'the poor manufacturers of Nuneaton' and their hope for 'increased employment, and a reduction in the price of bread'.[38] However, he went on to explain that great care has to be exercised in alterations to the Corn Laws in order to achieve the results wished for because even the experts did not agree.[39] Peel was wary of taking action that would cause increased fluctuations in prices whose negative effects could outweigh any benefits from slightly lower prices. Fluctuations in food prices, he argued in this period, were greater than the fluctuations in the supply which was supposed to cause them. In 1840 he looked to the sliding scale to stabilise prices:

> Now neither upon this point would he pretend to deny that there had been great fluctuation in the price of corn, greater fluctuation than he wished to see in an article of such general consumption, but at the same time he doubted whether it would not be found upon examination that there had been a great or greater steadiness under the sliding scale, as it was called, than could be hoped for under any other system.[40]

At this time, he did not believe that full-blown free trade would stabilise prices:

> With respect to the fluctuations in price I confess, having paid my best attention to his subject, that I have great doubts whether your expectations, that free trade in corn will produce a great fixity in price will be realised... The main object to be attained is a comparatively fixed price.[41]

In 1842 he was still following this belief:

> ...prices are more peculiarly affected by influences which fluctuate, and must of necessity be uncertain—... it appears to me that the strict principles of free trade cannot be applied without danger to the interests of the community.[42]

Initially he was influenced by his President of the Board of Trade between 1841 and 1844, Robinson, who by this time had become known as the first Earl of Ripon. Ripon was a believer in 'reciprocity' rather than full free trade.[43] He advised Peel against unilateral reductions in tariffs. Most notably, on 7 October 1841, he wrote to Peel advising against reform of the Corn Laws as 'it would not be liked by our friends either in or out of Parliament' and that 'it would be most dangerous, if not fatal, to take any course that would make us habitually dependent on foreign countries for our supply of bread and corn'.[44] In a letter dated 29 November 1841 Ripon stated that previous experience showed that reciprocity was the only policy that worked to persuade other countries to reduce their tariffs on British goods.

> We have tried ineffectually to induce them [foreign governments] to open their doors by the partial openings from time to time we have made: mere example has not operated but offers of conditional advantages may have a very different effect and if we can get some one important state to come to an understanding with us, others will be obliged to follow.[45]

By contrast, as Colin Matthew pointed out, Gladstone was ideologically driven: once convinced of the case for unilaterally reducing tariffs, he even attempted to challenge Peel on 'corn law revision' and then threatened resignation when he did not get his way.[46] These events indicate that there were conflicting ideas within the Board of Trade, with Gladstone as a unilateralist free trader and Ripon as a multilateralist.[47]

Ripon tended to avoid conflict within the Board of Trade by deferring arguments with Gladstone to the prime minister, which gave Gladstone an opportunity to persuade Peel of the correctness of his views.[48] As a result of this access, Gladstone was increasingly successful in persuading Peel of the case for unilateral tariff reductions. Peel came to be convinced that his principal aim, to lower prices, was not put at risk by slight imbalances of trade, which Ripon's slow path to free trade through bilateral agreements was intended to guard against.

The 1842 budget, in which Peel's new government cut 750 out of 1200 import duties and re-introduced the income tax, was intended to lower food prices while eliminating the UK-wide budget deficit.[49] The Whig experiment of raising tariffs to reduce the budget deficit in 1840–1841 had failed to produce sufficient revenue. Peel used this experience to justify reducing them instead, but with the same aim of a balanced budget.[50] His rhetoric as leader of the opposition during this period blamed the size of the deficit on Whig mismanagement.[51] In an attempt to silence such criticisms, in May 1840, Baring, the Whig chancellor of the exchequer, introduced a 5% increase in Customs and Excise Duties and 10% in Assessed Taxes to reduce an estimated deficit of £1,851,000. This was the first budget in decades to increase import duties on this scale.[52] Although these reforms benefited rural areas including Ireland, where the Repeal of the Union movement enjoyed little support, and West Wales, where the economically driven Rebecca riots abated, manufacturing suffered and United Kingdom's economy began to contract.[53]

Peel carefully considered whether a fall in prices would cause a fall in wages in both agricultural and commercial sectors and came to the conclusion that:

> the wages of the agricultural labourer did not vary in a direct ratio with the price of corn. He was speaking then of agricultural labourers only, and he thought he had proved his assertion to be founded in fact. But in speaking of the manufacturing and not of the agricultural labourer, he (Sir R. Peel) said he thought he could show that at many times and in many cases the wages of the manufacturing labourer had varied in an inverse ratio to the price of corn.[54]

Peel's support for free-trade ideas therefore developed over a period and he put it into practice only when economic circumstances were right and when he was sure it would serve his purpose of improving the condition of the working classes. As Gladstone himself pointed out to his father, he did not make Peel a 'free trader'; the prime minister made the decision to repeal the Corn Laws himself at the end of 1845 after his protégé had resigned as President of the Board of Trade much earlier that year for unrelated reasons.[55] Nevertheless, his intention was still to introduce it gradually, in contrast to the Whigs who were offering full free trade immediately.[56]

The 'repeal' of the Corn Laws, and also the Banking Acts, were only partial in nature and this shows how Peel was trying to introduce legislation which was intended to only have moderate effects—in effect a gradualist approach. Privately, Graham explained to Croker, in 1845, the overall aim of a gradualist approach to lowering food prices and how it seemed to have succeeded so far:

> ...we have laboured hard and not in vain to restore the prosperity of the country, and to give a measure of security to the Aristocracy by improving the condition and diminishing the discontent of the great Mass of the People. We have affected this without inflicting any real injury on the Landed Proprietors...[57]

The idea was to moderate and stabilise food prices without harming the agricultural sector. For instance, Peel's 'repeal of the Corn Laws' was in fact only a half measure. Peel only reduced part of the sliding scale of duties with his changes of 1842, smoothing out the scale at its lower end. Even in Peel's 1846 legislation, it can be seen from Fig. 2.1 that duty still rose as prices dropped below a certain level.

That was to ensure that food prices would drop far enough to help Ireland, which at this time was going through the Great Famine, while

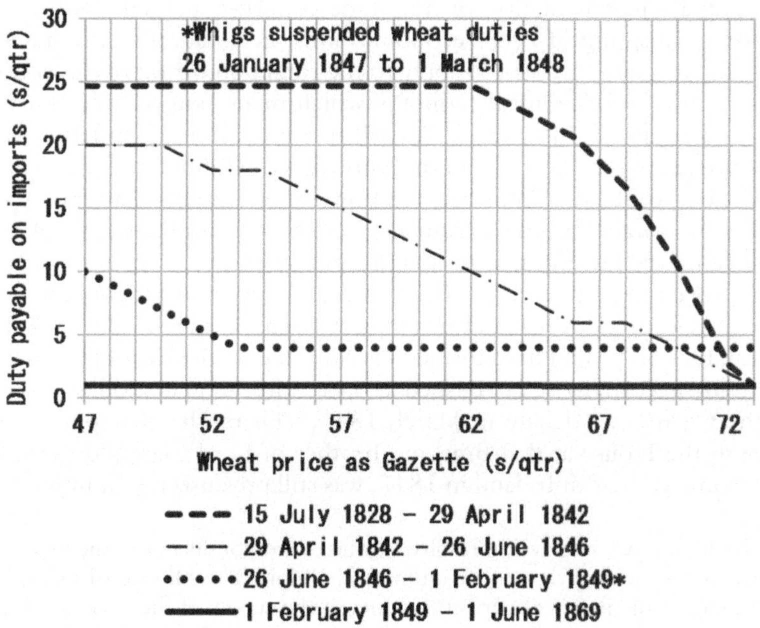

Fig. 2.1 Duty payable per quarter for foreign imports of wheat according to price in shillings/quarter 1828–1869[58] (*Sources* 9 Geo. IV. c.60; 5 & 6 Vict. c.14; 9 & 10 Vict. c.22)

not destroying the livelihoods of farmers across the United Kingdom. Repeal of more of the sliding scale was provided for in the legislation but had to wait until 1849. And even then a duty of one shilling per quarter was retained.

Peel's phased approach to introducing low tariffs in 1846 caused him to be attacked from both sides of the debate. As well as the protectionist members of his own party on one side, he was attacked by the Whigs for not bringing in free trade in one step. If this happened, Peel believed the agricultural districts, including Ireland, would suffer, and it was better that free trade was introduced slowly by a Conservative government than all at once by a Whig government, who, he worried, were more guided by liberal '*laissez faire, et laissez passer*' dogma than a well thought out economic aims and policy.[59]

Hilton has indicated that the *laissez faire* attitudes Peel might have had were generally 'social' in nature.[60] As far as economic policy is concerned, his gradual implementation of free trade confirms such an ideology was not the mainspring of Peel's economic aims. Peel had explicitly stated in 1845 he 'was not prepared to apply to the rural population of this country those principles of political economy which many hon. Gentlemen were disposed to do'.[61] In contrast, Russell had written an open letter to his constituents in the City of London (known as the Edinburgh letter) on 22 November 1845, declaring 'observation and experience have convinced me that we ought to abstain from all interference with the supply of food' and urging the government to unite to put an end to 'a system which has been proved to be the blight of commerce, the bane of agriculture'.[62] On failing to form a government in January 1846, Russell jeered at Peel for fearing that he 'would have formed his Ministry on the basis of a complete free trade in corn, to be established at once, without gradation or delay'.[63] In the Corn Laws debate in March 1846, Villiers, the champion of free trade in the House at that time and brother of Lord Clarendon who was to become viceroy of Ireland in 1847, was still pressurising for immediacy:

> The House has very wisely resolved to take into consideration the protective system with a view to its ultimate abolition. The Ministerial measure recognises the policy of perfect freedom in the supply of the necessaries of life to the people of this country; but it has postponed the full application of that principle until the 1st of February 1849. In my opinion that delay is not called for. It is my conscientious belief that the full advantage of

> the Ministerial scheme may be extended to this country at once, without danger or inconvenience to any class of the community.[64]

In response, Peel said he would ignore all other points except 'the question whether it be desirable that the repeal of the corn duties should be immediate, or whether they should continue, as Her Majesty's Government propose, for a period of three years', showing how important the issue was for him.[65] He explained that the legislation was dual purpose, helping Ireland and changing permanently the import duties. Although tariffs were only to be slowly reduced on grain, immediate and complete reductions on Indian corn and rice were designed to help Ireland.[66] The three-year delay before a further reduction was, he said, to avoid 'a panic greatly depressing the price of wheat' and to 'meet the wishes...of the agricultural interest'.[67] Peel also proposed several measures, including government loans and relief to rural districts from the cost of pauperism, to help boost agricultural efficiency so as to 'enable the landed interest to meet the competition' from foreign corn producers over this time.[68] Peel had explained his plans in much the same way to Prince Albert who had noted in a memorandum, quoted in full at the start of this chapter, that:

> Sir Robert has an immense scheme in view... He will deal with the whole commercial system of the country. He will adopt the principle of the League, that of removing all protection and abolishing all monopoly, but not in favour of one class and as a triumph over another, but to the benefit of the nation, farmers as well as manufacturers.[69]

2.3 Currency

In short, Britain's move towards free trade was influenced less by *laissez faire* social theory, but more by Peel's intended desire to promote stability while simultaneously protecting the interests of the labouring poor through lower food prices. Likewise, the intentions behind his other major and long-lasting economic reform of the 1840s, reform of the British currency and the Bank of England's charter, was also driven less by pure Currency-School theory and more by the belief that this was the method by which financial stability and stable prices could be promoted and future banking crises avoided. As we shall see, these intended objectives, at least as far as the banking sector was concerned, failed to be delivered in practice. Nonetheless, these aims were very sincerely intended by Peel.

The controversies over currency which dominated Peel's era in the nineteenth century arose from the period of the Napoleonic wars. In 1717 Sir Isaac Newton, the master of the Royal Mint, established a new mint ratio between silver and gold that had the effect of driving silver out of circulation and putting Britain on a gold standard. This gold standard was maintained by the Bank of England until the Napoleonic Wars: its bank notes could be converted on demand to the equivalent sum of gold coin. However, in 1797, when there were rumours of a French invasion of Britain, banks were besieged by holders of bank notes trying to exchange them for gold. Even the Bank of England faced a stoppage as its holdings of gold reduced to around £1.1m. The then government, under William Pitt the Younger, faced borrowing at a rate of 6.7% and took emergency measures to ban notes being converted to gold coin and these were confirmed in the Bank Restriction Act (37 Geo III, c.45).[70] The measures were extended several times in 1803. Finally on 15 December 1803 they were set to continue until six months after a definitive treaty of peace.[71] The war against France lasted until 1815, but disagreements with America after the War of 1812 prolonged the period of hostilities to January 1819. Resumption was therefore due to take place in July 1819.

When the legislation containing this timing had been laid down, the return to gold had been seen as essential for the stability of the currency as bank notes were losing their value against gold and for prices which were inflating. However, in 1819 the exchanges for currency and price of gold were unstable. Nicholas Vansittart, Liverpool's chancellor of the exchequer until early 1823, resisted a return to 'cash payments', the system where the Bank of England guaranteed to exchange banknotes, on demand, for gold. So committees were appointed in the British Parliament to investigate the advisability of returning to what was, in effect, a gold standard.[72]

Evidence given to the Committees differed as to the benefits of convertibility of the pound to gold at a fixed value and the inevitable restriction in the number of notes this would entail. Alexander Baring, a partner in Baring Bros. and Co. and a Banking-School opponent-to-be of the Bank Charter Act of 1844, pointed out that a reserve of gold would have to be kept by banks to fund payments. It followed that notes would have to be limited, by the judgement of banks, according to the number for which the limited gold available could provide a guarantee.

In contrast, David Ricardo, now seen as one of the major inspirations behind what later became ideas of the Currency School, considered such a restriction would be beneficial. He had produced a pamphlet blaming the depreciation of pound notes on the high number of notes issued. Questioned on the new circumstances he persisted in arguing that 'from whatever cause a bad exchange arises it may be corrected by a reduction in the amount of currency'.[73]

The use of the word 'exchange', as Ricardo does here, has multiple meanings in nineteenth-century banking. It can refer to the balance of trade, an exchange rate, as it does here for gold, but as 'foreign exchanges' it can refer to flows of gold or bullion between countries. While the restriction of note issue was to become a central Currency-School idea, Ricardo also acknowledged concepts which were to form part of Banking-School thinking: the commercial demand for notes and the restriction of the international mobility of gold coin. He considered that the quantity of circulation should be determined both 'upon its value and the quantity of business which it has to perform'.[74] He had to return to the House of Commons to amend his advice that international mobility of gold should be allowed to suggest that a 'seignorage', or charge upon the coining of gold should be made to pay for the Mint's costs, which would inhibit the export of gold coin.[75]

Immediate opposition to Ricardo's Currency-School views came from Nathan Rothschild, a banker, who foresaw 'considerable deflation' and Samuel Gurney who preferred notes to be secured by a mixture of 'loans to government, commercial bills and bullion'.[76] Even so, Peel, the chairman of the House of Commons Committee formed to decide this issue, saw the move to convertibility as a step towards stable food prices. He recommended a return and in May 1819 introduced the Bill for the Act of Resumption.[77] His solution for the possible instability as the new exchange rate was imposed was similar to his approach to free trade: a policy of gradual introduction.

Under the Act, cash payments were to be resumed at the latest by 1 May 1823. However, between 1 February 1820 and 1 May 1823 notes would be cashed at a rate which increased from the current value based on the price of gold to around the Treasury target or 'par' (i.e. £1 note = £1 gold coin). This was intended to set the fixed exchange at the desired rate from May 1823. After this time, the United Kingdom would be on a gold standard with a fixed exchange rate with any other country pursuing the same policy. The Act of Resumption also declared the trade in bullion to be free, in other words, providing the opportunity for free capital movement linked to the gold standard.[78]

This legislation cured an immediate problem: the depreciation of the value of bank notes against gold coin, which had lost up to a quarter of their face value by 1814, as shown in Table 2.1.

The loss of value of British pound notes against gold was followed closely by the pattern of variation of the pound's exchange rate against other currencies (Fig. 4.2 compares the British pound to the French franc and American dollar). This demonstrates that the loss of value was confined to the pound and not a feature of other currencies at the time.

After the Act of Resumption, note-issuing banks were left to manage their own bullion reserves to ensure they had sufficient to exchange for notes on demand. There were two theories in existence to assist them, the competing concepts of the price-specie flow theory and the reflux theory. The theories implied different reactions to a crisis caused by a drain of bullion. The price-specie flow theory, favoured by those who tended to the Currency School, implied that in a balance of payments crisis, credit had to be restricted. This would lower domestic commodity prices, which would encourage exports that in turn would eventually return enough bullion to cover the drain. Those tending to the Banking-School position believed that restricting credit harmed commerce and that bullion flows could be curbed directly by increasing interest rates.

Among the latter was Henry Thornton, whose writings contain a mixture of ideas favoured by the Currency and Banking Schools. He saw that, if Britain was one of two countries which shared identical currencies, and it suffered a bullion drain:

Table 2.1 Loss of value of Bank of England notes against gold coin[79]

Loss on £100 in gold			
1801	£8 7s	1814	£25 3s
1802	£7 5s	1815	£19 14s
1803–1809	£2 3s	1816	£16 14s
1810	£13 9s	1817–1818	£2 13s
1811	£7 16s	1819	£4 9s
1812	£20 14s	1820	£2 12s
1813	£22 18s	1821	par (£0)

> ...the whole [amount of bullion] would not leave us; a high rate of interest would arise, and this extra profit on the use of gold, which would increase as its quantity diminished, would contribute to detain it here—some foreigners, probably, transferring property which would take the shape of the precious metals, or continuing to afford to us the use of it for the sake of this high interest.[80]

His theory was very different from the price-specie flow theory of the Currency School because that involved trade and commodity prices. In contrast, Thornton's theory was concerned with bullion as a means of investment, a very 'Banking School' concept. It raised the possibility of using interest rates to control capital flows if market interest rates could be changed by altering the Bank of England minimum discount rate, more commonly known as just the 'Bank Rate'.[81] Horsley Palmer, a well-respected Governor of the Bank of England in the 1830s, believed that this manipulation of interest rates was perfectly possible to achieve.[82] In a crisis, he thought, the market was sure to follow the Bank of England because other banks relied on it for additional liquidity when it was in short supply.[83]

However, Thornton also pointed out the dangers of interest-rate manipulation, either by setting it too high or too low too quickly. Doing so, he thought, could disrupt self-balancing systems, such as the price-specie flow theory and the reflux theory, by creating additional credit. Where different rates of interest existed, monies borrowed at one rate could be invested at the higher one and the resulting interest invested as deposits which were loaned as increased credit. He had in mind the Bank of England's discount rate, held below 5% by the usury laws, and the higher mercantile rate, which is the return produced by the private sector through, for instance, profits of trade or investment in property. This process would continue until, similarly to the law of one price, the different interest rates equalised through arbitrage.[84]

The usury laws were gradually relaxed in the early nineteenth century so that the Bank of England could raise the Bank Rate and discount at higher rates of interest than 5%.[85] Over this period, Palmer laid down the 'Palmer rule' about how the Bank of England should manage its reserves. It owed something to both Schools of thought. Under the rule the Bank should generally aim to keep a reserve equal to a third of its notes issued *plus* its deposits.[86] The notes and deposits made up the liabilities of the Bank. On the asset side it had its bullion reserve and securities.[87] As the bullion drain commenced, the Palmer rule required that the level of investment in interest bearing securities be maintained so that the reduction in bullion reserve bore down upon notes *and* deposits.

As it turned out, the Bank of England did not implement the Palmer rule fully and it was never fairly put to the test. However, Peel, Charles Wood, (chancellor of the exchequer 1846–1852), Robert Torrens (an economist) and Lord Overstone (also known as S. Jones-Loyd), an important Currency-School thinker, criticised the Palmer rule. When the Bank's charter came up for renewal in the 1840s, they pushed for a limit on note issue only, tied very strictly to the bullion reserve.[88] The Bank Charter Act of 1844 incorporated a requirement for the quantity of notes issued (which included notes held in reserve) to not rise above the amount of bullion and coin plus a fiduciary sum of £14m which was to be backed by securities. The limitation of note issue alone was justified by Peel as concentrating on the type of money which was most likely to affect commodity (including food) prices, Peel's ultimate target for stabilisation:

> There is a material distinction, in my opinion, between the character of a promissory note payable to bearer on demand, and other forms of paper credit, and between the effects which they respectively produce upon the prices of commodities and upon the exchanges.[89]

By not controlling all types of money Peel was following a moderate middle course, as with the removal of food tariffs gradually. The principle behind this provision was strongly influenced by the ideas of the Currency School. The Act also split the Bank into two departments: the issue department, to deal with the issue of banknotes, and the banking department, which acted as a commercial bank. Such a division had been called for since the suggestion of Thomas Joplin in 1823 that a national bank run by commissioners be set up to run the note issue, an idea he repeated in 1840 to look after the issues of country banks.[90] Ricardo drafted a proposal in 1834 for a National Bank along similar lines, but died soon thereafter.[91] Although Ricardo's bank would have been run by commissioners, it would still have carried out the commercial business of managing the government's debt.

However, Peel's solution here, once again, was very much one of half-measures. The true principle of separating out the currency function into a Currency Board run by commissioners was only put into action for the first time by the Third Earl Grey, advised by James Wilson, at the end of the 1840s in Mauritius.[92] It was one of three options considered for the pound sterling and the Bank of England when the Bank Charter Act was being planned in 1844. In the 'compromise' option chosen, the Bank of England's issue department contained the bullion and coins which backed the issued notes that were with the public and the reserve of notes held in the Bank. However, the gold was not all owned by the Bank. It could also be called upon by a variety of depositors with the banking department. The securities which backed the fiduciary issue were made up of £11.0151m of historic public debt and additional securities provided by the Bank. The additional securities were counted in the issue department. It is not clear whether they also appeared as part of securities in the banking department balance sheet, counted as an asset against which deposits were liabilities.[93] This was implied by George Clare, a banker writing in 1900, but has been seemingly contradicted by some recently published presentations of the data by the Bank of England.[94] The dual role of gold in the Bank's reserve was to cause problems as it fluctuated according to the withdrawal of deposits, which then put pressure upon the maximum number of notes that it could issue.

Even so, the restriction on note issuance in the Bank Charter Act of 1844 pleased the Currency School. At this stage they were not worried about bank deposits. Peel and others in Parliament did not see that the restriction upon deposits was useful because they could not see how idle bank deposits affected commodity prices.[95] Furthermore, the Currency School feared that the reduction in deposits could be carried out disproportionally so that the note issue was maintained.[96] After the 1847 financial crisis, they changed tack and saw deposits as an uncontrolled source of money. However, the deposits restriction pleased the Banking School because it bore down upon the excess credit which Thornton had suggested raised interest rates might bring.[97] That increase in interest rates would be necessary, the Banking School believed, to bring back bullion quickly from abroad when the drain had been 'external'. Although many Banking School inclined theorists, including Thomas Tooke, accepted the quantity theory of money and how it affected commodity prices, they argued that the differences in price variations actually observed were not large enough to bring bullion back home under the price-specie flow theory in the way Currency School believed would happen.

Peel's view that the 1844 Act would stabilise prices was supported by the theories of S. Jones-Loyd (Lord Overstone from 1850), the intellectual leader of the Currency School. Peel was present when Loyd gave evidence to the 1840 Committee on Banks of Issue. Loyd, who is said to have 'undoubtedly influenced' Peel, was closely questioned on prices.[98] He stated, after some pressure, that if the 1819 Act re-introducing a gold standard had been properly constituted 'considerable fluctuations in prices…would have been avoided'.[99] However, he was unwilling to say exactly whether prices would rise or fall because of other factors such as the success of harvests.[100] Peel's pronouncements in Parliament very much reflect the Loyd line, both being unwilling to predict price movements but showing an underlying belief that a gold standard exerted a downward pressure and brought stability to prices.

The 1847 financial crises and the failure to successfully raise enough loans to pay for famine relief in Ireland provoked Earl Grey to demand an enquiry on the commercial distress and the 1844 Act from Lord Russell, then prime minister.[101] Peel and Wood, as chancellor of the exchequer, who supported the former prime minister's main economic policies, dominated the Commons enquiries. Although the enquiry held by the House of Lords concluded 'that the Panic was materially aggravated by the operation of that Statute [the Act of 1844]', this opinion was ignored by the government, as it was entitled to do in the absence of the agreement of the House of Commons, where the same motion was defeated by just two votes.[102]

And, thus, by the narrowest of margins in Parliament, the Currency-School view and Bank Charter Act of 1844 survived. They eventually became the orthodox view on how the pound should be administered—with the exception of a few short periods of suspension during crises and the first world war—until Britain left the gold standard in 1931. Even then, its legacy endures. Substantial portions of the 1844 Act, which granted the Bank of England its monopoly over the issue of banknotes in England and Wales, are still in force today.[103]

2.4 Interest Rates

Although the Bank Charter Act of 1844 eventually triumphed, the matter of how to set interest rates has remained a point of contention between adherents of the Banking and the Currency Schools ever since. The context of this debate is starkly macroeconomic, namely the failure by politicians to raise taxes enough to cover the enormous cost of the Napoleonic Wars. Faced with Parliamentary resistance against tax rises on the scale necessary to defray the entire cost of the conflict, there was little choice but to resort to increased government borrowing. The result was that Britain's national debt soared from around 100% of GDP at the start of the war to some 260% by the time it ended in 1815. As a result, with the onset of peace, interest on the national debt came to take up over half of government expenditure from 1817 onwards (see Fig. 2.2). With such a large debt it was difficult to raise more funds for later emergencies, such as for Irish famine relief in 1847. To create fiscal capacity for such events, it soon became clear to policymakers that they needed to keep the overall cost of servicing the national debt affordable.

Various methods of reducing the rate of interest paid on government debt were attempted. One of these, pioneered in the early eighteenth century, was Sir Robert Walpole's sinking fund, which involved the government borrowing when rates were low to buy its own debt when it could do so at a discount and using some of the interest on it to

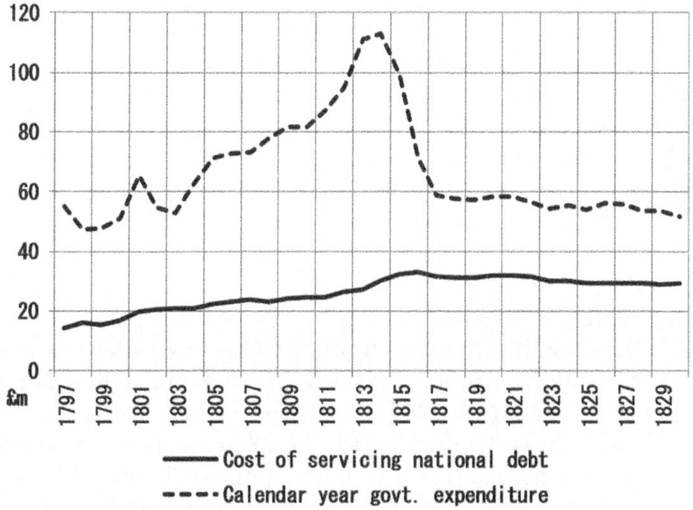

Fig. 2.2 Cost of interest on national debt and government expenditure 1797–1830 (£m) (*Source* B. R. Mitchell, *British Historical Statistics* [Cambridge: Cambridge University Press, 1988] pp. 575–593)

buy further debt. When William Pitt continued this idea the rates of interest became high, thanks to the war, and the scheme lost money. Eventually it was wound up in 1829. Long-term government debt was sold as consols, which paid a specified rate of interest, but which could only be redeemed when the government chose. Later chancellors, such as Graham and Goschen, redeemed consols when long-term rates were low and offered new consols paying a lower rate than before, which many investors accepted for lack of an alternative.

After the Napoleonic wars, the cost of servicing the wartime debt was borne disproportionately by indirect taxation. The income tax expired in 1816. The Corn Laws, the tariffs on grain imports the burden of which fell on the poor, made up some of the shortfall. However, this fiscal settlement was under strain by the end of the 1830s. The Whig governments of that decade struggled under public demands for lower indirect taxation as well as more public services provided by the state. The large losses caused by the introduction of Rowland Hill's new Penny Post service in 1840 brought matters to a head. A growing annual deficit increased the cost of government borrowing, raising the deficit further.

This experience—which Peel as leader of the opposition blamed clearly on 'Whig mismanagement'—hardened Peel's pre-existing thoughts on fiscal policy. From an early stage, Peel tended to favour direct over indirect taxation and made a 'balanced budget', in other words the idea that the Treasury should not run a fiscal deficit, a key objective of government. He re-introduced the income tax in 1842 to recompense for the government income lost through reduced tariffs. However, initially the legislation had to be renewed every three years. After his repeal of the Corn Laws split the Conservative Party in 1846 this led to problems. Subsequent weak minority governments found it increasingly difficult to renew it in Parliament, while raising the rate charged proved impossible. Matters, most notably, came to a head in 1847–1848 when more money needed to be found to continue to finance Irish famine relief. The Russell government had found in 1847 that raising a loan for relief from the City of London was very difficult with the 1844 Act in place. Meanwhile, raising the rate of income tax was almost impossible owing to a lack of a majority in Parliament, leaving the Treasury with only local taxation in Ireland as a source of finance for relief.[104]

So traumatic were the problems associated with Peel's macroeconomic policies and raising the Irish loan in 1847 that it inspired the parsimony of Gladstonian finance in subsequent decades. When Gladstone became chancellor of the exchequer in December 1852, at the very end of the Irish famine, he vowed to ensure the Treasury would never again have to go 'begging to the Bank'.[105] The Treasury needed to be, Gladstone wrote, 'provided with an instrument sufficiently powerful to make him [the chancellor of the exchequer] independent of the Bank and the City power when he has occasion for sums in seven figures'.[106] Building fiscal capacity through paying down debt and borrowing directly from the public by setting up the Post Office Savings Bank in 1861 was Gladstone's strategy.[107] And it is clear that the incident on Gladstone's mind was the Irish loan panic of 1847, when Wood tried to borrow a seven-figure sum to spend on Irish relief—£8,000,000—and found himself at the mercy of unnerved and unstable money markets in the City of London.

Nevertheless, even as successive governments sought to reduce long-term interest rates, the Bank of England began to use its influence to raise short-term interest rates via the Bank Rate to counter bullion outflows. The Bank never fully explained its decisions on interest rates and whether these were based on the theories of the Currency School or the Banking School. Most probably the Court of Directors decided on balance, with individual members of the Court having different reasons for their votes.

Occasional evidence given to government enquiries suggests that in the 1830s the normal response to bullion drains was to restrict credit, the favoured solution of the Currency School. The restriction on credit was supposed to reduce prices, increase exports and bring back bullion in payment. Palmer agreed in 1832 that raising the interest rate could be a short cut to raising prices 'with the increased value of money'.[108] This still assumed the Currency-School theory based on Hume's price-specie flow mechanism, but in 1848, commenting on the 1847 crisis Palmer was describing an effect whereby interest rates directly influenced the movement of funds between countries, and were at least partially responsible for international bullion flows, a position associated with the Banking School.[109] The differing pressures of government and bankers upon interest rates did not directly conflict because, as Palmer pointed out in 1832, there was little connection between the long-term rates that were of concern to government and the short-term rates that were of concern to bankers.[110] However, such a sudden disparity between the two sets of rates was just the situation that Thornton had described when he suggested that additional credit could be created by borrowing at one rate and investing at another.[111] It was this additional credit, he argued, that lay at the root of banking crises.

2.5 Conclusion

Peel's policies were intended to bring in an era of stability and prosperity. Some historians have since lauded him as the 'chief architect of the mid-Victorian age of stability'.[112] This interpretation has in recent decades become a dominant part of the liberally minded historical literature on why there were no revolutions in mid-Victorian Britain. In Peel's own era, those sympathetic to Currency-School policies promoted his reputation for having made Britain a commercially successful nation. Lord Northcote, who wrote in 1862 a review of financial policy since Peel's budget of 1842, expressed satisfaction that 'the last twenty years have witnessed… a marked development of the wealth and prosperity of the country'.[113] The Bank Charter Act of 1844, which Peel introduced, was credited with securing the reputation of the British pound by making it convertible into and linked to the value of gold. Tight fiscal policy and a downward pressure on interest rates helped to advance the goal of a 'minimum state', which contributed towards the paying off of the national debt. All these strands of policy came to be known as 'sound finance' a policy direction which was followed by Gladstone, and then survived beyond that time as 'the Treasury view'.

However, in reality, Peel's policy changes also brought a backlash which became known as the Banking School. If Peel's policies were about bringing Britain stability and prosperity, they were far from a complete economic success. The Banking School believed that the optimistic view that venerated Peel's policies and reputation ignored the fact that several banking crises and deep recessions seemed to repeat almost every ten years after his reforms were implemented. There may have been no political revolutions in mainland Britain in Peel's era, but economic, financial and banking instability continued nonetheless. Even before 1844, there was the very severe banking crisis of 1825 which followed the return of the pound to convertibility in line with Peel's recommendations of 1819–1821. In 1837 both America and Britain suffered a financial crisis, which have been seen by several scholars as being the result of the growing linkages between their banking systems. Further systemic banking crises (and near misses) occurred in Britain in 1847, 1855–1857, 1860–1861 and 1863–1866, all of which threatened the centralised banking system as legally established by the Bank Charter Act of 1844. So severe were these crises that in 1847, 1857 and 1866 this legislation needed to be suspended in order to return to stability. All three crises were followed by deep economic recessions involving sharp falls in GDP. In 1847 the commercial crisis at home also caused banks, financial systems and living standards to collapse across the British empire. In 1866 London's banking crisis had even more widespread effects, spreading financial contagion around the world and causing a deep slump in world trade, as recent research by Chenzi Xu of Harvard University has shown.[114]

After 1866, however, British banking and economic stability improved considerably—even though worries about comparative economic decline against America and Germany began to grow. There continued to be minor crisis in banking but they were not systemic. In 1873 high interest rates set by the Bank of England caused only a mild period of commercial bankruptcies and panic in the United Kingdom, while a seemingly deeper crisis took place in the United States. Afterwards, calm returned to British banking. At the time, the period seemed to be one 'Long Depression', but it can be analysed as a succession of minor crises, held remarkably in check by policymakers, in 1878, 1882, 1884, 1888, 1890 and 1896–1899.

Is it Peel and his new policy regime, or is it his critics associated with the Banking School, who were responsible for this turnaround and the birth of banking stability in Victorian Britain? This is the question that the remaining chapters of this book attempt to answer. The answer they reach casts doubt on Peel's reputation among both economists and historians as the 'chief architect of the mid-Victorian age of stability'.[115]

Notes

1. Prince Albert memorandum 25 December 1845, Royal archives microfilm 95709/5; A. C. Benson, Viscount Esher, *Letters of Queen Victoria, 1861* II (London: John Murray, 1908) p. 66.
2. Based on list in C. Read, 'The Political Economy of Sir Robert Peel', in J. Hoppit, A. B. Leonard, D. J. Needham (eds.), *Money and Markets: Essays in Honour of Martin Daunton* (Woodbridge: The Boydell Press, 2019) p. 72.
3. Ibid.
4. Ibid.
5. F. Williams, *Ernest Bevin* (London: Hutchinson, 1952) p. 217.
6. H. C. G. Matthew, 'Disraeli, Gladstone, and the Politics of Mid-Victorian Budgets', *Historical Journal* 22 (1979) 615–643; H. C. G. Matthew, *Gladstone, 1809–1874* (Oxford: Clarendon Press, 1988).
7. M. Daunton, *Trusting Leviathan, The Politics of Taxation in Britain, 1799–1914* (Cambridge: CUP, 2001) p. 81.

8. For biographical details see A. B. Erickson, 'Edward T. Cardwell: Peelite', *Transactions of the American Philosophical Society* 49 (1959) 8–11.
9. Cardwell to Peel, 20 May 1847, Peel papers, B.L., Add. MS. 40598 ff. 260–265.
10. Ibid.
11. Idem., f. 263.
12. 'Election Address to the Electors of the Borough of Tamworth', 15 July 1847, Peel papers, B.L., Add. MS. 40599 ff. 24–43.
13. The only (indirect) mention of the Bank Charter Act in Peel's published memoirs is R. Peel, in Earl Stanhope, E. Cardwell (eds.), *Memoirs by the Right Honourable Sir Robert Peel* II/III (London: John Murray, 1856–1857) pp. 300–301.
14. *Hansard*, 26 May 1820, I, c.577.
15. R. B. Jenkinson, 'Earl of Liverpool', in *A Few Observations for the Consideration of the Farmers of Great Britain ... By an Agriculturist* (High Wycombe: J. W. Burnham, 1826). Handwritten notes in B.L. copy.
16. N. Gash, *Lord Liverpool* (Cambridge MS: Harvard UP, 1984) p. 221.
17. W. D. Jones, *Prosperity Robinson: The Life of Viscount Goderich 1782–1859* (London: Macmillan, 1967) p. 109.
18. C. Read, 'Peel, De Grey and Irish policy 1841-44', *History* 99 (2014) p. 17.
19. Graham to De Grey, 8 March 1842, Graham papers, B.L., Add. MS. 79620 f. 34.
20. Ibid.
21. D. Ricardo, *The Works and Correspondence of David Ricardo* I, 1817 edition (Cambridge: CUP, 1951) pp. 159, 317–318; A. Smith, *Wealth of Nations* (Oxford: OUP, 1993) pp. 149, 208, 309; J. Chodes, 'Richard Cobden: Creator of the Free Market', in B. W. Folson (ed.), *The Industrial Revolution and Free Trade* (Irvington-on-Hudson, NY: Foundation for Economic Education, 1996) pp. 41–42.
22. Daunton, *Trusting Leviathan*, p. 81.
23. D. Irwin, 'Political Economy and Peel's Repeal of the Corn Laws', *Economics and Politics* I (1989) pp. 53–55.
24. E. J. Hobsbawm, C. Wrigley, *Industry and Empire: From 1750 to the Present Day* (New York: The New Press, 1999) pp. 40–41.
25. J. Wesley, *Thoughts on the Present Scarcity of Provisions* (London: R. Hawes, 1773).
26. Importation of Corn Act 1828, 9 Geo. IV c.60.
27. Memorandum by Herries on free trade, n.d. c.1830, Wellington papers, Southampton UL, WP1/1164/11.
28. *Hansard*, 19 March 1834, XXII, c.443.
29. *Hansard*, 15 March 1839, XLVI, c.757.

30. *Hansard*, 16 February 1842, LX, c.592.
31. Peel, *Memoirs* II/III, p. 102.
32. R. Peel, *Speeches of the late Sir Robert Peel, Bart., 1842–50* IV (London: Routledge, 1853) p. 835, Taxation of the Country debate, 12 March 1850; see also p. 833.
33. D. Eastwood '"Recasting Our Lot": Peel the Nation and the Politics of Interest', in L. Brockliss, D. Eastwood (eds.), *A Union of Multiple Identities: The British Isles c.1750–c.1850* (Manchester: Manchester UP, 1977) p. 35.
34. J. Bright, J. E. Thorold Rogers (eds.), *Speeches on Questions of Public Policy by Richard Cobden, M.P.* II (London: T. Fisher Unwin, 1908) pp. 580–581.
35. For example, 'Workers Wages in Barnstable Union', Peel papers, B.L., Add. MS. 40566 ff. 64–377b.
36. B. Hilton, 'The Ripening of Robert Peel', in M. Bentley (ed.), *Public and Private Doctrine: Essays in British History Presented to Maurice Cowling* (Cambridge: CUP, 1993) p. 71; R. Stewart, *The Politics of Protectionism: Lord Derby and the Protectionist Party 1841-52* (Cambridge: CUP, 1971) p. 35; *Hansard*, 5 June 1832, XIII, c.426.
37. P. Ghosh, 'Gladstone and Peel', in P. Ghosh, L. Goldman (eds.), *Politics and Culture in Victorian Britain: Essays in Memory of Colin Matthew* (Oxford: OUP, 2006) pp. 47–51.
38. R. Peel, *Tamworth Election: Speech of Sir Robert Peel, June 28, 1841* (London: John Ollivier, 1841) p. 12.
39. See Irwin, 'Political Economy and Peel's Repeal of the Corn Laws', p. 45 for more examples of Peel's opinion of political economists as disagreeing on this subject.
40. *Hansard*, 3 April 1840, LIII, c.523.
41. *Hansard*, 27 August 1841, LIX, c.419.
42. *Hansard*, 16 February 1842, LX, c.604.
43. Jones, *Prosperity Robinson*, pp. 249–251.
44. Ripon to Peel, 7 October 1841, Peel papers, B.L., Add. MS. 40464 f. 28.
45. Ripon to Peel, 29 November 1841, Ripon papers, B.L., Add. MS. 40863 f. 254.
46. Matthew, *Gladstone 1809–1874*, p. 66.
47. Jones, *Prosperity Robinson*, p. 278; Ripon to Peel, 29 November 1841, Ripon papers, B.L., Add. MS. 40863 f. 254.
48. Ripon to Gladstone, October 1842, Gladstone papers, B.L., Add. MS. 44731 f. 5.
49. N. Gash, *Sir Robert Peel: The Life of Sir Robert Peel after 1830* (London: Longman, 1972) p. 319; A. Howe, *Free Trade and Liberal England 1846–1946* (Oxford: OUP) p. 4.

50. 1841 budget: *Hansard*, 30 April 1841, LVII, cc.1295–1372; for tax changes see B. Hilton, 'Peel: A Reappraisal', *Historical Journal* 22 (1979) p. 597; Peel cutting tariffs to produce 'cheapness', B. Hilton, *Cash, Corn, Commerce: The Economic Policies of the Tory Governments 1815–1830* (Oxford: OUP, 1977) pp. 257–258, fiscal aim of balanced budget, p. 267.
51. *Hansard*, 15 May 1840, LIV, c.156.
52. D. Steele, 'Baring, Francis Thornhill, first Baron Northbrook (1796–1866)', *Oxford Dictionary of National Biography* (OUP, 2004), online edn, Jan 2008; L. Brown, *The Board of Trade and the Free-Trade Movement 1830–1842* (Oxford: OUP, 1958) p. 219.
53. W. J. O'Neill Daunt, *Ireland and her Agitators* (Dublin: J. Browne, 1845) p. 215, cited in P. M. Geoghegan, *Liberator: The Life and Death of Daniel O'Connell 1830–1847* (Dublin: Gill & Macmillan, 2010) p. 115; D. Williams, *The Rebecca Riots: A Study in Agrarian Discontent* (Cardiff: University of Wales Press, 1955) pp. vii, 189; A. Odlyzk, 'Collective Hallucinations and Inefficient Markets: The British Railway Mania of the 1840s' (2010) p. 32; B. R. Mitchell, *British Historical Statistics* (Cambridge: CUP, 1988) p. 837.
54. *Hansard*, 15 May 1846, LXXXVI, cc.631–632.
55. W. E. Gladstone to J. Gladstone, 30 June 1849, Glynne-Gladstone papers, Gladstone's Library, MS 229 ff. 132–135. I am indebted to Professor Douglas Kanter for being pointed in the direction of this letter and for a transcription.
56. *Hansard*, 15 May 1846, LXXXVI, cc.631–632.
57. Graham to Croker, 22 March 1845, Graham papers, B.L., Add. MS. 79618 f. 59.
58. Concept from: P. Sharp, '1846 and All That', *University of Copenhagen Department of Economics Discussion Paper*, 06–16 (2010) p. 7.
59. Russell explains the rise of '*laissez-faire*': *Hansard*, 2 April 1849, CIV, c.215.
60. Hilton, 'The Ripening of Robert Peel', p. 82.
61. *Hansard*, 2 July 1845, LXXXI, cc.1426–1427.
62. *Morning Chronicle*, 26 November 1845; *The Times*, 27 November 1845.
63. *Hansard*, 22 January 1846, LXXXIII, c.107.
64. *Hansard*, 2 March 1846, LXXXIV, c.422.
65. Idem., c.450.
66. Idem., c.451.
67. Idem., c.455.
68. *Hansard*, 27 January 1846, LXXXIII, cc.264–271.
69. Prince Albert memorandum 25 December 1845 Royal archives microfilm 95709/5; Benson, Viscount Esher, *Letters of Queen Victoria* II, pp. 65–66.

70. W. Pitt, Memorandum on debt n.d. c.1796, Chatham papers, N.A., PRO 30/8/197 ff. 50–52.
71. A. D. Gayer, W. W. Rostow, A. J. Schwartz, *The Growth and Fluctuation of the British Economy 1790–1850* (Sussex: Harvester Press, 1975) p. 79.
72. *Secret Committee on State of Bank of England with reference to expediency of resumption of Cash Payments report I* PP 1819 (202) III.3; *Report II* PP 1819 (282) III.3; *Secret Committee of the House of Lords on State of Bank of England reports I and II* PP 1819 (291) III.363.
73. *Secret Committee on State of Bank of England... I* PP 1819 (202) III.3, p. 133.
74. Idem., p. 133.
75. Idem., p. 227.
76. Idem., pp. 157, 175.
77. Idem., pp. 17–18.
78. Resumption of Cash Payments Act... 1819, 59 Geo. 3 c.49.
79. A. M. Andreadēs, *History of the Bank of England* (London: P. S. King, 1909) p. 242; *The Times*, 10 February 1826, 'The Market Price of Bullion'.
80. H. Thornton, *An Enquiry into the Nature and Effects of the Paper Credit of Great Britain* [1802 edition] (New York: Kelley, 1965) p. 331.
81. Thornton, *An Enquiry*, p. 331.
82. *Report from the Committee of Secrecy on the Bank of England Charter* PP 1831–1832 (722) VI.1, pp. 37, 44.
83. J. H. Palmer, *The Causes and Consequences of the Pressure upon the Money Market* (London: Pelham Richardson, 1837) pp. 37–38; see A. B. Cramp 'Horsley Palmer on Bank Rate', *Economica* 26 ns (1959) pp. 342–343.
84. Thornton, *An Enquiry*, pp. 335–336.
85. The maximum rate of 5% was set by the Usury Act 1714 (13 Ann. c.15). Bills of exchange, promissory notes, and discounting were gradually excluded by Usury Act 1840 (3 & 4 Vict. c.83), Usury Act 1841 (4 & 5 Vict. c.54), Usury Act 1843 (6 & 7 Vict. c.45), Usury Act 1845 (8 & 9 Vict. c.102), Usury Act 1850 (13 & 14 Vict. c.56) and Usury Laws Repeal Act 1854 (17 & 18 Vict. c.90).
86. *Report...* PP 1831–1832 (722) VI.1, pp. 11–34.
87. Bank of England daily account books, BoE archive.
88. *Report from Select Committee on Banks of Issue; with the minutes of evidence, appendix, and index* PP 1840 (602) IV.1, pp. iv–v.
89. *Hansard,* 6 May 1844, LXXIV, c.733.
90. T. Joplin, *An Analysis and History of the Currency Question* (London: Ridgway, 1832) pp. 178–81; 'Mr. Joplin's Circular to the Joint Stock Banks', *Hume Tracts* 1840, p. 1.

91. D. Ricardo, *Plan for the Establishment of a National Bank* (London: John Murray, 1834).
92. Wilson to Grey 17 October 1847, Earl Grey papers, Durham UL, GRE/B132/11/5 enclosed plan B145/D9.
93. Bank of England daily account books, 1851 on; *Second Report from the Secret Committee on Commercial Distress with Minutes of Evidence*, PP 1847–1848 (584) Appendix pp. 25–143.
94. G. Clare, *A Money Market Primer* (London: Effingham Wilson, 1900) pp. 16–17; Bank of England database Three centuries of data v.3 presents a separate balanced account for the Issue department, whereas the daily account books show this as a note limitation calculation only. See also B. Price, *Currency and Banking* (New York: Appleton, 1876) p. 66.
95. *Report… on Banks of Issue* PP 1840 (602) IV.1, p. v. The report, chaired by Charles Wood (Currency School) criticises Palmer for 'mixing up deposits and circulation'.
96. Idem., p. v, qq. 1890–1892, p. 156.
97. Idem., p. 4, J. B. Smith (Joint Stock banker in Manchester) regarded deposits and circulation as currency (liabilities). Smith and Loyd (Overstone) disagreed, *Merchants' Magazine and Commercial Review*, 5 July 1841, p. 27.
98. M. Reed, 'Loyd, Samuel Jones, Baron Overstone (1796–1883)', *Oxford Dictionary of National Biography* (OUP, 2004); online edn, Jan 2008.
99. *Report… on Banks of Issue* PP 1840 (602) IV.1, p. 258.
100. Idem., p. 258.
101. Russell to Grey, 26 November 1847, Earl Grey papers, Durham UL, GRE/B122/3/103; see also C. Read, *The Great Famine in Ireland and Britain's Financial Crisis* (Woodbridge: The Boydell Press, 2022) pp. 242–243.
102. *Report from the Secret Committee of the House of Lords on the Causes of Distress* PP 1847–1848 (565, 565-II) VIII Pt. III.1, 537, p. xlv.
103. 'Bank Charter Act 1844', http://www.legislation.gov.uk/ukpga/Vict/7-8/32 online [accessed 29 February 2020].
104. For the full background to this episode see Read, *The Great Famine in Ireland and Britain's Financial Crisis*, pp. 101–183.
105. J. Tomlinson, *Problems of British Economic Policy, 1870–1945* (Abingdon: Routledge, 2006) p. 46.
106. Undated fragment quoted in J. Morley, *The Life of William Ewart Gladstone* (Cambridge: CUP, 2011) p. 651.
107. Tomlinson, *Problems of British Economic Policy, 1870–1945*, pp. 46–47.
108. *Report…* PP 1831–1832 (722) VI.1, p. 52.
109. *First Report from the Secret Committee on Commercial Distress* PP 1847–1848 (395) VIII.1, VIII.379, p. 159.
110. *Report…* PP 1831–1832 (722) VI.1, pp. 30–31.

111. Thornton, *An Enquiry*, pp. 253–256.
112. Gash, *Sir Robert Peel: The Life of Sir Robert Peel after 1830*, p. 714.
113. S. H. Northcote, *Twenty Years of Financial Policy* (London: Saunders, Otley & Co., 1862) p. 1.
114. C. Xu, 'Reshaping Global Trade: The Immediate and Long-Run Effects of Bank Failures', *Harvard University Working Paper* (2019).
115. Gash, *Sir Robert Peel: The Life of Sir Robert Peel after 1830*, p. 714.

CHAPTER 3

The Ideas and Policies of the Banking School

> Now if we place in parallel columns, at the dates of the alterations of the Rate of Discount, the figures that represent the Reserve (of Bullion)…it will need no great amount of attention to discover:- *that up to the present time the proceedings of the Banking Department have been as nearly as possible wholly free from the control of that particular element of the rise and fall of the Circulation which was intended to operate with so much constancy and precision; while, on the contrary, the element really powerful, has been the degree in which the [interest-rate] policy of the Directors has led to the increase and decrease of the Banking (Bullion) Reserve.*
>
> —Thomas Tooke, *On the Bank Charter Act of 1844* (1856) pp. 85–86.[1]

Prior to the Bank Charter Act of 1844, there were a series of commentators who contributed to the Banking School's ideas. The main thrust of their ideas in comparison with those of the Currency School was that crises were caused by investment rather than trading flows of capital abroad. That situation made the linking of the quantity of banknotes to a bullion reserve unwise according to the Banking School. While the Currency School thought the restriction of credit in a crisis reinforced the action of the price-specie flow mechanism to bring back bullion into the country, the Banking School saw it as draining away permanently in foreign investments unless it was brought back by extreme measures such as high interest rates, which were in themselves undesirable because of the damage they caused to commerce.

C. Read, *Calming the Storms*, Palgrave Studies in Economic History,
https://doi.org/10.1007/978-3-031-11914-9_3

Henry Thornton had pointed out the possibility of international bullion flows for investment, the dangers of interest-rate disparity and the need for increased credit facilities in financial crises in the first decade of the nineteenth century.[2] Thomas Attwood of the Birmingham School opposed a currency tied to gold because he foresaw 'sovereigns that fly abroad'. He saw the Currency School as a privileged class from the nobility that subjugated what they regarded as the 'surplus population' for their own ends as opposed to what he characterised as the moral new breed of educated middle-class bankers.[3] Like Thornton, he believed a lack of investment opportunities led to unwise investments.[4] John Horsley Palmer, when Governor of the Bank of England in the 1830s, tried to avoid high interest rates with limited success. John Fullarton, in response to the proposals for the 1844 Act, pointed out that the price-specie flow mechanism would only operate in a closed system, and suggested that as the United Kingdom allowed free capital flows, unrestrained capital flows of precious metals could cause problems.[5]

These views will be discussed further in later chapters, but perhaps the most well-known champion of Banking-School opposition to the principles of the 1844 Act is Thomas Tooke, a political economist. Tooke, like most of the Banking School, preferred to analyse data and past experience to draw conclusions rather than proposing models which the Currency School preferred to do. As the quotation at the start of this chapter shows, he could not see any evidence that the Bank was controlling the circulation with its Rate but he could see a link between its bullion reserve and interest-rate changes.

None of these theorists had full access to the Bank of England data that could have confirmed the link they had identified. But now that the Bank of England has recently made this data publicly available, it enables their observations to be investigated in more detail. This chapter will excavate the ideas of the Banking School about interest rates, capital flows and financial crises. It will also present the available quantitative and qualitative evidence on which the Banking-School theory of financial crises was claimed to be based from the crisis of 1825 onwards.

3.1 The Banking School as a Reaction Against Peel's Policies

The Banking School was a diverse group of individuals who had drawn similar conclusions. It first really made its presence felt at the Committee on Banks of Issue held in Parliament in 1840.[6] Many witnesses expressed Banking-School views, at least in part. John Smith, a banker from Manchester, gave evidence that bills of exchange acted in the place of currency, except that they could not repay debt permanently.[7] Richard Cobden, a famous supporter of free trade, believed the problem in the 1830s was manias caused by large deposits.[8] He recognised the rate of interest as a factor for causing distress in times of pressure and suggested an increased stock of bullion in the Bank and taking measures such as raising interest rates promptly as a remedy.[9] William Wood, a trader from Manchester, also believed early action was necessary to prevent bullion leaving the country.[10] He suggested that a demand for notes by the sudden withdrawal of deposits could be counteracted by the sale of securities by the Bank to replace notes.[11] Richard Page, a financial author, included deposits in his definition of money and pointed to flows of bullion as a potential problem with linking the currency to gold.[12] George Muntz, an MP, suggested that a bullion reserve of 50% of circulation should be retained.[13] The Third Earl Grey and James Wilson, the editor of *The Economist*, a pro-free-trade newspaper, included this in a proposal for a currency system that formed the basis for the world's first currency board in Mauritius.[14] Muntz foresaw a dispute could develop between joint-stock banks and the Bank and thus predicted the situation which led up to the failure of Overend, Gurney & Co. Palmer, a former Governor of the Bank, described how the Bank had sent out bullion to America, which originated from France, and was invested in bills of exchange, but as the Bank of England's rate rose there was 'a sudden stoppage of trade to America'.[15] In 1839 Palmer described how the interest rate was used to discourage a bullion drain together with a sale of securities and the drawing of bills on Paris to counteract the export of bullion.[16]

Tooke, who is sometimes erroneously accused of contradicting the quantity of money theory, confirmed he agreed that a change in the global quantity of gold would change the value of gold in commodities but because the United Kingdom was an open country with free capital flows, prices should change the circulation, not circulation change prices.[17] He differentiated between the trading environment in which the amount of currency depended on the state of the exchanges and the state of the money market for investment which governed the rate of interest.[18] James Gilbart, a banker, also noted how a low rate of interest in the United Kingdom caused large sums to be invested in the United States in 1839; indeed 'all our panics have been preceded by a low rate of interest'.[19]

He also noted the 'American houses stopped' after Bank Rate rises by the Bank of England.[20] He was against lending for speculation (and the real-bills doctrine can be seen as a rule to lend for trade rather than investment where the value of the assets can be doubtful).[21] On the other hand he described the damage caused by interest rates that rose too high.[22]

Despite these various insights Sir Robert Peel chose to follow the Currency-School solution in 1844. As presented by Overstone in the enquiry, it offered the best hope for Peel's main aim: price stability. The Banking School's responses were too complex and disparate to provide a clear solution for Peel's objective of achieving price stability. Under the constraints imposed by Peel's new policy regime of the 1844 Act, there were numerous attempts by Banking-School theorists, businessmen and bankers to find ways to prevent systemic banking crises and to mitigate periodic mini-crises. Some were impracticable. For instance, major reforms, such as the creation of the world's first currency-board system for paper money in Mauritius, proved politically and practically impossible for Parliament to approve for the United Kingdom.[23] However, measures such as increasing the general level of the Bank of England's bullion reserve, recommended by Tooke, and Wilson in *The Economist*, were acted upon by the Bank.

The first test of the new legislation came in 1847 and as far as public opinion was concerned it failed. This reaction is summarised by a cartoon in *Punch* which portrayed Peel as 'Robert the Devil' for having paralysed the UK financial system just as finance for relief in Ireland from famine and the construction of railways was required.[24] After the 1847 crisis, enquiries were held in both Houses of Parliament, but Peel as leader of the opposition and Charles Wood as chancellor of the exchequer managed to protect the Bank Charter Act of 1844 from revision, and Currency-School ideas were victorious.

Nevertheless, some of the ideas of the Banking School began to gain favour, at least as far as concerning how the Bank of England managed interest rates. The Banking School's criticism of the Bank of England, that it did not raise interest rates soon enough when a bullion drain was forecast in early 1847, struck a chord with the financial press, and even Lord John Russell, the prime minister at the time.[25] Increasingly the Bank Rate became the favoured tool to attract and retain bullion in the Bank's reserve.

George Goschen's *The Theory of the Foreign Exchanges* (1861) described bullion flows in terms of the rate of exchange and disparities between the discount rate in different countries—in other words, that international capital flows were the product of the interest-rate parity theory. This was a Banking-School approach, in contrast to Currency-School theories, which tended to be based on trade flows and prices. Goschen recommended a minimum one percentage point rise in Bank Rate when the aim was to attract bullion. In 1866 this was attempted and found counterproductive as bullion importations were converted to notes, increasing the demand for them when they were in short supply. After that, rate changes by the Bank were moderated to small but frequent changes in prompt response to both bullion and note reserve fluctuations. The aim was to retain rather than attract bullion.

Walter Bagehot in his book *Lombard Street: A Description of the Money Market* (1873) popularised the revised set of policies adopted by the Bank, including acting as a central bank in times of credit shortage and discounting at a high rate to sound firms on the basis of collateral and rescuing banks in crises when there was little other option. The policy outlined by Bagehot was a compromise between the Currency and Banking Schools, therefore giving something to satisfy both shades of opinion. The high interest rate that Bagehot prescribed for crises limited credit and pleased those of a Currency-School disposition, but the certainty of credit being available to sound organisations from the lender of last resort mollified the Banking School.[26]

Even so, theoretical differences remained between the two schools of thought. For the rest of the nineteenth century, Banking-School commentators were searching the Bank of England's data for a link between interest rates, capital flows, deposits and financial crisis. The direction of their research contrasted with Currency-School and Classical theorists, including Carl Menger and Alfred Marshall, who concentrated on concepts of business cycles and static equilibrium theory connected with a trading environment.[27]

George Clare, a banker and a supporter of the Banking School's ideas, derided this point of view. He wrote in 1900: 'It is evident that but little weight attaches to the periodic rise and fall [of the bullion reserve] in connection with the every-day work performed by the currency, and that such ordinary demands may be left to take care of themselves'. He preferred to look into 'extraordinary demands' for credit, to identify the mechanism of crises.[28] He identified the Bank Rate as peaking in years of the most serious crises and noted that 'years of high average [bullion] Reserve are years of low average Bank-rate, and years of high average Bank-rate are years of low average Reserve'.[29] Another concern was 'floating money'—now more often called 'hot money'—whose flows appeared to cause problems during times of crisis. However, Clare's ability to analyse the mechanisms involved in this process was limited by his lack of available data, which was basically limited to what the Bank of England as a private profit-making organisation was willing to publish at the time.[30] His attempts to identify the exact cause of bullion flows were inconclusive because of this lack of data. Nevertheless, he noted that high interest rates attracted capital and identified an interest-rate-parity effect in 1890 between the French and British short-term rates.[31]

His conclusion concerning the existence of interest-rate parity between London and other European financial centres during the gold standard has recently been confirmed by Nils Herger using modern techniques.[32] Herger took weekly money-market data between 1880 and 1914 and found that between Amsterdam, Berlin, Brussels, London and Paris the return from discounting bills of exchange in the local money market was roughly equivalent to the return from investing in foreign currency bills.[33] In short, some form of arbitrage—whether from trade or, more likely during this period, information via telegram cables—kept short-term money-market rates similar across Europe.

Later theorists who regarded interest-rate movements to be as important as a price mechanism in causing capital flows included Knut Wicksell, a Swedish economist in the last decades of the nineteenth century. Wicksell believed that a frenzy of investment activity would arise if actual borrowing rates fell below the 'natural' rate of interest but developed this premise into a Currency-School policy of limiting investment at times of crisis. His ideas started from a similar observation to that which produced those of Thornton, but Thornton promoted lender-of-last-resort-style loans of banknotes to London bankers to expand credit in a crisis.[34] He warned against credit squeezes during a drain of gold. 'It is not the severity of the pressure which is to be the remedy' and believed 'it must be important to maintain, and to maintain carefully, the credit of the country, at that time in particular'. 'It belongs to the Bank of England, in particular, to guard and superintend the interests of the country in this respect'.[35]

Other economists in the twentieth century echoed the Banking School's ideas. John Maynard Keynes allowed for the possibility of both price and interest-rate mechanisms as causes for capital flows but pointed out that the effect of the interest-rate disequilibrium on them was greater than that of price-level disequilibrium. In the former case, 'the restoration of equilibrium may require not only a change in interest rates, but also a lasting change in income levels (and probably in price levels)', because both price levels and income levels were affected by investment choices.[36] Arthur Bloomfield, writing in the 1960s, differentiated between the role of both short-term (in 1963) and long-term (in 1968) capital flows under the pre-1914 gold standard and his studies noted the importance of the development of transatlantic capital flows in this system.[37] Another British economist, W. E. Beach, had shown that for the period between 1881 and 1913, the price levels of one country did not rise or fall in accordance with their previous behaviour. It was hitherto believed that the movement of gold would force all countries to follow the same pace through the business cycle if the price-specie flow mechanism was dominant.[38] After 1881 some other force was seen to have most influence and he identified this as the money supply, of which capital flows were an element.

The last half of the nineteenth century was the heyday of Banking-School policies. At the end of the century, they had been refined to such an extent that major banking crises no longer took place in Britain. However, as George H. Pownall, a leading figure at the Institute of Bankers and a follower of J. S. Mill and W. S. Jevons, warned in 1899: 'we have refined our methods of working until we are spinning a big top on a needle point'. The 'sensitive' money market he referred to was constantly adjusted by minor tweaks to the Bank Rate, but, as will be shown, the Banking School believed the development of commerce and the wealth of the nation was still held back by insufficient credit. 'Credit is a lever to move the world', Pownall proclaimed, 'but a lever must have something to rest on before it can exert its power'. 'When people want *cash*, "money at call and short notice" will not meet the case'.[39] What is clear is that followers of the Banking School believed the Currency School's limitations were still holding back British industry and trade, as well as acting as a contributor to economic decline.

3.2 The Banking School and Interest Rates

The commercial damage caused by the use of high or rapidly fluctuating interest rates to protect the Bank of England's bullion reserves became an increasing concern among the Banking School in the second half of the century. As early as 1848 Palmer admitted that he had heard of manufacturers who had had difficulty in executing foreign orders because of the high rate of interest charged by their banks for 'accommodation', or trade finance.[40]

The issue was taken up most famously by Sir Robert Harry Inglis Palgrave (1827–1919) in a paper published in 1873 and expanded into a book published in 1903, which analysed the Bank Rate from 1844 to 1900. He noted that the Rate had been changed 400 times compared with between 100 and 200 times for national banks in Europe. His thesis was that 'great instability in the rate of discount is a very prejudicial thing to the interests of commerce, and hence to those of banking'.[41] By making the cost of credit unstable, it made the expected returns from commercial investment less predictable and therefore less attractive, and forced firms to behave more conservatively. Palgrave was a self-educated country banker who became editor of *The Economist* in 1877. In spite of his practical background, he only narrowly lost out to the much more academic Alfred Marshall when a new Professor of Political Economy was being appointed at the University of Cambridge in December 1884.[42] Yet it was this competition between Marshall and Palgrave that symbolised the division between the two theories of crises.

Marshall's approach drew from both the Currency and Banking Schools, but his tendency was to the former and his methodology was theoretical. In contrast, Palgrave was more inclined towards the Banking School and his approach relied more upon observation and analysis of data than being based on abstract models. Marshall described the mechanism of how a gold outflow which lowered the Bank of England's reserves would cause economic problems still in terms of the price-specie flow model. He did mention investment, but only in relation to prices: the Bank would respond by raising its discount rate, and 'the result would be a check to speculative investments, a diminished demand for commodities, and a fall of prices'.[43] Marshall followed Mill's lead in explaining that 'the credit cycle breeds optimism which in turn breeds recklessness which in turn leads to crises and stagnation' and saw crises in terms of the business cycle.[44] From this, other economists have spent much research time in the twentieth century examining the periodicity of business cycles and crises to see if they are predictable over a certain period. However, their efforts have generally been without particular success.[45]

The Banking-School approach mentioned by Palgrave has more to do with capital flows. In short, he was interested in the 'influx and efflux of gold', investment abroad and the seemingly large amounts held in deposit accounts in the Bank of England.[46] It originated with Thornton's observations about the consequences of disparity between different types of interest rate. It was developed by T. H. Williams who in 1858 decried 'excessive conversions of floating into fixed capital' and Jevons in the 1860s who pointed to 'the varying proportion which capital devoted to permanent and remote investment to that...temporarily invested, soon to reproduce itself'.[47]

The ideas of Palgrave and his Banking-School antecedents on the mechanism of crises can be summarised as follows. Government pressure down on interest rates (to reduce its debt service costs) moved short-term interest rates well below long-term rates (and market rates). This triggered a search by investors for better returns for their available funds. It also incentivised speculators to borrow money at short-term rates for long-term investment. Funds flowed to investments with higher returns, which were often abroad, thus causing international capital flows. To stem the capital flows, interest rates in the country suffering the drain were increased and reached the same level as the investment abroad, adjusted for any transaction costs, fundamental risks, etc. This stopped the flow of investment. As the short-term rate rose above the long-term rate, speculators found themselves in a credit crunch at home. When short-term rates in investor and investment countries equalised and the flow of funds to the investment stopped, the value of the investment slumped. This caused the speculators to make losses and possibly fail. Because of the sharply raised rates and limited credit, thanks to the Bank Charter Act of 1844 in the case of England, ordinary commerce was adversely affected, and weak businesses could go insolvent or bankrupt because of an inadequate cash flow. This unstable response was encouraged by British insolvency law until it was reformed in 1869. Even if a firm owned a surplus of assets over liabilities on its balance sheet, if it ran out of cash it would have to declare bankruptcy. After a wave of bankruptcies, the now uninvested funds piled up in deposit accounts and created expanding credit to restart the cycle all over again as short-term interest rates fell below long-term ones.

A form of the Banking-School theory of crises as a self-perpetuating cycle was popularised as a cartoon in a short-lived journal called *The Money Bag* in 1858 after the Bank Charter Act of 1844 had been followed by two crises. It was called 'The Overstone Cycle of Trade' (Fig. 3.1) which at first glance appears to be illustrating Lord Overstone's description of crises.[48] However, *The Money Bag* was a Banking-School publication whose rubric championed its ideas: 'money's uses in the commonwealth of industry, should measure the supply of legal tender, not the ebb and flow of golden quicksands in Threadneedle Street'.[49] The cartoon is explicitly blaming Overstone's Currency-School restrictions for the crises, in contrast to his description of them as inevitable, but momentary, 'storms and tempests' that just had to be suffered.[50]

Overstone mentioned his analysis of crises while arguing with Palmer as to whether it was possible that the quantity of banknotes could be adjusted according to the bullion reserve in practice. The former suggested that during crises banks tended to issue too many notes in

Fig. 3.1 The Overstone Cycle of trade from *The Money Bag*, 1858 vol., between p. 112 and p. 113, fold out (Princeton University Library)

order to keep their customers happy. Overstone's description of a cycle of the 'state of trade' was as follows:

> First we find it in a state of quiescence, —next improvement, —growing confidence, —prosperity, —excitement, —overtrading, —convulsion, —pressure, —stagnation, —distress, —ending again in quiescence.[51]

The cartoon in *The Money Bag* shows a similar cycle but with some stages missing, conflated with others. 'Over-trading', for instance, was not a generally accepted concept for the Banking School and was probably omitted for this reason. The significant difference is the incorporation of a character at the centre of the cycle called 'the hard calculator' mentioned in *The Times*.[52] *The Times* had complained that government action had prevented 'the hard calculator' from making 12% or 15% from his gold. In ridiculing this, *The Money Bag*, made the cartoon of 'the hard calculator' resemble Lord Overstone, continuing the criticism made by Thomas Wakley in 1847 that his reforms in the Bank Charter Act of 1844 favoured the wealthy. As a medical reformer and founding editor of *The Lancet*, Wakley had criticised the enquiry before the Act as being similar to doctors having decided their diagnosis before examining the facts and 'the poor patient was John Bull'.[53] *The Money Bag* added a reason as to how the Act favoured the wealthy: by the interest earned in the periods of high rates. In the cartoon, the 'the hard calculator' carries a bag of gold which is full when interest rates are at 10% and nearly empty when the rates are at 2%. Thus the rate of interest and bullion holdings in the United Kingdom are put at the heart of the mechanism of the cycle. The commentary which accompanies the cartoon was designed for easy reading, but was at pains to point out that 'the whole "cycle" is in our opinion, connected with the pernicious monetary system now existing'—in other words the Bank Charter Act of 1844.[54]

How the cycle restarts is described, making the coming and going of crises a continuous process with one circuit of the cycle after another. This is in contrast to Overstone's description which suggests a single circular process. With little demand for money after a crisis 'it therefore accumulates in the Bank, and in the hands of money dealers'. It is added to by 'an enormous amount of commercial money, consisting of bills of exchange, cheques &c'. It is pointed out that 'the Bullionists falsely accuse the currency reformers [Banking School] of advocating an over issue of paper'. The answer given to this is that the Currency-School '"principle" necessarily involves over-issues, and consequent "over-trading" as they call it'.[55] The rest of the cycle is then described along Banking-School lines after the process has been shown as restarting in the manner that Thornton described of a disparity between interest rates, bullion being exported to pay for goods and to find a better rate of interest as a return, and so forth. After a period of 'Prosperity', comes 'Excitement' driven by low interest rates of 2% advertised on the front of a bank. There is a building boom in the background and over-optimistic investments are represented by the steam driven flying machine. Foreign-investment adventures are shown by the 'South Pole Warming Company'. As interest rates increase 'Convulsion' arises and the 'Royal Bubble Bank' explodes. 'Stagnation' follows with workers in front of the 'Workhouse' and a businessman hanging himself in a shop window; but the 'hard calculator' is happy with interest rates of 10% and a full bag of gold. 'Improvement' is driven by manufacturing leading to 'Confidence' in trade and so back to 'Prosperity'. The 'hard calculator' is unhappy with his 2% return, though, and the process restarts.[56]

Nevertheless, thanks to the survival of the Bank Charter Act of 1844, the ideas of the Currency School continued to overshadow those of the Banking-School ones in the public sphere, in spite of *The Money Bag*'s pointed criticisms. Among some modern scholars the Banking School has been completely forgotten, to the extent that a copy of *The Money Bag*'s satirisation of 'The Overstone Cycle' was incorporated into a printed edition of Overstone's writings in the 1970s as if the illustration was explaining and supporting, rather than criticising, his theories![57] Yet the Banking School had anticipated the type of problem described today in connection with the Carry Trade.

3.3 Testing the Banking School's Theories with Charts

It is easy to explain what the Banking School's ideas were. A much harder question is that of whether its ideas are really an accurate description or observation of economic trends in nineteenth-century Britain. This section shows, using charts, the economic context that led theorists associated with the Banking School to reach the conclusions that they did. The next section tests some of their hypotheses, analysing data only released relatively recently by the Bank of England, using econometrics, to assess whether their main claims really stand up to statistical scrutiny.

Through these two methodologies, it becomes much easier to see the economic and financial phenomena that the Banking School were trying to describe in their writings.

To be clear about what is being discussed it is necessary to clarify what was meant by 'financial crisis' and by 'economic downturn'. There is no accepted definition of a financial crisis. Most crises are a mixture of commercial, asset price and banking crises. A commercial crisis is one in which commercial firms cannot obtain credit to continue in business, either because it is not available or because it is too expensive. An asset-price crisis usually refers to excessive booms or busts in the value of property or shares and other securities. In a banking crisis, particularly a systemic one, a number of banks limit lending and credit at the same time and the collapse of banks may threaten the payments system. In short, the most important feature about financial crises is that they disrupt the normal channels of the banking system through which funds are passed from households to firms for productive investment opportunities. The reduction in economic activity resulting from a crisis usually impinges on most of the population as a decrease in their living standard. Many depressing effects have accompanied crises, including a decline in the value of firms and their shares on the stock market, such as seen during the global financial crisis of 2007–2009; a large decline in the price level, such as occurred after the Napoleonic wars; and a decline in the value of assets on which loans may have been made. In a domino effect, initial problems could then trigger others. For instance, banking crises are often triggered by the price of assets held by the institutions as collateral falling below the value of loans made on them. If the banks had not managed their balance sheets and loan portfolios with sufficient equity buffers to anticipate possible falls in value, they might not be able to liquidate assets sufficiently quickly to cover all their liabilities. When knowledge of this spreads in an uncontrolled manner, without any other guarantee or rescue in place, a bank run may ensue. At this stage suspicion and contagion normally spread between banks and sometimes several collapse, causing a wider-scale banking panic. During and after a panic, other banks then lend very carefully. This can constrain credit availability and raise market interest rates further, prolonging commercial distress among firms.

The definition of an economic downturn is more straightforward. A 'recession' is now accepted as meaning a successive two quarters of falling Gross Domestic Product (GDP). The data which are available for the nineteenth century tend to be annual rather than quarterly, so for the

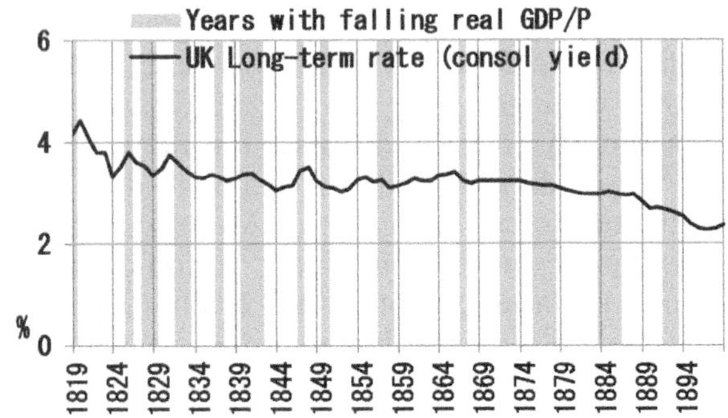

Fig. 3.2 UK long-term interest rate (consol yield) and years with real GDP per person lower than the previous year (*Source* Bank of England 'Three centuries of data' v.2, col. A4 N)

purposes of the present analysis a year of negative real annual GDP growth from the previous year is taken as a downturn[58] (Fig. 3.2).

There has been considerable discussion among economists about the relationship between interest rates and GDP growth. This has prompted controversy in the twentieth century between Keynesians and their Austrian critics about what sort of monetary policy should be adopted in a modern recession. Banking-School theorists considered long-term and short-term rates to move in mostly disconnected worlds from each other, as well as from economic growth. Palmer and Clare pointed out that the government is interested in reducing long-term rates, while bankers are interested in using short-term rates to manage bullion flows and obtain discounting business. In a crisis, both of them believed short-term rates increase and afterwards reduce as banks push them down to seek business and respond to government pressure. In contrast, long-term rates appear to have risen briefly in the main crises of 1847, 1857–1858 and in the run-up to 1866, but the trend reverses between crises to maintain an overall stable level between 1840 and 1866 (Fig. 3.3). After 1866 there was a steady decline in the period of the 'Long Depression'. There is no clear relationship between long-term rates and GDP, but the overall stability of the long-term interest rate in general is very apparent.

By contrast, short-term interest rates fluctuate widely. While they have no obvious relationship with GDP, the comparative rates in different countries do have an apparent relationship with crises. It was Palmer

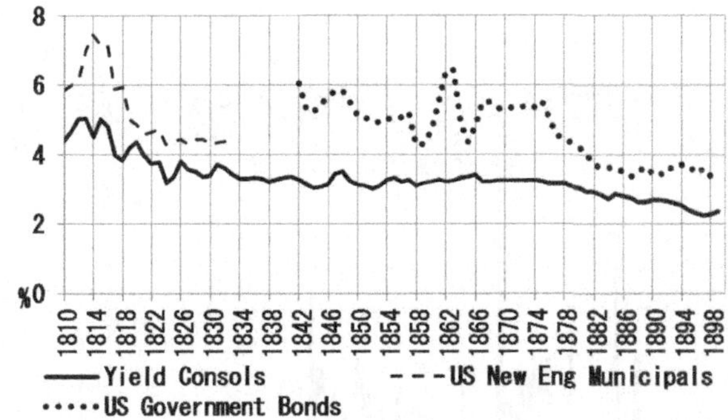

Fig. 3.3 Long-term interest rates for the United Kingdom and United States, 1810–1899 (*Sources* Bank of England 'Three Centuries of data' v.2.3, A19 P; S. Homer, R. Sylla, *A History of Interest Rates* [Hoboken, NJ: Wiley, 2005] pp. 300–312)

who pointed out that, in the 1830s, bullion flows to America suddenly stopped whenever interest rates in the United Kingdom rose.[59] Figure 3.4 shows that over the period 1836–1899 when US and UK nominal short-term rates drew together, a financial disturbance of this type would occur, consistent with such a stoppage. The difference between the two rates is shown as a proportion of the rates added together in the top line. The grey shaded vertical bars highlight periods in which the ratio is close to zero. These periods are the same as those in which financial disturbances took place. The particular value with which the ratio is compared is plus or minus 0.1 in the chart, but this can be varied to increase or decrease the resolution with which events are picked out.

As the countries' short-term interest rates moved together, the flows of bullion would have ceased, according to theories about arbitrage. Funds for investments would have dried up, leading to financial disruption. Thornton's and Jevons' ideas about where these flows came from suggested that they arose from periods before the crises when short-term interest rates were low.[60] In the theory, as developed by Wicksell, the short-term interest rate is compared with a 'natural' rate of interest, which is one when prices are stable, but the Banking School's theorists tended to ignore prices.

Wicksell's theory developed into the Austrian-School Business Cycle, which is very different from the Banking School's concept. Although low

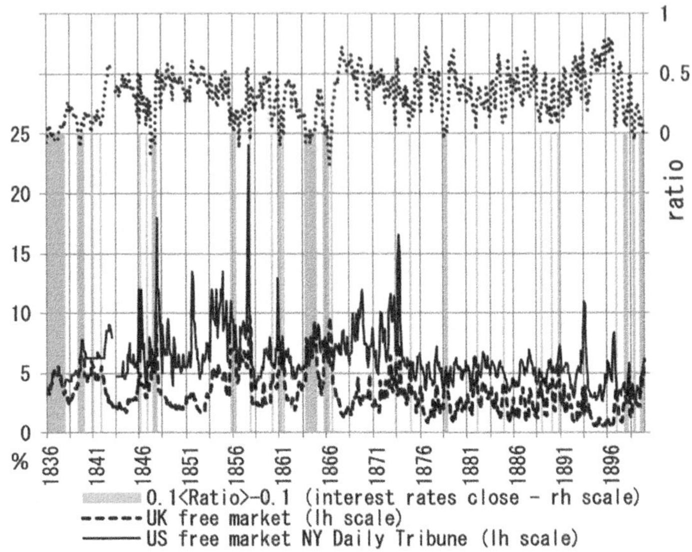

Fig. 3.4 A comparison of US and UK short-term free market interest rates 1836–1899. At the top, shown as a dotted line, is the ratio ([US rate] - [UK rate])/US + UK rates. Where this ratio falls between 0.1 and −0.1, the period is shown by the grey shaded bars (*Sources* Report from the Select Committee on bank acts PP 1857 [220] [220–1] X, Pt. I, Pt. II.1, pp. 463–464; ***Burdett's Official Intelligence*** [1894] p. 1771. US: *New York Daily Tribune*, 'Commercial and Money Matters' column)

interest rates kickstart a search for better returns in both theories, the Austrian model has several woolly concepts about how the boom stops and the 'natural' rate is a difficult statistic to calculate.[61] The theory of the Banking School is very clear: the boom stops as interest rates equalise, an event which can clearly be seen in the data.

Banking-School theorists usually compare the short-term with the long-term interest rate as the most stable rate available from actual data. It can be seen in Fig. 3.5 that before each period in which UK and US rates draw together and there is a crisis, there is a period of short-term interest rates lower than long-term ones. Thornton's ideas suggest that this would have provoked a search by investors for better investment yields and this would have generated bullion flows when these opportunities were abroad. The question then arises whether there was any sign of the excess credit that Thornton had suggested would occur after interest rates draw together. Clare pointed to the excess monies which appeared in the 'Other Deposits' account of the Bank of England, which mainly contained un-lent or uninvested funds of other British banks and firms, at around the time of crises as a sign of this.

This, for instance, can be clearly seen in the run-up to the financial crisis of 1847. In December 1845 British short-term rates rose above long-term rates. There followed a dramatic peak in 'Other Deposits', which excludes public and banking deposits, in January 1846, which may have been money reserved for investments such as railways and to purchase food from abroad. It soon fell again. The next large increase in 'Other Deposits' was in January 1858 after the Bank Rate rose suddenly in October 1857. The next sharp rise was in May 1866 alongside a sharp increase in Bank Rate in the same month, following several increases since October 1865. Each of the latter two crises (1857–1858, 1866) was accompanied by a permanent step up in the level of 'Other Deposits'. After the 1860s there were large increases in the Other Deposits, following increased earnings from investments abroad, which were not accompanied by crises suggesting that the earlier increases followed immediately on crises only causing another later on. The large increases in deposits at the same time as large changes in interest rates is consistent with Thornton's theories of excess funds being available as investment opportunities become unviable. They are also consistent with an iterative system whereby a cycle is constantly restarted as the funds are invested in riskier investments with the promise of higher yields as bank rates and market short-term rates fall below long-term ones.

The comparative intensities of the crises caused vary according to the measure used to assess them. Banking School inclined commentators preferred to measure banking crises as the ratio of Bank of England note reserve to total deposits. In 1866 *The Economist* discussed the note-reserve-to-total-deposits ratio. For a 'well managed bank', it reported, 'it is sometimes said that the reserve should present the ratio of one-third to the depositors' and many well-known economists have used the measure since that time.[62]

A systemic crisis is indicated by a very low note-reserve-to-total-deposits ratio, because the legality of the Bank's paper currency is under threat, and as without any bank notes in reserve it is unable to immediately meet its liabilities or function as a lender of last resort. It can be seen from Fig. 3.6 that the crises of 1847, 1857–1858 and 1866 occurred

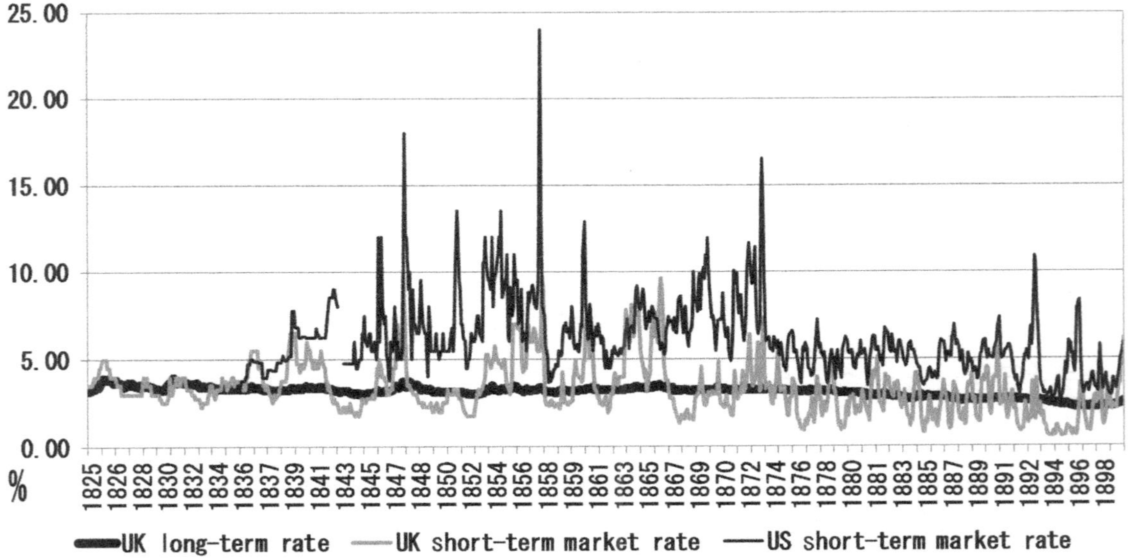

Fig. 3.5 A comparison of US and UK short-term free market interest rates 1825–1899 and long-term UK interest rates (*Sources* As Figs. 3.3 and 3.4)

during periods when this ratio reached very sharp and dramatic lows. In 1857 the low point of the ratio then would have been negative, –0.033, if the government had not temporarily increased the Bank of England's fiduciary issue (that did not need to be backed by bullion reserves) by £2m.

After 1866, with the adoption of revised policies by the Bank of England later approved of by Bagehot in *Lombard Street*, and those recommended by the Banking School, it can be seen the ratio remains above the 0.3 recommended by *The Economist*. The importance and long-lasting influence of this indicator can be seen in its use as late as the Cunliffe report of 1918, which still valued the ratio of note reserves to deposits as a measure to assess the immediate stability of the Bank of England.[63] Even in the interwar period, as the classical gold standard went through its death throws in Britain, the views and ideas of the Banking School in this respect remained influential.

In contrast, theorists inspired by the Currency School preferred to use the ratio of Bank of England bullion reserve to total liabilities (notes with public plus deposits) as an indicator of the seriousness of a crisis (see Fig. 3.7).[64] This was argued to better measure the long-term stability of the Bank, rather than short-term problems of squeezed credit, which the Banking School's rival indicator tended to highlight. The Currency School's favoured way of calculating their ratio changed over time. In

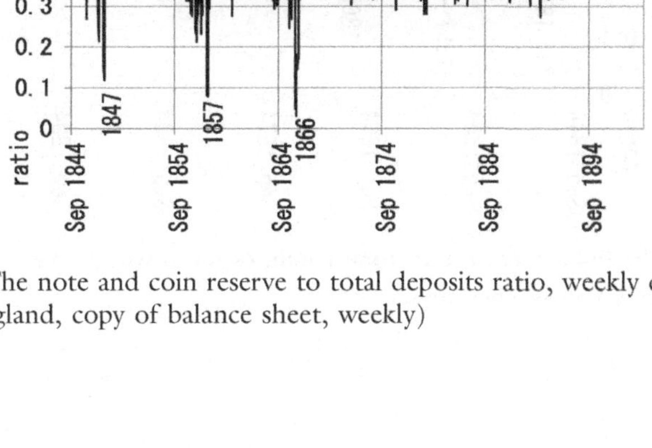

Fig. 3.6 The note and coin reserve to total deposits ratio, weekly data (*Sources* Bank of England, copy of balance sheet, weekly)

the 1840s the Currency School had not accepted deposits as money, only banknotes.[65] Opposing them, the Banking School, particularly Tooke, had argued deposits were money too and formed part of the circulation.[66]

After the financial crisis of 1866, the Currency School changed track and found that it was convenient to use them in their favoured ratio which minimised the seriousness of the financial crises which followed the Bank Charter Act of 1844 and assisted in defending the legislation when it came under attack. From a comparison of the total coin and bullion and note reserves, it is clear that the reduction in notes allowed under the Bank Charter Act of 1844 when the bullion reserve shrank fell mainly upon the note reserve, not the notes with the public.

This outcome is naturally what would have happened, as the reduction of the note reserve would be the easiest way of limiting the 'circulation'. However, this also sterilised the effect that note restriction may have had on the general public and businesses, and prevented the price-specie flow mechanism from fully operating, as pointed out by Wilson of *The Economist*.[67] More effective in limiting the supply of notes was the reduced discounting of bills. The Bank could not refuse its depositors notes without stopping its business, but it could refuse to discount bills for notes without defaulting on its obligations, and so protect its reserve. A comparison of the Bank of England 'Note Reserve' and 'Total Coin and

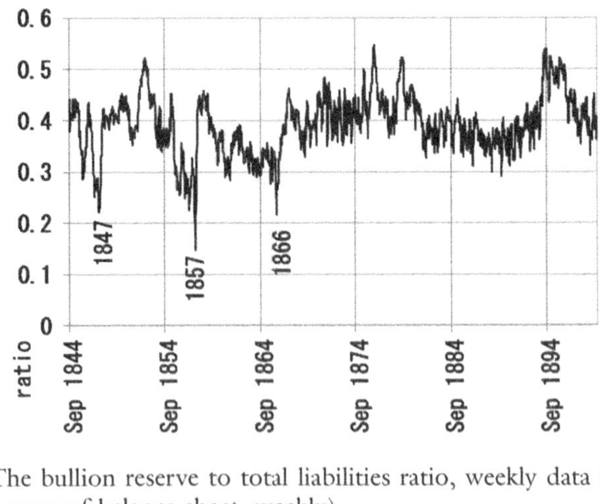

Fig. 3.7 The bullion reserve to total liabilities ratio, weekly data (*Source* Bank of England, copy of balance sheet, weekly)

Bullion' held in the Issue Department shows that the 'Note Reserve' fluctuated with the 'Bullion Reserve' and declined alongside it during crises (Fig. 3.8).

However, there is an anomaly in 1866. The bullion reserve does not fall with the note reserve in the way it did in 1847 and 1857. This is an indication of bullion being drawn into the country and being turned into notes at the time, as will be shown in Chapter 7 of this book. It was one of the very few periods when UK short-term rates rose substantially above US ones.

Another measure of the intensity of a crisis preferred by those supporting the Currency-School point of view and the principle of the gold standard was the proportion of banks which ceased operations annually during each crisis. The aim was to emphasise the high proportion which ceased in 1825 in comparison with 1847, to give the impression that the Bank Charter Act of 1844 had resolved the problem as far as banks were concerned. Neville Ward-Perkins was an enthusiast for the gold standard and spent many years exhaustively cataloguing Country Banks.[68] He claimed in 1950 that 'the financial crisis [of 1847] was exaggerated by the interested parties'.[69] However, his work was considered by his contemporaries, such as R. C. O. Matthews, as 'not very intellectual'.[70] A review of the data more recently shows that 10% of banks

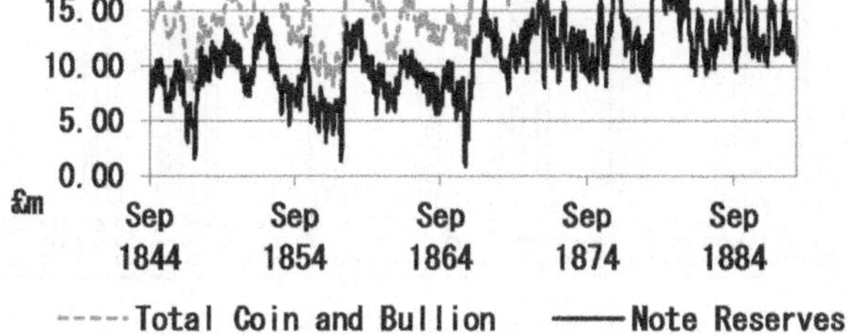

Fig. 3.8 The Bank of England Note Reserve and Total Coin and Bullion, weekly data (*Sources* Bank of England, copy of balance sheet, weekly)

went bust in the crisis of 1825, compared to 3.4% in 1847 and 4% in 1866.[71] So a significant number of banks continued to fail in crises after the banking legislation of 1844 came into force, with no downward trend seen between the 1844, 1857–1858 and 1866 crises.

Those who took into account Banking-School ideas of the need to provide good conditions for commerce were more interested in the effect of crises upon the wider economy. In contrast to Ward-Perkins' conclusion that the 1847 financial crisis was exaggerated by interested parties, the impact of 1847 on GDP per head was worse both in absolute and real terms than 1825. When real GDP per head is used instead of GDP per head (see Figs. 3.9 and 3.10), the 1837 crisis sees the largest percentage drop, and 1847 fares slightly worse than 1825.

However, recessions appear to be still clearly associated with the mini-crises that occurred in the period after 1866. Taken together with Fig. 3.6, showing the deep cuts into the note reserve up to 1866, it suggests that after the crisis that year, the Bank protected itself, but the country at large suffered, possibly from unstable interest rates, or lack of credit, the complaints of Palgrave.[72] This observation is consistent with some of the literature on the relative decline of the late Victorian British economy, which some economic historians have attributed to a financial sector more interested in stability and foreign investment abroad than in economic growth at home.

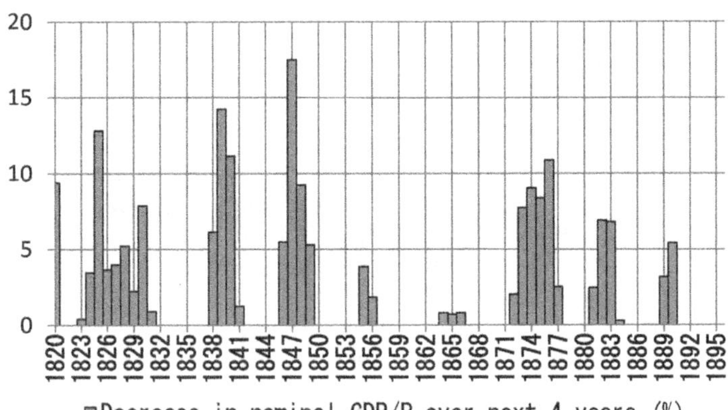

Fig. 3.9 Percentage decrease in nominal English GDP per head over next 4 years by year (%) (*Source* 'Three Centuries of data', A21 H)

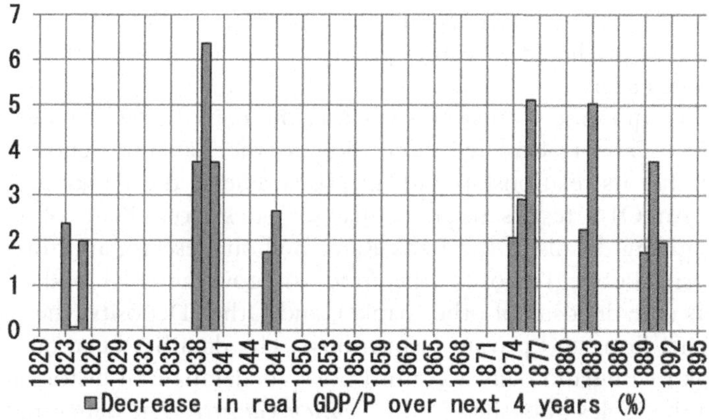

Fig. 3.10 Percentage decrease in real English GDP per head over next 4 years by year (%) (*Source* 'Three Centuries of data', A21 I)

3.4 Testing the Banking School's Theories with Econometrics

In considering the context of Banking-School theory as shown by econometrics it is important to distinguish between the various types of model and analysis available. Data series can be short term or long term. Short-term series cover only a period of a few years, but with frequent data-points, perhaps weekly. Long-term series may run over a period of over fifty years and be monthly or annual. Short-term series may pick up small-scale fluctuations, whereas long-term series will average these out to concentrate on overall movements. The type of model will also affect the type of fluctuation which is considered. Ordinary Least Squares (OLS) analysis is focused on overall trends and whether the series are correlated, but with time series this method can produce misleading positive results. To be secure in the results, the series must be stationary, and the regression must be free from heteroskedasticity and autocorrelation and the residuals (or errors) must be normally distributed. In the OLS regressions given, the calculations have passed these tests unless stated otherwise. An Augmented Dickey–Fuller test is used to establish the series are stationary, and a White's test for heteroskedasticity. Cointegration tests take into account the minor movements of the series and whether these are matched by the series being compared and they are more suited to non-stationary series. A causality test measures whether the points in a series can be predicted by earlier points in another series better than just in the series itself.

The first question to answer is whether the Bank Rate was raised whenever the bullion reserve fell, according to the Banking School's ideas, and whether its relationship with Deposits reflects the Banking School's theory. An OLS test is used to analyse series from Bank of England records giving details of the Bank Rate, Bullion Reserve, and three types of deposit: Public Deposits (the funds of governmental bodies) Bank Deposits (the deposits of other banks), and Other Deposits (the funds of the public, firms and private institutions). The data has been taken from the Bank of England daily account books, its database of historical statistics and the tables published in the *London Gazette*. The date range taken was 7 September 1844 to 21 December 1889 with 2364 weekly values in each series. It starts with just after the Bank Charter Act of 1844 and stops a decade before the end of the century.[73]

With the Bank of England Bullion Reserve as dependent variable, the results show a negative relationship at more than 99% certainty with the Bank Rate. This relationship is consistent with the Rate being raised in response to the Bullion Reserve falling, which confirms use of the Banking School's policy by the Bank. The Rate also has a 99% positive relationship with all three types of deposits which would be the case if the bullion had been mainly added to by means of deposits. Therefore, money deposited at the Bank rather than invested elsewhere calms crises by raising the Bullion Reserve, which gave the Bank a safety margin to lower its Rate again, thereby restarting the business cycle (Table 3.1).

Table 3.1 Results of OLS test with Bullion Reserve as dependent variable

Variables	*BoE Bank Rate*	*BoE Public Deposits*	*BoE Bank Deposits*	*BoE Other Deposits*	*Constant*
Coefficient	−1.0468	0.3264	0.4452	0.3484	9.8393
(Std. error)	(0.0327)	(0.0206)	(0.0310)	(0.4790)	(0.3546)
Significance	***	***	***	***	***

Asterisks indicate the significance of the result: *** > 99%, ** > 95%, * > 90%

Table 3.2 Results of OLS test with Bank Rate as dependent variable

Variables	*BoE Bullion Reserve*	*BoE Public Deposits*	*BoE Bank Deposits*	*BoE Other Deposits*	*Constant*
Coefficient	−0.2897	0.0374	0.3828	−0.0930	7.8248
(Std. error)	(0.0090)	(0.0114)	(0.0242)	(0.0169)	(0.1422)
Significance	***	***	***	***	***

$R^2 = 0.4161$

With the Bank Rate as dependent variable, the same relationship as above is seen with the Bullion Reserve and Public and Bank Deposits. However, the relationship with Other Deposits is the reverse of that with the Bullion Reserve as dependent variable, as it is negative. This is consistent with the surges of money into Other Deposits noticed by Banking-School commentators. This happens when short-term and long-term market interest rates converge, as opposed to the deposits rising or falling consistently with the either Bank Rate or the level of its Bullion Reserves. Other Deposits would include the accounts where spare cash would end up when profitable places to invest at a beneficial rate could no longer be found (Table 3.2).

A Granger Causality test can be used to gain information on whether the Bank Rate caused Bullion Reserve changes or vice-versa. The results (Table 3.3) suggest there was little difference with a small margin on the side of Reserve changes causing Rate changes. This also does not conflict with the scenario that the Bank followed the generally accepted policy of the Banking School of raising the Bank Rate to discourage bullion from leaving the country and that Rate increases provoked improvements in the Bullion Reserve (Table 3.3).

Table 3.3 Results of Granger Causality test: Bank Rate and Bullion Reserve

Causation *A > B A Granger causes B*	*f-value* *7 lags*	*p-value*	*Lag and significance*
Bullion Reserve > Bank Rate	51.039	0.0000	1, 2 of 7***
Bank Rate > Bullion Reserve	7.4602	0.0000	1 of 7***

Table 3.4 Results of Granger Causality test: Bank Rate and free market rate

Causation *A > B A Granger causes B*	*f-value* *2 lags*	*p-value*	*lag and* *significance*
Free Market > Bank Rate	15.361	0.0001	1, 2 of 2***
Bank Rate > Free Market	7.626	0.0803	2 of 2*

A Currency-School view was that the Bank of England was forced to change its Rate to follow the market rate. In contrast, Palmer, who is associated with the Banking School, argued that the Bank could influence the market rate with its Bank Rate. A Granger causation test to inform this conundrum is carried out, based on data from the Bank of England database, covering the period March 1836 to December 1899 monthly (766 values).

It suggests that while the Bank Rate did have influence, the market rate had the strongest influence. This means it was possible for the Bank to influence rates as Palmer hoped, but it was also possible for control of monetary policy to be taken out of the hands of the Bank by market forces, a fear of other Banking-School theorists such as Thornton and Tooke (Table 3.4).

To test the Banking-School proposition that UK and foreign interest rates might have interacted with short-term money to provoke crises when the rates equalised and investment money suddenly stopped flowing or reversed direction, a Probit estimation was carried out. A 'Crisis' series was constructed as a binary series that marks '1' against commonly recognised months of crisis and '0' elsewhere. The periods of crisis chosen are shown in Table 3.5.

The crisis series was used as dependent variable. US market rates were obtained from the *New York Daily Tribune*. The date range was March 1836 to December 1899 with 766 monthly values. The test produced the following model equation in order to fit the interest rates to the series of 'Crises':

$$\text{Crisis} = \underset{(0.537)}{-1.84} + \underset{(0.348)}{1.46} \times \text{UKFreeMkt} - \underset{(0.182)}{0.880} \times \text{USFreeMkt} - \underset{(0.266)}{0.228} \times \text{UKBkRate}$$

The model fitted 0 or 1 correctly against the subjectively estimated crisis series correctly 96.9% of the time. The UK free market and US free

Table 3.5 Crises months denoted by '1' in the Probit model

Date Range (months)	*Basis of choice*
June 1836–April 1837	Bullion drain in connection with investment in US
May 1839–October 1839	Bullion drain in connection with investment in US
April 1847–November 1847	Drains because of high food imports, Irish loan for relief, investment in railways
October 1856–November 1856	Gold from new sources drains to the East: India,
November 1857–January 1858	Ceylon and China
January 1861–July 1861	Bullion shipped to US as potential civil war threatened
December 1863–August 1864	Drains for investment in India including cotton
February 1866–August 1866	Drains to France, bankruptcy of Overend, Gurney & Co.
July, August, December 1878	Drains connected with the war in Afghanistan
November 1890	Drains for foreign loans, Baring Bros. in difficulties
December 1899	International competition for bullion

market rate series have a role in this with over 99% certainty, but the role of the Bank Rate is less important. However, if the same estimation is carried out without Bank Rate the fit is slightly worse, so the Bank Rate has some effect. The equation above that fits the series together sets a positive coefficient for the UK series but a negative coefficient for the US series for the free markets. The equation is therefore using a difference between the United Kingdom and United States in the same way that the graph showing interest rates coinciding during crises is intuitively analysed on a difference between the rates (Fig. 3.4).

The Probit and similar graphical analyses provide confirmation of Clare's theory that crises are coincident with high interest rates and Thornton's thesis that the convergence of different interest rates available for investment marks the start of a crisis. A model using only UK market short-term rates to predict the 'Crisis' series only produces a fit of 92.3%. Examination of a graph of predicted against given data for the 'Crisis' series shows that the model was giving weak predictions of additional marginal crises after 1866 and this was the source of a lack of 100% fit. This error is understandable because there were constant fluctuations or 'mini-crises', not full-blown systemic ones, after 1866.

The results described so far beg the question about whether it is possible to identify the capital flows of funds for investment that brought the interest rates together and stopped the flow of funds. If this was the case, there should be a relationship between flows of bullion and the difference between interest rates in the United Kingdom and the United States. Attempts to analyse this have historically proved frustrating but looking at this again confirms Clare's conclusion that short-term rates and long-term rates are linked to different systems. Short-term rate differences have no long-run relationship with bullion flows but can be shown to have a specific effect on them for short-run periods of a few years. The flows they influence are the specific flows between the countries for which the interest-rate gap is considered. By contrast, the difference between long-run interest rates for the same countries has a long-term relationship with the total flows in and out (added together) for one country, i.e. overall international economic activity. The long-term mechanism seems to have no relationship with crises, as Clare pointed out, whereas Banking-School theory links short-term interest rates to bullion flows and crises. Currency-School attitudes that refuse to acknowledge the Banking-School mechanism can only see crises as sporadic surprises based on particular events.

The analysis of short-term rates uses weekly data for gross bullion exports (less imports) from the United Kingdom to the United States and from the Bank of England daily account books in the period 3 January 1863 to 22 December 1899. US market rates were from the *New York Daily Tribune*, 'Commercial and Money Matters' column (author's series). The £/$ exchange rate is also used for comparison. The truncated series of US short-term rate and UK short-term rate is just non-stationary and to ensure this is not an issue first differences of the series are taken, which are stationary. This is because non-stationarity (an excessive trend or variation) can cause spurious correlations. An OLS regression gives a 95% certain correlation between the bullion flows between the United Kingdom and United States and the differential between their interest rates.

The first difference of 'Bullion Exports from UK to the US minus Imports from US' is the dependent variable and is regressed against the first differences of 'US Short-term rate minus UK Short-term rate' and the 'Exchange rate'. The exchange rate gives a 99% certain correlation (Table 3.6).

However, as the interest rate variable is only barely non-stationary and the main influence on this is variability through the panic period, it is worth noting the result of an OLS test with the variables as before but not differenced (Table 3.7).

Table 3.6 Results of OLS test with first difference of 'Bullion Exports from UK to the US minus Imports from US' as the dependent variable

Variables	*Δ £/$ exchange rate*	*Δ US-UK short-term interest rates*	*Constant*
Coefficient	−988.257	−40.474	0.1049
(Std. error)	(262.752)	(19.270)	(11.151)
Significance	***	**	

Table 3.7 Results of OLS test with 'Bullion Exports from UK to the US minus imports from US' as the dependent variable

Variables	*£/$ exchange rate*	*US-UK short-term interest rates*	*Constant*
Coefficient	−1453.92	−46.5967	194.306
(Std. error)	(374.350)	(6.955)	(15.877)
Significance	***	***	***

With all three variables a Granger causation test gives a 99% certainty result for the difference between short-term interest rates in different countries causing bullion flows (Table 3.8).

There was no causation indicated between the exchange rate and bullion flows. These results show that short-term interest rates in the United Kingdom and United States had a short-term direct effect on bullion flows between the two countries, particularly when the data are examined at a high-resolution level. However, the long-term rates of the two countries also appear to have had a longer term effect on the direction and total level of bullion flows entering and leaving the country. This is consistent with the Banking School's treatment of long- and short-term

Table 3.8 Results of Granger Causality test between interest-rate difference and bullion flows and interest-rate difference and exchange rate (all first differenced)

Causation *A > B A Granger causes B*	*f-value* *12 lags*	*p-value*	*Lag and significance*
Δ Interest Rate diff > Δ Bullion flows	15.361	< 0.0001	4 of 12***
Δ Exchange Rate > Δ Bullion flows			no causation

rates as belonging to separate mechanisms, with only periodic interaction. The difference in short-term interest rates between two countries influences the capital flows between those countries at high resolution over the short term, including during crises. However, the difference between long-term rates in different countries is linked to the total flows in both directions, in other words the total trade and investment activity of one country over a long-term period. The series used for the analysis are: total bullion flows in and out of the United Kingdom, ratio of difference to total of US and UK long-term interest rates, the CPI price index and GDP per person.[74]

Regressions with various other series were investigated such as bullion flows between the United States and United Kingdom and net interest rates for one country, but the best OLS results were from regressing logs of the series as follows.

Total capital flows in and out of UK against the difference between US and UK long-term interest rates, CPI price index and GDP per capita. Logs were taken because there were some non-stationarity elements within the series which could give false results.

The dependent variable is 'Total capital flows in and out of UK'. The period of the data is January 1858 to December 1899, monthly (42 terms). The results are shown in Table 3.9. There must be some doubt in this test because of the possibility of spurious correlation due to the structure of the series.

The equation of the model is:

$$\underset{}{\text{l\_Gr.flows}} = \underset{(1.07)}{15.3} + \underset{(0.126)}{0.579} \times \text{l\_US} - \text{UK Lg.Term} + \underset{(0.291)}{0.807} \times \text{l\_GDP} - \underset{(0.658)}{2.93} \times \text{l\_prices}$$

Table 3.9 Results of an OLS test with log 'Total capital flows in and out of UK' as the dependent variable

Variables (logs)	*US-UK long-term interest rate*	*GDP per capita*	*CPI price index*	*Constant*
Coefficient	0.5791	0.8071	−2.9259	15.3478
(Std. error)	(0.1259)	(0.2906)	(0.6585)	(1.0694)
Significance	***	***	***	***

$R^2 = 0.4295$

Table 3.10 Results of an augmented Engle-Granger test with log 'Total capital flows in and out of UK' as the dependent variable (m = million)

Variables (2 lags)	*US-UK long term interest rate/total*	*GDP per capita*	*CPI price index*	*Constant*
Coefficient	212.074m	1.3805m	−112.69m	105.33m
(Std. error)	(47.598m)	(0.5078m)	(27.376m)	(38.94m)
Significance	***	***	***	**

Residuals test: test statistic: tau $\tau = -4.44507$, asymptotic p-value 0.01873

From graphical evidence spurious correlation appears unlikely, but confirmation is sought by carrying out an Engle-Granger test for cointegration. The series are all non-stationary under an ADF test and the results for the cointegrating regression and test for unit roots in the residuals are as shown in Table 3.10.

The results confirm that the difference between US and UK long-term rates moves consistently with the general level of bullion flows in and out of the United Kingdom when adjusted for GDP per person and the price level. This result explains why long-term rates are so stable. It is because they are affected by long-term and holistic factors. Short-term rates, by comparison, are affected by immediate and very specific factors: the net bullion flows between particular countries. The main interaction between the two types of rates appears to be in a crisis when variations in short-term rates can give a 'kick' to long-term rates in a specific direction.

3.5 Summary of Conclusions

Despite the victory of the Currency School's ideas embodied in the Bank Charter Act of 1844, the Banking School's ideas continued to be used in attempts to understand serious systemic banking crises and other less serious types of financial crises. The Banking School's theory of crises operated through interest rates and international bullion flows and the recycling and multiplication of funds through deposits. A review of available data by means of graphical and econometric analysis has shown that there is some reason to take the theories of the Banking School seriously. There are also signs that Banking-School policies were used to militate against the possibility of crises. After 1866 the Bank of England resorted to prompt but minor Bank Rate fluctuations to influence the balance in its bullion reserve. The changes were frequent, as Palgrave pointed out, about twice the frequency of those made by central banks on the continent. He linked this to a general malaise in commercial confidence during the 'Long Depression', but it was less traumatic than the series of systemic crises before 1866.[75]

This policy followed the type of mitigation that would have arisen from the Banking School's understanding of crises. The frequent changes in the Bank Rate caused the UK short-term market rate to oscillate around the long-term rate. There were only short periods when the British short-term rate was much lower than the long term; small but frequent Bank Rate rises helped close the gap before they could cause large or persistent bullion drains. Henry Huck Gibbs, when Governor of the Bank of England in the 1870s, confirmed that this policy of constant minor adjustments was in use and that alongside considerations of the bullion reserve, the size of the note reserve in relation to liabilities was also monitored very carefully.[76] Short-term rates in the United States after 1866 became less extreme in both their level and variation, which assisted the Bank in trying to influence market rates. When American short-term market rates started to rise again in the 1890s, British rates generally shadowed them at a slightly lower level suggesting that rates were being raised just sufficiently to prevent capital leaving the United Kingdom for the United States.

The following chapters examine the financial crises of the nineteenth century in detail, showing the signs of the mechanism of crises described by the Banking School. In particular, they place the equalisation of interest rates in crises and consequent variations in capital flows at the centre of the narrative of each. Chapter 9 shows that these phenomena returned in the second half of the twentieth century and became well-known to traders as the 'Carry Trade'.

Notes

1. T. Tooke, *On the Bank Charter Act of 1844* (London: Longman, 1856) pp. 85–86.
2. H. Thornton, *An Enquiry into the Nature and Effects of the Paper Credit of Great Britain* [1802 edition] (New York: Kelley, 1965) pp. 331–336.

3. T. Attwood, *Distressed State of the Country* (Birmingham: Beilby, Knott and Beilby, 1829) pp. 4, 8.
4. Idem., pp. 11, 45.
5. J. Fullarton, *On the Regulation of Curriencies* (London: John Murray, 1844) pp. 58–62.
6. *Report from Select Committee on Banks of Issue; with the Minutes of Evidence, Appendix, and Index* PP 1840 (602) IV.1; *Committee of Secrecy on Banks of Issue: First Report* PP 1841(I) (366) V.1.
7. *Select Committee...* PP 1840 (602) IV.1, pp. 9, 29.
8. Idem., p. 33.
9. Idem., pp. 35–36.
10. Idem., p. 48.
11. Idem., p. 52.
12. Idem., pp. 64, 77.
13. Idem., p. 94.
14. Colonial Office confidential print, Wilson Report on Mauritius Currency, Colonial Office papers, N.A., CO 882/1 XVIII ff. 309–320.
15. Idem., p. 117.
16. Idem., p. 120.
17. Idem., pp. 299–300.
18. Idem., p. 305.
19. J. Gilbart, *An Inquiry into the Causes of the Pressure on the Money Market During the Year 1839* (London: Longman, 1830) p. 12.
20. Idem., p. 7.
21. Idem., p. 32.
22. Idem, p. 39.
23. Wilson to Grey 17 October 1847, Grey papers, Durham UL, GRE/B132/ 11/5 enclosed plan B145/D9.
24. *Punch*, 29 May 1847, pp. 221–222; A. E. Scribe, G. Delavigne, *Robert-le-Diable, an Opera in Five Acts: With an Easy Translation, Line for Line with the French* (London: H.N. Millar, 1847) p. 49.
25. *The Times*, 7 April 1847, p. 3; J. Wilson, *Capital, Currency and Banking* (London: The Economist, 1847) p. 206.
26. 'Very large loans at very high rates are the best remedy for the worst malady of the money market', W. Bagehot, *Lombard Street: A Description of the Money Market* [1873] (Westport: Hyperion Press, 1962) pp. 27–28.
27. R. W. Garrison, 'The Austrian Theory of the Business Cycle', in D. Glasner, *Business Depressions* (New York: Garland, 1997) pp. 23–27.
28. G. Clare, *A Money-Market Primer and Key to the Exchanges* (London: Effingham Wilson, 1900) p. 57.
29. Idem., pp. 8–9.
30. Idem., p. 30.

31. Idem., p. 100; G. Clare, *The ABC of the Foreign Exchanges* (London: Macmillan, 1911) pp. 90–95.
32. N. Herger, 'Interest-Rate Parity Conditions During the Era of the Classical Gold Standard', *Swiss Journal of Economics and Statistics* 154 (2018).
33. Ibid.
34. D. Laidler, 'Two Views of the Lender of Last Resort: Thornton and Bagehot', *Papers in Political Economy* 45 (2003) p. 68.
35. Thornton, *An Enquiry*, p. 88.
36. J. M. Keynes, *Collected Writings of John Maynard Keynes* V (Cambridge: CUP, 2013) pp. 293–294.
37. A. L. Bloomfield, *Patterns of Fluctuations in International Investment Before 1914* (Princeton: Princeton University, 1968) pp. 14–41; *Short-Term Capital Movements Under the Pre-1914 Gold Standard* (Princeton: Princeton University, 1963) pp. 34–50.
38. W. E. Beach, *British International Gold Movements* (Cambridge, MA: Harvard UP, 1935) p. 170.
39. All quotes from G. H. Pownall, 'Bank Reserves', *The Economic Journal* 9 (1899) p. 400.
40. *Report from the Secret Committee of the House of Lords on the Causes of Distress* PP 1847–1848 (565, 565-II) VIII Pt.III.1, 537, pp. 88–89.
41. R. H. I. Palgrave, *Bank Rate and the Money Market in England, France, Germany, Holland, and Belgium 1844–1900* (London: John Murray) p. viii.
42. D. Reisman, *Alfred Marshall's Mission* (London: Palgrave Macmillan, 1990) p. 51.
43. J. A. Schumpeter, *Business Cycles* I (London: McGraw-Hill, 1939) pp. 143, 198; S. Kuznets, 'Review of Shumpeter's Business Cycles', *American Economic Review* 30 (1940) 257–271; A. Marshall, J. M. Keynes (ed.), *Official Papers of Alfred Marshall* (London: Macmillan, 1926) p. 158.
44. A. Smith, *Wealth of Nations* (Glasgow Edition of the *Works* of Adam Smith, Oxford: OUP, 1976) pp. 437–438; A. W. Mullineux, *Business Cycles and Financial Crises* (Ann Arbor: University of Michigan Press, 1990) p. 64.
45. In particular, the long-wave theories of the business cycle associated with Simon Kuznets and Nikolai Kondratieff have fallen into disfavour among mainstream economists during the twentieth century. See, for instance, S. N. Solomou, *Economic Cycles: Long Cycles and Business Cycles Since 1870* (Manchester: Manchester UP, 1998).
46. Palgrave, *Bank Rate and the Money Market*, pp. 44–45, 212.
47. T. H. Williams, 'Observations on Money Credit and Panics' [1858], in T. H. Ashton, *Economic and Social Investigations in Manchester, 1833–1933*

(London: King and Son, 1932) p. 72; W. S. Jevons, *A Serious Fall in the value of Gold* (London: Stanford, 1863) p. 10. See F. A. Hayek, *Business Cycles Pt. I* (Chicago: University of Chicago Press, 2012) p. 263.

48. *The Money Bag*, 1858 vol., between pp. 112 and 113. For the description of the theory see pp. 111–114, for the liquidation of foreign balances, p. 290.
49. Idem., inside front cover.
50. S. J. Loyd (Lord Overstone) *Remarks on the Management of the Circulation* (London: P. Richardson, 1840) p. 104.
51. Idem., *Reflections Suggested by a Perusal of Mr. J. Horsley Palmer's Pamphlet on the Causes and Consequences of the Pressure on the Money Market* (London: Pelham Richardson, 1837) p. 44.
52. *The Times*, 24 November 1857, p. 5.
53. *Hansard*, 15 December 1847, XCV, cc. 1148–1149; D. P. O'Brien, *The Correspondence of Lord Overstone* (Cambridge, CUP, 1971) pp. 401–402. *The Money Bag* added a reason as to how the Act favoured the wealthy: by the interest earned in the periods of high rates.
54. *The Money Bag*, 1858 vol., p. 113.
55. Idem., pp. 113–114.
56. Idem., pp. 112–114.
57. D. Besomi, 'Graphical Representations of Overstone's Cycle of Trade', in N. Salvadori et al. (eds.), *Classical Political Economy and Modern Theory* (Abingdon: Routledge, 2013) p. 301; O'Brien, *The Correspondence of Lord Overstone*.
58. Bank of England, Three centuries of data v.3, c. A10 B.
59. *Select Committee*... PP 1840 (602) IV.1, p. 117.
60. W. S. Jevons, 'On the Frequent Autumnal Pressure in the Money Market and the Action of the Bank of England', *Journal of the Statistical Society of London* 29 (1866) 240.
61. A modern confirmation of the thesis that low rates induce more risky investing has been provided by Y. Ma, W. Zijlstra, 'A New Take on Low Interest Rates and Risk Taking', *VOX, CEPR Policy Portal*, 7 March 2018.
62. *The Economist*, 13 October 1866, p. 1196; C. A. Phillips, *Bank Credit: A Study of the Principles and Factors Underlying Advances made by Banks to* Borrowers (New York: Macmillan, 1924) p. 81; R. S. Sayers, *Modern Banking* (Oxford: OUP, 1938) p. 34; R. Dornbusch, J. A. Frenkel, 'The Gold Standard and the Bank of England in the Crisis of 1847', in M. D. Bordo, A. J. Schwartz (eds.), *A Retrospective on the Classical Gold Standard 1821–1931* (Chicago: University of Chicago Press, 1984) pp. 233–276, 245.
63. Cunliffe Report, *First Interim Report of the Committee on Currency and the Foreign Exchanges* PP 1918 (Cd. 9182) para. 4, p. 3. The report

was overtly Banking School referring to the apprehensions caused by the 'limitations of the Act of 1844', para. 28, p. 8.

64. W. E. Huffman, J. R. Lothian, 'The Transmission of Business Cycles', in M. D. Bordo, A. J. Schwartz (eds.), *A Retrospective on the Classical Gold Standard 1821–1931* (Chicago: University of Chicago Press, 1984) p. 471.
65. R. Torrens, *A Letter to Thomas Tooke* (London: Longman, 1840) pp. 11–15.
66. T. Tooke, *History of Prices* I (London: Longman, 1838) p. 152.
67. *Hansard*, 30 November 1847, XCV, c. 430.
68. M. Dawes, C. N. Ward-Perkins, *Country Banks of England and Wales* (Canterbury: Chartered Institute of Bankers, 2000).
69. C. Ó Gráda, *Black '47 and Beyond: The Great Irish Famine in History, Economy and Memory* (Princeton: Princeton UP, 1999) p. 79; C. N. Ward-Perkins, 'The Commercial Crisis 1847', *Oxford Economic Papers* 2 (1950) p. 89; C. N. Ward-Perkins, 'Review', *Economica* 16 (1949) p. 386.
70. Ward-Perkins, 'The Commercial Crisis', p. 94; see R. C. O. Matthew's assessment of Ward-Perkins' approach as not very intellectual, quoted in J. S. Lyons, L. P. Cain, S. H. Williamson (eds.), *Reflections on the Cliometrics Revolution* (Abingdon: Routledge, 2008) p. 157.
71. Sources: Dawes, Ward-Perkins, *Country Banks of England and Wales*; *Bankers' Almanac and Year Book*; checked with I. Bond 'The British Banking Population 1790–82', in M. Hollow, F. Akinbami, R. Michie (eds.), *Complexity and Crisis in the Financial System* (Cheltenham: Edward Elgar, 2016) pp. 99–103.
72. R. H. I. Palgrave, *Bank Rate and the Money Market in England, France, Germany, Holland, and Belgium 1844–1900* (New York: Dutton & Co., 1903) pp. viii–ix, 225 (revised edition).
73. Further details of the tests are given in the Appendix.
74. Price index Bank of England, Three centuries of data, A26 T (1770–1869); GDP per person, Bank of England, Three centuries of data, A4 M (UK incl. S Ireland [1830–1920]).
75. Palgrave, *Bank Rate and the Money Market*, p. 225.
76. B. Price, *Chapters on Practical Political Economy* (London: Kegan Paul, 1878) pp. 551–558.

CHAPTER 4

The Crises of 1825 and 1837–1839

> The Bank had not kindled the fire, but, instead of attempting to stop the progress of the flames, it supplied fuel for maintaining and extending the conflagration.
>
> —Thomas Tooke, *A History of Prices and of the State of the Circulation*, II (1838) pp. 178–179.[1]

> The hon. Gentleman concluded by moving as an amendment to the order of the day, the following resolution: 'that in the opinion of this House the present system of currency is not efficient to meet the wants and protect the interests of the community'.
>
> —Thomas Attwood, MP, of the Birmingham School, *Hansard*, 5 June 1837, XXXVIII, c. 1205.[2]

In the generally accepted view among historians, originally associated with the Currency School, the 1825 crisis is seen as 'the first Latin American debt crisis' because over-optimistic investments in newly emerging economies are presented as the cause of the problem.[3] Larry Neal has extended this interpretation to emphasise the poor information on which those investments were based.[4] The international nature of the 1825 crisis marked a significant change from the crises in the United Kingdom of 1810–1816, so this story goes. The crises of 1810–1816 were believed to have been localised and mainly caused by weather conditions, trading after a poor harvest and the effects of war. By contrast, the causes of the

C. Read, *Calming the Storms*, Palgrave Studies in Economic History,
https://doi.org/10.1007/978-3-031-11914-9_4

1825 crisis were strongly influenced by global economic conditions, not just what was happening in Britain.

The Banking School provides an alternative—and in overall terms more convincing—narrative of this crisis, which has gone mostly unremarked upon in the more recent academic literature on this event.[5] In this version, 'the first Latin American debt crisis' was more the result, not the cause, of financial problems in Britain. The real root of the 1825 crisis could be found at home, as a malfunction of the monetary policy that the Bank of England had adopted after the pound returned to a convertible gold standard in 1821, as result of Sir Robert Peel's recommendations. The 1825 crisis helped to develop the Banking School's emerging theory of financial crises: that they were the eventual negative consequence of an excess of funds looking for better returns in an environment of low interest rates. The crisis of 1837 then proved a very good example of this in action. This chapter, using the full range of qualitative and quantitative sources now available, outlines a revised narrative of these two crises.

4.1 1825: An Overview of the First Crisis of the Gold Standard Era

The Banking School's theory of crisis appeared, in a nascent form, following the reattachment of the pound to gold. Before 1825 there was an extended period in which British short-term interest rates were lower than long-term ones. British long-term rates were under downward pressure from the government. The gold standard had been implemented in the United Kingdom only a few years before in 1819–1821 along with free capital flows, and this was why it was felt the problems of 1825 were different from those in 1810 and 1816. After 1810 the trade balance headed into negative territory and bullion drained out of the Bank of England. However, the flexibility provided by a floating exchange rate meant that the resulting pressure was relieved by a falling pound. In contrast, in 1825, the bullion drain was due to a decreasing trade balance and to investment funds leaving the United Kingdom, resulting in a loss of control of interest rates. They had to be raised to protect bullion reserves and deter investment capital flows seeking high returns, initially an idea associated with the Banking School, but then adopted by Currency-School theorists after 1847.

The position in 1816 was a mixture of mainly exchange rate but also interest-rate adjustment. In other words, between 1810 and 1825 the exchange-rate problems of a non-gold standard era were steadily replaced with the interest-rate problems which the Banking School believed were characteristic of a period with currencies run on a basis akin to a gold standard. Although European countries did not formally adopt a gold standard until the 1870s and the United States is generally viewed as not running a de facto one until the 1830s, most countries backed their currency with bullion (gold, silver or both) after the Napoleonic wars in order to provide stability. This, in effect, created a gold standard between countries, but it could be broken by fluctuations in exchange rates. In addition, if there were reasons for the currency to devalue or if credit dried up, then trade and transfers of capital had to be carried out by bullion. Trading in bullion was the most fixed and rigid gold standard there was, because the price of everything was related to gold.

Politicians and economists at the time were divided into two camps. In this era, the Currency School inclined group of policymakers included Lord Liverpool, Peel and Huskisson. Their solution to the crisis was to further restrict note circulation. The small £1 and £5 bank notes issued by country banks were blamed and their issue was to be stopped, but due to opposition from Wellington and Herries in the Cabinet, the implementation of this was slightly delayed. The Bank was to sell Exchequer bills, further reducing available money. The buying and selling of government debt could be used in a Currency-School or Banking-School manner. Selling debt was seen as reducing the price of credit instruments and raising interest rates, buying it was viewed as having the opposite effect. Decreasing credit substantially in a crisis was a Currency-School policy but the subtle use of it to control market rates by bringing them up to the Bank Rate (minimum discount rate) and discourage drains of gold became a Banking-School policy. The buying of debt in a crisis was also a Banking-School policy. The Banking-School response was supported by many merchants and traders and was articulated by Thomas Attwood, who described himself as 'a Banker, and a manufacturer of "*worthless rags*" as Lord Goderich [Frederick John Robinson] and Mr. Cobbett have called me'.[6] Thomas Tooke supported the government legislation in 1825, but after the event, in 1829, changed his mind and argued against restrictions on banknote circulation.

Attwood and his supporters in what became known as 'the Birmingham School' have been labelled as protectionist, but their hostile attitudes to free trade are a distraction from the more forthright and sincerely-held views aligned with the Banking School they held about currency and monetary policy. In his speech at Birmingham Town Hall on 8 May 1829, Attwood ridiculed the Bank of England's management of the currency and called for the issue of a government-backed paper currency not tied to gold.[7] He criticised the proposed withdrawal of small notes after May 1823, included in Peel's legislation of 1819, saying that it was inevitable that money would become short when 'the *sovereigns* would *fly abroad*', in other words when there was a bullion drain.[8] He supported Lord Castlereagh's concession to agricultural interests in legalising small notes past 1823. However, the Bank of England did not make use of this permission, until it issued small notes during the 1825 crisis.

Attwood claimed that the small notes had been part of the solution to the crisis, not part of the problem, and criticised renewed attempts in 1826 to stop their issue.[9] He viewed the commercial problems in the country as an '*underproduction of money*' not '*overproduction*' of goods.[10] He blamed the restriction of money for the victimisation, through unemployment, of 'what is blasphemously called, the "*surplus population*"'.[11] Echoing Thornton's theories, he described how crises start from accumulations of excess money in times of low interest rates.[12] Attwood explained these in terms of a lack of opportunities for investment and how the situation leads to unwise investments.

He attributed the success of the Currency School's views to support from newspapers and journals in which 'the proprietors are often *stock-jobbers*, interested in the national plunder'.[13] *The Times* was particularly forthright in its support of Currency-School ideas. Attwood found its position not only economically but also morally objectionable for several reasons. *The Times* presented the crisis as not really significant and soon to pass: 'it creates in our minds no great terror as a *national* evil'. It snootily placed the blame on country bankers: 'many of them mere retail shopkeepers... deluging the provinces with millions' of small notes while the 'Bank of England' was 'without the issue of a single one or two pounds note'.[14] In response, Attwood contrasted what he saw as the distant and uncaring attitudes of the upper classes who held senior banking positions in London, with the hard-working businessmen and country bankers in the provinces. (Notably, the same moral tone was echoed by *The Economist* in 1855 when Overend, Gurney & Co. challenged the Bank of England for supremacy in banking.) In Attwood's analysis, the crisis in 1825 was due principally to bullion flows out of the country which were influenced by 'foreign circumstances', not just those at home. These, if left unfettered, could have led to 'national bankruptcy' if the Banking School's methods of issuing small notes and of the Bank of England buying Exchequer Bills had not been used to ease the pressure on credit.[15]

Huskisson responded to Attwood's calls for the repeal of the Country Bankers Act of 1826 saying that this action 'by allowing an unbounded circulation of small notes, would again cause universal distress'.[16] The Act had restricted note issue to larger banks more than 65 miles from London and allowed the Bank of England to set up branches. An Enquiry was offered as a palliative. At the Enquiry, Horsley Palmer, then Governor of the Bank of England, explained his rule of operating the Bank according to the state of the foreign exchanges, and of moderating the flow of bullion, firstly by buying or selling government securities, next by adjusting the Bank Rate and then by restricting discounts.[17] This rule of thumb influenced the future actions of the Bank and incorporated Banking-School ideas in that it aimed to hurt commercial business as little as possible while influencing flows of bullion and protecting the convertibility of the currency.

Samuel Jones-Loyd (Lord Overstone from 1850), a Manchester banker, also gave evidence to the Enquiry. He was to become a leading light in the propagation of the Currency School's ideas, particularly in the lead up to the Bank Charter Act of 1844. In 1832 his views were more moderate and he had some sympathy for some of the Banking School's ideas. He recognised the disparity in interest rates, market rates being below the Bank of England's discount rate and believed publication of the Bank's accounts would help reduce panics. He even supported the idea of Palmer standing as MP for the City of London.[18] On the question which divided some members of the Schools in 1844, as to whether prices varied according to the quantity of currency, he avoided the question: 'that question involves a variety of very difficult considerations, which require much more examination'.[19] Samuel Gurney gave evidence that he did not favour attempts to remove disparity and fluctuations in the value of money and it is notable that the bill broking business of the Gurney family went on to make use of the disparity of interest rates in its business.[20] In general, his views appeared more 'Currency School' than Overstone's were, at least at this stage.

This chapter will highlight indications that the underlying cause of the 1825 crisis was a surge of flows of capital abroad seeking investment opportunities and that those flows arose from reductions in interest rates in Britain. The problem of understanding at the time was that no records were kept of bullion imports into Britain and no one knew how much was in the country. The concern of bankers and politicians in Britain over bullion was centred on the reserves of the Bank of England rather than the amount of gold in the country as a whole. Yet, with a lack of any data on the latter, the two were often conflated. Every dip in the Bank's reserves brought a panic that all the gold was disappearing out of the country in a situation when notes had to be convertible by the Bank to the precious metal on demand.

The Bank initially reduced the credit it offered, but as the drain persisted, it was forced to return interest rates to the 5% maximum in the last resort. This put stress on commerce and contradicted the government policy of maintaining a national budget without a deficit which required lower interest rates to decrease the payments on the national debt.[21] Most of the bankruptcies were in 1826 after the Bank of England raised rates from 4 to 5% on 13 December 1825. By the end of that month, the bullion drain reversed.[22] The number of bankruptcies soon tapered off. Of the bankruptcies in 1825, 70% were in December and, of those in 1826, 72% were before the end of March.[23] The Banking School thought all these events were linked, but apologists for the Currency School saw them as 'co-incidental', the viewpoint mentioned in some modern histories that include the crisis.[24]

The origins of this crisis can be traced back to monetary policy, namely the government's attempt at financial repression. In the early 1820s the government bore down on interest rates because, after a fall in government spending after the Napoleonic Wars, there had been a sharp rise in the proportion of government revenues which had to be applied to servicing the swollen national debt. The government reduced debt payments by cancelling high-yield government bonds and reissuing them at a lower rate. The Bank of England followed on by reducing its Bank Rate from 5 to 4% in June 1822 to help these efforts. As William Quinn and John Turner have recently noted, the Bank also released more money onto the market by purchasing the Dead Weight Annuity, security that had been originally issued to delay some of the cost to the Treasury of military pensions from the Napoleonic Wars.[25] As a result of these policies the money supply soared; the Bank's note issue rose by 25% in the three years to February 1825, and that of the country banks swelled by around 50% between 1823 and 1825.[26]

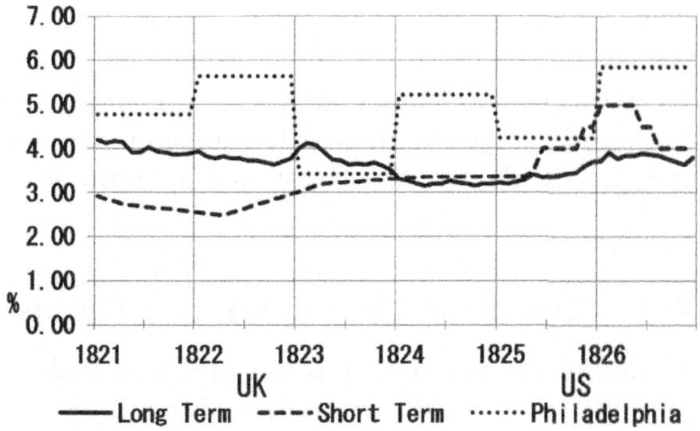

Fig. 4.1 UK short-term interest rate and long-term rate (monthly) and Philadelphia discount rate (annual) (*Sources* Three centuries of data v.3 cols. M10 K and M9 N; H. Bodenhorn, H. Rockoff, 'Regional Interest Rates in Antebellum America', in *Strategic Factors in Nineteenth Century American Economic History* [Chicago: University of Chicago Press, 1992] p. 167)

As wartime restrictions on capital flows of bullion had been fully lifted by Peel in 1821, much of the bullion and coin in Britain was exported out of the country. Investors looked for better returns abroad than those available at home where interest rates were under downward pressure from the government.[27] The bullion flooded onto the continent and to South America, where bond yields were spiralling. French government debt offered a steady 5%, higher than the return of around 3% available from the British equivalent.

More exotic investments seemed to offer even greater rewards. Bonds from Peru rose from 6% in mid-1825 to an illusory 25% in April 1826 for the unwary. In the United Kingdom, in mid-1825, the Bank of England, concerned at its bullion drain, squeezed credit and put pressure on other London and country banks. Many payments and transfers of capital had to be made in gold rather than by credit, producing the conditions of a tight gold standard. Despite government wishes, the Bank of England was forced to raise its official rate from 4 to 5% in December 1825, matching the returns of French bonds and bringing down even more banks and in turn the Latin American loans.

Even at this early point after the return of convertibility, the characteristics of future crises, as later pointed out by the Banking School, can be identified (Fig. 4.1). Not only is there a prolonged period before

1824 when short-term rates are lower than long-term rates (which had themselves been reduced), but the discount rate in Philadelphia, the main banking centre of the United States at the time, equalised with those in the United Kingdom in 1823, signalling trouble ahead for British investors and the American schemes and institutions in which they invested.

4.2 The Run-Up to the 1825 Crisis

As gold convertibility was resumed and full capital mobility was allowed from 1819, the Banking School's theories about international capital flows would become more relevant. In the circumstances of the balance of trade becoming out of equilibrium, an adjustment would tend to be by a change in interest rates instead of the exchange rate. Interest rate changes were increasingly linked with unstable flows of investment capital which caused bullion drains from the Bank of England.

This is indeed what the data show. Figure 4.2 reveals that the main change in exchange rate took place between 1808 and 1816, after that there were only small fluctuations on an annual average basis. Looking at the gold price, Fig. 4.3 shows that the exchange rates were not merely being made to appear stable after 1817 by the franc, dollar and pound moving together but by their steadiness of their value against gold. So, Peel's slow lead into a fixed exchange rate was reasonably successful in that it provided exchange stability after 1817. It should be noted however that this was on an annual average and that between 1816 and 1821 there were short-lived fluctuations that unsettled investors at the time.

The crisis of 1825 and the lead up to it from the wars against Napoleon and America can be divided into three periods of balance-of-trade deficits. These are labelled 1, 2, and 3 in Fig. 4.4. The start of the first large main variation in the exchange rate is matched by the first and smallest of these three periods of the balance of trade decreases or deficits in the case of the merchandise balance of trade.

The trade balances both exclude bullion. Very approximate estimates of bullion flow are shown in Fig. 4.4. These are necessarily vague proxies because it is not possible to differentiate between bullion which is the current account (payments for goods) or capital account (investment flows) and official figures for bullion imports were not kept. The story they point to is nonetheless an interesting one.

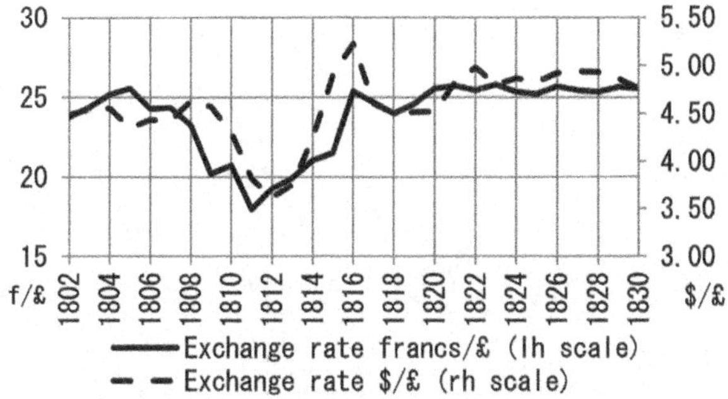

Fig. 4.2 Exchange rate of the UK £ with the French franc (lh scale) and US $ (rh scale) 1802–1830 (*Sources* L. H. Officer, 'Exchange Rates', in S. B. Carter et al. (eds.), *Historical Statistics of the United States*, 5 [Cambridge: CUP, 2006]; *Journal de commerce*)

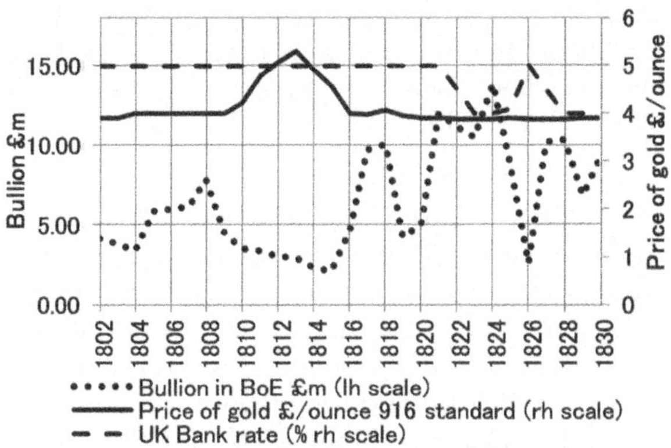

Fig. 4.3 Bullion reserves, including coin, in the Bank of England, UK Bank rate and the price of gold 1802–1830 (*Sources* R. Thomas, and N. Dimsdale. [2016]. Three centuries of data v.2.3, Bank of England cols. A19 B, A13 F)

All three trade deficits have corresponding periods of bullion drain from the Bank of England, similarly marked A, B, and C on Fig. 4.4, suggesting that they are linked. The first balance of trade deficit of 1810 coincided with a long running drain running up to 1817. The balance of trade oscillated around zero, but the forces that brought it there are not to do with interest rates. That was because the gold standard was not

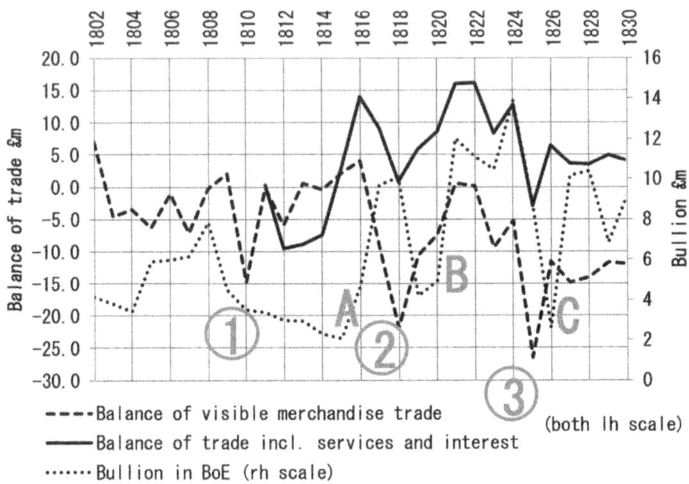

Fig. 4.4 Bullion and coin in the Bank of England compared with balance of trade with and without services and interest 1802–1830. Trade depressions are marked 1, 2 and 3, bullion drains A, B and C (*Source* Bank of England Three Centuries of data v.2.3, col. A13 F, A24 N, S)

yet in effect and the correction mechanism to the balance of payments occurred by the fluctuation of exchange rates, as can be seen in Fig. 4.3. Much silver found its way to Asia towards the end of this first drain taking advantage of the difference in exchange rate for it in different countries. The drain included some foreign bullion from those who had thought Britain a safe place for their funds during the war but were now looking to export it. The drain was large and long-lived for this reason, and because of the exportation of coins, adding to the flow of payments for the importations of food in 1810. The first trade deficit is solely around 1810 and is connected with grain imports which produced an external drain, but the exportation of coin would have appeared to be an internal drain as the coin was withdrawn from banks internally. At the time, the drains were noted as a sign of the general condition of a drain from the country. The coincidence of bullion and trade fluctuations provides some support for Currency-School theories of the price-specie flow mechanism, explaining its popularity in the period after the 1825 crisis.

Figure 4.5 shows that the balance of trade in bullion was positive (i.e. exports were greater) throughout most of the period except 1826, 1827, and 1830. This suggests that overall flows of bullion were significant, on average about £3m a year). The best guesstimate from the period of the amount of gold coin in the country before the Bank restriction was at least £20m, but this was enough, together with bullion in the Bank, to fund the net exports.[28]

This first small deficit and associated sizeable bullion drain was partially counteracted by the prolonged period of exchange rate fall which also ran up to 1817, in that cheaper prices would have encouraged exports and reverse payments. But for the next two deficits, this was not possible as the exchange rate was intended to be fixed.

So the second and third dips both were associated with flows of trading payments while interest rate differentials increasingly caused flows of investment capital until they were counteracted by the moving together of interest rates. This suggests that the mechanisms later suggested by the Banking School may have played some role here. The second drain arose from another food shortage in 1816 and large importations of grain. The third drain in 1825 was, by contrast, mainly the product of a search for better yielding foreign investments after the government and banks began to bear down on interest rates from 1822 onwards through the Bank Rate. As a result, the Bank of England's bullion reserve fell below £3m in 1825.

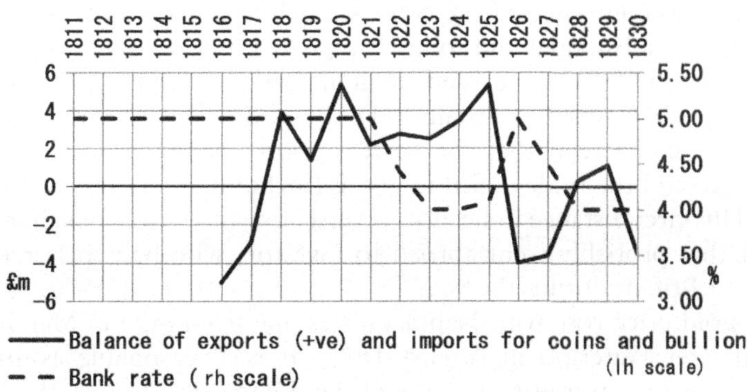

Fig. 4.5 Balance of trade of bullion, approximate estimate, Bank rate, annual average (*Sources* A. H. Imlah, *Economic Elements* [Cambridge, MA: Harvard University Press, 1958], 'Three Centuries of data')

While the drawing together of yields on the stock exchange warned of the investment flows adding to the second period of problems, the drawing together of the nominal interest rates of France and England, was to the Banking School a sign of investment flows which would drive the third and worst crisis in 1825. The Bank of England dropped its interest rate from 5 to 4% in June 1822 and the government began to repay and reissue consols at lower interest rates in 1822–1823. This environment of lower rates caused an international search for better yields and the interest rates of France and England moved together when bullion left the United Kingdom for France as a loan so that France could pay the British government war reparations and avoid famine. The Bank was forced to reverse its official interest rate cut and put it back up to 5% in December 1825. At that point, loans made to Latin American countries—including one for a country that was a hoax and did not exist—then went sour. Although some more recent commentators regard this hoax as the cause of the 1825 crisis in Britain, by chronology it was more of a consequence.

4.3 The Bullion Drain of 1810

This complex series of events, involving three separate bullion drains, is often conflated in descriptions of the crisis so the stages will now be explained in more detail. The first drain, in 1810 (marked as '1' on Fig. 4.4), was composed of the coin as much as bullion and, as shown in Fig. 4.3, was substantial and long-lasting. At the start, there was a small merchandise trade deficit caused by grain imports. About 1.5m quarters of grain were imported to Britain in 1810, six times that for the following year.[29] It can be seen that the trade surplus, including services, drops below zero and the trade deficit in goods (including bullion) just after this point. This circumstance indicates a reverse flow of services which includes interest that probably went abroad to investors who had sheltered their bullion in Britain during the war.

The gold price rose with Napoleon's escape from exile in March 1815 and fell after Waterloo in August 1815. It is a reasonable assumption therefore that the war was the cause of the rise in price. In turn that meant that gold coins used by the general population in the United Kingdom appeared high in value against the deflated notes. New coins were often sent abroad to be sold, therefore causing the drain, and there was a shortage of coins in London and with which to pay Wellington's soldiers abroad. Tradesmen were even encouraged to issue their own tokens so that they could give change. In particular, there were large exports of silver coins to Asia in the period immediately before 1816 as this was profitable and legal at the time. The process of a currency devaluation rebalancing a balance of trade deficit by increased exports was thus coincidentally overtaken by the much quicker process of the exportation of the coin. Worse still the bullion drain was enormous and was accompanied by nearly 40 bankruptcies of bankers over the period of the drain (Fig. 4.6).

The stock market also fell reaching a low point at the end of 1816 as shares were sold to apply the money in what was thought to be a more profitable manner. The Bank of England contracted the amount of commercial paper it had under discount by 65% from 1816 to 1817 and the number of British Banks decreased by 12.5% from 1814 to 1816.[31] The Coinage Act of 1816, however, mitigated the problem and firmly pointed the way to a gold standard by establishing the sovereign as legal currency and making any clipped coin illegal with a value only as scrap.[32] Silver could only be used in coinage where the face value of the coin

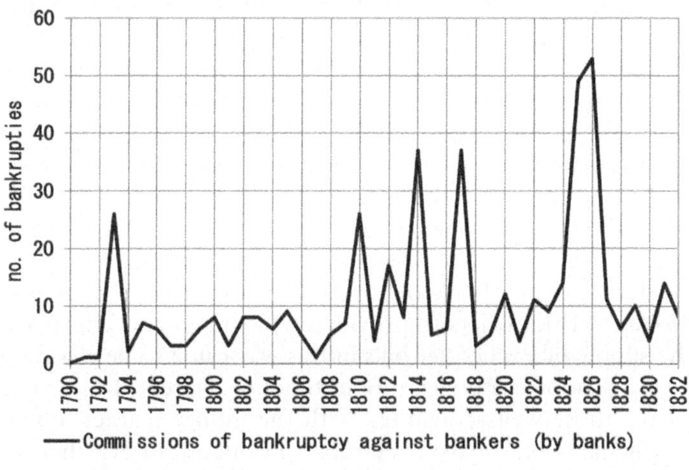

Fig. 4.6 Commissions of bankruptcy against bankers in England (by bank as opposed to individuals). A common error is mixing earlier individual and later bank bankruptcy data[30] (*Sources* Reports respecting the Bank of England resuming Cash Payments PP 1819 [291] III.363 p. 426; Country Banks PP 1826 [94] XXII-5, p. 6; Private Banks PP 1833 [489] XXXI.201, pp. 2–3)

was more than the market value of the silver, making its exportation or melting down for the silver uneconomic.

4.4 The Drain of 1816–1818

The next drain, of 1816–1818 (marked as '2' in Fig. 4.4), was preceded by a dip in the trade balance in goods, which went into deficit, while the trade balance including services also dipped but just remained positive. A bullion drain started shortly afterwards. These fluctuations were a sign of imports necessary to deal with a serious food shortage in 1816.

That year has been called 'one of the blackest years in agricultural history'—an apt description for what is commonly known as 'the year without a summer'.[33] Now thought to be caused by ash from the eruption in 1815 of Mt. Tambora, a volcano in present-day Indonesia, the poor harvest was widespread in Europe and, as a result of this dearth, the quantity of food imports into the United Kingdom soared from 1816. Food prices, which had been falling, suddenly rose. The labouring poor were hit across the board. Falling yields hit agricultural employment; factory workers also saw their real incomes dented by the higher prices.

Robinson's Corn Laws, by which when prices went above a certain level, foreign grain was admitted duty free meant that the ports were open for wheat, rye, barley and Indian corn from 15 November 1816 for a year, and opened again after 15 February 1818. The imports of grain for 1816 were lower than expected because a considerable quantity was diverted to France and some grain was even exported there from England, as French ports opened duty-free in August 1816.[34] In response to the economic crisis, Nicholas Vansittart wanted to set up a system based on loans, either Bank of England mortgages or Exchequer bills, to give loans to landowners to provide employment and improve agriculture. The supply of Exchequer bills in this way came to be associated with the Banking School as a policy tool in times of distress. The proposal was opposed by 'those well acquainted with the money market' on the basis that the scheme 'would have been more productive of evil than good'.[35] The scenario was to be replayed almost exactly in 1847 during the Great Famine in Ireland. On the earlier occasion such loans were argued to be not possible because credit was in short supply as a return to convertibility approached and a bullion drain was in progress, whereas during the Great Famine, although the bullion drain was less severe, the fear of a credit crunch was greater.[36] In this way, the wider economic-policy regime constrained fiscal room for manoeuvre and directly impacted the relief offered by the government.

The recovery in 1817–1818 is generally seen as being due to the good harvest of that period and optimism of manufacturing in general. However, some of the exporting was speculative and on long credit; the flow of monies back to the United Kingdom was not expected immediately. The drain did not stop with the recovery because the Bank of England started phasing in the gold standard and noteholders were only too anxious to cash in their notes for gold at reasonable rates. In 1816 the Bank took initial steps towards resumption and paid gold on some older bank notes. At the same time restrictions on exports of bullion were lifted in 1819 and the balance of the price of gold and exchange rates made it profitable to export gold, encouraging another bullion drain that year.

4.5 The Drain of 1825

The drain of 1825 (marked as '3' in Fig. 4.4) started with a large merchandise trade deficit; from then onwards this measure of the balance of trade tended to remain negative (at official prices) for decades to come (Fig. 4.3). However, it can only be considered when it includes trade-in services along with interest payments from abroad. This measure theoretically should have remained around zero if it was an estimate of the balance of payments. However, the figures do not satisfactorily deal with bullion and investment flows leaving Britain. The accumulated balance of British-owned assets abroad increased steadily from £104.4m in 1825 to £2,295m in 1895.[37] It might be said that the United Kingdom increasingly became the world's bank rather than the world's workshop during the Victorian era. Nevertheless, these flows of capital between nations which could at this early time very quickly even up the balance of payments were also thought to be the cause of instability and financial crises in the eyes of the Banking School. The figures are awkward to interpret because it is difficult to categorise the flow of bullion into investments, payments and non-money flows.[38] Certainly, the drain in 1825 discussed here was principally caused by the exit of bullion sent abroad by investors seeking the better returns available there in the face of reducing rates at home. This marks it out as substantially different from the drains of 1810 and 1816–1818, which were driven far more by trade than investment flows.

The cause of low rates in the United Kingdom was the government attempting to mitigate the fiscal effects of the debts which had been accumulated during the Napoleonic Wars. This debt had increased from over £355m in 1797 to over £816m (216% of nominal GDP) in 1816.[39] The interest payments as a proportion of total government expenditure had increased over a similar period from 25.8% to a massive 46.1%.[40] When the return to convertibility was being implemented in 1819, the problem posed by Britain's huge debt load was being addressed by bearing down on interest rates.

At the same time, the government lost the income to service these debts from a number of sources. The main contributor to servicing this debt had been what was frequently called 'the income tax', in fact, a property tax, of 5%. The war malt tax had also helped. At the beginning of the session of 1816, the government proposed to continue the property tax for two years and the malt tax for five years. Nicholas Vansittart, the chancellor of the exchequer, proposed the measure in the House of Commons. He argued that the property tax 'was a tax more upon the rich than the poor' and that continuing it would be 'the least objectionable of any tax that had ever been proposed' following the general policy of the government of protecting the labouring population (as described in Chapter 2).[41]

However, the rich were not impressed. The Corporation of London, for instance, considered that the effect of the taxes would be 'ruinous' in view of 'the depressed state of the agricultural interests' and particularly when 'the manufacturing and trading interests [were] equally depressed, and equally borne down by the weight of taxation'.[42] The property tax was defeated by a large majority (238 to 201) in the House of Commons and the malt tax proposal was dropped afterwards.[43]

The loss of income from taxes left a hole in government income of between £17m and £18m, a quarter of expenditure.[44] In 1816 distress from harvest failure was such that long-term loans could not be raised at reasonable rates. The government, nonetheless, did eventually engage in distress-relief measures despite considerable opposition. An issue of Exchequer bills (short-term loans) was made for the relief of the poor and the encouragement of public works, the rate being about 3% and repayment due by 5 April 1818. This left the government very vulnerable as short-term loans had to be renewed regularly at the rate current at the time, and at what rate that might be was unknown. With interest repayments as a significant proportion of expenditure, the country could be pushed further towards bankruptcy if rates went too high. The bankruptcy of countries was not unknown at the time. France had defaulted on most of its debts in 1789 during its Revolution.[45] Austria had suffered a catastrophic state bankruptcy due to inflation in 1811. Its paper war currency was replaced with a new one only for a further crisis and revaluation to occur in 1816. Following Britain's victories in 1815, its political classes did not want to emulate the financial failings of its shattered continental rivals.

The solution followed in Britain was to increase the proportion of 'funded' debt which was backed by long-term loans such as consols which were perpetual and could only be repaid when the government chose to do so. This contrasted with the 'unfunded' debt of Exchequer bills and short-term loans. The disadvantage was, of course, that the long-term debt normally attracted a higher interest rate than short-term loans, notionally because of the greater risk to the investor being parted for a longer time from his capital sum, and these high rates became fixed and were not able to be reduced. In 1815 unfunded debt was around 7% of the total, but by 1830 it had dropped to 3.2%.[46] The rebalancing of government debt towards funded long-term loans and away from unfunded short-term loans may have increased the stability of the country's finances, but it also decreased the flexibility for loans to be raised in a time of distress.

However, Robinson, who became chancellor of the exchequer in 1823, developed a method of reducing the rate on long-term loans. Holders of, say, 5% bonds would be told that at a certain date they were to be repaid, but at the same time they would be offered a replacement bond at a lower rate, say 4%. As this was done at a time when the prevailing interest rate was equal to or lower than the new rate, the investors had little choice but to renew at the new rate and, certainly, this was the most convenient course of action for them. This method was continued by Henry Goulburn and by George Goschen when they were chancellors. In 1844 a Parliamentary paper calculated that a saving of about £3m in interest a year had been achieved in the period 1822–1844, just over 10% of the interest payable on the national debt.[47]

The sinking fund had originally been intended by William Pitt for paying off the national debt. He paid off bonds with a million pounds each year from available surpluses and saved the interest in the fund which was then used to redeem more bonds. The sinking fund also became used to obtain loans as bonds from the money market to pay off the consols at a high rate while gambling they would be purchased at the lower rate. But Pitt's original plan did not last and a deficit had been run for some which could mean that the cost of interest on loans raised to buy back the consols was more than the interest saved on the lower rate repurchased consols. When there was no surplus, the sinking fund itself was maintained by raising loans and then it was used to defray the national debt. The sinking fund was also always a target for funding any particular crisis that came along and was less under Treasury control than other funding. Because of these problems, and others, the sinking fund was abandoned in 1832.

The action of bearing down on long-term interest rates rebalanced how the cost of the debt fell on the different classes. Whereas the inability of the government to continue the high taxes from wartime had benefitted the rich, the amount paid to the wealthy in return for loaning their capital had been reduced by the reduction in rates. In a further clever move, Robinson placated the tax-hating wealthy by reducing taxes when he could, but did it in areas such as tariffs on manufacturing that also provided employment for the poor.

However, the wealthy, who had become used to a steady and safe rate of interest of around 5% for the last couple of decades, were prompted by the Bank of England cutting its Rate to 4% in June 1822 to look for better investments yields. There was a surplus of bullion and coin held by individuals as well, and these circumstances caused the yield rates of certain reliable stocks and shares to be drawn together with consols in an early internal version of interest rates moving together internationally, in the manner later recognised by the Banking School, over the period 1819–1823 (Fig. 4.7).

This was first noted by Larry Neal who also used econometric analysis to show that the series before and after the pulling together of rates were dislocated and not continuous.[48] This dislocation is consistent with

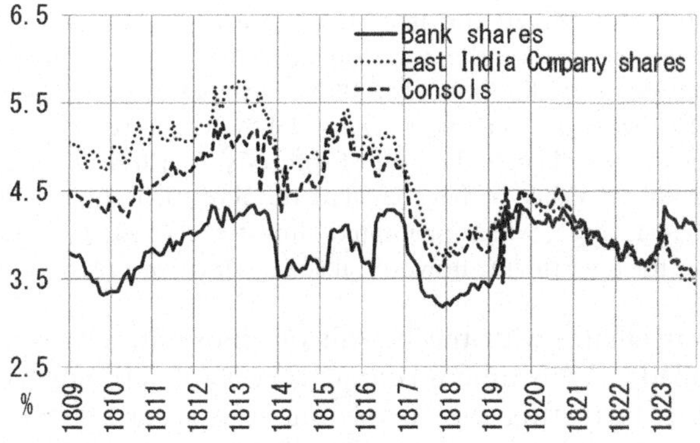

Fig. 4.7 Yield estimated from prices for Bank of England shares, East India Company shares and consols 1809–1824. The rates are drawn together over the period 1819–1823 (*Sources* L. Neal, *The Rise of Financial Capitalism* [Cambridge: Cambridge University Press, 1990] pp. 254–257; *Course of the Exchange*)

the moving together of the rates being caused by a very different set of economic circumstances than the rest of the time. It is consistent with surplus funds being available in the period when short-term rates were less than long-term rates (Fig. 4.1), as the Banking School's theories describe.

As a result of better times, Robinson gained the nickname 'Prosperity Robinson', a title buoyed up by the same rhetoric which he used to talk up the economy[49]:

> Looking forward, then, to the future result of this state of things, as connected with our commercial interests, I may confidently say, 'The wide, unbounded prospect lies before me' without being compelled to add, with the poet, that 'shadows, clouds and darkness rest upon it'. We have seen the opening of a brilliant dawn and we may anticipate without hesitation the steady and glowing splendour of a meridian sky.[50]

Unfortunately for investors the bearing down on interest rates by the government was to invite back 'shadows, clouds and darkness' very shortly. Palmer firmly blamed Robinson's bond rate reductions for the crisis ('excitement') that it induced in 1825:

> I have always considered the first step towards the excitement was the reduction of interest upon the government securities; the first movement in that respect was, I think, upon £135,000 of five per cents which took place in 1823. In the subsequent year, 1824, followed the reduction of £80m of four per cents… That reduction of interests, one fifth in one case and one eighth in the other to have created the feverish feeling in the minds of the public at large, which prompted almost everybody to entertain any proposition for investment, however absurd, which was tendered.[51]

Palmer was talking with the benefit of hindsight. The largest foreign investment made at this time was quite successful, although it did have a rough patch at first. After the Napoleonic war, according to the Treaties of Convention which were concluded on 20 November 1816, France had to pay reparations to Great Britain in a number of payments, altogether about 125m francs, or £5.25m in British currency, as follows:

During the year	*Francs*
1816	15m
1817	27.5m
1818	27.5m
1819	27.5m
1820	27.5m

This was Britain's share of total reparations of 700m francs (£29m) that France had to pay, the remainder being payable to Austria, Prussia and Russia.

In addition, France had to pay for an army of occupation and Britain's share of this was around 11.8m francs (£0.5m) a year.[52] In order to pay this amount, at first the French government ran a deficit and financed it with cash advances from British loan contractors secured against French *rentes* to be sold on to banks or the money markets. However, the rates of interest payable in France were high at first because of the insolvency of former Bourbon regimes. Two British banks, Baring Bros. and Hope & Company helped set up a foreign loan to overcome this with an advance to France of 100m francs in return for *rentes* which were successfully marketed. This was followed by a number of issues, some directly by the French, which were traded in France and London.[53]

Figure 4.8 shows the theoretical yield based on the sale price as published in the *Course of the Exchange* at the time. Foreign investments in the French national debt were not like the 100% secure consols of the British government and part of the theoretical yield might be a risk premium on top of the interest rate dependant on the reputation of the bond. The *rentes* had a coupon rate of 5% and it can be seen from Fig. 4.8 that from 1819 to 1824 they fell from 7.5 to 5%. This fall in yield, or gain in price, was a sign of strength rather than weakness. The French government's finances were fairly robust after the war and the national debt was low compared with that of England, so it was not surprising that any risk premium had gradually evaporated and that the bonds were trading at par. They continued to do so into the future and were a successful investment.

However, for Britain, the immediate consequences were not so bright. In December 1825 there were large capital flows accompanied by international interest rates moving together. This occurred in the circumstances of free movement of capital (bullion moving in considerable quantities to France) and a relatively stable exchange rate. The Bank of England had dropped its official Bank Rate to 4% in 1822, but in December 1825 it was forced to put it back up to 5% to prevent bullion drains seeking the 5% yield of the now stabilised French *rentes*. The free market rate in London kept pace. The recovery in London's stock market was immediately choked off as domestic securities were sold in preference to other types of investment.

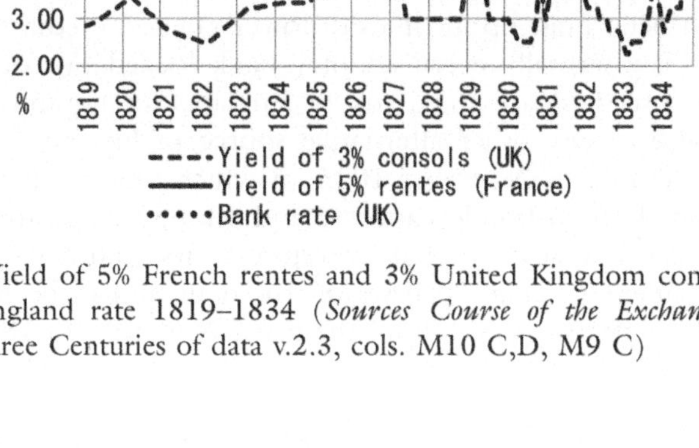

Fig. 4.8 Yield of 5% French rentes and 3% United Kingdom consols and the Bank of England rate 1819–1834 (*Sources Course of the Exchange*, Bank of England Three Centuries of data v.2.3, cols. M10 C,D, M9 C)

4.6 The Wider Consequences of the 1825 Crisis

The effect on English country banks of the raised rate was the last straw that broke the camel's back. Country banks had been suffering from problems since the summer of 1825. However, it was the Bank's tightening of credit conditions in early December that was responsible for the intensity of the problems that the English banking sector suffered that month, which continued into the start of 1826. It is from this period that the crisis gained its notoriety in British banking history.

English country banks were for the most part small and poorly capitalised, and specialised in giving minor loans to local businesses. When the Bank of England's charter was renewed in 1709 it was given a monopoly of joint-stock banking. Its country bank cousins were limited to no more than six partners if they issued notes and, in any case, could only form as unlimited-liability partnerships, not as joint-stock companies. This limitation ensured they were low risk in that they covered only a small area geographically, but they were subject to local pressures and crises as well as national ones. The business model was to exchange as many notes as possible for investors' coin or bullion and then reinvest that money to earn interest. The notes bore an inscription 'I promise to pay the bearer the sum of ...... on demand', but if noteholders wished to exchange them for coin all at once, such as when there were investment opportunities abroad or when news of another country bank failing came in, it caused a run on the bank. The bank could turn to a London bank, which would in turn approach the Bank of England for a loan to tide things over until assets could be liquidated.

However, when the Bank restricted its lending and increased its Rate in December 1825, even if the country banks obtained a loan, the likelihood was that they would not be able to keep up with the payments, as their business had been built up in times of lower rates. A credit crunch thus ensued that saw virtually every country bank locked out of the credit market and forced to ask the Bank of England for liquidity assistance in the absence of any other alternative source of finance.[54] The panic reached a peak on 14 December 1825, at which time many banks were forced to close both in London and provincial England.[55] After that date, the panic began to ease as the Bank reversed course and began to lend to banks more liberally again.[56] However, the damage had been done and bank failures continued throughout the first few months of 1826.[57] John

Turner estimates that, in total, nearly a fifth of the English banking system failed during the crisis.[58]

The Times of 20 July 1826 later described how an English bank failure started a domino effect of Latin American states, most newly independent from the Spanish Empire, defaulting on loans raised in London:

> The news of the failure of Mssrs B A Goldschmidt and Co. reached Bogota previous to the 19th May by an express sent on from Carthagena, but was only known to the executive and a few individuals who obtained letters by that mode; but the regular mail, which left England on the 15th February had not arrived...The attention of the government had, however, been drawn to its approaching difficulties in finance by having learnt that all attempts on the part of the Peruvian Deputies Mssrs. Paredes and Olmedo to raise money in Europe had failed. It will be recollected that the proceeds of this loan, if raised, were to be applied in the discharge of the debt to Colombia incurred by Peru for the assistance in achieving independence of the latter country.[59]

The Colombian government was relying on Peru to raise a further loan in order to pay them interest on their previous borrowings. This would enable Colombia in turn to service the interest on their own debt that had been issued in England. They had few funds to hand and otherwise could not afford to do this, so a default was inevitable. The Colombian loan bond, which had been trading at a price of 92.5% of face value in March 1825, fell to 26% in July 1826. Peru bonds fell in price from 88.5% to 23% of their face value over the same period.

In 1820 Colombia had been the first Latin American country to issue bonds in London. Their first loan was for around £2m. 1822 saw loans taken out by Colombia, Chile, Peru and the fictional Poyais.[60] The last was a fraud by a Gregor McGregor who raised £200,000 by offering bonds as a loan to a purely imaginary country supposedly in Latin America.[61] The bonds were sold at a price of 80% at a return on the face value of 5% or an effective 6.25% yield in September 1822 and were quoted in *The Times* and *Course of the Exchange* in October and November. McGregor's fraud was discovered when survivors of a party of settlers he sent to what was actually the Black River in Belize returned

Table 4.1 Loans raised for foreign states that defaulted, 1821–1825[63]

Loans raised for foreign states that defaulted

Year of issue	*Country*	*Face rate %*	*Issue yield %*	*Theoretical yield to maturity November 1827 %*	*Amount issued in London £m*	*Default from*
1821–1822	Spain	5	8.9	50.9	12.9	May 1824
1822	Chile	6	8.6	23.1	1.0	September 1826
	Colombia	6	7.1	25.5	2.0	May 1826
	Peru	6	6.8	23.0	0.45	April 1826
	Portugal[a]	5	5.7	7.0	1.5	June 1828
1823	Spain	5	16.7	71.4	1.4	May 1824
	Buenos Aires	6	7.1	12.6	1.0	January 1828
1824	Colombia	6	6.8	21.8	4.75	January 1826
	Greece	5	8.5	30.3	0.8	January 1827
	Mexico	5	8.6	11.9	3.2	October 1827
	Peru	6	7.3	23.0	0.75	April 1826
1825	Greece	5	8.8	32.8	2.0	January 1827
	Guatemala	6	6.8	–	1.43	February 1828
	Mexico	6	6.7	11.0	3.2	October 1827
	Peru	6	7.7	23.5	0.62	April 1826

[a]Transferred to Brazil in 1825 as part of the independence settlement

to London and the whole story was announced in the press as 'complete humbug'.[62]

The episode illustrates what little information investors had in this period with which to judge the credit-worthiness of bond issues. The source of short-term 'hot money' in this period was the inexperienced private investor, rushed into obtaining a share of the high returns which seemed to be on offer. By the end of 1825, Latin American countries as a group had borrowed over £20m.[64] The loans were not taken out just by governments, but also by private investors exploring opportunities to start mining enterprises in order to exploit the natural resources of the area.

Nevertheless, however fragile the economies of the new Latin American states were, it was the crisis among England's country banks that triggered the problems in Latin America by stopping further loans which would have helped to perpetuate the refinancing of the region's sovereign debts. *The Times* recorded the steady meteoric rise in market interest rates in London from April 1825 due to an 'inexplicable panic'.[65] By 14 December 1825, they were quoting the effective rate at around 50%, and even as the panic abated on 24 December, it was 8–10%.[66] These rates surpassed the rates provided by the Latin American loans (Table 4.1) and, as the Banking School's theory suggested, capital flows reversed. As a result, Latin America was starved of further loans. Share prices of British mining interests in Mexico plummeted and a major stock market crash in London followed. By 1829 Spain, Portugal, and all of Latin America had defaulted, except for Brazil which only defaulted on their sinking fund for paying Portugal's bonds (Table 4.1).

As the bondholders would now not receive interest payments or they would be much reduced as arrears built up, the price of their bonds nose-dived. Theoretically, comparing the bond prices and face value returns, the yields on the bonds were very high but in actual fact their only value was if the countries concerned continued or resumed payments. Renegotiation was decades away in most cases which meant that the actual returns, when there were some, were low, taking into account the period with no payments. The whole affair after 1825, therefore, contributed to the lowering of nominal returns on capital rather than raising them as investors searching for higher yields had originally hoped.

Capital flows from Britain to Latin American countries fell sharply. In 1825, compared with export of 80% of its gold to France, only 0.5% went to 'Foreign Colonies on Continent of America' and 6.8% to Brazil. These events had an influence on market interest rates in London but had little impact on the Bank Rate because of the usury laws.[67] France received 80% of an enormous 1.13m ounces of gold exported to foreign countries in 1825. In both 1823 and 1824 only just under 0.3m ounces in total had been exported in gold each year. The large 1825 exportation occurred just before French and British interest rates were drawn together in December 1825, showing how high capital flows preceded the pulling together of interest rates (Fig. 4.8).

The interest rates of countries which also received sizeable quantities of bullion exports, such as Holland and Italy followed British rates closely over the period of the mid-1820s. The United States received a mere 0.12% of the total in 1825 but had received 4.4% or 207,484 ounces in 1822 but Sidney Homer and Richard Sylla document that yields on federal government debt fell from 5.9% in 1819 to 4.25% in 1824, closing in on the Bank of England's official rate in 1824–1825.[68] It appeared that equalising interest rates had affected bullion flows, as the Banking School's theories suggested. Philadelphia's banks' earnings on assets similarly dipped from 5.7% in 1816 to 4.24% in 1825 and regional interest rates in the United States followed.[69] America had experienced a crisis in 1819, but this was more to do with internal speculation and the setting up of the Bank of the United States. By 1825 many American merchants and banks, especially those in New York, had developed close financial ties to their counterparts in Britain. In 1825 New York's securities markets experienced a boom which was at least partially stimulated by events in the British and Irish stock market where many new companies were floated as joint-stock companies. The panic in London limited credit in America in late 1825 and early 1826 through these connections. However, there was no generalised banking crisis in the United States, at least in part because the Second Bank of the United States worked with its New York branch to provide credit to the banking community there.[70]

The 1825 crisis was caused, in summary, by an excess of funds looking for better returns in an environment of low rates. The surplus of bullion produced large capital flows seeking investment opportunities. As the source of these flows changed from just experienced bankers to include short-term and inexperienced investors, interest rates moved together. Initially, this indication of the cessation of arbitrage in investments appeared in internal investments and then internationally, between France and Britain, then Latin America, and to a certain extent in other countries in Europe and America. When international capital flows stopped, a stockmarket bubble burst in London and a credit crunch ensued, which then spread to Latin America and elsewhere in the world.

After the crisis, the Country Bankers Act of 1826 promised to usher in a Scottish-style banking system in provincial England, based on competition. After an experiment in Ireland in 1825, the Country Bankers Act 1826 lifted some of the restrictions because of the chaos of 1825 and allowed the establishment of joint-stock banks provided they were at least 65 miles from London.[71] The Bank of England opened provincial branches competing with note-issuing joint-stock banks. However, this was amended by the Banking Act of 1833 which made only the Bank of England's notes legal tender. Joint-stock banks were allowed to set up in London as compensation. This series of reforms meant that banks became larger and therefore did not fall in the numbers seen in 1825–1826 again in the nineteenth century. However, that should not minimise the serious nature of later financial crises. In these the Bank of England's ability to honour its legal obligations was threatened; they also had significant negative consequences for the British empire and the rest of the world, even if the City of London and the Country Banks themselves emerged relatively unscathed.

Even so, the British economy's connections with other countries, in terms of trade and investment, continued to grow, which would prove to be a future vulnerability for the British financial system. In particular, Britain's trade with its former colonies in North America grew particularly strongly it was between these countries (the United Kingdom and the United States) that interest-rate equalisation would appear in its strongest form in the next crises in the 1830s.

4.7 The Crises of 1837–1839

The structure of the 1830s crises also reflects Banking School's theories about cycles of crises. In 1832 the so-called 'Bank war' in the United States (a political struggle that developed over the issue of rechartering the Second Bank of the United States) and a disparity in rates attracted bullion away from the United Kingdom. The rates then equalised and the flows stopped, causing brief problems, particularly for banks, in the United States. The same happened in 1837 when rates in the United Kingdom, United States and France drew together from mid-1836. Bullion returning from France, as well as money from the large sum paid by the British government to compensate slave owners for emancipation, were invested abroad in the United States where rates were higher in 1836. However, as rates equalised, the United States became short of gold as flows from British investors were no longer lured by higher American returns. The American government reacted by insisting that it must be paid in specie and not by any credit instrument. The shortage of gold caused a crisis in the United Kingdom and United States. The process was repeated at the end of the 1830s, in 1839.

The Currency School and the Banking School produced different explanations of the causes of the crises in the 1830s. Loyd (Overstone) argued, in a Committee on Banks of Issue in 1840, that a potential crisis was avoided after a bullion drain between May 1830 and May 1832 because credit was restricted, whereas this was not the case for drains of 1835–1837 and 1838–1839.[72] Such arguments were opposed by Palmer, who confirmed that the Bank had not restricted credit in 1830–1832, and by a Scottish surgeon and banker, John Fullarton.[73]

Fullarton's book, *On the Regulation of Currencies* (1844), greatly influenced the ideas and theories of the Banking School. He emphasised the complexity of the forces behind the 'periodical hurricane' of financial disorder and the need to understand them.[74] He supported the principle of the 'reflux' of currency and the impossibility of over-issue of a convertible currency. He explained that differences in rates of interest between countries could cause the movement of bullion by attracting bills or investment to the most advantageous rate. He, therefore, concluded that the Bank could control flows by influencing the market rate of interest.[75]

All these opinions were by now standard among the Banking School. However, Fullarton also attempted to draw together the two schools of thought by reconciling Tooke's outburst in the 1840 Enquiry that he doubted that the quantity of circulation 'operate[d] upon prices at all', as suggested by the 'partisans of the currency theory' (the Currency School).[76] He did this by pointing out that the direct relationship between the quantity of money and commodity prices only operated in a closed system. In an open system, other factors would come into play. He took 'the case of a nation having no commercial intercourse with its neighbours' and a 'circulation "which preserves a high rate of exchangeable value merely by the limitation of its amount" and compared it with a country more advanced in its commercial relations, and with its monetary system on a more improved footing, possessing already a full metallic circulation of standard weight and fineness, an unrestrained traffic in the metals and a mint open for coinage…'.[77] He concluded that the quantity of circulation effect of prices would be easy to see in the former but not in the latter because to 'add permanently to the note circulation of the country' it would be necessary to spread the effect 'throughout the world'. However, 'the prices of all commodities, estimated in bank-notes, would after a time, infallibly rise'.[78] The synthesis of the theories of the two Schools in *The Economist* and the writings of Walter Bagehot later in the century were later a natural development from these insights.

More aggressive was the attitude of Henry Burgess who edited a newsletter called *Circular to Bankers* between 1828 and 1850. The *Circular* was the mouthpiece of a lobby group which combined country (private) bankers and merchants. After 1832, joint-stock banks were added and the newsletter became a public journal in 1835.[79] It aligned itself with the Banking School, being against the Bank of England having control of the currency. Its editorials concentrated on the adverse effects of high interest rates and the disparity between different rates of interest on the basis that this led to financial instability in the 1820s.[80] But the problem of interest rates was taken further with an accusation that the Bank of England, by the manipulation of rates in the 1820s and 1830s, attempted to destroy the competition with its commercial services.[81] Backing this up was a moralising attitude that Burgess's group of bankers worked for their living, rather than inheriting it, and cared for the productive classes of the economy.[82] Some of this attitude may have arisen from its anti-slavery Quaker financial backers.[83] They contrasted with the 'old' school Bank of England Governors and Directors some of whom were seen as part of the wealthy nobility who did not have to work, who did not appear to care for society in general, some being slave-owners, and kept the working classes in Britain repressed with Currency-School policies. *The Economist*, founded in the 1840s by James Wilson, a Scottish Quaker, was to revive this theme in the 1850s.[84]

To an extent, this was a reaction to Lord Liverpool's angry denunciation of country bankers as 'the most rotten, the most insecure, the very worst in every respect, that could possibly be conceived'; the then prime minister had blamed them for the crisis in 1825.[85] Nevertheless, it also arose from the fact that by 1836 the Bank of England had lent so significantly to the government that it had little credit left for commercial purposes. This opened opportunities for private banks but, on the basis of Banking-School insights, Burgess had a warning for all types of banks about the pitfall of profiting from the disparity between different rates of interest and for using money gained from short-term loans for long-term investments. It was to be a prophetic warning, particularly for the events of 1866 as well as in 1836.

> Specific loans of money for long periods require markets amply supplied with bills and mercantile securities, to render them beneficial to the borrowers. Hence Bill-brokers, and banks that carry on a similar trade to theirs, may eagerly seek money at a low rate of interest for the current profit to be gained by it. These parties would do well to reflect, very deliberately, on the expediency of availing themselves of such loans, and on the safe and proper methods of applying them. If they should be unexpectedly withdrawn, or raised in the rate of interest from three to five or six per cent, their own connections might be thereby placed in a very awkward predicament.[86]

The main criticism of the government by Burgess, was that after the abolition of slavery in its directly held colonies in October 1833, it had taken out a large loan of £15m to compensate slave owners, which had drained the Bank's resources.[87] The government had also persuaded the Bank to make foreign investments including 'the transmission of British capital to the United States', which accounted for much of the capital flows in the 1830s.[88]

4.8 The Effect of the Slavery Abolition Act of 1833

The Slavery Abolition Act of 1833 made the purchase or ownership of slaves in the British empire (except for the East India Company's territories) illegal. Monetary compensation was provided for former slave owners of up to £20m, most of which was funded by issuing extra government debt in London. This large sum, some 4.6% of Britain's GDP, had been haggled up from a smaller loan by the slave owners in negotiations that preceded the legislation's passing. The decision to give the slave owners compensation from public funds was controversial at the time, an issue that has returned to widespread public attention over the past decade as a result of the 'Legacies of British Slavery' project at University College London.[89] Yet it also had another particularly baneful effect on ordinary Britons in that it helped to trigger and exacerbate the bullion drain and banking crisis of 1836–1837. This has been overlooked by historians to date but will be explored in this section.

There was concern at the time that the raising of such a large loan and the payment of the compensation would cause problems with the currency and credit. Attwood was anxious to know 'whether this loan of fifteen millions was to be paid in paper money or in gold and if in gold where it was to come from'.[90] The *Circular* was concerned that it would lead to a shortage of credit for other purposes such as the construction of railways.[91]

As it turned out, there were considerable difficulties in raising the loan. Originally, there were thirty people invited to a tender meeting in various groupings including Baring Brothers, Reid, Irving & Co., Mssrs. Ricardo, and the Rothschilds and Montefiore, but before the meeting all serious contenders except Rothschild had withdrawn. This made negotiation difficult for Thomas Spring Rice (later Lord Monteagle), the new Whig chancellor of the exchequer. However, he did manage to chip away at the terms that the Rothschilds originally proposed. The payments were to be made in 3% consols, with a notional return of 3.5% and an actual yield of 3.875%. Rothschild's only organised the loan rather than investing its own money in it; most of the funds came from investors who had signed up before the tender, which then had to be collected. Such was the Rothschilds' reputation that the *Circular* reckoned they received initial applications for a portion of the loan at the rate of 7 to 1 compared to other tenderers.[92] (The Bank of France's official rate was 4% continuously through this period.)

The subsequent portions of the loan were successfully fulfilled but at a cost. The concerns about the effect of the loan on the Bank of England's bullion reserve and note circulation were shared by many. Figure 4.9 shows that from the passing of the Slavery Abolition Act a drain took place that was partly internal and indicated an expectation of credit problems. The *Circular* anticipated that 'the money paid to the owners of slaves will be received by men who have very little connexion with bill-brokers, with manufacturers, or with the Stock Exchange' and that much of the money would therefore go abroad and be badly invested, which turned out to be the case.[93] The journal also expected a fast paying-in of the money and slow abstraction, an idea that can be considered to gain some support from the data presented in Fig. 4.9, which appears to show a link between slave compensation payments and gently falling bullion reserves.[94]

4.9 The Two Schools and the 1830s Crises

The effect of capital flows for investment and the associated drains can be seen using the Banking School's method of analysis by looking at the

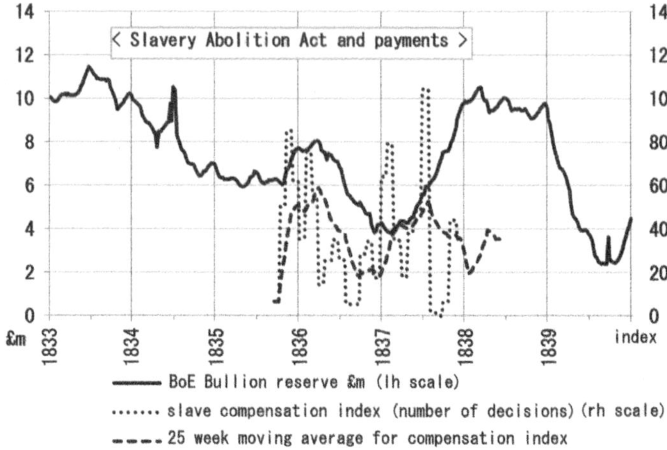

Fig. 4.9 Bank of England bullion reserve, weekly 1833–1840, slave compensation activity index based on payments and decisions per month with 25-week moving average (*Sources* Committee on Banks of Issue PP 1840 [602] IV.1, pp. 120–242; Accounts of Slave Compensation Claims PP 1837–1838 [215])

comparative rates of interest in the different countries. Interest rates in the United Kingdom and the United States moved together in 1831–1832 and again in 1836–1838 (Fig. 4.10). Meanwhile, British and French official rates started off the same at 4% and free market rates moved towards each other but did not meet until the middle of 1836.

The points of equalisation of interest rates coincide with periods of large international flows of bullion. However, more than that, as an extension of the trend in the late 1820s, they are particularly associated with times when credit becomes short and payment has to be made by transfers of bullion and coin representing short-term money. In France, in July 1830, there was a revolution, known as *Trois Glorieuses*, in which the monarchy was replaced. This was followed by the seccession of Belgium from the Netherlands in another revolution. This upheaval arose during a time of a trade depression when the wages of factory workers fell or stagnated; many labourers returned to the countryside to find work only to be confronted with a failed harvest.[95] The United Kingdom did not escape unrest entirely and there were riots in the agricultural districts.[96] However, it was from the United Kingdom that flows of bullion flowed to

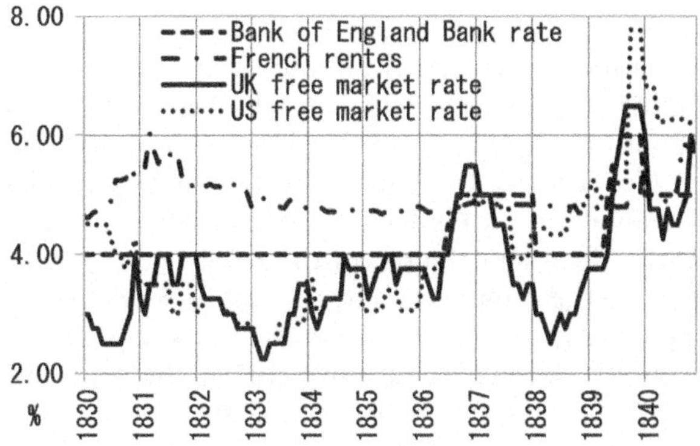

Fig. 4.10 Bank of England Bank rate, yields of French rentes and US and UK free market interest rates 1830–1841 (*Sources New York Price Current*, *Philadelphia Price Current*, *Richmond Enquirer*, Bank of England Three Centuries v.2.3, col. M9 C, Course of the Exchange)

the European states as their governments and banks raised interest rates in an effort to stabilise their economies. *The Times* of 17 September 1831 published data for the exportation of bullion from London between the last week in June and the first week in September 1831. Out of £0.807m of gold 79% went to Russia or probably there via Hamburg.[97] At this time Hamburg competed with London as a conduit for flows of bullion, but London gradually came to overshadow its German financial rivals.

The point in mid-1832, when the rates in the United Kingdom and the United States converged at around the same level, is at the time when President Jackson vetoed the renewal of the charter of the Second Bank of America, an attempt to found a central bank. From 1831 there had been continuous exchanges of bullion in connection with trade and investment and much cooperation between London Banks and the Second Bank of America. It was only when the 'Bank War' between President Jefferson and Nicholas Biddle of the bank heated up over whether to renew its charter and bullion was in demand, that American and British rates converged. Another international-payments shock came in 1836 when France paid an indemnity owed to the United States for its attacks on shipping in the Napoleonic period. This involved a sizeable bullion transfer and also may have aided the convergence of interest rates in Britain, France and the United States.

In Britain, despite bankers having learnt some lessons from the 1825 crisis, the similarity of the American and British rates appears to have crept up on most bankers and politicians who started to quarrel amongst themselves about how best to control bullion drains purely on an internal basis. Palmer, Governor of the Bank over the critical period 1830–1833, followed his 'Palmer rule'. Under this policy, which was in place in the Bank from 1827, the cash liabilities of the Bank were to be invested one-third in bullion, at the minimum, and the rest in accessible or short-term securities. Importantly, the capital assets of the Bank, which could not be liquidated promptly, known as 'deadweight' at the time, were not part of the equation and were not to be increased if the note: security ratio was too low. Palmer was very proud of the fact that the bullion drain of 1830–1832 stabilised itself with bullion returning apparently without the Bank taking any action. To some Palmer had 'cheated' because during the bullion drain the Bank had withdrawn notes from circulation and bought Exchequer bills with them to obey the Palmer rule, thus reducing the note circulation and boosting interest rates by decreasing available credit at the same time.[98]

Overstone (Loyd at this time) of the opposing Currency School, agreed that in the run-up to 1832 from 1830:

> Although during this period the bullion in the Bank was diminished from twelve millions to five millions, yet in the progress of this reduction, as there was no excitement, and no undue credit given by the banks in the interior of the country, the interest of money gradually rose from 2 1/2 to 4 per cent; and then without discredit or distrust of any kind, the bullion returned to the coffers of the Bank, and money nearly resumed its former value.[99]

However, Loyd used the example of 1830–1832, to support his case that Palmer had reduced the note circulation as if the currency was limited on the basis of bullion reserves. Loyd's view was to influence Peel when he constructed the Bank Charter Act of 1844 with its partial bullion-limited note circulation. However, Palmer's policy had influence as well and was adopted elsewhere in the world, most notably wholesale as 'the Forstall system' in February 1842 in Louisiana.[100]

To the Currency School, the 1830s presented a picture of a continuous trade deficit for the United Kingdom with four dips. Two of these caused the balance of trade, including services and interest, to go into negative territory. Each of these four dips was, as in the 1820s, followed by a bullion drain (Figs. 4.12 and 4.13). The exchange rate between the pound and the United States dollar, although varying down in 1834 and up in 1837 was still stationary over the decade (Fig. 4.11). The payments with bullion which became necessary when credit became disturbed would have fixed the effective exchange rate more rigidly, as only one currency was in use: gold. To those in charge at the time, a change in rates was regarded as the last resort to prevent bullion drains from the central banks. However, in the end, this was the action that they were forced to take. Trade still had an effect on bullion flows, supporting the Currency School's theories to some extent.

The first dip in the balance of trade from 1830 and drain of bullion in 1831–1832 coincided with imports to deal with distress in England and rising trade and investment flow of capital to America, France and Russia (Fig. 4.12). In 1833–1834, the dip in the balance of trade and bullion drain which followed occurred at the same time as an export drive to America where, due to a recession, the take-up of goods was slow and the bullion was equally slow in coming back to London in payment. The United States had a continual demand for gold in this period, some of which, it was suspected, was eventually invested in the purchase of slaves as well as land. This made the Banking School fear that American plantations using slaves would undercut British plantations using free labour, and, worse still, would do it with funds from British investors. The *Circular to Bankers* launched a tirade against President Andrew Jackson who proposed to use the postal service to stop anti-slavery tracts being

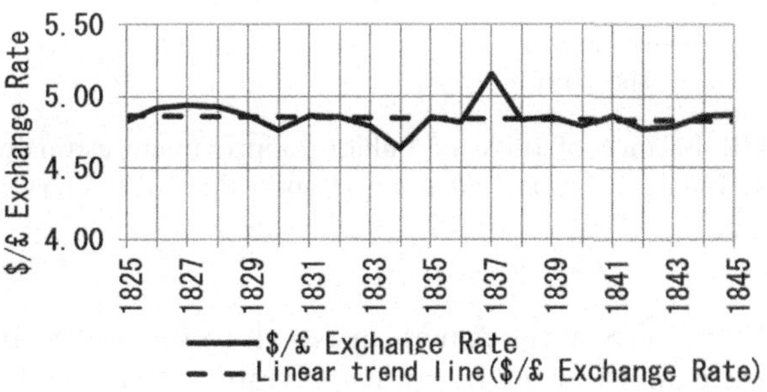

Fig. 4.11 $/£ exchange rate 1825–1845 and linear trendline (*Sources* As Fig. 3.2)

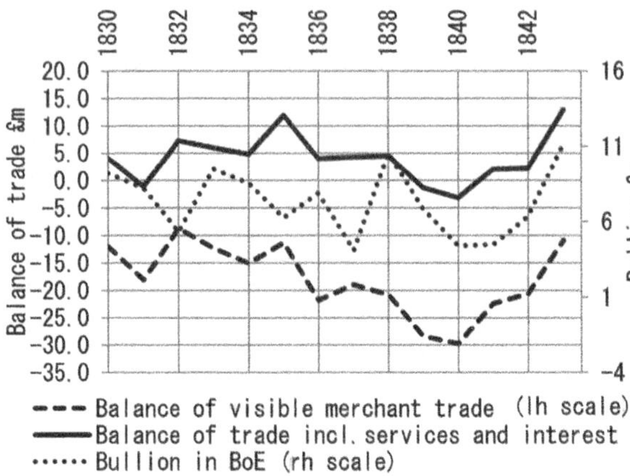

Fig. 4.12 Bullion and coin in the Bank of England compared with the balance of trade with and without services and interest 1830–1843 (*Source* Bank of England Three Centuries of data v.2.3, col. A13 F, A24 N, S)

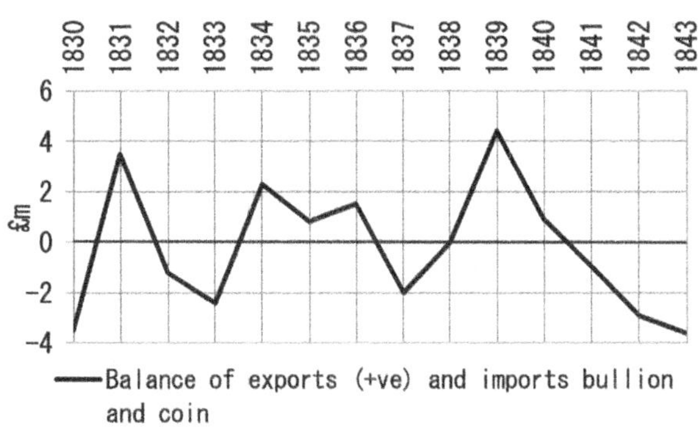

Fig. 4.13 UK Balance of trade of bullion, approximate estimate 1830–1843 (*Source* A. H. Imlah, *Economic Elements* [Cambridge, MA: Harvard University Press, 1958])

sent from abolitionists in the American North to the South. It considered it 'the fiercest exhibition of the spirit of tyranny ever openly manifested by a public Ruler… for the purpose of trampling on a principle cherished and held even in sacred veneration, by a great proportion of the people of Great Britain'.[101]

The *Circular* warned that in contrast to past experience, the United States was financially strong and was 'about to assume an attitude which will make England...feel the manifestation of her pecuniary power'.[102] The *Circular's* analysis was proved true, in the opinion of the Banking School, when later in 1836 the Bank Rate in Britain had to be increased to provoke a return of bullion. It followed the American rate which had risen because of the 'Specie Circular'. This order was issued by America's Secretary to the Treasury in July 1836 and required the inexpensive government land which was being sold in the West to be paid for in specie. Before this, the rush to purchase had caused a large amount of credit paper to build up in the US Treasury, which was of little use in making international payments. The closing down of credit caused a rise in market interest rates to above 5%. It was just before this point that American and British rates equalised, with America dominant along the lines described in the *Circular* and so bullion flows from the United Kingdom ceased, all of which caused a business panic and crash in American financial markets.

In 1836 there was a third dip in the balance of trade and a bullion drain followed in 1837 which was mainly to the United States. The years 1836 and 1837 were canal-building boom years in America. Indiana, Illinois, Massachusetts and Michigan built new canals in 1836 and 1837, while New York, Ohio and Pennsylvania planned to extend their systems.

In Britain, the recovery from the bullion drain happened after free-market interest rates rose from their low point. This avoided an extensive banking crisis in Britain but was what cut off bullion flows to the United States. Currency and Banking Schools both claimed this recovery as a victory for their principles. The Currency School claimed a restriction of credit had rebalanced the trade bullion flows. Meanwhile, the Banking School insisted that market rates of interest had followed the Bank Rate up and prevented investment flows to the United States from the United Kingdom.[103]

The imports of bullion to the United Kingdom which followed again came from France, rather than being returned from the United States. This can be seen from the available data on interest rates; the British interest rate over 1837–1839 equalled that of the United States, but French ones were lower than British ones in late 1837 (Fig. 4.10). Banks called in their loans and property prices fell, causing more loans to be called in. The new joint-stock banks in Britain, particularly in Northern areas such as Lancashire, had lent heavily to merchants involved in the cotton business and banks started to collapse.

When President Jackson had moved the Treasury funds in the Bank of America to state, so-called 'pet' banks, the new institutions started issuing their own notes. Some were backed by bullion, but others were not. These 'shinplasters' depreciated against specie, and all had their own exchange rate with bullion and with each other. The depreciation caused the government concern because public lands, which had been cleared of their indigenous population and were being sold to settlers cheaply, were being sold in exchange for some of these notes. Jackson therefore had the 'Specie Circular' issued on 11 July 1836, which insisted the lands had to be paid for in specie. This accelerated the worthlessness of the notes and increased their use rather than decreasing it as intended. The discount on the notes typically increased from 1–3% to 15–18%.[104] New York banks suspended payments in gold on 10 May 1837 and financial panic and run on banks ensued. Demand for specie soared and added to the demand for it entering the country. Most of the US banks suspended payment in specie and 618 failed in 1837.[105] Biddle's new bank was suspended in 1839 and failed in 1841. In the United States payments in gold were suspended and even individual states defaulted on their loans taken out in London which caused more banking turmoil. The cotton industry was affected and there was a 25% drop in raw cotton prices between February and March 1837.

The last drain of the 1830s, which started in 1838 and went on into the early 1840s, has already been described by R. C. O. Matthews as being caused by a flow of 'hot money'.[106] Investment went from Britain to France and America, where interest rates were up to 2.5 percentage points higher in 1838 (Fig. 4.10). In addition, the price of wheat went above the level where it was allowed to be imported at a nominal duty in August 1838 and remained there for most of 1839. Bullion was needed to pay for these increased imports. The Bank of England raised its interest rate to 6% following a rate hike in America to halt the export of bullion there. Palmer in the 1841 Enquiry referred to a 'sudden stoppage' of trade and flows to America consequent on interest-rate changes and the use of security sales to counter a credit shortage.[107] Despite this, the United States managed to achieve a net import of bullion from 1833 to 1838 (Fig. 4.14). This time the bullion was very slow in returning to the Bank of England's vaults. The United Kingdom was becoming the main

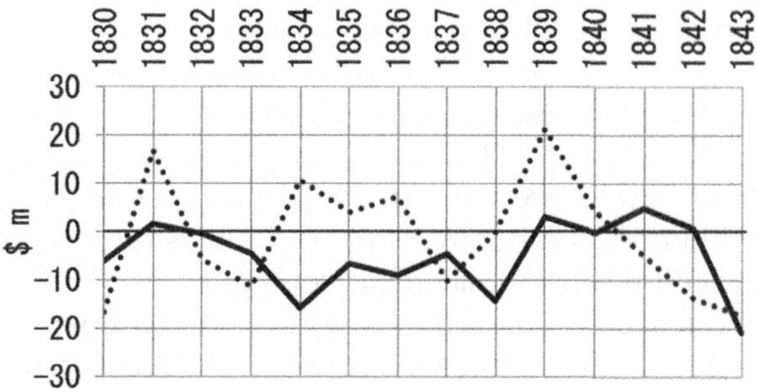

Fig. 4.14 US balance of trade of specie and UK in $, 1830–1843 (*Source* D. North, *The United States Balance of Payments, 1790–1860* [Princeton: Princeton University Press, 1960])

conduit for international flows and the Bank of England was finding it less easy to influence financial conditions in its own country.

Although there was still evidence to support Currency theorists of the time who assumed that trade and prices alone influenced capital flows and therefore bullion drains, there was a growing body of evidence to support Banking School's ideas that investment flows were becoming an increasingly significant factor. In 1840 the *Merchants' Magazine* noted that:

> the bank...lost...about six millions of bullion, which certainly could not all of gone in payment for corn, because the value of the wheat bought and imported in those six months [first half of 1839] would not exceed three millions of pounds, or only half of the value of the bullion sent away, and blamed 'large importations of American securities of all kinds which found a ready market here while English securities were scarce.[108]

4.10 Consequences of the 1830s Crises

One consequence of the 1830s crisis was to permanently roll back the usury laws which had effectively limited interest charged by the Bank of England to 5%. The Bank of England Act of 1833 exempted bills of exchange and notes for up to three months from the old limit.[109] There followed a series of legislation gradually relaxing the usury laws until they were finally repealed in 1854.[110] This was to open the way to high rates of interest in future crises, a situation welcomed by Overstone (Loyd) of the Currency School.[111] The *Circular to Bankers*, putting forward a Banking-School view, depreciated any restriction on rates but foresaw that 'a system of things so complicated and artificial' as the new patchwork of exemptions would result in 'malignant consequences'.[112]

The consequences of the crises for the real economy were indeed malign. In spite of a brief recovery between 1837 and 1839, economic downturns followed the 1839 crisis in both the United Kingdom and United States. The cotton industry, which had boomed in the early 1830s, suffered. The price of cotton in the United States fell due to the increase of supply and the British textile industry suffered from overcapacity.

The important trade link of cotton exports coming from the United States to mills in the United Kingdom, meant economic problems were shared after 1840 when the negative effects of the interest-rate synchronisation in 1839 had otherwise dwindled. In Britain, handloom weavers went to the wall and unemployment increased (Fig. 4.15). Other industries, such as iron smelting, also reduced activity along with employment and this depression worsened into 1840–1841 (Fig. 4.16). In Lancashire, the West Riding of Yorkshire, the Midlands and West Scotland distress was particularly felt and was followed by a series of Chartist meetings seeking to widen the electorate to include working men. The Charter was published in 1838, a Convention was formed, and its petition to Parliament was made in July 1839, but in September the Convention disbanded. However, conditions for workers worsened and it was said their wages were hardly able to cover the price of food.[113]

America had its share of protests as well, including the 'anti-rent' wars in rural estates around New York. In 1841 and 1842 eight states and the Territory of Florida defaulted on their debts. In that environment, most states were unable to assist their distressed citizens or continue with public works projects that would have provided employment.

In conclusion, the crises of the 1830s provide ample evidence that an early version of the Carry Trade was operating. The crises of 1837 and 1839 spurred the development of the Banking School's theory of crises. In both crises, bullion flows developed initially from the United Kingdom to the United States, where interest rates were higher. Free market rates in

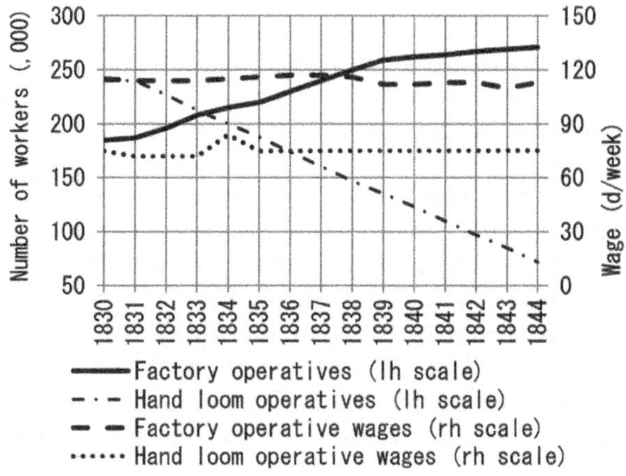

Fig. 4.15 Number of cotton factory operatives and wages by type (hand or machine) 1830–1844 (*Source* G. H. Wood, *History of Wages in the Cotton Trade* [London: Sherratt and Hughes, 1910] pp. 127–128)

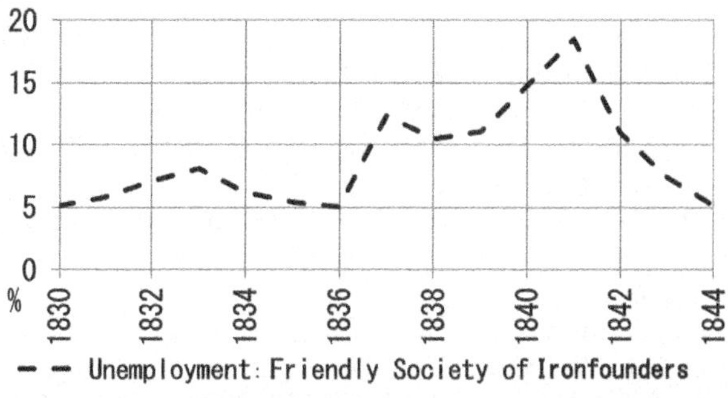

Fig. 4.16 Percentage unemployment in Friendly Society of iron-foundry workers 1830–1844 (*Source* Report on Trade Unions PP 1890–1891 [c.6475] XCII.73, pp. 522–523)

the United Kingdom rose to meet those in the United States and together they met the French rates and eventually exceeded them. These circumstances caused strong flows of capital from France, through the United Kingdom, to the United States followed by starvation of further flows as the rates equalised. It was these flows which caused a large and damaging drain of bullion out of the Bank of England, which culminated in it having to seek a loan from the Bank of France in 1839. Going cap in hand for financial assistance to the central bank of a foe defeated just 24 years before was a humiliation that few acquainted with the episode in the City of London forgot.

Such was the psychological impact of this event on the banking community that the effect of the 1847 crisis was to cause a political reaction and aversion to loans beyond its true significance by size. In 1847 the size of the bullion drain and of the Irish loan to fund relief were relatively small compared to those in the 1830s, but the aversion and sensitivity were already laid down. In addition, Peel's Bank Charter Act of 1844 was to insist on the publication of the Bank's reserves in a specific format, so any minor variation could be picked upon by the public and converted into a panic. The result was a significant crisis in 1847, whose consequences were catastrophic for both Ireland and the wider British empire.

Notes

1. T. Tooke, *A History of Prices and of the State of the Circulation* II (London: Longmans, 1838) pp. 178–179.
2. *Hansard*, 5 June 1837, XXXVIII, c. 1205.
3. F. G. Dawson, *The First Latin American Debt Crisis: The City of London and the 1822–25 Loan Bubble* (New Haven: Yale UP, 1990).
4. L. Neal, 'The Financial Crisis of 1825 and the Restructuring of the British Financial System', *Federal Reserve Bank of St. Louis Review* 80 (1998) p. 63.
5. The exception is a relatively brief mention in a recent chapter about the 1825 crisis in W. Quinn, J. D. Turner, *Boom and Bust: A Global History of Financial Bubbles* (Cambridge: CUP, 2020), see pp. 41, 52–53.
6. T. Attwood, *Distressed State of the Country* (Birmingham: Beilby, Knott and Beilby, 1829) p. 2.
7. Idem., p. 3.
8. Idem., p. 4.
9. Bank Notes Act 1826, 7 Geo 4 c. 6.
10. Attwood, *Distressed State of the Country*, p. 8.
11. Idem., p. 11.
12. Idem., p. 45.
13. Idem., p. 15.
14. *The Times*, 13 December 1825, p. 2.
15. Attwood, *Distressed State of the Country*, pp. 51, 65–66.

16. W. Huskisson, *Speeches of the Right Honourable William Huskisson* (London: John Murray, 1831) p. 588.
17. *Report from the Committee on the Bank of England Charter* PP 1831–1832 (722) VI.1, pp. 12, 15–16.
18. Overstone to Norman, 5 November 1832 in D. P. O'Brien, *The Correspondence of Lord Overstone* (Cambridge: CUP, 1971) p. 203.
19. Idem., pp. 234–235, 237–238, 242–243.
20. Idem., pp. 249–252.
21. M. R. Daugherty, 'The Currency-Banking Controversy: Pt. 1', *Southern Economic Journal* 9 (1942) 142.
22. *The Times*, 14 December 1825, p. 2, 24 December 1825, p. 2.
23. *Country Banks* PP 1826 (94) XXII-5, p. 6; *Private Banks* PP 1833 (489) XXXI.201, pp. 2–3.
24. B. Hilton, *Mad, Bad and Dangerous People?* (Oxford: OUP, 2008) p. 302.
25. Quinn, Turner, *Boom and Bust*, p. 52.
26. Ibid.
27. Bank Restriction Act 1797, 37 Geo. 3 c. 45.
28. T. Tooke, *A History of Prices and of the State of the Circulation* I (London: Longmans, 1838) p. 131.
29. *Account of Quantity of Grain, Meal and Flour Imported and Exported 1792–1814* PP 1814–1815 (87, 88, 89) X.469, p. 10.
30. J. D. Turner, *Banking in Crisis* (Cambridge: CUP, 2014) p. 52.
31. *Report...* PP 1831–1832 (722) VI.1, Appendix 59, p. 54; I. Bond 'The British Banking Population 1790–82', in M. Hollow, F. Akinbami, R. Michie (eds.), *Complexity and Crisis in the Financial System* (Cheltenham: Edward Elgar, 2016) p. 99.
32. A. Redish, 'The Evolution of the Gold Standard in England', *Journal of Economic History* 50 (1990) pp. 802–803.
33. B. Hilton, *Corn, Cash, Commerce: The Economics Policies of the Tory Governments 1815–1830* (Oxford: OUP, 1977) p. 30.
34. D. G. Barnes, *A History of the English Corn Laws: From 1660 to 1846* (London: Routledge, 2013) pp. 161–62.
35. Lord Liverpool to Lord Kenyon 27 May 1817, Liverpool papers, B.L., Add MS 38267 ff. 12–13.
36. J. E. Cookson, *Lord Liverpool's Administration: The Crucial Years 1815–1822* (Edinburgh: Scottish Academic Press, 1975) p. 99; C. Read, 'Laissez-Faire, the Irish Famine, and British Financial Crisis', *Economic History Review* 69 (2016) pp. 423–424; C. Read, *The Great Famine in Ireland and Britain's Financial Crisis* (Woodbridge: The Boydell Press, 2022) Chapters 3 and 4.
37. Bank of England Three centuries of data v.3, A46 D, including information from A. Imlah, *Economic Elements in the Pax Britannica* (Cambridge, MA: Harvard UP, 1958).

38. A. Imlah, *Economic Elements in the Pax Britannica*.
39. B. R. Mitchell, *British Historical Statistics* (Cambridge: CUP, 1988) pp. 575–593; Bank of England Three centuries of data v.2.3, cols., A3 C.
40. Bank of England Three centuries of data v.2.3, A17 K L.
41. *Hansard*, 13 March 1816, XXXIII, c. 240.
42. *Hansard*, 13 February 1816, XXXII, cc. 433–34.
43. *Hansard*, 18 March 1816, XXXIII, c. 451.
44. *Memoranda Respecting the Proceedings of Government as to the Unfunded Debt from the Year 1815* PP 1842 (104) XXVI.251, p. 2.
45. E. N. White, 'The French Revolution and the Politics of Government Finance, 1770–1815', *Journal of Economic History* 55 (1995).
46. *National Debt Funded and Unfunded 1817–1844* PP 1845 (12) XXVIII.197, p. 3.
47. *Debt*... PP 1845 (12) XXVIII.197, p. 2.
48. Neal, 'The Financial Crisis of 1825', p. 57; L. Neal, *The Rise of Financial Capitalism* (Cambridge: CUP, 1990) pp. 254–257.
49. W. D. Jones, *'Prosperity' Robinson* (London: Macmillan, 1967) p. 100.
50. *Hansard*, 21 February 1823, VIII, c.200.
51. *Report*... PP 1831–1832 (722) VI.1, p. 47.
52. *Hansard*, 1 March 1816, XXXII, cc. 1038–42.
53. P. E. Austin, *Baring Brothers and the Birth of Modern Finance* (Hoboken: Taylor and Francis, 2015) p. 12.
54. Quinn, Turner, *Boom and Bust*, pp. 54–55.
55. Ibid.
56. Ibid.
57. Ibid.
58. Turner, *Banking in Crisis*, pp. 53–54.
59. *The Times*, 20 July 1826, p. 2.
60. V. Allan, 'The Prince of Poyais', *History Today* 2 (1952) 53–58.
61. T. Strangeways, 'The Poyais Bubble', *Quarterly Review*, XXVIII (London: John Murray, 1823) 158–161; see also D. Sinclair, *The Land That Never Was: Sir Gregor MacGregor and the Most Audacious Fraud in History* (Cambridge, MA: Da Capo Press, 2004).
62. *The Times*, 21 October 1823, p. 3.
63. *Fortune's Epitome*; *Course of the Exchange*; J. W. Gilbart, *History and Principles of Banking* (London: George Bell and Sons, 1905) p. 60.
64. G. L. Kaminsky, 'The Centre and the Periphery: Two Hundred Years of International Borrowing Cycles', *Banco de España seminas* (2018) p. 5.
65. *The Times*, 15 April 1825, p. 3.
66. *The Times*, 14 December 1825, p. 2; 24 December 1825, p. 2.
67. *Account of Quantity of Gold and Silver Bullion, Coin and Plate Imported and Exported*, 1815–24 PP 1825 (204) XX.215.

68. S. Homer, R. Sylla, *A History of Interest Rates* (Hoboken, NJ: Wiley, 2005) pp. 282–285.
69. H. Bodenhorn, H. Rockoff, 'Regional Interest Rates in Antebellum America', in C. Goldin, H. Rockoff (eds.), *Strategic Factors in Nineteenth Century American Economic History: A Volume to Honor Robert W. Fogel* (Chicago: University of Chicago Press, 1992) pp. 159–187, 167.
70. E. Hilt, 'Wall Street's First Corporate Governance Crisis: The Panic of 1826', *NBER Working Paper* 14892, pp. 7, 10.
71. 1825 6 Geo 4 c.42; 1826, 7 Geo. 4 c.46.
72. *Committee on Banks of Issue* PP 1840 (602) IV.1, pp. 218–219.
73. Idem., p. 22.
74. J. Fullarton, *On the Regulation of Currencies* (London: John Murray, 1844) p. 4.
75. Idem., pp. 64, 81, 137, 142.
76. *Committee…* PP 1840 (602) IV.1, p. 298; Fullarton, *On the Regulation of Currencies*, p. 58.
77. Idem., pp. 60–62.
78. Idem., p. 58.
79. D. J. Moss, 'Circular to Bankers', *Victorian Periodicals Review* 25 (1992) 129–136.
80. *Circular to Bankers*, 16 September 1836, pp. 65–68.
81. Idem., 16 September 1836, p. 68.
82. Idem., 4, 25 July 1834.
83. Moss, 'Circular to Bankers', p. 131.
84. *The Economist*, 23 June 1855, p. 671.
85. *Hansard*, 17 February 1826, XIV, c. 462.
86. *Circular to Bankers*, 9 September 1836, p. 59.
87. Idem., 3 February 1837, p. 236.
88. Idem., 3 February 1837, p. 234.
89. https://www.ucl.ac.uk/lbs [accessed 23 May 2022].
90. *Hansard*, 3 August 1835, XXX, c. 24.
91. *Circular to Bankers*, 31 July 1835, p. 12.
92. Idem., pp. 9–12, 28 August 1835 p. 44; *The Times*, 30 July 1835, p. 5.
93. *Circular to Bankers*, 31 July 1835, p. 12.
94. *Committee on Banks of Issue* PP 1840 (602) IV.1, pp. 120–242; *Accounts of Slave Compensation Claims* PP 1837–1838 (215).
95. P. Pilbeam, 'The Economic Crisis of 1827–1832 and the 1830 Revolution in Provincial France', *Historical Journal* 32 (1989) 332.
96. G. Rudé, *The Crowd in History: A Study of Popular Disturbances in France and England, 1730–1848* (London: Serif, 2005) p. 150.
97. *The Times*, 17 September 1831, p. 2.

98. J. H. Palmer, *Causes and Consequences of the Pressure Upon the Money Market* (London: Pelham Richardson, 1837) p. 6.
99. *Committee*... PP 1840 (602) IV.1, p. 219.
100. M. G. Madeleine, *Monetary and Banking Theories of Jacksonian Democracy* (Philadelphia: Immaculata College, 1943) p. 162.
101. *Circular to Bankers*, 1 January 1836, p. 187.
102. Idem., p. 188.
103. See PP 1840 (602) IV.1 *Report from Select Committee on Banks of* Issue: Banking School: John Smith, p. 2 (Bank of Manchester) raising of interest rates, rejection of bills to America; Tooke, bullion flows, rate of interest, pp. 363–364; Currency School: Loyd (Overstone), circulation, prices, value of money, pp. 259–260, 319.
104. Contemporary listing journals: *Shipping & Commercial List (and New-York Price Current); Thompson's Bank Note and Commercial Reporter; Bicknell's Reporter, Counterfeit Detector, and General Prices Current.*
105. R. C. McGrane, *The Panic of 1837* (Chicago: Chicago UP, 1924) p. 93; H. M. Hyndman, *Commercial Crises* (London: Swan & Co.) p. 46.
106. R. C. O. Matthews, *A Study in Trade Cycle History: Economic Fluctuations in Great Britain 1833–42* (Cambridge: CUP, 1954) p. 98.
107. *Committee*... PP 1840 (602) IV.1, pp. 117, 120.
108. *London Atlas*, 16 November 1839, quoted in *The Merchants' Magazine and Commercial Review*, September 1840, annual volume, p. 234.
109. Bank of England Act 1833 3 & 4 Will IV c. 98 s. 7.
110. Usury Act 1837, 1 Vict. c. 80, Usury Act 1839 2 & 3 Vict. c. 37; Usury Act 1840, 3 & 4 Vict. c. 83; Usury Act 1843, 6 & 7 Vict. c. 45; Usury Act 1845, 8 & 9 Vict. c. 102; Usury Act 1850, 13 & 14 Vict. c. 56; Usury Laws Repeal Act 1854, 17 & 18 Vict. c. 90.
111. *Report from the Secret Committee of the House of Lords on the Causes of Distress* PP 1847–1848 (565 565-II) VIII Pt. III.1, 537, p. 191.
112. *Circular to Bankers*, 19 May 1837, p. 354.
113. N. Gash, *Aristocracy and People: Britain 1815–1865* (Cambridge, MA: Harvard UP, 1979) p. 210.

CHAPTER 5

The 1847 Crises

> The famine was the primary cause of our distress… Then comes the Bill of 1844… We want a vessel that can breast the storm and ride out a gale of wind in safety; but the Bill of 1844 foundered [in] the very first sea that struck it.
>
> —Mr. William Brown, MP for South Lancashire, merchant and banker, *Hansard*, 17 February 1848, XCVI, cc 834–835.[1]

The 1847 crises in April and October were the first that followed the 1844 and 1845 Banking Acts and were seen at the time as a test of that legislation. Sir Robert Peel, the prime minister who designed the legislation and passed it through Parliament, intended that it would improve financial stability as well as further his goal of low food prices for the labouring classes.[2] The Acts restricted note circulation by the Bank of England to an initial amount backed by government securities, plus the remainder which had to be backed by bullion in the Bank of England's reserves. They were a victory for the Currency School's views, which were aimed at preventing deterioration in the value of notes against gold coins and producing some stability in prices. To show that the rules were being followed, the Acts required that tables of notes in circulation and bullion reserves in the Bank were published in the *London Gazette* on a weekly basis. These tables were republished and analysed in newspapers such as *The Times* and *The Economist*.

C. Read, *Calming the Storms*, Palgrave Studies in Economic History,
https://doi.org/10.1007/978-3-031-11914-9_5

The public was therefore aware of the progress of a bullion drain and they took their own steps to protect their position. This seems to have comprised two separate courses of action: to have withdrawn more than the usual amount in banknotes and to have made increased short-term deposits in the Bank of England. The aim was to ensure as much access to liquidity as possible in a situation in which gold was being drained out of the Bank and the number of notes allowed into circulation was being reduced. Unfortunately for the Bank, this meant that they had to run down their own store of notes to the minimum and had little spare to meet increased demand from general commerce, withdrawals from the increased level of deposits that had been made with them or to finance expenditure by the Treasury when it began to struggle to issue new debt or refinance existing borrowings.[3] It is these deposits, combined with an initial plan to use loose monetary policy and fiscal stimulus to pay for Irish famine relief, which the Banking School then blamed for the next financial crises in 1847.

Twice during 1847, the Bank came close to running out of notes, in April and October. In the October crisis the Bank Charter Act of 1844 was suspended temporarily for the first time to relieve the pressure on the Bank of England. Both incidents were triggered by bullion drains, but the low level of notes was more serious. They amounted to being close to a 'systemic' failure, one in which the whole legal regulatory framework of the banking system might collapse, and the payments system along with it. Under the newly implemented Bank Charter Act only the Bank of England remained able to issue notes in England. Other banks had only small reserves of bullion and notes. And so, if the Bank of England was forced by law to stop payments, the whole banking system of the United Kingdom would have been at risk of collapse. This possibility is why the panics of 1847 threatened to be one of the worst financial crises of the nineteenth century in Britain.

5.1 An Overview of the Crises

There were many influences that caused the capital flows and the bullion drains associated with the panics of 1847. Wheat prices rose and larger volumes had to be imported because of harvest failure, particularly but not limited to potatoes. Investment into railways in the United Kingdom was seen as a sound and profitable investment and became what has been described as a 'mania'.[4] India received a loan at 5% to set up a banking system and France, which suffered a grain shortage in late 1846 that amounted to famine, required loans and exports of bullion in order to fund its food imports.

There were plenty of critics of the 1844 Act who had their particular interpretation of what exactly caused the crises of 1847. David Morier Evans, a financial journalist working for *The Times* in this period, brought the newspaper towards a Banking-School viewpoint briefly before it returned to supporting the Currency School. He wrote a book on the 1847 crises, explaining the background influences of a strong demand for funding for the construction of railways and the need for the large importations of food. However, significantly, the market was coping with these demands 'until it was ascertained... the necessities of Ireland through the failure of the potato crop would have to be satisfied by the national treasury' and 'the negotiation of a loan [seemed] a matter of extreme probability'.[5]

The catastrophe of the Irish Famine, in which around a million excess deaths are said to have occurred, seems to have had more influence than other demands on financial matters. The Irish Famine can be said to have started in the autumn of 1845 under Peel as prime minister. His generous relief policies—based on the traditional methods previously used by Dublin Castle to relieve famine—were substantially funded from the large budget surplus accumulated under Peel's austerity drive of the previous few years. However, a more catastrophic harvest in the autumn of 1846, combined with an impending recession in Britain, raised the need for more spending in Ireland at a time when tax receipts from Britain were beginning to fall. Within a few months of Lord John Russell taking over as prime minister in July 1846, it became clear that there was no longer a budget surplus from which Peel's policies could continue to be funded. Attempts to raise a loan to pay for further relief spending coincided with a bullion drain and the first plunge in the note reserve to total deposits ratio of the Bank of England in April 1847.[6] The timing suggested that fears concerning the effects of spending the loan fuelled the April drain, just as had happened with the loan issued to compensate slave owners in the 1830s. Although wheat prices and railway investment were significant factors in the second drain in October, it still arose from importations linked with the famine in Ireland and harvest shortfalls in the rest of the United Kingdom.[7]

On 8 May 1847 James Wilson wrote in *The Economist* an article which explained why the markets thought that the Irish loan would cause unmanageable bullion flows:

> During the next five months the whole of the eight million loan for Ireland will be abstracted from the capital of the country, and being chiefly if not wholly, destined for the purpose of provisions will in reality be sent out of the country to meet out foreign payments. The money it is true goes to Ireland first where it is expended on provisions [but eventually] is transmitted to the United States to pay the balance of trade caused by the imports of food.[8]

The reaction of Charles Wood, the chancellor of the exchequer, to difficulties over the first loan was to make not only the Irish landlords, but also the Irish middle classes, pay for poverty and relief in Ireland. Relief funding from the British government was suddenly cut at the beginning of May 1847 and replaced by local funding raised from the rates (land taxes). Wood and Peel saw the Bank Charter Act of 1844 as sacrosanct, and rebuffed attempts to reform it in light of the crisis. The Russell government realistically had little other political choice because it did not have a majority in Parliament and relied on Peel and his followers—who saw the legislation as an important part of his legacy—to stay in power.[9]

Although Wilson set up *The Economist* primarily to pursue the cause of free trade, he was also stridently opposed to the Bank Charter Act of 1844. However, he preferred the currency to be run by independent banks (a view sometimes called the Free Banking School). The Third Earl Grey, War and Colonial Secretary in Russell's government from July 1846, was also opposed to the 1844 Act, but had championed a government-run currency in his pamphlet *Thoughts on the Currency*, published anonymously in 1842.[10] His pamphlet directly addressed the problem of bullion flows for investment by the unwary by suggesting gold coin should not be exported. In 1848 Grey blamed the 1844 Act for 'an obvious deficiency of disposable capital in the country' which meant that 'it would have been impossible for the Government to have gone into the market to borrow money' for emigration schemes including those to relieve Ireland.[11]

The *Circular to Bankers* predicted in June 1845 that the 1847 crisis would happen on the basis of the low interest rate on consols and large amount of available funds.[12] This was essentially the Banking School's theory of crises and assumed that funds would flow abroad, and the capital flows would cause interest rates to move together, followed by a sudden halt when they were equal.

This scenario is what occurred with flows going to the United States and the interest rates in the two countries moving together, as shown in Fig. 5.1. In October 1847, at the height of the second drain, *The Circular* rounded on politicians and experts who had testified at the 1841 Enquiry, saying that none of them had 'any clear conception of the nature of the subject he dealt with, or any idea whatever of the ultimate consequences of such an iron rule as that by which the people are now oppressed'.[13] By contrast, Loyd's view of the situation, in defence of the Currency School's ideas, was that 'the whole community was frightened out of its senses by a rate of 7 or 8%—and their ignorant panic broke down everything'.[14]

The Enquiry in the House of Lords into the 1847 crisis recognised that there was a purpose to the restrictions of the 1844 Act but concluded that 'an attempt to enforce by law, under all circumstances, one fixed and inflexible rule for the management of a national bank of issue seems

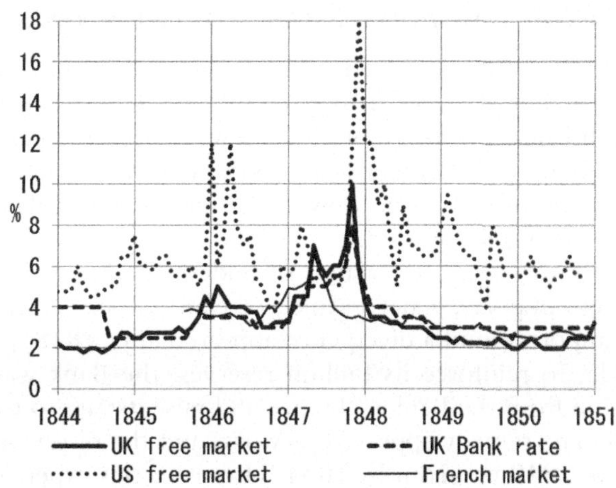

Fig. 5.1 French, UK and US market interest rates and UK Bank of England official rate Jan. 1844–Jan. 1851 (*Sources New York Daily Tribune*, Bank of England Three Centuries of data v.2.3, col. M9 C, *The Economist*, L. J. Loutchitch, *Des Variations de l'Intérêt en France de 1800 à nos jours* [Paris: Félix Alcan, 1930] pp. 42–45)

inconsistent with the best written authorities, with the general principles of economical science, as well as with the testimony of many witnesses of practical knowledge and experience'.[15] The criticisms of the Bank Charter Act of 1844 were also a widely held and understood view among the public. *Punch* published a cartoon at the time of the first drain showing 'Robert the devil' paralysing 'John Bull' (a metaphor for the British economy) with the Bank Charter Act, based on characters in an opera popular at the time.[16]

However, as it turned out the 1847 crisis secured in place the ideas of the Currency School as embodied in the Bank Charter Act. The influence of Peel and Wood meant that the Enquiry in the House of Commons rejected the motion 'that in the opinion of this Committee, the laws for regulating the issue of bank notes payable on demand aggravated the commercial distress in England in the year 1847', albeit only by two votes.[17] However, as the House of Commons held precedence over the House of Lords, the Bank Charter Act was safe—but undeservedly so, according to the intellectual thought of the Banking School.

5.2 The First Phase of the Crisis

The decade of the 1840s started with a very low balance in the Bank of England's bullion reserve, around £4m. This drain was just during a period of high wheat prices. Figure 5.2 shows that on the basis of annual averages, the bullion drains in 1840–1841 and 1847 coincided with the surge in the price of wheat and dips in the measures of balance of trade as large amounts were imported.

Figure 5.3 shows that the balance of trade in bullion generally varied with the wheat imports, a net balance of exports occurring in years of high wheat imports (until a divergence appeared after 1848). At the start of the decade, to reinforce its bullion reserves, the Bank was forced to borrow bullion from the Bank of France and raise its rate to 6% to attract gold inflows. The remedy appeared to work, and the reserve rose from a low of £4m in 1840 to £16m by 1844. However, this experience left the banking community in the City of London nervous about the effects of large wheat imports.

These nerves were sorely tested after 1845, when the potato blight appeared in both Great Britain and Ireland at the same time as a series of other unrelated crop failures occurred in northern Europe. In 1846–1847 the Bank was wary about running down its bullion reserve. With the new responsibilities of the Bank Charter Act of 1844, it had even greater

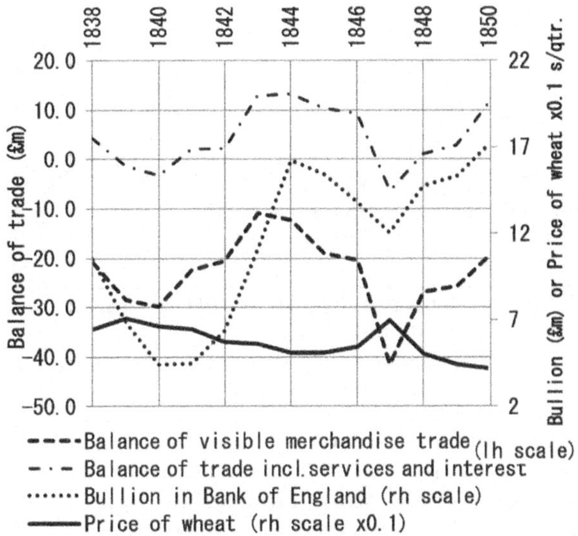

Fig. 5.2 Bullion and coin in the Bank of England compared with balance of trade with and without services and interest 1838–1850 (*Sources* Price of wheat PP 1850 (460) LII.287, p. 2, Bank of England Three Centuries of data v.2.3, col. A13 F, A24 N, S)

reason to avoid low reserves as it meant decreasing the note circulation in the country and causing a scarcity of credit. This would affect business adversely.

The Bank, as a profit-making firm, also had a financial interest in keeping its rates low. If interest rates were raised significantly to stem a bullion drain, its banking department would lose custom to rival bill discounters offering lower rates. Although the 1844 Act separated the accounts of the banking department's lending activities from the issue department's currency-management functions, it crucially did not separate the decision-making of the two departments, thereby creating a clear conflict of interest. Although the harvest failures from 1845 and the subsequent Railway boom and bust provide the background to the crises in 1847, it was the perverse incentives towards a loose monetary policy that the Bank of England's regulatory regime created, plus the Treasury's fiscal expansion to help Ireland, which provided the triggers for panic.

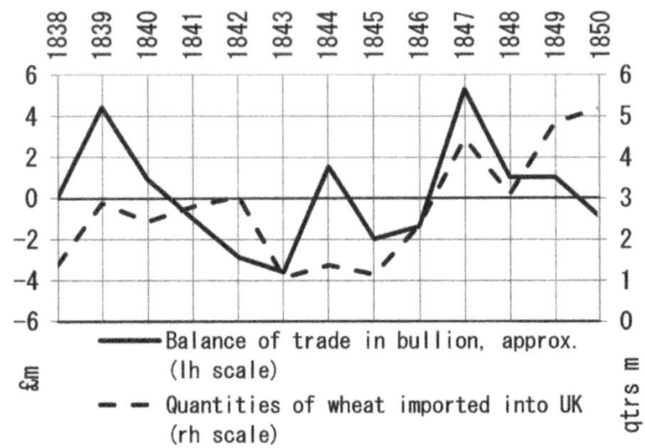

Fig. 5.3 Balance of trade of bullion, approximate estimate 1838–1850 (*Sources* Price of wheat PP 1850 (460) LII.287, p. 3, A. H. Imlah, *Economic Elements in the Pax Britannica: Studies in British Foreign Trade in the Nineteenth Century* [Cambridge, MA: Harvard University Press, 1958])

The Bank of England adopted a policy of loose monetary policy soon after the Bank Charter Act was passed in 1844. In September that year the Bank of England lowered its discount rate to 2.5%. With indications of a poor harvest and the appearance of the potato blight across Great Britain and Ireland, the Bank raised its rate to 3% on 16 October 1845 and then to 3.5% on 6 November 1845 to forestall a bullion drain. Its bullion reserve had been falling from June 1845 when it had stood at £16.05m to around £13.5m in November 1845. After the Bank Rate rose, the reserves recovered to £15.88m in August 1846.

However, at that point, with what seemed to them a good reserve of bullion, and a more than adequate reserve of notes and coins, they reduced their rate of interest to 3%. They had about £16m of bullion in their coffers, and a note reserve (those kept back from the public but included in the 'circulation') of about £9.5m, suggesting to the directors of the Bank the existence of about £5m or £6m of capital in the shape of bullion, 'not wanted as a commodity for the purpose of trade, and forming the basis of an amount of issue beyond what was required by the public'.[18] Nevertheless, as events were to show, this outlook was over-optimistic.

The reduction of interest rates by the Bank in August 1846 was followed by an expansion of credit—a phenomenon that worried Banking-School commentators such as Wilson at the time.[19] It fuelled further an existing boom in sales of railway shares which offered potentially good returns on investment, particularly sought after since Peel's chancellor of the exchequer, Henry Goulburn, had managed to reduce the rates on consols by repaying and reissuing them. Initially, there was an accumulation of deposits of railway money in the London banks, which eased the credit position, but further instalments or 'calls' were due and these were to stretch the resources of some investors, who had misjudged their size, and also strained credit generally.

From August the state of things changed for the worse. The harvest of 1846 was also plagued by failure; the spring crops were also very short of expectations. The potato crop in Ireland was almost completely wiped out, and it became necessary to import large stocks of food to feed the population. This meant wheat in England, but cheaper Indian corn from America for the general populace in Ireland where public and private resources for relief were too short to buy anything else.

From mid-1846 the calls on the railway shares began to build up and the demand for capital overtook supply. The price of cotton rose in the autumn of 1846 from deficiency of the crop, and the high price which people had to pay for their food reduced the demand for manufactured goods. From the end of the summer, a steady drain of gold took place from the Bank of England. Hoping that it could avoid crippling credit markets in London and worsening the situation caused by crop failures in the country at large, the Bank of England delayed taking any action. It thought its stock of bullion was so large, that it was able to allow the drain to proceed. There was also a lingering belief from the 1830s that drains were self-balancing. By January, however, the bullion reserve had fallen to below £13m and the Bank raised its rate of interest first to 3.5%, in January 1847, and then to 4%.

Even so, the drain of bullion continued. This was the first drain, which reached a trough in April 1847. These movements can be seen graphically in Figs. 5.1 and 5.4. The note reserve to total deposits ratio, as has been discussed in Chapter 3, represents the proportion of deposits for which the Bank still has notes, within the allowance of the Act, to offer if the deposits are withdrawn. Essentially it is a measure of the liquidity of the Bank, or how near it is being legally bankrupt from the point of view of cashflow. It was highlighted by Rudi Dornbusch and Jacob Frenkel to demonstrate the serious nature of the crisis, in terms of the availability of banknotes, better than the movements of the bullion reserve, also shown in Fig. 5.4.[20]

There are some quite unusual features about these data. Firstly, the first interest rate rise is tracked exactly by the French market rate but the second is ignored by the French rate (Fig. 5.1). This is because the French were competing with the United Kingdom not only for corn, in early 1847, but for bullion whereas in October, the French obstructed the export of bullion using capital controls. In October imports from the

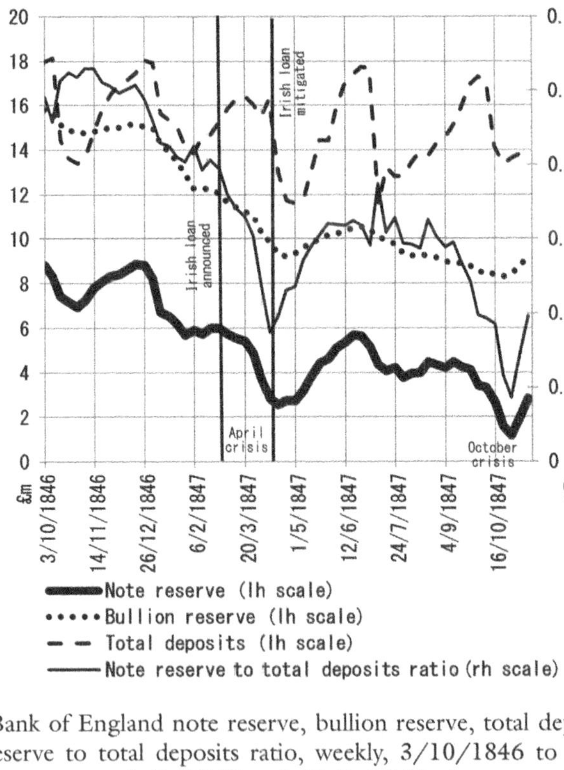

Fig. 5.4 Bank of England note reserve, bullion reserve, total deposits (all £m) and note reserve to total deposits ratio, weekly, 3/10/1846 to 13/11/1847. Vertical lines represent 1/3/1847 and 17/4/1847, the announcement of the loan and reported third reading of the Poor Relief (Ireland) Bill 1847 (*Sources* Dornbusch, Frenkel, 'The Gold Standard' pp. 261–62; PP 1847–1848 (584) VIII.505 Pt. I, app. 6, pp. 16–21)

United States and investment flows caused a heavy outflow of bullion from the United Kingdom. Secondly, the timing of the sudden increase in demand for notes and its equally sudden abatement in April primarily coordinated with attempts by Charles Wood, Goulburn's replacement as chancellor of the exchequer in the new Whig government, to raise an £8m loan to fund relief in Ireland, which he announced in Parliament on 1 March 1847 (Fig. 5.4).[21]

By then, lower than expected tax revenues in Great Britain and a need for more relief spending in Ireland as the famine worsened had eliminated the budget surplus that Peel and Goulburn had bequeathed the new government only the previous year. This forced Wood to seek two loans to fund Irish relief that year; the first, worth £8m, became known as the Irish loan, but it was to be raised on the credit of the entire United Kingdom. Ireland only had £6.009m in notes in circulation and £1.889m of bullion reserved in its banks, suggesting to investors in the City of London that, itself alone, the Irish economy nor banking system could not support such a loan.[22] Ireland's bullion reserve was not a requirement of the 1845 Act, as the circulation was not enough to require any notes to be backed by bullion. Instead, it was what banks judged that they needed to fulfil the requirements of the 1828 Act that effectively made all unstamped notes repayable in gold on demand.[23]

What made Ireland's plight as well as Britain's trade deficit worse was that France had been suffering wheat shortages since July 1846 and, in addition, autumn storms in northern France had wiped out some of that autumn's crop. The French then had to import foreign grain and the government was willing to pay high prices to forestall a political revolution in its cities. Market reports in contemporary newspapers, as well as the government's own grain broker, Eric Erickson, commented that foreign imports into Britain and Ireland intended for consumption at home were drawn away to France while still in customs bond.[24] Charles Trevelyan, the assistant secretary to the Treasury, expressed frustration at the situation.[25] In 1848 Britain became a net exporter of grain to France for the first time in contemporary living memory.[26] It was not only food that was drawn to France, but just as importantly, British bullion as capital flows, including some of the Bank of England's own reserves. This drain was in progress just as the British government began its efforts to raise the Irish loan.

From 1846 until the end of January 1847, the Bank of France's bullion reserves decreased by 173m francs. On 31 December 1846, the specie it held was under 71m francs. During the month of October 1846, 53m francs had been paid out, and in November 43m francs. The Bank of France used its government stock to buy 45m francs worth of bullion (about £2.25m).[27] On 14 January 1847, it put its rate up to 5%, ahead of the Bank of England's 4%. Under these conditions some bullion must have moved to France from the United Kingdom, but because of lack of information, the British government seemed unconcerned by this. However, the amount would have been outweighed by the size of the Irish loan at £8m.

Palmer, the former Governor of the Bank of England, wrote to *The Times* on 29 April 1847, using the pseudonym the 'Vindicator', pointing out how advances on loans for Irish relief could induce financial panics by suddenly producing a drop in the Bank of England's bullion reserve because its balance was published in the weekly tables in the *London Gazette* as required by the 1844 Act.[28]

> I will suppose a case. The Chancellor of the Exchequer has calls on him for money to carry on the works there, or may have to pay for corn to feed the people, has not a farthing on his account, and comes to the Bank and asks an advance to the amount of the next instalment of the loan, or upon any other receipt he may expect in a few days- say to the amount of £2,000,000... If this should happen the day before the publication of the account what a panic may be raised by interested parties?

As he pointed out, the possibility of a panic depended on how quickly any such advance was repaid and the nature of future demands. This letter was written shortly after a recovery in the bullion reserves which coincided with an indication that changes to proposed Irish Poor Law legislation would slow down the use of loan payments, the implication of his letter being that this was a good thing for the credit situation.

Dornbusch's and Frenkel's analysis tends to confirm Palmer was correct that there was a link (Fig. 5.4).[29] The announcement of the Irish loan on 1 March 1847, followed two weeks later by the first reading of the Poor Relief (Ireland) Bill, which dealt with how the money would be spent, corresponds to a collapse in bullion reserves at the Bank of England and also a crisis depicted by a low note reserve to total deposits ratio. The beginning of the crisis coincided with the announcement of the Irish loan; the crisis only began to fade in April after the government executed a U-turn on funding Irish relief that slowed down the rate at which the loan was spent and increased the share of advances that local taxpayers in Ireland were required to repay.

The third reading of the bill corresponds with a complete reversal of the downward trend of bullion reserves to the exact date of its announcement in the papers, 17 April 1847. At the commencement of the bill's progress it was generally assumed about half of the Treasury advances for relief were to be funded by central government grant and the rest provided as a loan (as with the Poor Relief (Ireland) Act that February).[30] The bill proposed outdoor relief of the able-bodied but destitute poor, a potentially costly commitment in a country in which three million people previously reliant on potato farming had since seen their livelihoods all but wiped out. During the third reading of the bill, it became clear that the entire loan was to be repaid by the propertied classes of Ireland, landlords and tenant farmers, and that the money would only be released slowly, as the Poor Law Commissioners could control whether outdoor relief was given.[31] Irish landlords also amended the bill to restrict the eligibility of the poor for relief.[32]

The link between how quickly the Irish Loan was likely to be spent and financial confidence (or lack of it) was a very serious blow to the Russell government's plans for relief in Ireland. It meant that, not only would it be difficult to raise a further loan, but for the purposes required, the £8m loan taken out was virtually useless because it could not be expended quickly. Suddenly all the plans about cutting Treasury funding and costs in general that had been slowly put together over the previous period of declining finances were implemented in a rush at once. Massive relief cuts, the largest proportion at one time during the famine, were made 1–8 May 1847 (40% of employment on the public works), as contemporary Treasury maps show, and in due course the public-works schemes were replaced with soup kitchens and then relief provided by Poor Law Unions.[33] This contrasts with a 20% proportion which was reduced slowly from 20 March to the end of April, to ensure that there were enough agricultural workers to sow the next season's crops.[34] Despite being considered since January 1847, the relief legislation transferring more of the costs onto the Poor Law had been delayed by landlord protests, but was now implemented 'as rapidly as possible', as Peter Gray has pointed out.[35] The Poor Relief (Ireland) Bill (which became the Poor Relief (Ireland) Act 1847 c. 31 of 8 June 1847), and Poor Relief (Ireland) (No. 2) Act 1847 c. 90, of 22 July, transferred relief costs to the poor-law system and separated it from that of England, in order to remove the liability from the government's main balance sheet and placate the London financial markets, for whom the level of uncertainty about the total cost of public relief efforts was so threatening.[36]

That calmed commercial matters, but due to the government's assumption that it was entirely the Irish loan that caused the crisis and the lack of awareness of any drain to France which may have contributed to the panic, Wood as chancellor assumed there was no future in any further attempts to raise loans for Irish relief in the prevailing economic crisis. As Russell later admitted to his lord-lieutenant in Dublin, 'Now without borrowing and lending we could have no great plan for Ireland – and much as I wished it, I have got to see that it is impracticable'.[37]

That may well have been a reasonable assumption, if Peel's Bank Charter Act was to be maintained in force. The loan was intended to be paid out in 12% instalments between 9 April and 15 October 1847, which implied a significant amount of money coming onto the food market quite quickly.[38]

Tenders were to be submitted by 1 March 1847, and a large group of wealthy capitalists was invited to a meeting with Wood. In the event the tenders of Baring Bros. and Co. and N. M. Rothschild and Sons were accepted as they were the only suitable. Their offers were at the level of 89.5% of 3% consols stock, whereas Irish stock had originally been offered.[39] Although the loans had been contracted, the monies still had to be raised from the market and this extended over the period of credit shortage in April 1847 and second panic in October. The records in the Baring Archive show that, before the contracting of the loan at the beginning of March, Barings had raised promises of the money from investors quite easily. Over a hundred offers were refused and some applicants only received a third of their offered allocation. However, as the April difficulties developed, deposits had to be paid and the list of those actually paying shows considerable changes from the offers accepted only weeks ago.[40] Interest rates had increased and credit had become tight; moreover, Wood had decided the deposits could not be paid by discounting stock. Wood wrote to Russell on 14 April 1847 with an indication Barings were have difficulties collecting the funds, 'certainly they have reason to reject the terms of the loan, and they not unnaturally complain of anything and everything'.[41] The records of subscriptions suggest that groups of investors such as the staff of the Bank of England bought into the loan on a virtually charitable basis to help stabilise the financial system.[42] Grey recorded in his diary that he visited Wood at home on

7 March 1847, less than one week after the loan was contracted, 'where I found the two Rothschilds very anxious something will be done after an increased demand for capital and fall in government securities'; 'Wood showed me letters from Ireland more frightful than ever'.[43]

The Rothschilds had set up the British Association for the Relief of the Extreme Distress in the Remote Parishes of Ireland and Scotland, in early 1847.[44] At this time, as the loan became so difficult to collect, the need for the Association was clear. As a charity, it ran many of the soup kitchens and food depots up to mid-1848 which bridged the early shut down of government relief that was provoked by a financial and commercial crisis that paralysed credit and the British currency system. Even so, the Association closed down in 1848, well before the end of the famine and in a period in which the effects of reduced harvests and disease were still taking their toll.

The Banking School's evidence to the enquiries on the 1847 commercial distress mainly blamed the Irish loan for the April crisis. Alexander Wylie who represented business in Liverpool, which was particularly badly hit by commercial distress, blamed price rises in food on 'the Irish loan, or a great part of it, being thrown upon the market'.[45] Charles Turner, representing Liverpool merchants, was asked what he believed caused the commercial distress in Liverpool. 'The fundamental cause I believe to be the famine', increased imports of food, bills of exchange limited by a scarcity of credit, had to be paid for in bullion, he explained. 'How do you consider the Government loan [Irish loan] aided in increasing the pressure?' he was asked. He answered that the loan was 'a very proper course for the Government to pursue; but it is clear that if Government had not issued that loan, the same importation of food would not have taken place'.[46] He did not blame the 1844 Act, however, mainly the loan. George Muntz from Birmingham believed the Bank made a mistake in not 'increasing the rate in the months of October and November 1846...'; 'I have always supposed that they were influenced by a wish to assist the government in making the [Irish] loan'.[47]

James Morris and Henry Prescott, Governor and Deputy Governor of the Bank of England, confirmed that the interest rate rise was deferred to ease the rate at which the Irish loan was raised. It was queried whether this had been fair to those bidding for the loan because afterwards the rates went up.[48] Morris and Prescott were of the opinion that the Bank Rate should have been raised earlier. They believed the cause of the April pressure was the famine and consequent importation of food. The result was 'an almost total prostration of credit'.[49]

Some historians have accused the Country Bankers of linking the panic to the Irish loan for self-serving reasons, and Wood and the Treasury of using the crisis simply as an excuse for pursuing the policy of *laissez-faire* that they desired all along. But the threat to the public finances from the crisis and the loan was a real one. This can be clearly seen by zooming in on the unexpected troubles that the government had in refinancing its Treasury bills that year.[50] Treasury bills were a form of short-term government debt issued on a regular basis to pay for the interest on the national debt and other expenditure when there was not sufficient government cash flow. Usually, there were few issues with finding buyers for this debt. However, thanks to the shortage of credit in the first crisis of 1847 and the Irish loan crowding out the debt market, in the run-up to paying the April dividends on the national debt there was a shortfall of £2.5m in a sale of Treasury bills. The Bank of England was forced to step in instead and provide £2m of funds to the Treasury as deficiency bills, reducing its note reserves further when they were already under severe pressure.[51] This worsened the note reserve to total deposit ratio that Dornbusch and Frenkel highlighted as a sign of the seriousness of the crisis at the Bank of England. Given this and Wood's fear that the opposition could exploit the situation as a repeat of the Whig fiscal mismanagement of the public finances in the 1830s, it is clear that his protestations to his colleagues that further borrowing and spending for Ireland were a risk to the public finances were based on genuine apprehensions. As he wrote to the lord-lieutenant of Ireland in August 1847:

> ...assistance to Ireland means only a further loan and in the present state of the money market and depression in all our manufacturing towns, this is out of the question. Ireland must keep herself somehow or other. This, at least, is certain: the public funds of this country will not. I plead guilty to being very hard hearted.[52]

However, worse was to come. During the second crisis, the government had a shortfall for the October dividends that it was unable to finance from the sale of Treasury bills because of the panic in the money market. This time the Bank of England, whose note reserve was again under severe pressure, was unable to step in to fill the gap. The Treasury spent half the Irish loan covering these other liabilities, squeezing the amount left for relief efforts in Ireland further.[53]

5.3 The Second Phase of the Crisis

The Bank of England found that the drains caused by the Irish loan left them with reserves too low to be able to provide sufficient funds for the payment of the next round of railway share calls and so took the 'severe step' of restricting the amount of discounts.[54] Reserves only recovered slightly before the bullion drain from the Bank of England recommenced at the end of July. On 5 August 1847 the Bank increased its discount rate to 5.5% and this was enough to trigger commercial and mercantile failures. First to fall were those involved in the corn trade, under pressure from falling cereal prices, which had begun to tumble. In May wheat was 102s 5d per quarter and by 7 August the price had fallen to 75s 6d per quarter. Bill brokers and other merchants, banks and brokers followed. Morier Evans lists over 450 firms that failed between August 1847 and December 1848.[55] In Ireland the commercial community that had benefited from sales of food at high prices in 1845 and 1846 was suddenly in a difficult financial position. They had bought stocks of grain at high prices which they could now only sell at a loss or raise credit and hope prices would rise again. All Irish banks found themselves under pressure to provide coins, which were already scarce due to the increased amount needed for payments for public works. The Bank of Ireland had made an arrangement with the other Irish banks to provide coins in times of shortage and had to import £0.2m in gold coins from Britain in order to honour their commitments.[56]

Wood, as chancellor of the exchequer, tried to convince the Bank of England that it should not worry about the diminution of the note reserve because of the increase at the same time in private securities held by the Bank.[57] However, the Bank knew that these securities could not necessarily be sold at the rate required to satisfy the demand for liquidity.

Meanwhile, the wholesale cost of grains imported into the United Kingdom continued to increase, even as prices began to slide in the summer of 1847. The figures for total costs were announced in Parliament. They were, without any allowance for profit, for the six months from June 1846 to January 1847, £5.139m, and from January to July 1847, £14.184m, but during the three months from July to October, the sum paid for corn imported was £14.240m. The highest corn imports were therefore during the three months the pressure in the money market was the greatest. In 1843 the United Kingdom had imported no grain at all from the United States. In 1847 it imported 16% of its needs from there.[58]

Events conspired to ensure that these exports were paid for in bullion rather than any credit or exchange arrangement. On 6 August 1846 the Second United States Independent Treasury Act had been passed and government business could only be done in specie. Payments included the tariffs on traded goods and because of this, payments for exports were generally required to be paid for in bullion by suppliers. As the United Kingdom was operating under the Bank Charter Act of 1844 with the pound linked to bullion this meant trade was carried out under a tight gold standard. Interest rates in the United Kingdom rose to meet those in the United States in April. Demands for liquidity to pay for corn, pay calls for railway shares, supply–demand from France and contribute to the Irish loan all played their part by causing drains. Now flows to the United States suddenly faltered due to the reversal of investment flows causing a sudden, but temporary drop in the value of the dollar. The *Mississippi Free Trader* reported the fall of the dollar against gold was up to 50% and the banks would only accept payment in specie.[59] The effect was so short that monthly exchange-rate data from London shows a dip of only a few per cent.[60]

The Second United States Independent Treasury Act had been passed as a result of America's war with Mexico over territory. Texas had been annexed in 1845 and President James Polk, who had been elected on an expansionist platform, persuaded Congress to declare war on Mexico on 13 May 1846. Mexico City was captured by the United States in September 1847 and negotiations over a peace treaty began. The direct cost of the war to the United States has been estimated at around $70m and about $38m was raised in Treasury notes. Interest rates soared from August 1847. The Treasury notes issued to raise the capital were at a rate of up to 6% and it was expected that the price of them would increase when the Mexicans had been defeated making a capital gain when sold. This added to the flow of bullion from the United Kingdom. As an indication of the volume of flow, the net importation of coin and bullion into the United States for 1847 amounted to $22.2m compared with a net importation of $0.127m in 1846.[61] This was from all countries, but the United Kingdom would have provided a significant proportion.

When the United Kingdom started to collect better information about the destination of bullion after 1847, it was discovered that sizeable flows were making their way to France and Germany.[62] That suggests the flows from Britain to America were bigger than in the available data for the 1840s.

So concerned were bankers about the situation created by the 1844 Act that a City of London petition against the Bank Charter Act was presented to the House of Commons by Baring and mentioned in the *Bankers' Magazine*.[63] It was described as causing 'much vexation to the Currency Philosophers' (or Currency School) who depended on 'currency dogma' rather than those who had practical banking experience. The journal states that it was received in the Commons with 'cheers' in spite of the 'angry attempts' of the Currency School to 'weaken the effect' of the document. Yet this incident is barely mentioned in the *Hansard* record, a sign of the official repression of Banking-School views that was to come.[64] *The Times'* fuller report of the petition, includes its suggested remedies of a relaxing power to be managed by the Government, and the issue of some notes against silver bullion.[65]

From its recovery to around £10.5m in June 1847, the bullion reserve of the Bank of England reduced to £8.4m by the beginning of October. The note reserve dropped to a lower point than it had been in April. Wood described the situation at the beginning of October as follows:

> I came to London on the 2nd of October, I found the whole city in a state of the greatest excitement and alarm. For one day, the continuation was at the rate of 60 per cent per annum. I certainly never passed through so painful and anxious a period as the three weeks which succeeded that day. My time was occupied in seeing persons of all descriptions from the moment I came down in the morning until I went to bed at night. Parties came to me and represented that it was perfectly impossible that the loans could be repaid to the Bank; that if the Bank relied upon such repayment for the payment of the dividends, they would be disappointed; that the Bank dared not sell the securities on which the advances had been made, and, consequently, that it was impossible that the public credit could be maintained during the next week.[66]

'The payment of dividends' referred to the government paying interest on its existing debt. Treasury bills were normally raised for this if the government did not have enough cash, and failing this the Bank of England filled the gap with deficiency bills. In this case, those bills could not be raised either as the Bank's note reserve was so low and as it was struggling to obtain repayment of other loans owed to it because of the ongoing credit crunch.[67] The situation showed how serious the second crisis really was to the public finances.

It was at this time that Irish MPs were told that there was no cash for any further assistance to Ireland. In order to raise revenue for the Treasury, the Recovery of Public Monies (Ireland) Bill had been raised to obtain repayment of the original Irish loan via the Irish Poor Law Boards except in certain hard-hit areas.[68] John O'Connell sent a circular letter to all provincial Irish newspapers saying, 'We are told *there is no money in the Treasury!* Yes, that has been repeated to us over and over again within the last few weeks. THERE IS NO MONEY—THERE IS NO MONEY TO KEEP THE PEOPLE ALIVE!!!'. O'Connell accepted there was a problem, stating that local organisation would have to step into the void to combat starvation.[69] It was at this point that Trevelyan, the Treasury civil servant in charge of relief efforts, briefly broke ranks with the government and wrote to *The Times* to ask the public for charity.[70]

Meanwhile, in the City of London, the 'Week of Terror' from 16 to 23 October 1847 brought matters to a head. Several banks, thought to be well run, suspended payment. Many of these banks had lent money for the purchase of food to be grown in foreign countries and these assets could not be realised promptly. Investment had gone abroad, particularly to the West Indies, Mauritius and Asia, to grow crops to supply Britain. This had produced a glut of some commodities, such as a two years supply of indigo from India in stock.[71] *The Times* of 25 October 1847 described how:

> In the West Indies and the Mauritius as well as in India itself, advances which…led to this consequence came into the hands of the houses in questions…The natural consequence was that these houses which had thus foolishly locked up their capital in such (immediately) unrealizable property, carried on their business by means of credit than by means of their own money were not prepared to meet the great convulsions in the money market.

On 25 October 1847, in a Treasury letter to the Bank that was widely publicised, Lord Russell and Wood (with Peel's approval) announced the government's intention to maintain 'the vital principle of preserving the convertibility of the Bank-note' but in practice to promise that no action would be taken if the restrictions of the Bank Charter Act of 1844 were breached.[72] To ensure that the Bank of England's gold reserves returned to a level where it could maintain the gold standard and the Bank Charter Act, the government 'recommended' (in effect 'told') the Bank to raise official interest rates to 8%, a record high since the Bank's foundation in 1694.[73]

> Downing-street, Oct. 25, 1847.
>
> Gentlemen—Her Majesty's Government have seen with the deepest regret the pressure which has existed for some weeks upon the commercial interests of the country, and that this pressure has been aggravated by a want of that confidence which is necessary for carrying on the ordinary dealings of trade.
>
> They have been in hopes that the check given to transactions of a speculative character, the transfer of capital from other countries, the influx of bullion, and the feeling which a knowledge of these circumstances might have been expected to produce, would have removed the prevailing distrust.
>
> They were encouraged in this expectation by the speedy cessation of a similar state of feeling in the month of April last.
>
> These hopes have, however, been disappointed, and her Majesty's Government have come to the conclusion that the time has arrived when they ought to attempt, by some extraordinary and temporary measure, to restore confidence to the mercantile and manufacturing community.
>
> For this purpose, they recommend to the Directors of the Bank of England, in the present emergency, to enlarge the amount of their discounts and advances upon approved security, but that, in order to retain this operation within reasonable limits, a high rate of interest should be charged.
>
> In present circumstances, they would suggest that the rate of interest should not be less than 8 per cent.
>
> If this course should lead to any infringement of the existing law, Her Majesty's Government will be prepared to propose to Parliament, on its meeting, a Bill of Indemnity.
>
> They will rely upon the discretion of the directors to reduce as soon as possible the amount of their notes, if any extraordinary issue should take place, within the limits prescribed by law.
>
> Her Majesty's Government are of opinion that any extra profit derived from this measure should be carried to the account of the public, but the precise mode of doing so must be left to future arrangement.
>
> Her Majesty's Government are not insensible of the evil of any departure from the law which has placed the currency of this country upon a

sound basis; but they feel confident that, in the present circumstances, the measure which they have proposed may be safely adopted, and at the same time the main provisions of that law, and the vital principle of preserving the convertibility of the Bank-note, may be firmly maintained.

We have the honour to be. Gentlemen,

Your obedient humble servants, (Signed) *J. Russell, Charles Wood.*

To: The Governor and the Deputy-Governor of the Bank of England.

This letter is interesting in that it includes a number of features that were to be repeated in similar letters issued in future crises, which formed the basis of Walter Bagehot's recommendations on how to run a lender of last resort. It combines the Banking-School policy of extending credit as much as is necessary, provided that it is on good security, with the Currency-School limitations of a high discount rate. The high rate, to the Banking School, would also have had the advantage of drawing in bullion to the country and increasing the Bank's bullion reserves.

The move had the desired effect and the 8% rate did not last long; by July 1848 it had reduced to 3.5%. The United States Treasury allowed customs charges to be paid in Treasury bonds from November 1847, which had a similar effect to the Bank of England's letter in the United Kingdom, helping rates in the United States to fall to around 5% by 1850. Even so, pressure on banks was reported by the *New York Herald* in January 1848.[74] The Bank of England's Bank Rate was reduced further and was down to 3% for much of 1849. The Bank's bullion reserve increased from around £8m at its lowest in 1847 to vary consistently at above £12.5m for the rest of the decade.

The letter states that the Bank was to pass profits from the increased rate to the government but there is no record of this happening. The Bank's income from short loans and advances from August 1847 to August 1848 was £112,000 compared with an annual average of £33,000 over the following similar years.[75] This pattern persisted in future crises.

Among Peel's papers is a collection of notes, including his speeches, concerning the Currency and the Bank of England, which is similar to those on other subjects gathered together to be published in his memoirs. However his *Memoirs*, as published, only deal with the questions of Catholic Emancipation and the Corn Laws, matters of currency are not mentioned, a sign that even Peel regarded the Act of 1844 as not one of his successes. Peel wanted history to remember his economic legacy in glowing terms, not the emerging protest about the 1844 Act, particularly in the aftermath of the crisis of 1847. As Richard Gaunt, a biographer of Peel, has described, 'Peel did not merely hope for his reward in heaven—but in history'.[76]

It has been described in Chapter 2 how the discussion of the 1844 Bank Charter Act was repressed after Peel was informed of how unpopular it was.[77] Both Peel and Cardwell did their best to remove the relationship between the Bank Charter Act and financial crises of 1847 from the historical record.[78] Peel's advocacy for legislative action to help Ireland later on during the famine, including the Rate-in-Aid Act which spread the load of local taxation more evenly, the Encumbered Estates Act which freed up land ownership and model farms to improve agriculture, may well have been attempts to assuage any guilt he may have felt at the negative effect, as it turned out, of his economic policies on Ireland.

5.4 The Consequences of the Crisis

Fear that another banking crisis caused by bullion flows was on the way meant that the 1847 Irish relief reductions were never reversed. From August 1847 Wood became wary of loans:

> In order to lend or give to Ireland we must borrow. It may be necessary to do this...but it will be well to avoid borrowing again if we can.[79]

The alternative was to raise income tax, but after 1847, it became difficult politically to get the income tax renewed, let alone raise it, as neither the Peelites nor the Irish Repeal-of-the-Union-ers were willing to support the government on the issue.[80] The Repealers were not even willing to give up Ireland's income-tax exemption in exchange for a higher rate on British taxpayers to help fund relief. Peel, meanwhile, feared that a higher income-tax rate could be diverted from relief towards accelerating the gradual path of tariff reductions outlined in his Repeal of the Corn Laws in 1846.[81]

The resulting lack of funds caused a sharp reduction in government expenditure in the aftermath of the 1847 crises. Loans advanced for Irish relief amounted to £4.08m in 1846–1847 and £2.139m in 1847–1848, but were almost completely ended by March 1848.[82] Treasury grants from central government funds for Irish relief also sharply fell after 1847, from £0.8525m in 1845–1846, £0.682 in 1846–1847, and £0.975m in 1847–1848 to just £0.390 in 1848–1849.[83] After 1849, central government assistance for Irish relief was virtually non-existent. The reductions coincide with the peak in famine-related mortality, which workhouse data suggest occurred in the winter of 1848–1849.[84]

In addition, a nervous Wood sent Peel information in July 1849 that suggested their plans were failing, as part of communications with him over free trade matters and legislation such as the Navigation Laws.[85] Large quantities of foreign wheat were being imported and Poor Law reports showed that there was intense distress in the agricultural districts.[86] Wood pointed out wheat imports for the entire United Kingdom in the 1848–1849 period were over three times those of 1846–1847, which were believed to have triggered the bullion crisis, and the Poor Law reports 'disclose[d] a good deal of distress in the agricultural districts from want of employment'. Wood realised that the social benefits of their policies would be less than expected; 'small, unskilled farmers will have the fate of hand loom weavers: and though the people at large will be most materially benefited, I am afraid that there must be a good deal of class suffering'.[87] This realisation that the lower classes would suffer appears to have been news for both parties, and against their original intentions. However, bullion outflows prevented the government from reversing its 1847 decisions because of Wood's fears that more Irish relief expenditure—or even discussion of it—might trigger yet another financial crisis. Yet the quantities of wheat imported continued to rise without associated bullion flows or a repeat of the crisis (Fig. 5.3), suggesting that manufacturing was improving but also that investment flows were beginning to take over in importance from trade flows.

The effects of the Irish famine, inadequately relieved by local financing, persisted beyond 1850. From peak to trough, Ireland's GDP fell around 25% during the crisis. As a result, around a million Irish people probably died and more than a further million emigrated. Lower agricultural yields and raised levels of emigration out of Ireland persisted after the famine throughout the rest of the nineteenth century.[88] Combined with increased local taxation levels on land, much of Ireland became unattractive for investment. Some of rural Ireland's subsequent economic underperformance may be laid at the door of the Bank Charter Act of 1844; Britain's monetary policy did not suit Ireland's needs. Even so, the rest of the United Kingdom suffered under these policies too. Unemployment is estimated to have risen by about a third from 1846 to 1847 and after falling for the next two years surged again in 1850.[89] Evans lists over 450 commercial firms and banks, in the United Kingdom and abroad that he claims became insolvent due to the 1847 crisis.[90] One of the firms was Jevons, Sons & Co., which went bankrupt in early 1848 and forced one of the partners Thomas Jevons, father of the economist William Stanley Jevons, to obtain employment elsewhere.

The effect of the 1847 crisis on the colonies has been largely ignored by historians but it was truly devastating. Most colonies, particularly former slave-plantation islands, had rudimentary monetary and banking systems and these were brought to their knees by the failure of their banks, including the West India Bank and Planters' Bank, as a result of contagion from the credit crunch in London.[91] The contagion from the second crisis of 1847 helped to crush the wages of ordinary labourers in British sugar colonies in the Caribbean by as much as half.[92] Not only did such failures impoverish workers and cripple the plantation owners, but they also dissuaded the newly freed labouring population from engaging in wage labour or non-subsistence agriculture. Before the crisis, many had saved up banknotes to club together and buy land for their own villages, but as the Governor of Trinidad reported with the colonies' 1847 blue book, 'the failure of the West India Bank has prevented many of the peasantry from becoming purchasers, as great numbers of that class had horded their notes; there appears to be still a great prejudice amongst them against entrusting their money to the savings bank'.[93] The carefully saved notes had proved worthless when the issuing bank failed. Failures occurred in India and the East Indies, generally, as well. The populations found their food supplies at risk because the credit to import food was not available; it had failed with the many agents that operated trade with the colonies.[94] Most workers had to accept pay cuts and grow their own food, ending up little different from the subsistence peasantry in Ireland. The exception was, perhaps, Mauritius, for which a financial rescue was arranged, and a new currency launched.[95]

Dismayed by the effect of the 1847 crisis on the colonies and on Ireland, the Third Earl Grey set up a currency board in Mauritius, where a government currency had been requested. After a slow start, currency-board schemes spread throughout the British empire. Mauritius was the first currency board.[96] In the 1850s Prince Edward Island rejected the idea and New Zealand abandoned an experiment with one, but James Wilson set up India's currency as a partial currency board in the 1860s and the Ceylon currency was taken over by commissioners of currency from private banks in 1884.[97] The Falklands set up similar systems in 1899, Bermuda in 1915, Gibraltar in 1927, and the Irish Free State in 1928, and Hong Kong in 1983. In 1945 the number of currency-board-like systems reached over 45 globally.[98] Eventually, even Britain nationalised its central bank in the 1940s, a concession to the Mauritian model of government ownership, even though the Bank of England continued with a central-bank currency model.[99] The currency-board arrangements have generally been seen as a success (except for a notable failure in Argentina, which had a long history of financial problems under various currency systems). Kurt Schuler has shown by an analysis of 155 countries including over 99% of the world's output that countries with currency boards performed better, judged by output growth, than those with central banks.[100] So although Grey was unable to benefit Ireland during its famine with his innovation, the lesson learnt from 1847 can be said to have assisted many developing countries around the world since.

The 1847 crisis undoubtedly influenced Karl Marx in his authorship of the *Communist Manifesto* in 1848, not regarded by policymakers as significant at that time, but which certainly became so later. Marx predicted that the 'proletariat' would demand 'the centralisation of credit in the hands of the state by means of a national bank'.[101] His assertion that crises were 'inherent within the present system' provoked a disparity of views on how to mitigate them based around the contrasting ideas of Currency School and the Banking School. Those influenced by the latter hoped that their suggestions on how to prevent crises would provide stability—averting the potential for a Marxian revolution or similar—more effectively than did Peel's Bank Charter Act of 1844.

Notes

1. *Hansard*, 17 February 1848, XCVI, cc. 834–835.
2. C. Read, 'The Political Economy of Sir Robert Peel', in J. Hoppit, A. B. Leonard, D. J. Needham (eds.), *Money and Markets: Essays in Honour of Martin Daunton* (Woodbridge: The Boydell Press, 2019) pp. 78–83.
3. C. Read, *The Great Famine in Ireland and Britain's Financial Crisis* (Woodbridge: The Boydell Press, 2022) p. 145.
4. G. Campbell, 'Government Policy during the British Railway Mania and the 1847 Commercial Crisis' in N. Dimsdale, A. Hotson (eds.), *British Financial Crises Since 1825* (Oxford: OUP, 2014) pp. 59–68.
5. D. M. Evans, *The Commercial Crisis 1847–48* (London: Letts, 1849) p. 55.
6. C. Read, 'Laissez-faire, the Irish famine, and British financial crisis', *Economic History Review* 69 (2016) 411–434.

7. Read, *The Great Famine in Ireland*, pp. 101–183.
8. J. Wilson, *Capital, Currency and Banking* (London: The Economist, 1847) p. 206.
9. See Read, *The Great Famine in Ireland*, pp. 168–173 for the full story.
10. Anon. (Earl Grey), *Thoughts on the Currency* (London: Ridgeway, 1842); Wood to Grey, 10 January 1843, Grey papers, Durham UL, GRE/B105/3/55; Pennington to 'author of "Thoughts on the Currency"', 9 January 1843, Grey papers, Durham UL, GRE/B105/3/56, passed from Wood to Grey.
11. Earl Grey, Memorandum to Cabinet, 14 April 1848, Grey papers, Durham UL, GRE/B144/20.
12. Evans, *The Commercial Crisis 1847-48*, p. 13.
13. *Circular to Bankers*, 15 October 1847, p. 137.
14. Overstone to Reeve, 7 November 1857, in D. P. O'Brien (ed.), *The Correspondence of Lord Overstone* (Cambridge: CUP, 1971) p. 769.
15. *Report from the Secret Committee of the House of Lords on the Causes of Distress* PP 1847–1848 (565 565-II) VIII, Pt. III.1, 537, p. xliv.
16. *Punch*, 29 May 1847, pp. 221–222; A. E. Scribe, G. Delavigne, *Robert-le-Diable, an Opera in Five Acts: With an Easy Translation, Line for Line with the French* (London: H.N. Millar, 1847) p. 49.
17. *First Report from the Secret Committee on Commercial Distress* PP 1847–1848 (395) VIII. 1, VIII. 379, p. viii.
18. *Hansard*, 30 November 1847, XCV, c. 382.
19. *The Economist*, 6 December 1845.
20. R. Dornbusch, J. A. Frenkel, 'The Gold Standard and the Bank of England in the Crisis of 1847', in M. D. Bordo, A. J. Schwartz (eds.), *A Retrospective on the Classical Gold Standard 1821-1931* (Chicago: University of Chicago Press, 1984) pp. 233–276.
21. *Hansard*, 1 March 1847, XC, cc. 612–14.
22. J. W. Gilbart, 'On the Laws of the Currency in Ireland', *Journal of the Statistical Society of London* 15 (1852) 316, 322.
23. The Bank Notes Act, 1828 9 Geo. 4 c. 23 for England; c. 24 for Ireland.
24. Documents are contained in ING Baring Archives HC3.16 and HC3.75; Trevelyan papers, Erickson files, N.A., T64/365A/1-3.
25. Trevelyan to Barings, 8 July 1846 and 27 August 1846, ING Baring Archives, HC3.75.
26. *Tableau décennal du commerce de la France avec ses colonies et les puissances étrangères/1847/56*, Pt. 1 (Paris, 1856).
27. A. Liesse, *Evolution of Credit and Banks in France* (Washington: Government Printing Office, 1909) pp. 56–57.
28. *The Times*, 29 April 1847, p. 6; for the identity of the 'Vindicator' see *The Spectator*, 1 May 1847, p. 11.
29. Dorbusch, Frenkel, 'The Gold Standard'.

30. Poor Relief (Ireland) Act 1847 (10 & 11 Vict. c.7).
31. *Hansard*, 16 April 1847, XCI, cc. 915–917; Idem. c. 879.
32. Ibid.
33. Trevelyan papers, N.A., T64/ 370 C/3.
34. Treasury Minute 11 March 1847, *Report of Commissioners of Public Works (Ireland)* PP 1847 (834) XVII, pp. 4–6; Earl Grey noted in his diary 'relief works had failed because the Irish of all ranks had thwarted [them] in every way', 2 February 1847, Grey papers, Durham UL, GRE V/C3/13.
35. P. Gray, *Famine, Land and Politics* (Dublin: Irish Academic Press, 1999) p. 283.
36. Landed Property Improvement (Ireland) Act 1847 (10 & 11 Vict. c. 32); Poor Relief (Ireland) Act 1847 (10 & 11 Vict. c. 31); Poor Relief (Ireland) (No. 2) Act 1847 (10 & 11 Vict. c. 90).
37. Russell to Clarendon, 24 February 1849, Oxford Bodleian Library, Clarendon papers, Ms. Clar. dep. c. 126, also cited in P. Mandler, *Aristocratic Government in the Age of Reform: Whig and Liberal 1830–52* (Oxford: OUP, 1990) p. 252.
38. *The Era*, 28 February 1847, p. 11.
39. *Yorkshire Advertiser*, 4 March 1847.
40. Irish loan, unsuccessful and successful applications, ING Baring archive HC3.75A.1, 2; List of allocations and deposit payments, ING Baring archive 3.75A.7.
41. Wood to Russell 14 April 1847, Russell papers, N.A., PRO 30/22/6C ff. 80–86.
42. Letters of application from staff of the Bank of England, with lists of allocations, ING Baring archive, HC3.75A.6.
43. Grey's diary, 7 March 1847, Grey papers, Durham UL, GRE/V/C3/13.
44. N. Ferguson, *The House of Rothschild*, I, *Money's prophets, 1798-1848* (Harmondsworth: Penguin, 1999) Chapter 16, p. 443.
45. *Report from the Secret Committee of the House of Lords*... PP 1847–1848 (565 & 565-II) VIII Pt. III.1, 537, q. 2144, p. 246.
46. *First Report from the Secret Committee on Commercial Distress*..., PP 1847–1848 (395) VIII Pt. I.1, p. 50.
47. Idem., p. 101.
48. Idem., p. 230.
49. Idem., p. 205.
50. For the more about deficiency bills and the crises, see Read, *The Great Famine in Ireland*, pp. 145, 155, 166.
51. H. M. Boot, *The Commercial Crisis of 1847* (Hull: Hull UP, 1984) p. 50.
52. Wood to Clarendon, 15 August 1847, C.U.L., Hickleton papers, MS MF A4.186, reel 1523.

53. Read, *The Great Famine in Ireland*, pp. 155, 166.
54. *Hansard*, 30 November 1847, XCV, c. 384.
55. Evans, *The Commercial Crisis, 1847-48*, Appendix, pp. lxxxiv–ci.
56. F. G. Hall, *History of the Bank of Ireland* (Dublin, Hodges, Figgis & Co., 1949) pp. 218–219.
57. *Hansard*, XCV, 30 November 1847, c. 387.
58. *Grain, Flour, & c. RETURNS of the Quantity of Grain and Flour* PP 1849 (588) L.403.
59. *Mississippi Free Trader*, 22 June 1847, p. 2.
60. Bank of England Three centuries of data v. 3, c. M15.
61. *The Merchants' Magazine and Commercial Review*, April 1848, p. 427.
62. *Gold and Silver Bullion* PP 1854 (516) XXXIX.439, pp. 2–3.
63. *Bankers' Magazine*, August 1847, p. 325.
64. *Hansard*, 13 July 1847, XCIV, c. 236.
65. *The Times*, 14 July 1847, p. 3.
66. *Hansard*, 30 November 1847, XCV, c. 386.
67. *The Economist*, 15 January 1848, p. 57; *Return of Number and Amount of Exchequer Bills issued, June 1847-48* PP 1847-48 (454) XXXIX.153, p. 5.
68. *Hansard*, 10 July 1847, XCIV, c. 153; *The Times*, 3 September 1847, p. 3.
69. *Athlone Sentinel*, 1 October 1847, p. 3.
70. *The Times*, 12 October 1847, p. 5.
71. *The Times*, 25 October 1847, p. 8.
72. Russell and Wood to Morris and Prescott, 25 October 1847, in D. M. Evans, *The Commercial Crisis 1847*, p. 87.
73. S. H. Northcote, *Twenty Years of Financial Policy* (London: Saunders, Otley & Co., 1862) pp. 381–382.
74. *New York Herald*, 26 January 1848, p. 2.
75. J. Clapham, *The Bank of England* II (Cambridge: CUP, 1970) p. 435.
76. R. A. Gaunt, *Sir Robert Peel: The Life and Legacy* (London: I. B. Tauris & Co., 2010) pp. 160, 201.
77. For biographical details see A. B. Erickson, 'Edward T. Cardwell: Peelite', *Transactions of the American Philosophical Society* 49 (1959) 8–11.
78. The only indirect mention of the Bank Charter Act in Peel's published memoirs is R. Peel, *Memoirs by the Right Honourable Sir Robert Peel* II/III, Earl Stanhope, E. Cardwell (eds.), (London: John Murray, 1856–1857) pp. 300–301.
79. Wood to Russell, 26 August 1847, Russell papers, N.A., PRO 30/22/6E ff. 218–221.
80. Wood to Russell, 25 August 1847, Russell papers, N.A., PRO 30/22/6E ff. 211–214.

81. Peel encouraged Wood to run a deficit instead. Wood to Peel, 26 February(?) 1848 partial letter, Graham papers, B.L., Add. MS. 79713 f. 34.
82. *Public income and expenditure* PP 1861 (402) XXXIV.139.
83. *Public income and expenditure* PP 1851 (62) XXXI.159.
84. T. W. Guinnane, C. Ó Gráda, 'The Workhouses', in T. Dyson and C. Ó Gráda (eds.), *Famine Demography* (Oxford: OUP, 2002) p. 44.
85. Various letters Wood to Peel, May 1849, Peel papers, B.L., Add. MSS. 40601 ff. 277, 281, 284, 288, 290.
86. Wood to Peel, July 1849, Peel papers, B.L., Add. MSS. 40602 ff. 1–4.
87. Idem., ff. 11–14.
88. K. H. O'Rourke, 'Did the Great Irish Famine Matter?', *Journal of Economic History* 51 (1991) pp. 1–2.
89. Bank of England Three centuries of data v.2.3, A27 R.
90. Evans, *The Commercial Crisis 1847-48*, pp. lxxxix–ci.
91. Disgracefully, the Colonial Bank used its better knowledge of banking to sabotage the other banks when at their weakest. The Bank of England's treatment of Overend's was to be similar. Calvert to Rennie, 1 May 1840, Colonial Bank Correspondence, University of the West Indies Archives, C/1840/13.
92. For instance, in Barbados, *Past and Present State*... PP 1847–1848 (1005) XLVI. 1, pp. 65–66.
93. *Past and Present State of the Colonies* PP 1847–1848 (1005) XLVI.1, p. 171.
94. For colonial agents affected by the 1847 crisis, see the revised listing of stoppages and failures and the Appendix which contains many of their accounts in the second edition of Evans' *The Commercial Crisis 1847-48* [1849] (Newton Abbot: David & Charles, 1969).
95. Read, *The Great Famine in Ireland*, pp. 229–276.
96. K. Stukenbrock, *The Stability of Currency Boards* (Frankfurt am Main: Peter Lang AG, 2004) p. 61.
97. R. Chalmers, *A History of Currency in the British Colonies* (Colchester: John Drury, 1972) pp. 35–36.
98. Stukenbrock, *The Stability of Currency Boards*, p. 55.
99. S. H. Hanke, 'Exchange rate regimes and capital flows: currency boards', *Annals of the American Academy of Political and Social Science* 579 (2002) 87–105, p. 89.
100. K. Schuler, 'Should developing countries have central banks? Currency quality and monetary systems in 155 countries', *IEA Research Monograph* no. 52 (London: Institute of Economic Affairs, 1996) pp. 1–126.
101. K. Marx, F. Engels, J. C. Isaac (eds.), *The Communist Manifesto* (New Haven: Yale UP, 2012) p. 91.

CHAPTER 6

The 1857–1858 Crisis

> I feel satisfied that after what has occurred, the Act of 1844 cannot stand as it is. It is, I hold, impossible for it so to stand. That Act, as experience has shown, requires alteration in order to obviate difficulties and dangers which, if we leave them without a remedy, will increase every day, and will beset with peril, as long as they are suffered to continue, the very principles of the Act itself.
>
> —William Ewart Gladstone, *Hansard*, 11 December 1857, CXLVIII, cc. 645–646.[1]

The Bank Charter Act of 1844 survived the crises of 1847, although only narrowly.[2] Yet Sir Robert Peel, who saw the legislation as one of his key legacies, did not survive to see the next severe crisis, in 1857–1858. On 29 June 1850 he was thrown from his horse while riding near Buckingham Palace and died three days later as a result of his injuries.[3] In the absence of Peel, the debate between the Currency and Banking Schools diverged on the best way to deal with the problem of the major banking panics, which were now appearing regularly every ten years. This chapter explores how this debate evolved between the 1847 and 1857–1858 crises, explains the role of capital flows to France, America and Asia in triggering another panic, and what the consequences of the crisis were for Britain and its empire.

C. Read, *Calming the Storms*, Palgrave Studies in Economic History,
https://doi.org/10.1007/978-3-031-11914-9_6

6.1 The Currency School's and Banking School's Ideas in the 1850s

The viewpoint associated with the Currency School was most vigorously promoted by Marmaduke Sampson, *The Times'* City correspondent from 1846 to 1871. The previous correspondent, Thomas Alsager, had been more balanced in his views. His assistant, David Morier Evans, had leaned towards the Banking School. However, in the 1850s, Evans was dragged towards the views of Sampson, his new manager, before he left to try and make a career elsewhere. This reshuffling of personnel sharpened the views of the Currency School and gave them an influential platform with which they could disseminate their ideas to the public.

The Currency School's remedy for crises was to expose fraudulent and incompetent investment opportunities. Unlike the Banking School, it did not criticise the Bank of England or the Bank Charter Act of 1844. Sampson blamed crises mainly on corruption and greed but otherwise accepted periodic disturbances as part of economic reality.[4] Support of the Bank Charter Act should be a matter of national pride, he wrote, and the temporary high interest rates in a crisis were perfectly bearable.[5] More than that, other Currency-School theorists suggested that they might be helpful in clearing away less efficient firms and institutions as a form of creative destruction *avant la lettre*. Lord Overstone claimed in a speech after the 1857 crisis that if the Act had been maintained only 24 hours longer, 'the whole of the vicious system [American banking system, Scottish and Irish notes] to which he had referred would have been got rid of by the crumbling to atoms of the institutions that fostered it'.[6] What needed to be done was to expose schemes that were not genuine or sound.

Alas, those delivering this message became corrupt themselves. Sampson was Secretary to the Committee of Treasury at the Bank of England at the time he joined *The Times*, in today's terms, a clear conflict of interest.[7] He had no qualms about using any advantage his many contacts and jobs in the world of banking and journalism might bring. Sampson was eventually dismissed from *The Times* in 1871, following the discovery that he had received large payments from the financier, Albert Grant (also known as Abraham Gottheimer) in exchange for not criticising the companies the financier set up, which often failed.[8] On his death, *Reynold's Newspaper* noted 'for years past he [Sampson] had turned his position to corrupt purposes'.[9]

By contrast, the Banking School's ideas can be clearly found in the articles published by *The Economist* on the 1857 crisis. The first principle was to use interest rates to draw in bullion when a crisis was approaching. *The Economist* congratulated the directors of the Bank of England in acting promptly by raising the 'rate of interest' to '10 per cent without any suggestion from the Government' … 'sufficient to subdue the foreign drain, and thus indirectly to make money more abundant for home purposes'.[10] This action was in contrast to 1847 when they delayed raising the rate, resulting in a much sharper and commercially damaging hike when it could no longer be postponed further. *The Economist* agreed that convertibility of notes to gold was necessary, but queried whether the specific restriction on note circulation of the Act of 1844 made matters worse: 'the existence of this arbitrary limit does materially aggravate the difficulty of the *crisis*, by increasing it into panic'.[11]

The Economist also criticised the Currency School directly, in 1857 blaming 'a certain class of *doctrinaires*' who 'refer every commercial crisis and its disastrous consequences to "excessive issues of bank notes"'. However, it also suggested that both the '*Currency* school', who wanted notes restricted, and '*Birmingham* school', who wanted them freely available, concentrated too much on the quantity of circulation. Instead, it pointed to the variations in interest rate and unemployed capital as the cause of 'imprudent credits', 'imprudent advances', and 'capital absorbed in unproductive and profitless speculation'.[12] This observation harked back to Thornton's theories and previous Banking-School ideas about how crises commenced due to a disparity between interest rates. The way to halt this was to keep notes convertible and interest rates stable, 'however much credit may be abused, however recklessly capital may be dealt with, however extensive and disastrous the speculations undertaken', *The Economist* continued, 'there can be no "excessive issues" of paper money so long as it is convertible into gold'.[13] This implied that the reserve of capital held for the nation's banks had to be far larger and this issue was taken up by Walter Bagehot as a writer and then editor at *The Economist*.[14]

Sampson and his assistant Evans tried to claim the moral high ground by writing up examples of frauds and failed investment schemes. In 1845 in his book *The City*, Evans emphasised the precautions that were taken by institutions such as the Stock Exchange to avoid fraud, but by 1859 he was cataloguing 'a complete record of the astounding frauds and forgeries, with other attended circumstances, which have of late so frequently startled the commercial community from their propriety' in another book *Facts, Failures and Frauds* (1854).[15] Sampson wrote a pamphlet notionally against slavery, but he was still concerned about the 'certain ruin which must result from diminished production' after abolition. Other commentators criticised Sampson for lingering sympathy for slave owners; John Stuart Mill, a political economist, accused his articles for *The Times* of encouraging railway investment which supported mines that used slave labour, while simultaneously being a director of a Brazilian railway company.[16]

Sampson's loose attention to probity was also exposed in a libel trial against him and *The Times* (*Rubery v. Grant*).[17] He had received £2500 in 1871 and around £5000 in 1872 not to criticise Baron Albert Grant's companies and the prosecution provided details of the relevant articles.[18] Evans at the *Standard* was implicated in a similar way in *Twycross v. Grant* but this may have been due to spite and he was dead by that time and could not defend himself, whereas Sampson admitted he had received money.[19] Although the main publicist of Currency-School attitudes had gone when Sampson left *The Times*, the same editorial policy continued when he was replaced as City correspondent by Arthur Crump, who wanted no more discussion of currency controversies, including from Earl Grey.[20] Crump was later dismissed by *The Times* after receiving a cheap loan from the Bank of England to sway its coverage in the Bank's favour.[21]

The Economist was more concerned with the moral issues of ensuring a sufficient supply of credit was available in order to avoid future crises and the suffering that they caused. The paper supported the rise of the new joint-stock banks because they provided an alternative source of credit for trade, as well as competition for the Bank of England. However, this meant that joint-stock banks had to live up to the high standards expected of them. Competing with the Bank of England was difficult because the Bank held influence over interest rates and access to credit in a crisis. *The Economist* would have preferred the bullion reserve to have been held by individual banks and managed by them. However, as the situation had arisen that most of it was held by the Bank of England, the Bank was 'almost morally compelled to give large amounts of temporary accommodation' to compensate for its advantages.[22]

In particular, *The Economist* treated the bill broking firm of Overend, Gurney & Co. with sympathy because of its ability to compete with the Bank of England, even as things started to go wrong for it in the 1850s.[23]

In 1825, while the Bank restricted lending and discounting severely, Overend's had proved a lifeline to many banks and other organisations by making short-term loans. This made it popular with *The Economist* when compared with the Bank, which it saw as the preserve of 'aristocracies and hierarchies' and the 'satisfied and indolent' classes.[24] Overend's and similar organisations, as champions of the moral force in banking, were expected to adhere to a strict code of upwardly mobile middle-class conduct: 'to keep rigidly to engagements, to be punctual in the performance of contracts, to pay debts the very day they are due, to live frugally and within their means, to accumulate capital, and gather increasing influence in society'.[25] In addition, Overend's leading figures such as Samuel Gurney represented the anti-slavery lobby, whereas the Bank and its followers were seen as including some who were prepared to countenance commercial relations with slave-owning industries around the world.[26]

However, the Bank, with its deposits on which it paid no interest and virtual control of now widely varying short-term discount rates, held the upper hand in the commercial-banking game. Overend's had moved from being brokers who did not actually lend money to discounters who borrowed money at a low rate and lent it at a higher one, making use of the disparity between rates. The new variability in rates was incompatible with that. Overend's and organisations such as them found it increasingly difficult to make their business model work under the new interest-rates regime, when defaulting clients left short-term funds locked up in unsellable long-term investments.[27] This situation led to catastrophe when Overend's became insolvent in 1866 and it became clear the Bank of England's primacy was unassailable. Much was made later in the century by supporters of the Currency School of the demise of Overend's, as a morality tale about fraud in banking, but little was said about the motives behind the propagation of the Currency School's ideas in *The Times* in the 1850s.

6.2 An Overview of the 1857–1858 Crisis

The conventional and Currency-School view of the 1857–1858 crisis, repeated in most recent historical scholarship, is that it started in the United States with the failure of the Ohio Life Insurance and Trust Company on 24 August 1857.[28] Over September and October 1857 a banking crisis erupted in New York, and it was said, at the time, 62 out of 63 commercial banks suspended payment on their notes. The scarcity of money in 1857 can be seen by the very high peak of the US market short-term paper interest rates shown in Fig. 6.1.

However, looking at Figs. 3.4 and 6.1, UK short-term interest rates had been below or similar to long term rates from March 1848 to June 1853 and then US and European interest rates had been moving together since late 1853. This was consistent with the Banking-School theory of crisis that low short-term rates provoked a search for higher yields abroad, thereby causing international bullion flows. Exchange rates were relatively stable throughout the period and, it was changes in interest rates that were consistent with the crisis once again. Peter Temin has already noted that an overall lack of capital in the United States in 1857 could not have been the problem that caused the crisis in the United States. Indeed, as the rest of this chapter will show, the problem was with the sudden halt in capital flows, rather than the overall quantity of capital, as interest rates drew together.[29]

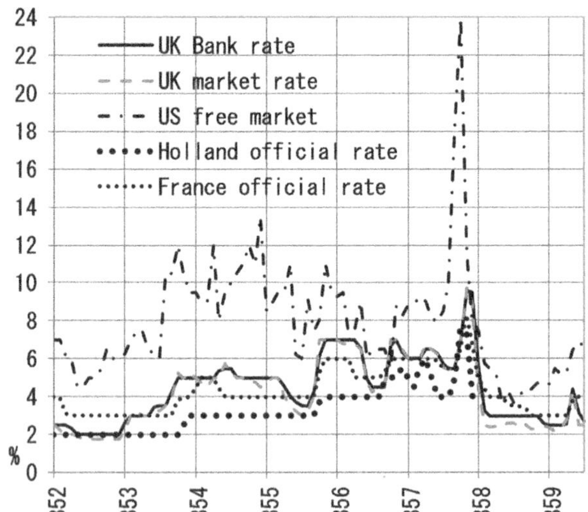

Fig. 6.1 Short-term interest rates in the UK, US, Holland, and France, January 1852–July 1859 (*Sources* Calculated from R. H. I Palgrave, *Bank Rate and the Money Market in England, France, Germany, Holland and Belgium 1844–1900* (London: John Murray, 1903); *The Economist*)

The Banking School's theories looked to bullion flows, interest rates, and France in this period for explanations about instability in the financial system. Thomas Tooke and William Newmarch devoted much of volume 6 of their *History of Prices* published in 1857 to the Bank of France and its arrangements to obtain bullion.[30] Figure 6.1 shows that from 1852 to 1855 France's and the Bank of England's official rates moved around each other as they competed for bullion. In the 1840s data on the importation and exportation of bullion had been hard to come by. However, this improved in the 1850s, led by the *Morning Chronicle* and *Daily News*. Their figures were recorded in the Bank of England's daily account books until official statistics were available. From this source, Fig. 6.2 shows that, because of sources of new gold, from late 1852 and into 1853, imports of bullion to the United Kingdom equalled and exceeded exports but despite this a bullion drain started from the Bank of England that went into 1855.

There was considerable competition among European countries for gold in the early 1850s because they all wished to boost their economic development at the same time. They quickly adopted the practice of

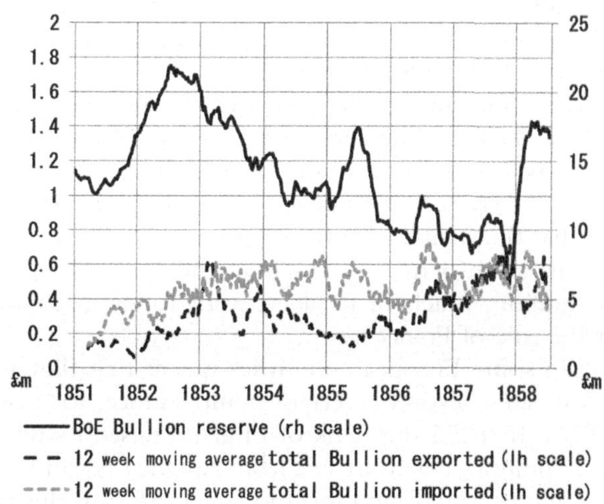

Fig. 6.2 Balance of weekly exports and imports of bullion and coin and Bank of England bullion reserve, 1851–1858 (*Sources* Bank of England daily account books; Gold and Silver bullion PP 1854 [516] XXXIX.439, pp. 8–15)

adjusting interest rates to follow each other, but this moderated flows and countries had to adopt policies to overcome this, such as France which effectively bought bullion at a premium using bills of exchange. In the United States attempts were made to lower interest rates to aid the development of the country, particularly in the West. In the early 1850s, British investors used payments in exchange for their imports into the United States to buy investments there.

As American interest rates came down and European rates rose eventually they met in 1855 and 1856. These events meant that, according to the Banking School's ideas, arbitrage of investment flows would halt as there was no advantage in investing in the United States, particularly with the increased risk of investments there. British-owned securities in America were liquidated, and the bullion was brought back to the United Kingdom. An indication of this can be seen in contemporary falls in American bank shares and in a fall in their bullion holdings. Alongside other domestic problems in the American banking system, this caused serious currency problems. The downturn in the United States which followed, in time, rebounded on banks and brokers in Britain that dealt with America.

However, in the new statistics available on bullion flows, the effect cannot be distinguished from the flows of new gold. Gold had been discovered in California and Australia and this resulted in bullion flows from both areas to the United Kingdom.

Thomas Weguelin and Sheffield Neave, the Governor and Deputy Governor of the Bank of England, told an Enquiry into the Bank Acts in March 1857, before the peak of the crisis, that these discoveries added over £79.3m to the stock of European bullion, between 1851 and 1856, but admitted that the Bank had suffered an overall bullion drain of about £5m during this same period.[31] Much of the new gold passed out to Europe, and bullion, much of it silver, went to Asia, yet they seemed unclear over the role of France.

Legislation in some European countries meant that they were unable to raise interest rates beyond a certain point. France, for instance, set a maximum of 6%. In 1855 the Bank of England raised its Rate above 6% when a peak of bullion, newly arrived from America began to drain away, as new opportunities were found for it in late 1855. But this rate was not enough to reverse the bullion drain, so the Bank increased its rate at the end of 1856 causing the crisis. The high level of rates did not hold back the drain sufficiently and it was raised even higher to 10% as American rates soared in 1857. The Bank of England's bullion reserves peaked in

1859 and then fell sharply at the beginning of the next drain that went on to 1861 (Fig. 6.4).

The price-specie flow mechanism received a boost in reputation because the 1850s showed the highest proportional rise in prices before the crises and a similar fall in prices afterwards, compared with other crises that century. The indication for the Currency School was that bullion flows in payment for trade still had a significant role in international flows and prices. However, this interpretation of the data was challenged by William Jevons in 1863 who pointed to the increased supply of gold.[32] The oscillation of prices in step with crises ceased in 1866 (Figs. 6.3 and 7.2). Up until then, trade remained the dominant factor, but the importance of investment flows was increasingly making Banking-School theory more important. In questioning the Governors of the Bank of England about the crisis, a Parliamentary Committee exposed a difference of opinion about Bank policy in moderating bullion flows. In answer to the question as to whether action to check a foreign drain had consisted of raising the rate of interest or reducing the term of commercial loans, Weguelin, Governor until 1857, replied:

> There is a difference of opinion amongst the Directors. I look more to the restraint which is placed upon the term of bills than to the rate of interest. The restraint upon bills according to my view acts in this way; in the first place, it renders difficult the negotiation of bills of a long date, and thereby tends to diminish the number of bills which are drawn at that date because it is not convenient for importers to import produce, unless they have sufficient time to be able to realise the produce in order to meet the bills.[33]

This attitude was centred around the use of bullion as payment for trade and ignored the now increasing consequences of investment flows. Neave, the Governor that followed Weguelin, thought that both methods were used by the Bank, but linked the limitation of credit with the view of David Ricardo that bullion flows were moderated by changes in the value of money and on prices:

> Now I think the Court look upon them rather as simultaneous and concurrent measures. Those who take the view with Mr. Weguelin, that the limitation of the term of the bills is a stringent measure and a very effective measure as regards the exchanges [i.e. balance of trade], do not lose sight of the important and real effects of it, which consists chiefly in raising the

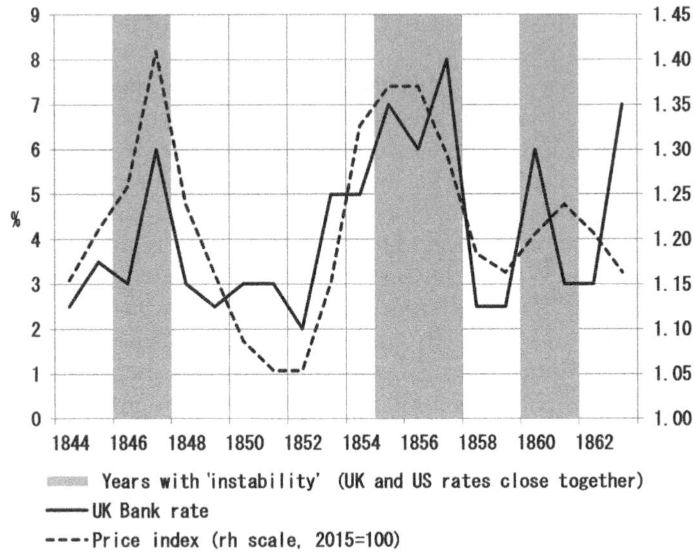

Fig. 6.3 The coincidence of price-index rises and high Bank rates plus bullion drains (years with instability) in the UK in the 1850s (*Source* Bank of England Three Centuries of data v.2.3, cols. A13 F, M9 C)

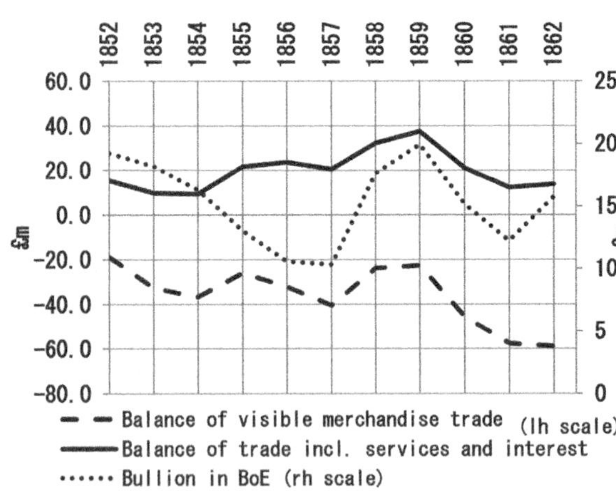

Fig. 6.4 Bullion and coin in the Bank of England compared with balance of trade with and without services and interest 1852–1862 (*Source* Bank of England Three Centuries of data v.2.3, col. A13 F, A24 N, S)

value of money. But the Court look mainly to the raising of the rate of interest as the mode of protecting the bullion.[34]

Figure 6.4 shows that the 1857 drain took place in the context of a dip in the balance of trade. There was a recovery in 1859 which was in parallel with high investment-based bullion flows with total flows in and out of the United Kingdom of around £72m. There was a large fall during the next year to around £48m. Changes in total flow were now becoming as much a predictor of drains as the balance of trade. A considerable increase in the trade deficit occurred in 1861 despite there being a surplus when services and interest are included. Those events were related to the start of the American Civil War and the abandonment of the value of the dollar tied to gold, commonly known as 'the Greenback period'.

The Crimean war, which lasted from late 1853 to early 1856, also provoked hostilities between the Banking School and the Currency School, among themselves as well as between each other. *The Economist* led the charge on the issue of how the war, which was to cost around £49m, was to be paid for in a leading article entitled 'The Finance of the War: Loans or Taxes'.[35] James Wilson, who no doubt at least influenced the article as both editor of the paper and chief secretary of the Treasury, and perhaps mindful of the chaos caused by the attempts to raise a loan for the Irish famine in 1847, counselled that the cost should be raised mainly by taxes. He pointed out that paying by taxes meant that 'the war would not cost the country a shilling more than was actually expended upon it' whereas a loan would be 'abstracted from the existing capital of the country' and therefore reduce credit.[36] In general, John Stuart Mill, a supporter of the Banking School, concurred but disagreed with Wilson over whether an excess of bullion (the reserve was rising in mid-1855) indicated excess savings that enabled loans to be raised safely.[37] Overstone remained confident when, in 1856 he wrote a paper on the 1844 Act for George Cornewall Lewis, the chancellor of the exchequer, claiming that, despite the war, there was enough bullion to 'effectually suppress… all alarm or anxiety'.[38] However, writing in private to Gladstone, in 1855, he had been demanding interest rate rises, alarmed at the bullion flows: 'our Gold is all going to the Mediterranean, and our Silver to India and China- if nothing remains- What then?'[39]

In the end, loans and taxes were used to finance the Crimean war in a two-to-one ratio. The total war expenditure by the British government was nearly £90m.[40] In spite of their size, there were few problems raising the loans. The comparative success of the Crimean loan owed much to lessons learned from the Irish famine and an improved strategy for its issuance. The debt was originally issued on a short-term low-rate basis as Exchequer bills in order to avoid the kind of problems experienced when the Irish loan of £8m was taken out in 1847.[41] Interest rates were raised to 7% to ensure the availability of bullion at the time, except in the United States where this extra demand contributed to the withdrawal of bullion from the banks.

Furthermore, the loans had been taken in tranches at market rates, without attempts to repress the rate as Wood had done for the loan for Ireland. The expenditure of the loan for the war, which mainly was spent on domestically produced arms and soldiers' wages, did not turn out to have the potential consequences on trade that the famine loan did.

6.3 Bullion Flows to France and the Continent

Looking at the various regions causing the bullion flows in detail, the movement towards Europe was initially the strongest. Many European states wished to modernise and expand their economies in the 1850s and saw the United Kingdom as the model with which they were in competition.

France was Britain's closest trading partner and exerted a strong influence on bullion flows. Napoleon III, the nephew of the original Napoleon, wanted to build France into a proud and modern state, but his approach was to copy the best ideas of other nations including Britain rather than confront them. Quentin Hughes has pointed out that his grand tree-lined avenues used in the reconstruction of Paris owe something to the main street of Southport, the English seaside town in which Napoleon III once stayed.[42] The rebuilding of Paris under the direction of Baron Haussmann and his other improvements had a heavy cost and he planned to fund this by modernising the economy, making it more open to trade and by reforming the French banking system.

The British example was followed even to the extent of tracking the interest rate of the Bank of England. When the rate rose above 6%, the limit previously imposed for social reasons, French law was changed to allow it to happen. The policy of the Bank of France however confused its British counterparts by seeming to aim to acquire as much bullion as possible but not to reduce its notes in proportion to the outflow of bullion. However, over the course of 1857, the volume of credit in France decreased by about half and businesses suffered a slump as they did in the United Kingdom. At its lowest point on 20 November 1857, the Bank of France had only a third of its notes in circulation backed by bullion, having in one week lost around £1m.[43]

From the early 1850s, in France, as in the United States, silver coin was replaced with gold. *The Economist* believed this change swallowed up much of the new sources of gold found in Australia and California.[44] The reason given was that the increased supply briefly made gold the cheaper metal, silver then fell in price and was exported to Asia where most currencies were based on it. Britain operated as a conduit for these flows and the Bank had to adjust interest rates carefully to prevent its reserve from being drawn out with the flows. France had only just learnt to adjust its interest rate after many years of keeping it the same. France's share of the bullion exports from the United Kingdom is shown in Table 6.1.

The year 1857 saw the export of £7.107m total gold and silver to France, according to the Bank of England's records, although the Committee on the Bank Acts was told a lower figure.[46] At first, this seems an exception to the normal search for higher returns as United Kingdom and French rates were keeping pace with each other. However, the *Merchants' Magazine* in the United States explained that the Bank of France had lost patience with interest rates and was buying gold at a premium. It had made contracts with M. St. Paul and others to provide a sum of £4m by purchasing in Paris Prussian bills on London using bills on Paris. Claims were forwarded to London, the cash realised and the specie sent to Paris, all in secret so that the Bank of England could not track or prevent it.[47] £1.8m of the bullion France received in 1857 was

Table 6.1 Percentage of bullion exported from UK, imported by France 1851–1857[45]

% Exports of bullion from United Kingdom to France		
Year	*Gold*	*Silver*
1851	30.5	27.5
1852	31.7	8.0
1853	16.6	2.4
1854	80.7	4.0
1855	85.0	6.9
1856	67.6	6.1
1857	61.6	0.7

converted to silver and shipped to the East to pay for the Crimean war.[48] In 1858 £10.637m and in 1859 £15.44m of bullion was sent to France from the United Kingdom.[49] The large capital flows which included this bullion, started another bullion drain from the Bank of England, which caused problems at the beginning of the 1860s. The annual average of bullion in the Banks of England and France 1852–1860 is shown in the following table (Table 6.2).[50]

With information from the Bank's daily account books, it shows that France recharged its coffers after 1857 through the United Kingdom. The Cobden-Chevalier Treaty of January 1860 reduced tariffs between the countries and encouraged trade, which produced further bullion flows between the two countries. Some began to flow in the other direction to the United Kingdom £2.73m in 1858 and £7.3m in 1859 and in 1861 there was a net flow of £1.14m.[52]

Other European countries received large shares of the bullion which passed through Britain. In 1851 and 1852, Portugal took about a tenth of the bullion exported, thanks to its new gold coinage there. In 1854 it adopted a classical gold standard. Exports to the Netherlands and into some of the German states also surged after it was discovered that their gold reserves were deficient:

> In the case of both of those banks [Hamburg and Amsterdam], are not all the notes which they issue represented by bullion actually existing in their coffers?—Yes; that was the supposition, but it was found not to be the case in the bank of Amsterdam at the time of the events which followed the

Table 6.2 Annual Average of bullion (£m) in Banks of England and France 1852–1860[51]

Annual Average of bullion (£m) in:		
Year	*Bank of England*	*Bank of France*
1852	20.7	23.6
1853	17.4	18.0
1854	13.9	16.2
1855	14.3	13.6
1856	11.2	9.0
1857	10.1	9.2
1858	17.7	18.4
1859	17.9	22.7
1860	15.2	20.0

French Revolution; the bullion in deposit in the bank of Amsterdam was found to have been deficient.[53]

Belgium also acquired a sizeable portion of the gold as it set up its economy to follow Peel's model. Stefano Ugolini has identified this as a Mundell–Fleming 'trilemma' and noted that Belgium escaped it by using circulating bullion as a 'buffer'.[54] This makes an interesting comparison with the United Kingdom in 1857. Figure 6.4 shows that the Bank of England bullion reserve increased suddenly in 1858, after the crisis, by £10m. This came from other Bankers' deposits which rose from £2.51m to £10.25m from 10 October 1857 to 13 January 1858. The international flows of bullion, in the same figure, cannot have supplied this amount over 1857; externally, it can only have built up over 1854–1856. Unlike Belgium, where the main bank could rely on bullion recirculating, in the United Kingdom it was stuck in other banks. There need not have been any crisis, it appeared, if the 'other banks' had co-operated. The Bank took revenge by barring bill brokers such as Overend's and other banks from receiving discounts for bills or other advances from its 'discount window' in certain periods from March 1858. This turned the 'competition' in the UK banking system into discord.

6.4 Capital Flows and the United States

Looking closely at the capital flows between Britain and America, it can be seen that the financial crisis of 1857–1858 in both countries was caused by the rise and fall of a carry trade between the two.

In the 1840s there was relatively little British investment in America. The City of London was wary of the United States, because, although the public debt of the country had mostly been paid off by the mid-1830s, previous exports to America, which had been supplied on credit, had not been paid for in full, and this inhibited future investment. As a result, capital inflows into the United States were negative for four years of the 1840s and the trade and specie balance was negative for five.[55]

However, the discovery of gold in California in 1848 brought a renewed bout of optimism and triggered a flood of British investment exploiting a carry trade. Investors thought that there would now be no shortage of bullion to back up payments on loans by railway companies and manufacturers and traders foresaw a boom in the requirements for tools and equipment for prospectors. By 1853 net capital movements into the United States had peaked at 56m dollars (Table 6.3), but then fell sharply. The Bank of England daily account books show that the United Kingdom received around £7.451m in bullion from the United States in 1855, £8.687m in 1856 and £7.697m in 1857.[56] The weekly importations together with a 12-week moving average are shown in Fig. 6.5, which shows that flows to the United Kingdom increased after 1853, when money returned to the United Kingdom because of the high interest rates during the Crimean war. The subsequent peak in 1854 is also consistent with the start of the war and those in mid-1855 and 1856 with British and American interest rates converging, rendering foreign investment no longer being advantageous, in accordance with the Banking School's theories.

Table 6.3 Capital movements into US (imports + ve) $m[57]

Capital movements into US (imports + ve) $m

Year	*$m*	*Year*	*$m*	*year*	*$m*
1851	6	1854	42	1857	17
1852	16	1855	15	1858	−23
1853	56	1856	12	1859	26

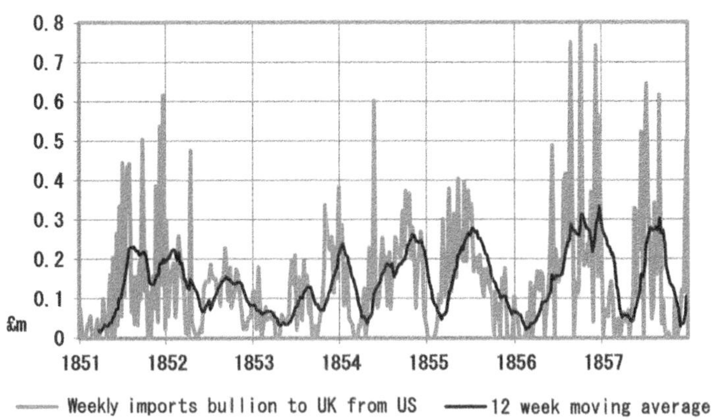

Fig. 6.5 Imports of bullion from America to the United Kingdom, 1851–1857 (*Source* Bank of English daily account books)

In 1853 investments in American railways seemed attractive. *Herapath's Railway and Commercial Journal* reported that dividends over the previous 18 years amounted to between 6% and 8% annually.[58] In 1835 1100 American miles had been built; in 1840 there were 2800, and in 1850, 9000. Lines were encouraged by land grants, tax exemptions and other incentives. A land grant was the offer by the federal government of Western land to provide an American firm security for a loan to purchase materials for railroad construction.[59] As British investors provided a great deal of these funds and British manufacturers exported much of the equipment to America, British investment abroad can be said to have helped British exports. However, their good times came to an end in 1853–1854, when railroad shares began to slide when the capital was first withdrawn. Some firms in the West collapsed in 1857, although others recovered.[60]

By contrast, mining was a very risky investment, but one that attracted a great deal of British capital seeking higher returns. Between 1849 and 1853 shares in nearly 120 public companies seeking to mine gold in Australia and California were offered through London. Some were mining companies and others intended to carry out ancillary tasks such as refining, buying and selling the gold. The capitalisation of the companies was over £15m but in the end, only around £1.75m of investment was received by 42 of them.

The shares became very popular in 1851–1852 and the papers forecast a bubble. By late 1853 it was obvious that something was wrong as the shareholders of many companies could not get details of their activities and financial position.[61] Agua Fria Mining Company, for example, raised over £77,000 but eventually failed.[62] The mine was leased to it by Colonel Frémont, the owner of the estate, through Palmer Cook and Co. for seven years. *The Times* of 11 October 1851 gave the mine the following write-up, probably authored by Sampson, after the company was floated on 5 October 1851:

> It is situated to the south-east of San Fransisco in the Maripoea district, and, according to the prospectus, the vein of gold quartz to be explored is supposed to be of an average thickness of four feet... Specimens of the vein... have been assayed at the United States' Mint and in London and have also been tested at the Bank of England and would give a gross value of £370 per cwt. Almost inexhaustible profits are therefore held out as the prospect of bringing machinery to bear upon this single spot.[63]

According to *The Times*, the company's share price reached as high as 1 1/8 to 1 1/4 on 7 January 1852. However, by March 1855, the company was only just surviving on further loans at 15% interest and little further money was forthcoming. The British public had learned to steer clear of cheap shares promising high yields. On 1 November 1855, they had fallen to the rock bottom price of 1/8 to 1/4 and shortly afterwards ceased being quoted.[64]

American banks suffered badly because they not only held the specie, but had British money invested in them as well. The *Merchants' Magazine* reported in November 1855 that the total specie in New York banks had amounted to $15.298m on 4 August 1855, but fell to $9.919m by 29 September 1855.[65] Circulation and monies discounted only fell about 2%, provoking Currency-School criticism of the American banks that they had not reduced their note issue in line with their bullion reserves.

Bank shares showed a dip in price in 1855 just as American and British interest rates moved together, as shown in the examples in Table 6.4, and a similar drop occurred in October 1857. Two months after the Ohio Life Insurance and Trust Company failed in August 1857, other banks followed its lead. New York banks had to send increasing amounts of specie to banks in the interior of the country as the rush to redeem notes increased after the Bank of Pennsylvania failed on 25 September. Eventually, they had to suspend specie payments. Other businesses unable to obtain credit failed. New York was the worst hit in this respect with more than 6% of all businesses failing as a result of the crisis, followed by Boston and Philadelphia, the main commercial centres. States further inland, such as Wisconsin, also fared badly with 4.52% of businesses failing.[67] The lesson that the Banking School drew from this was that when interest rates move together, it is the high-yielding investment (in this case the American side) that suffers most as funds stop flowing. Of course, the weakest and least genuine firms fail first, and there were other factors that determined why some banks went bankrupt and others not, but it is clear that the rise and fall of a carry trade explain the timing of the crisis.

6.5 Capital Flows to Egypt, India and China

From 1853 capital began to flow east in preference to America. Egypt received 74% of the silver flowing out of the United Kingdom, partly to fund the beginnings of the Alexandria to Cairo railway line.[68] British investment into Indian railways also grew strongly. Investors were made

Table 6.4 Example falls in US bank shares in the period October–November 1855[66]

US Bank Share falls		
Name of Bank	*Quotations (high to low)*	*Period of fall*
Exchange Bank of Virginia, Richmond	105 to 100	19 Oct.–26 Oct. 1855
Farmers Bank, Richmond	105.5 to 95	9 Oct.–26 Oct. 1855
Bank of Virginia, Richmond	73 to 70	14 Sept.–9 Oct. 1855
Baltimore Bank	103 to 98	24 Nov.–8 Dec. 1855
Atlas Bank, Charleston	107 to 103	24 Nov.–8 Dec. 1855
Blackstone Bank, Boston	106.5 to 103	27 Sept.–27 Oct. 1855
Boston Bank	60 to 58	27 Sept.–4 Oct. 1855

to feel secure by a government of India guarantee of the return of the face value of the shares. For example, when the railway was running, if the net profit was 4% and the face value 5%, the government would have to make up the shortfall of 1%. However, if the net profit was 7%, the government would not have to contribute but would receive 1% and the remaining 6% would be paid to shareholders. The government's 1% would go to pay off its previous contributions with interest. When this was done, the shareholders were to receive all the profit. Government payments were laid off against receipts due from India to the British government to minimise transfers.

The yields offered by these securities were attractive compared with safe investments at home such as consols (Fig. 6.6). By 1859 the Indian railway companies' capitalisation exceeded £168m of which £27m had been paid in, indicating the success and scale of the enterprise.[69] However the East India Company had become corrupt, profiting from hypothecation loans used as a type of carry trade, and insensitive to local customs. In 1857 the Indian sepoys rose in revolt against high-handed and oppressive Company rule—particularly its ignorance of their religions—and it took excessively brutal action by the Company's army to restore order

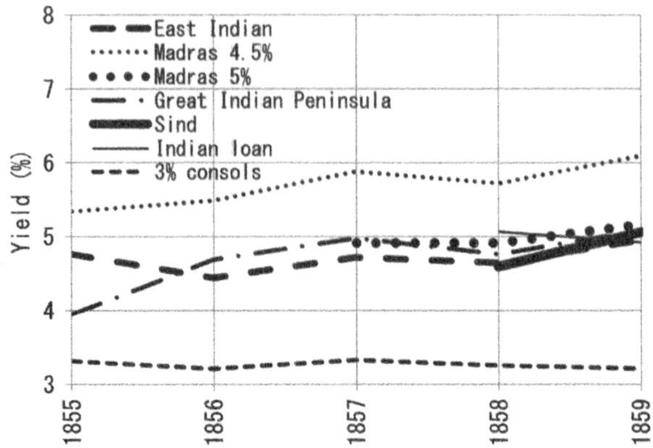

Fig. 6.6 Average annual yield for Indian Railway Securities and the Indian loan 1858, 1855–1859, compared with the yield from UK consols (*Source* Report to the Secretary of State for India in Council on Railways in India PP 1860 [2669] LII.635 p. 28)

and regain control of its 'possessions'. Following this failure of management, the British state formally took over the East India Company's rule in India. The railway shares show only a slight drop in yields over this period and they start climbing again almost immediately along with the 'Indian Loan' which was to contribute towards the cost of the war and the buying out of the East India Company's shareholders. Of course, the first thoughts of the government, on taking over India were of a fiscal squeeze. As the Earl of Ellenborough put it:

> It is the duty of the person, whoever he may be, who is placed at the head of Indian affairs in this country, to endeavour so to reduce expenditure in India as to make that expenditure, if possible, come within the revenue. That, undoubtedly, is his first duty; and, above all, I desire and trust that we shall effect the object of relieving this country from any burden on account of India.[70]

James Wilson was appointed as the first financial member of the Viceroy's Executive Council in India. He put in place a new banking system, a new currency, a reformed system of public accounts and the country's first income tax. He proposed a currency backed one-third by bullion and a variable amount of securities that allowed the circulation to expand with commerce, in accordance with his Banking-School views and in disagreement with the Bank Charter Act of 1844. They made use of a non-government commissioner to run the currency but were less 'free Banking' than Wilson's usual prescriptions were. His new policy regime was challenged by Charles Wood, who was by now the Secretary of State for India. However, Wilson's proposals managed to win over the British press, thanks, in part, to the publicity and support that *The Economist* unsurprisingly gave them.[71]

The arrangement increased opportunities for involvement of the Bank of England in Indian finances and enabled it to increase its stocks of bullion in the 1860s and weather financial crises more effectively after 1866. However, at first, the Bank was sceptical of the opportunities that the British government's direct takeover of India offered. In March 1858 the Court of Directors moved and seconded that the Governors be empowered to tender for a portion of the New Indian Loan up to £1m, upon which an amendment was moved:

> that it has always been a practice with the Bank of England to rely upon the security of no governments excepting the British, unless to a limited extent, as respects India bonds.
>
> That in conformity with the above practice, this Court has uniformly refused to purchase or advance upon Colonial Bonds, unless they possess an Imperial Guarantee.
>
> That the proposed Indian Loan has no legal security excepting that furnished by the Revenue of India and consequently falls within the above practice.[72]

This reaction was in line with the general opinion of the Currency School at the time. The *Times* commented that 'India must provide for her own pecuniary wants in the same manner as Canada, Australia, or any other possession', as it appeared legislation would limit the Indian loan to being raised in India.[73] Nevertheless, demand from British investors for Indian debt proved to be strong. An Indian loan of £5m was advertised in London on 13 August 1859 at 5% and was subscribed at between 97 (3% discount) and par (0% discount) within 10 days.[74]

Although Britain's increasing financial linkages and flows to India were the most notable trend during this period, a good deal of British capital also went to China. The East India Company had developed a triangular trade, which helped to pay for the export of goods from China to the

United Kingdom without the need to move bullion. Goods such as tea (to which the British were rapidly becoming accustomed, if not addicted) arrived in the United Kingdom, manufactured goods were transported to India and opium, grown in India, was transported to China to feed the definite addiction there and pay for the original exports of goods such as tea.

There was criticism of this trade in England and resistance to it in China, which culminated in the opium wars between 1856 and 1860.[75] Over the period of the war, it was necessary once again to pay for Chinese goods with bullion. Overall, the east received £10.9m in silver from the United Kingdom in 1856 and £16.4m in 1857.[76] After dealing with the 'mutiny' (or 'Great Rebellion' as it is now known) in India, Britain dispatched forces to Canton in a joint operation with America, French and Russian forces (now all allies rather than foes) against China.[77] The Chinese gave in and agreed to a treaty giving trading and various other rights, but when they dragged their feet once again in implementing it, Admiral Sir James Hope shelled the Chinese forts at the mouth of the Peiho River in 1859. The next year Emperor Xianfeng's Summer Palace in Chengde was looted and destroyed. The Chinese were thus forced to implement the agreement, relieving some of the pressure on the Bank of England's bullion reserves and aiding the recovery of Britain's financial system after the 1857–1858 crisis.

6.6 The Worst Period of the Crisis

Bullion flows in the early 1850s had only a minor effect on interest rates which was put down to the introduction of the transfer of monies between banks by cheques drawn on the Bank of England rather than by bank notes.[78] The Clearing House for cheques, which had started in 1773 as a room in the Five Bells public house, was moved to a permanent home in Lombard Street in 1833. Some joint-stock banks, allowed to be created under the 1833 Banking Act, were admitted as members of the Bankers' Clearing House in 1854. This step reduced the number of banknotes in circulation needed for interbank transfers and thereby increased effective circulation.

The problem in 1857, however, was also a lack of credit when banks could not cash their assets immediately. News of the problems of the Ohio Life and Trust Company arrived on 8 October and the timing and speed of the bullion drain suggests that it was caused by banknote holders anxious to exchange them for gold, fearing that bank failures would spread. The Bank Rate was raised to 7% on 29 October 1857. The July 1858 Parliamentary Committee reported:

> Before 8 October the tidings from America had become very serious; news of the suspension of cash payments by the banks in Philadelphia and Baltimore was received; cotton bills were reduced to par, and bankers' drafts to 105; railroad securities were depreciated from 10 to 20 per cent; the artisans were getting out of employment; and discounts ranged from 18% to 24%. The transactions between America and England are so intimate, and so large, the declared value of British and Irish produce exported in 1856 to the United States having been £21,918,000, while the amount of securities held by English capitalists in America was by some persons estimated at £80m that this serious state of commercial disorder there could not but produce in this country great alarm.[79]

The news from the United States caused runs on the banks in Glasgow, Liverpool and London where most American business was done. On 27 October 1857 the Borough Bank of Liverpool closed its doors and on 7 November the commercial house of Messrs. Dennistoun & Co. suspended payment. The Borough Bank in Liverpool was linked to Dennistoun of Glasgow, through common directors and shareholders, and the cotton business in America. Dennistoun had branches in London, France, Melbourne, New York and New Orleans. The Western Bank of Scotland failed on 9 November, and on 11 November the City of Glasgow Bank temporarily suspended its payments. Failures also spread inland to include those that did little business with America directly. The Northumberland and Durham District Bank failed on 26 November, and the Wolverhampton Bank for a time suspended payment from 17 November.[80]

An important difference between the attitudes of the Schools as to why the stoppages and bankruptcies took place emerged from these events. The Currency School's attitude, already expressed by Overstone in 1855, was that high interest rates were 'a necessary price' for maintaining convertibility and should be tolerated as such.[81] *The Economist* published an article in 1860 that pointed out that 'a banker gets, speaking generally, [this referred mainly to the Bank of England] much money for nothing, but a bill broker pays a high rate for every sixpence left with him' and the brokers needed to make specific checks when discounting. High interest rates therefore were an issue for the bill brokers and small banks.[82] As the Bank Rate rose above the long-term rate any money raised in the short-term market and invested long-term was at risk. High interest rates shortened the time which an institution in trouble had in which it could borrow and keep running while it realised time-dependent investments. The Borough Bank had not carried out *The Economist*'s checks, but many did not at that time.

Bonamy Dobree, deputy Governor 1857–1859, kept a diary in which a basic account for the Borough Bank is recorded as he assessed its application for assistance, along with others.[83] It gives an insight into how interest rates made it easy for banks and firms to fail in crises. The Borough Bank's accounts appear in his diary as follows:

Boro' Bank				
Dr			*Cr*	
Capital pd. up		£1,000,000	Cash and good bills	168,000
Lost		400,000	Funds	220,000
[Net capital pd. up]		600,000	Open & readily collected	350,000
Deposits		1,200,000	do. requiring time	1,258,000
Liabilities in Bills				
	3,500,000			
Good	2,668,000	832,000		
Acceptances	50,000			
Outstanding credits	350,000			
		2,632,000		1,996,000

The accounts show that the Bank had shareholders' equity left of minus £36,000 on liabilities of £2.032m to depositors and bill holders: a situation that it could not recover from while financing itself on debt at a high rate of interest. £1m of the discounted bills was with Overend's of which £0.3m was doubtful. On 29 October 1857 David Chapman visited Dobree, seeking reassurance that they could rely on the Bank for 'unlimited assistance', but he was told that 'loans to brokers must depend on the circumstances at the time'.[84] Nevertheless, the Bank of England offered the Borough Bank a loan if a suitable guarantee bond could be raised, but this arrangement did not materialise.

The Western Bank of Scotland had already had a chequered history. In 1834, only two years in business, it had to be supported by a £0.1m loan from the main Edinburgh banks, because of its low reserves and indiscriminate lending. Similar shortcomings caused difficulties in 1847, but that time the Bank of England had to come to the rescue with a £0.3m loan. The bank collapsed in 1857, due to the failure of three major customers, owing between them £1.2m. The Bank was criticised for preferring to lend to a few large traders rather than small local ones, which would have spread the risk and not left the Bank waiting for a large proportion of its funds at a time of high interest rates.[85] Customers did not lose out as other Scottish banks supported them, but the bank's shareholders lost their whole investment and became liable for the bank's debts.

The government was panicked into suspending the 1844 Bank Act again and a letter to the Bank of England was issued on 12 November 1857, in the following terms:

> Gentlemen, Downing-Street
>
> Her Majesty's Government have observed with great concern the serious consequences which have ensued from the recent failure of certain Joint Stock Banks in England and Scotland, as well as of certain large mercantile firms, chiefly connected with the American trade. The discredit and distrust which have resulted from these events, and the withdrawal of a large amount of the paper circulation authorised by the existing Bank Acts, appear to Her Majesty's Government to render it necessary for them to inform the Directors of the Bank of England, that if they should be unable in the present emergency to meet the demands for discounts and advances upon approved securities without exceeding the limits of their circulation prescribed by the Act of 1844, the Government will be prepared to propose to Parliament, upon its meeting, a Bill of Indemnity for any excess so issued.
>
> In order to prevent this temporary relaxation of the law being extended beyond the actual necessities of the occasion, Her Majesty's Government are of opinion that the Bank terms of discount should not be reduced below their present rate.
>
> Her Majesty's Government reserve for future consideration the appropriation of any profit which may arise upon issues in excess of the statutory amount.
>
> Her Majesty's Government are fully impressed with the importance of maintaining the letter of the law, even in a time of considerable mercantile difficulty; but they believe that, for the removal of apprehensions which have checked the course of monetary transactions, such a measure as is now contemplated has become necessary, and they rely upon the discretion

> and prudence of the Directors for confining its operation within the strict limits of the exigencies of the case.
>
> We have, &c. (Signed) *Palmerston, G. C. Lewis.*
>
> To the Governor and Deputy-Governor of the Bank of England.[86]

Three days later, by 15 November, bullion in the Bank had increased to £4.23m. In 1847 it was not found necessary for the Bank Directors to use the permission so given to them to exceed the limits on notes imposed by law, but that necessity in 1857 actually arose. Dobree's diary of 14 November, notes that 'all the notes in the Banking department are exhausted'.[87] The fiduciary issue was increased to the extent of £2m beyond the previous legal limit and was used between the weeks of 18 November and 23 December 1857. The Bank's note reserve, according to the original limit, was actually negative: –£0.85m in the first week and –£0.08m in the second. After the letter was issued, matters improved very quickly, and at the end of the year, the note reserve was £6.06m on the original basis of the law.

6.7 The Consequences of the Crisis

In parallel with the crisis, a debate had been taking place about renewing the Charter of the Bank of England. There was a group of MPs who considered that the Bank should be held responsible for the losses incurred by commerce, and there was a prospect that the Bank would be sued for damages. Those who protected the Bank preferred to talk about a Bill of Indemnity. Gladstone, by then in opposition, attempted to defuse this argument by emphasising the support the Bank had given to other banks and commerce. However, he also suggested that the Bank should feel guilty over its profits made by the increased rate and these should be returned to the government.[88] Gladstone as chancellor of the exchequer again in 1859 did try to bear down on the Bank's charges for providing services to the government, but it is not clear whether any excess profits found their way to the Treasury. This was one of the factors that triggered the Bank to compete more fiercely with its rivals and to be more proactive in expanding its own business, to make up for the squeeze on their income from rival discounters as well as from the government. This sowed the seeds for the next crisis in 1866.

The Economist of 20 February 1858 pointed out that exports had fallen in 1857, contrary to the theories of the Currency School, which suggested

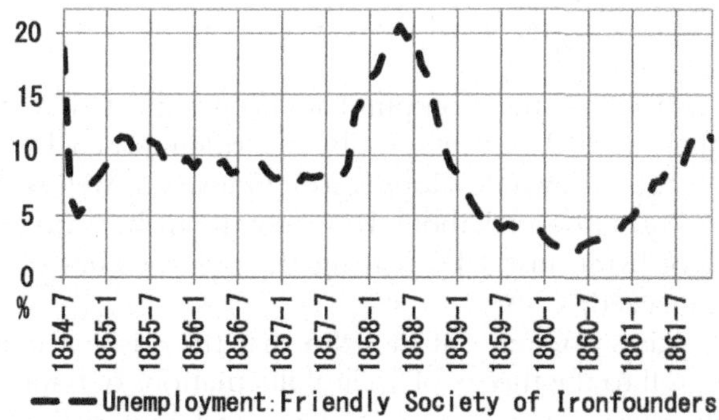

Fig. 6.7 Unemployment among member of Friendly Society of Ironworkers from July 1854 to December 1861 (*Source* Statistical Tables and Report on Trade Unions PP XCII 1890–1891 [c.6475] pp. 522–523)

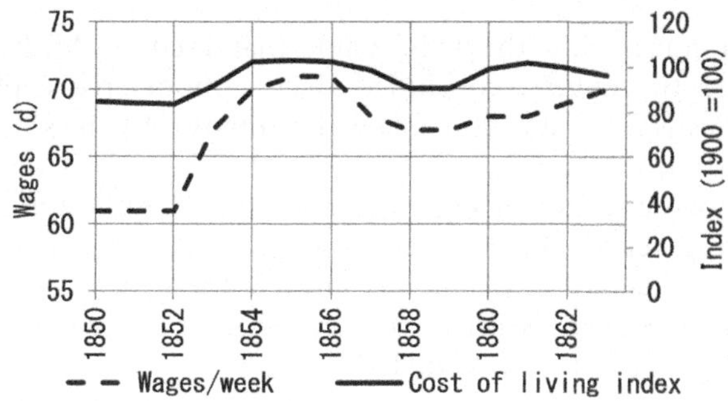

Fig. 6.8 Average wages/week compared with cost-of-living index (*Source* Bank of England Three Centuries of data v.2.3 cols. A26 K, A26)

that they should have risen and prices fallen.[89] The article concluded that it was then not the balance of trade that mattered but 'the balance *of payments*', or the actual flows of money and bullion, emphasising that Banking-School considerations of investment flows as well as trading flows needed to be taken into account.

The events of 1857 caused a noticeable rise in unemployment in heavy manufacturing, up to 20% among ironworkers (Fig. 6.7). Workers in Scotland and Wales were particularly affected, as contemporary reports in *The Times* and *Mining Journal* recorded.[90] One of the well-known steel makers of this period, Naylor Vickers & Co. of Sheffield, suspended operations (Fig. 6.8).[91]

About a quarter of their output had been exported to the United States and they were disadvantaged by a tariff imposed by the United States to protect their own developing iron industry as well as the financial disturbance. Wages dropped about 15% over the main period of the crisis and the cost of living just 10%, leaving the real incomes of the general population squeezed.

J. R. T. Hughes pointed out in 1956 that the crisis of the 1850s did not conform well to the theory of cyclical fluctuations of trade and its relationship with depression and crises[92]. This can be interpreted as another sign of the change from a cycle of crisis linked to prices as the main influence upon interest rates to a main influence of investment opportunities. Whatever the mix of influences, the Banking School believed that the consequent change in rate exacerbated the commercial and banking failures.

It was in considering the 1857 panic that Frederic Mishkin, writing in the twentieth century, concluded that 'a monetarist explanation of financial crises is...not able to explain the timing of panics'. He gave an explanation based on an asymmetric information analysis that saw bank panics 'as a consequence of high interest rates'.[93] Although very similar to the Banking School theory of crises, the Mishkin explanation does not focus on the equalisation of interest rates as the trigger—one identified by the Banking School earlier in the century and one which they saw as clearly playing out in the crisis of 1857–1858.

Notes

1. *Hansard*, 11 December 1857, CXLVIII, cc. 645–46.
2. *First Report from the Secret Committee on Commercial Distress* PP 1847–1848 (395) VIII. 1, VIII. 379, p. viii.
3. D. Hurd, *Robert Peel: A Biography* (London: Phoenix, 2008) pp. 383–384.
4. M. B. Sampson, *The Currency under the Act of 1844... from the "City" Articles of The Times* (London: John Van Noorst, 1858) pp. 8–9, 81–82.
5. Idem., pp. 20–22.
6. *Hansard*, 3 December 1857, CXLVIII, cc. 78–79.
7. *The Bankers' Magazine and State Financial Register*, 1847 volume, p. 61.
8. *Mining Journal*, 23 January 1875, p. 100; J. Taylor, 'Watchdogs or Apologists? Financial Journalism and Company Fraud in Early Victorian

Britain', *Historical Research* 85 (2012) 649; Idem., 'Financial crises and the Birth of the Financial Press 1825–80', in *The Media and Financial Crises* (Abingdon: Routledge, 2015) pp. 209–211.

9. *Reynold's Newspaper*, 8 October 1876, p. 2.
10. *The Economist*, 14 November 1857, pp. 1257–1258.
11. Idem., 21 November 1857, p. 1287.
12. Idem., 28 November 1857, p. 1313.
13. Idem., 28 November 1857, pp. 1313–1315.
14. Idem., 28 November 1857, pp. 1316–1318; W. Bagehot, N. St. John-Stevas (ed.), *The Collected Works of Walter Bagehot* IX, (London: The Economist, 1978) pp. 373–374, 377; Idem., X, pp. 379–380. The concern appears in Bagehot's first writings in *The Economist* which appear as letters to the editor from 'A Banker'. He became editor in 1861.
15. D. M. Evans, *The City or the Physiology of London Business* (London: Baily Bros., 1845) pp. 29, 44; Idem., *Facts, Failures and Frauds* (London: Groombridge & Sons., 1854) p. iv.
16. M. B. Sampson, *Slavery in the United States* (London: S. Highley, 1845) p. 10; Mill to Christie, 12 September 1864, in J. S. Mill, F. E. Mineka, D. N. Lindley (eds.), *The Collected Works of John Stuart Mill* XV—Part II (London: Routledge and Kegan Paul, 1972).
17. D. Kynaston, *The City of London* I (London: Pimlico, 1994–5) pp. 267–8; *Globe*, 1 April 1875, p. 4; *Daily News* 22 December 1874, pp. 3, 19 January 1875, pp. 3–4; Articles found to be libellous *The Times* 18, 20 November 1872, 20 December 1872.
18. *Rubery v. Grant and Sampson*, verdict reported in *Daily News* and editorial, 19 January 1875, pp. 3–4.
19. *Twycross v. Grant* reported in *Daily News*, 8 July 1876, p. 3; 12 July 1876, pp. 3–4; Evans was mentioned being given £50 at the *Standard,* Sampson received £275, *Morning Post*, 8 July 1876, p. 3, *Lloyd's Illustrated Newspaper*, 9 July 1876, p. 7.
20. Henry Grey to Grey, 22 February 1886, Grey papers, Durham UL, GRE/B90/1/93.
21. D. Kynaston, (abridged D. Milner), *City of London: The History* (London: Chatto & Windus, 2012) p. 158.
22. *The Economist*, 28 November 1857, p. 1317.
23. *The Economist*, tended to give Overend's explanations full coverage when the bill broker's clients had led them into questionable positions; examples: 19 (p. 544), 26 (pp. 572–574) May 1855, 2 (p. 594), 23 (p. 671) June 1855, 14 July 1855 (p. 756), 22 December 1855 (p. 1410), 25 December 1858 (p. 1427).
24. *The Economist*, 23 June 1855, p. 671.
25. Ibid.

26. Samuel Gurney of Overend, Gurney and Co. was a supporter of the Anti-Slavery Convention and was included in the painting of members by B. J. Haydon, *National Portrait Gallery* (1840); In 1833, some directors of the Bank of England had been included in a publicly available list of those who received compensation as slave owners PP 1837–1838 (215) XLVIII. 331.
27. Examples: *The Economist* records that in 1859, Overend's discounted bills at 2¼%, placed endorsements on them, using their name to make them more reliable, and let them out to other dealers at 1 7/8%: 'profit 3/8%', *The Economist*, 12 February 1859, p. 178; In 1855, Overend's had managed to obtain 5% for a short term loan from Sir John Paul because 'his creditworthiness was tarnished' when money was available on call from 3% to 3.5%, *The Economist*, 14 July 1855, p. 756. On default remaining funds were often locked up in long-term investments.
28. C. W. Calomiris, L. Schweickart, 'The Panic of 1857: Origins, Transmission, and Containment', *Journal of Economic History* 51 (1991) pp. 807–809.
29. P. Temin, 'The Panic of 1857', *Intermountain Review*, 6 (1975) 1–12.
30. T. Tooke, W. Newmarch, *History of Prices* VI (London: Longmans, 1857) pp. 1–134.
31. *Report from Select Committee on Bank Acts*, PP 1857 Session 2 (220 220–221) X Pt. I.1, p. 3.
32. W. S. Jevons, *A Serious Fall in the Value of Gold* (London: Stanford, 1863).
33. *Report*... PP 1857 Session 2 (220 220-1) X Pt. I.1, p. 31.
34. Idem., p. 33.
35. *Hansard*, 6 March 1856, CXL, cc. 1932–33, cc. 1948–9; *The Economist*, 20 January 1855, pp. 53–54.
36. Ibid.
37. *The Economist*, 14 April 1855, p. 389.
38. D. P. O'Brien, *The Correspondence of Lord Overstone* (Cambridge, CUP, 1971) p. 670.
39. Idem., p. 626.
40. *Report*... PP 1857 Session 2 (220, 220–2211) X Pt.II–1, p. vi.
41. Exchequer Bonds Act, 1854 17 Vic c. 23; O'Brien, *The Correspondence of Lord Overstone*, pp. 667–664, p. 626; facing p. 64.
42. *The Times*, 25 April 2000.
43. *Report*... PP 1857 Session 2 (220, 220–221) X Pt.II, p. 1x.
44. *The Economist*, 13 December 1851, p. 433.
45. Bank of England daily account books 1854–58; *Gold and Silver bullion* PP 1854 (516) XXXIX.439, pp. 8–13.
46. *Report*... PP 1857 Session 2 (220, 220–221) X Pt.II, Appendix no. 12, p. 404; Bank of England daily account book, 1857.

47. *Hunt's Merchants' Magazine and Commercial Review*, November 1855, pp. 600–601.
48. *Report...* PP 1857 Session 2 (220, 220–221) X Pt.II, Appendix 12, p. 404.
49. Bank of England daily account books, 1858, 1859.
50. F. Jourdan, 'The Effect of the Gold Supplies on the Foreign Exchanges Between the United Kingdom and Foreign Countries, and on the Price of Silver', *Journal of the Statistical Society of London* 24 (1861) p. 52.
51. Bank of England daily account books, 1852 to 1860; Jourdan, 'The Effect of the Gold Supplies'.
52. Bank of England daily account books, 1852 to 1860.
53. *Report...* PP 1857 Session 2 (220, 220–221) X Pt.II, p. 189.
54. S. Ugolini, 'The Origins of Foreign Exchange Policy: The National Bank of Belgium', *European Review of Economic History* (2012) p. 70.
55. D. North, 'The United States Balance of Payments', in *The Conference on Research in Income and Wealth* (Princeton: Princeton UP, 1960) p. 605.
56. Bank of England daily account books 1856 and 1857, figures originally from *Morning Chronicle*.
57. Bureau of the Census, *Historical Statistics of the United States,* series U18–25.
58. *Herapath's Railway and Commercial Journal*, 9 April 1853.
59. S. F. Van Oss, *American Railroads and British Investors* (London: Effingham Wilson, 1893).
60. Calomiris, Schweikart, 'The Panic of 1857', 807–834.
61. J. Woodland, *Money Pits: British Mining Companies in the Californian Gold Rushes of the 1850s* (Farnham: Ashgate, 2014) pp. xi–xii.
62. Woodland, *Money Pits*, p. 247.
63. *The Times*, 11 October 1851, p. 3.
64. *The Times*, 7 Jan 1852, pp. 3, 13 September 1854, pp. 5, 27 December 1854, 1 November 1855.
65. *Hunt's Merchants' Magazine and Commercial Review*, November 1855, p. 595.
66. eh.net/database/early-u-s-securities-prices/ [accessed 3 August 2020].
67. Calomiris, Schweikart, 'The panic of 1857', p. 814.
68. *Gold and Silver bullion* PP 1854 (516) XXXIX.439, pp. 12–13.
69. Ibid., pp. 38–39.
70. *Hansard*, 19 March 1858, CXLIV, c. 415.
71. S. Bhattacharya, *The Financial Foundations of the British Raj* (New Delhi: Orient Longman, 2005) p. 87.
72. Bank of England court of directors minutes, 25 March 1858.
73. *The Times*, 15 March 1858, p. 7.
74. Bank of England daily account book.
75. *Hansard*, 9 March 1857, CXLIV, c. 2049; 4 April 1859, CLIII, c. 1377.

76. Bank of England daily account books.
77. J. Y. Wong, *Deadly Dreams: Opium and the Arrow War (1856–60) in China* (Cambridge, CUP, 1998) pp. 9–10, 43–66.
78. *Select Committee on the Bank Acts* PP 1857 (220 220–221) X PtI.1, p. 60.
79. *Report from the Select Committee on the Bank Acts* PP 1857 (381) X Pt.II, p. xxxviii.
80. *The Bankers' Magazine* and *The Times*, various issues.
81. S. J. Loyd (Lord Overstone), *Tracts and Other publications* (London: Longman, 1858) p. 355.
82. *The Economist*, 2 September 1860, p. 896.
83. Diaries of Bonamy Dobree, Bank of England archives, page after 25 October 1857.
84. Idem., 29 October 1857.
85. *Glasgow Herald*, 23 October 1857, p. 6.
86. *Select Committee on Operation of Bank Acts, and Causes of recent Commercial Distress* PP 1857–1858 (381) V.1, p. lv.
87. Diaries of Bonamy Dobree, Bank of England archives, 14 November 1857.
88. *Hansard*, 4 December 1857, CXLVIII, cc. 145–179; 9 December 1857, CXLVIII, cc. 444–445.
89. *The Economist*, 20 February 1858, p. 194.
90. *The Times*, 6 July 1857, *Mining Journal*, 18 July 1857, 1 August 1857.
91. *The Engineer*, 13 November 1857, p. 372.
92. J. R. T. Hughes, 'The Commercial Crisis of 1857' *Oxford Economic Papers* NS8 2 (1956), pp. 218–220.
93. F. S. Mishkin. 'Anatomy of a financial crisis', *NBER Working paper* no. 3934, p. 15.

CHAPTER 7

The Uncertainties of the 1860s and the Crisis of 1866

> If we delegate to the gentlemen in Threadneedle Street the power of hoisting at the right time the storm signal, there ought to be some means of protecting those who suffer damage from that signal being kept flying needlessly long.
>
> —Edward Watkin, MP for Stockport, chairman of railway company, *Hansard*, 31 July 1866, CLXXXIV, c. 1716.[1]

The financial crisis of 1866 is famous in British banking. It was the last major systemically important banking crisis in Great Britain resulting from the Bank of England's use of monetary policy for 107 years until the secondary banking crisis of 1973–1975. It also saw the last high-profile or major bank run in British history for 141 years, until Northern Rock suffered one during the global financial crisis of 2007–2009.[2] One explanation for the disappearance of major crises in late Victorian Britain is that this situation was the result of a cartel that was later formed in banking to prevent excessive competition and risk-taking.[3] However, economic historians have since found that the return from capital in banking was not out of line with other sectors, in what would otherwise be a tell-tell sign of a particularly cartelised industry.[4] Another explanation is that the Bank of England adopted what later became 'Bagehot's dictum' during the crisis of 1866. That is for the Bank to lend on good securities 'quickly, freely, and readily', though at a penal rate of interest, to prevent runs on the

C. Read, *Calming the Storms*, Palgrave Studies in Economic History,
https://doi.org/10.1007/978-3-031-11914-9_7

country's financial institutions.[5] Emergency lending by the Bank, totalling £4m during the collapse of Overend, Gurney & Co., Britain's largest bill discounter, in May 1866 prevented a much larger crisis.[6] However, as Sabine Schneider has convincingly pointed out in a recent article, the Bank's evolving approach to crisis lending in the 1860s was much more shaped by its profitmaking objectives and its quest to preserve its autonomy from the Treasury.[7] To build and maintain public confidence in the country's financial system to prevent crises under Walter Bagehot's dictum, the Bank would need to pre-commit to 'lender of last resort' lending during periods of crisis. The problem is that the Bank never officially committed to this in the 1860s; many on its court of directors after the 1866 crisis still opposed it taking on such a role. Anthony Hotson has already pointed to the evolution of market practices other than Bagehot's dictum for the rise of British banking stability.[8] This chapter provides a fuller explanation for the events of 1866, one which suggests that the Banking School's other ideas about crises played a much greater role in the Bank's development of its policies to prevent them in the 1860s and beyond.

The ideas of the Banking School in this era can best be understood in the context of what its intellectual opponents were arguing. After the collapse of Overend's and with it the Banking School's hopes that it could rival the Bank of England, the Currency School was in an arrogant state of ascendency. Lord Overstone was in regular contact with George Norman, a director of the Bank from 1821 to 1872 throughout the period, pushing his philosophy.[9] The Currency School's response to the 1866 crisis at its most banal was voiced by Hammond Chubb, secretary to the Bank of England for 30 years from 1847.[10] In a lecture to the Statistical Society published in 1872, he responded to three criticisms of the Bank Charter Act of 1844 in a dismissive tone. To the complaint that extreme variations in interest rates were damaging commerce, he replied that this was 'nothing to do with the Act'; to the call for a note issue that expanded with commercial needs, he queried 'what kind of trade' wanted to be carried on outside 'safe limits'?; to the suggestion from traders that they had a right to access discounting of their bills of exchange, Chubb described this process as 'trading beyond their means'.[11]

Those serious commentators associated with the Banking School came back however with compromise solutions, which turned out to be the ones that calmed the storms at the end of the century. The crisis of 1866 is often quoted as providing the *raison d'être* of central banks. The Bank of England, as the narrative goes, provided lending facilities for other financial institutions after Overend's failed and 'inspired Bagehot's principles for lender of last resort' some of which 'can still be seen in the Bank of England's approach to liquidity assistance today'.[12] This viewpoint has been most enthusiastically propagated by the Bank of England itself almost as if it was its own invention. However, Bagehot's dictum is a compromise between the Currency-School and Banking-School positions: maximising the credit available to commerce, but maintaining some limit and restraining moral hazard by using a high rate.[13]

Bagehot's 'principles for lender of last resort' have received credit for the lack of systemic banking crises after 1866, but there are additional reasons for this stability. The increase in the reserves of the Bank of England is an important one. So is the gradual integration of short-term and long-term interest rates between the United States and United Kingdom which decreased capital flows and therefore volatility which might have caused sudden bullion drains from the Bank of England.

More importantly however, the Bank of England managed its Bank Rate in a more subtle manner using very prompt but minor variations in the rate, in response to fluctuations in their bullion reserves (Fig. 7.1). The price level stopped fluctuating in time with interest rates and the occurrence of crises or disturbances, and it began to decline in a less volatile fashion than it had before (Fig. 7.2). In line with this trend, the total bullion flows in and out that the United Kingdom experienced exceeded its trade deficits in goods and services. The total activity with the United States continued as a moderate but important part of international bullion flows passing through the United Kingdom (Fig. 7.3). Total bullion flows capture both imports and exports of capital as flows reverse in a crisis and the measure is therefore generally high in periods of crisis and minor events. On the basis of the Bank's ratios of cash to total assets and of note reserves to total deposits, 1866 can clearly be seen as the last crisis of the nineteenth century that threatened the legal currency system (Figs. 3.6 and 3.7).

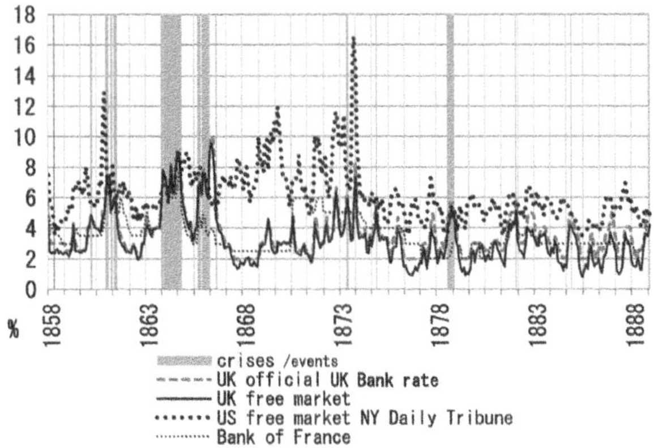

Fig. 7.1 Short-term interest rates in the UK, US and France 1858–1889 (*Sources New York Daily Tribune*, Bank of England Three Centuries of data v.2.3, col. M9 C, *The Economist*, L. J. Loutchitch, *Des Variations de l'Intérêt en France* [1930], NBER database)

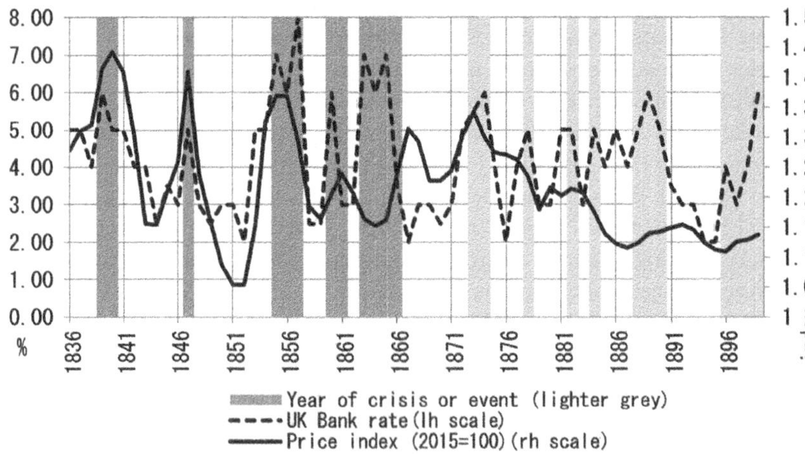

Fig. 7.2 UK Bank rate and CPI price index (2015 = 100) against the occurrence of crises and disturbances after the 1860s (*Sources* Bank of England, Three Centuries of data v2.3, sheet A19 column B, sheet A26 column S; disturbances are as author's equalisation of interest rates analysis)

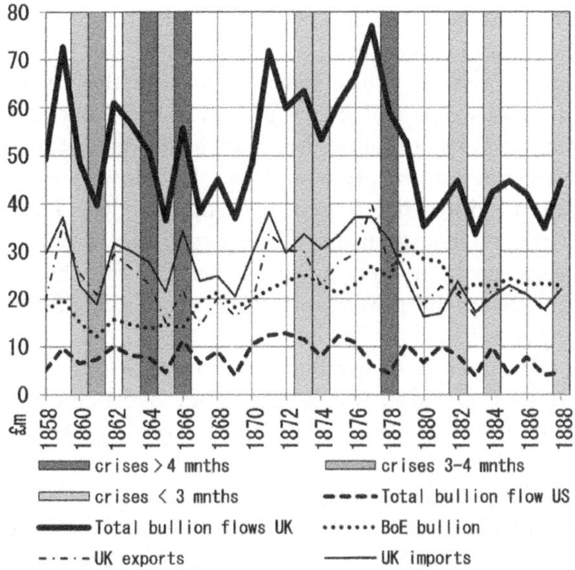

Fig. 7.3 Total bullion flows in and out of the UK compared with crises, as identified by UK and US interest rates moving together (*Sources* Bank of England daily account books, analysis in Chapter 3)

7.1 The Banking School and the Crisis of 1866

Bagehot's preferred solution was in fact different from the arrangement of the Bank of England acting as a lender of last resort. Bagehot agreed with the Free Banking School that, in an ideal world, banks would learn to regulate themselves if they were allowed to go bust, but in reality, a change to that situation would be very difficult to achieve because of the history and tradition of the English banking system. As he summed up:

> I have tediously insisted that the natural system of banking is that of many banks keeping their own cash reserve, with the penalty of failure before them if they neglect it. I have shown that our system is that of a single bank keeping the whole reserve under no effectual penalty of failure. And yet I propose to retain that system, and only attempt to mend and palliate it…I propose to retain this system because I am quite sure that it is no manner of use proposing to alter it.[14]

The current system, he argued, was only to be retained because of the practical difficulties of changing it, despite its flaws, not least thanks to the opposition such a reform would have faced from the Currency School. At the time he was writing, Bagehot indicated the Bank of England was assumed to be not at risk of failure because as guardian of the government finances it was believed that it would not be allowed to go bankrupt. It is important to note that Bagehot, along with the Banking School, was not in favour of this situation of being 'too-big-to-fail' (James Grant has recently suggested the contrary, incorrectly[15]) but that it was a given premise, arising from the power and influence of the Bank defended by the Currency School.

However, the directors of the Bank back in 1866 acted as if they were not at all sure their position was secure. They had been keeping weekly official records of bullion flows in and out of the country since 1858 as their position as both a private bank and holder of the bullion and note reserves of the United Kingdom seemed precarious. Both Banking and Currency School factions within the Bank, from their actions, realised that they had to influence the large capital flows in and out of the United Kingdom to ensure that their meagre bullion reserve was not washed away with the tides. Their only policy tools were interest rates and the availability of credit.

To assist in this process, in 1861, George Goschen, a director of the Bank and later to be chancellor of the exchequer, published a book, *The Theory of the Foreign Exchanges*.[16] It took the principle of gold points (the interest rate at which it is as cheap to settle international accounts in bullion as it is to buy bills of exchange) and used it to estimate the scale of interest-rate adjustment necessary to influence bullion to move between countries. He indicated that it was necessary to use steps of at least one percentage point. His book had to be revised in a second edition to overcome complaints from the Currency School, but it became influential. The crisis of 1866 was almost the only time in the nineteenth century that to solve a bullion drain, the Bank Rate was raised well above the American rate. Some commentators from both Schools noted that this change was immediately followed by inward flows from the United States but also by an excessive demand for notes, making the crisis worse in terms of banknote availability (Fig. 7.4). William Fowler, a banker in Lombard Street, pointed out that, at this time, almost £5m more in notes, had been 'absorbed' than in 1857.[17]

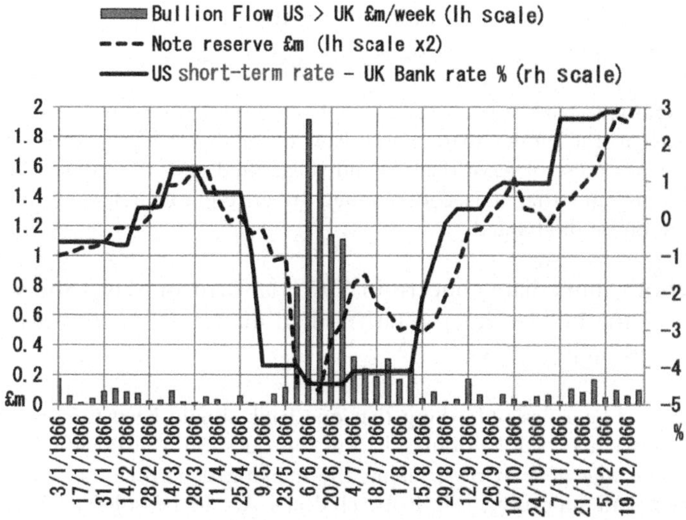

Fig. 7.4 US–UK Short-Term Rate, Bullion Flow from US to UK (£m per week) for 1866, Bank of England Note Reserve (£m) (*Sources* Bank of England daily account books, *New York Daily Tribune*, NBER database, *The Economist*)

Bagehot was aware of this situation and his replies to enquiries made by William Gladstone, the chancellor of the exchequer during the 1866 panic, as to whether there was really a crisis confirmed the explanation of what caused the panic given above. Bagehot sent an initial 'Note on the City crisis' to Gladstone which described 'A complete collapse of credit on Lombard St.' and 'large orders for notes…by Country Bankers'.[18] However, a letter almost two weeks later described the situation as 'a little different from that the first appearance of facts might suggest…I have no doubt at all that the panic of last Friday [18 May] was 80 per cent at least a deposit panic and not more than 20 per cent a note panic…'.[19]

This analysis meant the Bank was being put under pressure from the influx of bullion being turned into notes, not just from domestic demand for notes. J. Gurney Hoare of Barnetts, Hoares, Hanbury & Lloyd Bank, which was mainly involved in the cotton trade, also described the situation as one of large deposits of bullion being exchanged for notes.[20] Fowler reckoned that the bullion had 'arrived at the very moment it was most needed', but *The Economist* pointed out that it could prove to be a very short-term respite:

> The remittance of the precious metals from distant places gives a momentary ease to the money market and leads to an augmentation of the Bank reserve, we must observe that the aid so granted is in the highest degree precarious, and that it is compensated by an equivalent liability...which must soon be discharged.[21]

Bagehot's immediate concern in *The Economist* in May 1866 was over the size of the bullion reserve rather than matters of central banking or what caused bullion flows:

> Whether it be a desirable thing that one bank should keep the reserve of the country may well be doubted...But this question is not to the purpose now. The *aggregate reserve*, taking the banking department of the Bank by itself and supposing [Sir Robert] Peel's Act to be still in force, was insufficient.[22]

The Bank had already started to take a number of steps to increase its reserves, a policy that Bagehot in 1873 saw as having been essential to the Bank of England's success.[23] These included increasing the income of the Bank from activities such as discounting, and expanding its services into parts of the British empire such as India.

Other Banking School inclined commentators analysed data and also came to conclusions different from the Currency School's position. William Jevons, an economist whose father became bankrupt during the 1847 crisis, used an early example of graphical analysis to link instability and the Bank Rate. He queried how far the fluctuation in prices in the 1850s was caused by the adjustment of the Bank Rate and how much by the new finds of gold.[24] In France Clément Juglar, a statistician, had followed the British government's enquiries into financial crises and his later research identified cycles of investment into fixed capital, which coordinated with low official rates, again consistent with Henry Thornton and the Banking School's concerns. Examining the coincidence of crises in European countries, he concluded that 1864 was the period of real crisis in Britain and 1866 was a late symptom of the same disturbance.[25] Back in Britain, Robert Patterson, a journalist who was strongly opposed to the Peel's Act of 1844, examined rates of interest and flows between the United Kingdom and France. Between 1858 and 1864, France adopted the policy of frequent movements of interest rate to prevent bullion from moving out of the country. In 1866 it moved to a low interest rate, but did not lose gold bullion, enabling it to hold the low rate through the crisis, a position the Currency School considered 'impossible' according to Patterson (see Fig. 7.1).[26] There were suspicions of the obstruction of bullion exports, or in other words, informal capital controls, although there was no official legislation for this.[27]

The conflict between the different moral values of the Currency School and Banking School during this period were exposed by a court case about human-rights abuses in the Caribbean. Edward Eyre, Governor of Jamaica, had brutally repressed protests in October 1865 for better treatment of the workers on the island led by Paul Bogle, a Baptist deacon. Martial law was declared and over 400 people were killed, many flogged, and houses burned. Bogle's sponsor, George Gordon, a mixed-race member of the colonial Assembly, was executed for treason after a court martial. The incident, which came to be known by historians as the Morant Bay rebellion, was widely disapproved of in the United Kingdom and Eyre was recalled and an Enquiry set up. John Stuart Mill took over the chair of the Jamaica Committee to call for the prosecution of Eyre for murder, a change in the use of martial law, and 'to arouse public morality against oppression generally, and particularly against the oppression of subject and dependant races'.[28] The ex-Governor was defended successfully by a group championed by Thomas Carlyle, who was even by the standards of the era insultingly racist, despite being a popular author. Lord Overstone supported the defence of Eyre 'contributing £200 to Eyre's legal fund'.[29] *The Economist* was not only concerned about the action taken in Jamaica of 'deliberate cruelty and malignity' but 'should there be a riot in London or Birmingham, Glasgow or Dublin, the "Governors" there for the time being have in Mr. Eyre a model'. The 'crimes and blunders of the poor' of Jamaica should have received 'the justest treatment' because of their disadvantages.[30] No doubt *The Economist* had in mind the Hyde Park riots of March 1866 against the failure of the Reform Bill. Overstone continued to believe that the public should 'acquiesce in the existing state of things', a constant Currency School demand in contrast to the Banking School's optimism and belief in a better future even in the face of Overend's demise.[31]

7.2 The Background to the Crisis of 1866

Moving back to the run-up to the crisis of 1866, it is clear that the financial problems of this era were exacerbated by a search for yield because of low rates of the sort the Banking School had by this stage long warned about. The world was an uncertain place in the 1860s with the prospects of war in Europe and civil war in America, making the global economic environment volatile. Tensions in the United States tended to cause flows of bullion out of the country, through the United Kingdom towards Europe, where it was needed as war broke out between Prussia and Austria. Low short-term rates, 2.5%, prevailed in Britain from the end of the 1850s until 1861, triggering a search for higher yields. There were minor surges in interest rates in 1859 arising from a loan to India and disturbances on the Continent, but rates reached 8% in late 1861 and late 1863 and 9% twice in 1864 to stem bullion drains towards France and India. According to the Banking School, these interest-rate hikes caused a French crisis in 1864 and problems in India in 1866. Overend's was reconstituted in 1865 as a limited company, but this failed on what became known as 'Black Friday' (11 May 1866) due to cash-flow problems when it was refused credit by the Bank of England. That decision was not queried by the Banking School, but there was a feeling that the Bank had encouraged the situation and made a profit from it, an accusation denied by the supporters of central banks who have emphasised the assistance provided more widely to other institutions in 1866. To the Currency School, Overend's humiliation was the end of the Banking School's challenges to the supremacy of the Bank of England, but more than that, the failure of a banking system based on the philosophy of mitigating crises rather than putting up with them. The Currency School now had to be appeased rather than challenged. This section of the chapter explores in detail the interest-rate moves and bullion flows that provided the backdrop to Overend's demise and the crisis of 1866.

Over the course of March and April 1859, there was a bullion drain from the Bank of England and reserves fell from £19.246m on 9 March to £16.383m on 11 May. Bank of England rates rose from 2.5% to 3.5% on 28 April and to 4.5% on 5 May, falling by stages back to 2.5% by 14 July. The interest rate movements were reflected on the continent. On 19 May 1859 interest rates in Hamburg rose from 2% to 4%.[32] They then fell back, reaching 1.5% by the end of June.[33] Hostilities broke out between the Austrians and the Piedmontese supported by France from

26 April 1859 causing the Bank of Vienna to suspend specie payments and coinciding with a large flow of capital from America through Britain to the continent. In the week commencing 8 June imports of bullion from the United States to the United Kingdom reached over £1m and in the same week two-thirds of a million were exported from Britain to France.[34]

While all this was happening two large loans were being raised. One was the Indian loan (referred to in the previous chapter) and one was a loan raised by the Russian government in all the major capitals of Europe. The Indian loan was the result of the costs of a military presence in India but also of the precarious state of Indian finances as they were transferred from the East India Company to the Secretary of State for India under the British government. Previous loans for India had been raised locally, but that source became exhausted after the 1858 loan and on 14 February 1859, Lord Stanley introduced a bill into the Commons to authorise the Government to raise a loan of £7m to top up the finances for the year, and Lord Derby followed this up with a request for a further £5m on 25 March. After the chaos of the Irish loan in 1847, a bullion drain was to be expected by the Bank in association with loans to India, and this contributed to the rate increase on 28 April. British investors tended to shy away from subscribing to the Russian loan, unlike other countries where it was more successful, as the new Indian bond issue proved to be a more popular alternative.[35]

After 1859 there was a brief period of calm and prosperity in the United Kingdom. Cotton prices had stabilised. The fate of Liverpool Borough Bank and the liability of its directors had prevented cotton prices rising because it tied the hands of 'the speculators who, with the assistance of the Liverpool banks, used to get up an inflation upon the slightest pretext'.[36] By 1860 the British economy was booming and nearing full employment. The cotton industry prospered and commodity prices rose in response. However, in the final quarter of 1860, uncertainty resumed with the prospect of civil war in America and its effect on cotton prices.

While the economy seemed calm and prosperous on the surface at the end of the 1850s, the competition between the new joint-stock banks and the Bank of England began to develop into a disagreement with destructive consequences. The Bank was influenced by the way it was organised under Peel's 1844 Bank Charter Act. It was composed of a banking department which acted as any private bank making dividends for its shareholders and an issue department which was intended to operate in the public interest. As a private company, the Bank had to maximise its profit by discounting as many profitable bills as possible at the highest rate possible. As the bank of issue for England, it had to manage its note issue according to its bullion reserves as stipulated by the Act and was further obliged to do this in a way that did not damage commerce. As part of this, it was necessary to adjust interest rates to retain adequate bullion. Further, its status as the main bank of issue obliged it to make credit available when credit became tight because it was seen as having the power to do so, yet as the government's banker, it had to remain solvent at all costs.

The Currency School's narrative of the crisis of 1866 focuses on Overend's rather dissolute new management, their carelessness in checking those requesting loans or discounts and their alleged fraud in the transfer of the business to limited liability status in 1865. The Banking School points to additional factors. In the 1850s joint-stock banks were drawn by their clients into a business model which relied on obtaining credit at a low rate and lending it at a higher rate. The increasing use of Bank Rate to influence bullion flows led to a more variable short-term rate which disturbed this model. In addition, when rates were particularly low, there was pressure to find higher earning investments for the money which built up.

The Economist was sympathetic to Overend's plight as minor scandals emerged from it in the late 1850s, because of its vulnerability to the Bank of England's policies, but it was shocked and disappointed when the full picture emerged in 1866. Overend's directors came to believe that the Bank was purposefully adjusting its rate to destroy its competition in bill broking and this was reinforced by the Bank's decision to exclude bill brokers from their discount facilities in certain situations. The Bank made increased profits from prolonged periods of high rates. Its desire to take market share from the likes of Overend's was shown by the reorganisation of its discounting and small loans department to reduce costs and increase its capacity in this area in 1863.

Matters came to a head in 1860 when the Bank raised its interest rate on 29 March 1860 during dividend season, something that by convention it never did, and which was seen as an attack on the rival bill brokers, as this was the period in which they were mostly short of liquidity.[37] This resulted in a show of strength by Overend's and joint-stock banks in which a large amount of Bank notes were withdrawn at once to try and trigger an artificial crisis. The story of this has become one of traditional folklore at the Bank of England, illustrated and embellished by anecdotes involving blackmail notes from Overend's which gives a justification for the Bank refusing assistance to them in 1866.[38]

Britain was not the only country where there were tensions between central banks and bill brokers at this time. Some commentators point to the parallel example in France of *Crédit Mobilier*, which financed much of the rebuilding of Paris and many foreign projects, but which faded away after France adopted British practice and frequently adjusted the Bank of France rate after 1857.[39] It also nearly collapsed in the crisis of 1866. The mutual frustration between the English banks and bill brokers may have understandably arisen from the system imposed by the Peel's Act of 1844 and the consequent constant adjustment of interest rates. However, Overend's were still making £0.2m in annual operating profits on their discounting business in 1866, and their underlying problems arose from the historic debt of the former firm before it adopted limited liability. On this basis, some of the Banking School believed the bill broker should have been offered assistance by the Bank of England.

The problems at Overend's went back as far as May 1855, when *The Economist* reported the case of Daniel Davidson and Cosmo Gordon, who had defaulted on £0.5m, escaped to Malta and had to be brought back. It was stated that David Chapman of Overend's discovered some of the bills that they had discounted for the pair were against fictitious goods in October 1853 but had allowed the bills to circulate in the market in case 'it raised a panic in the market'.[40] This provoked a lecture on morality from *The Economist*, but they did not censure Overend's.[41] By contrast, *The Times* was always ready to criticise Overend's who were competing with the Bank of England by offering lower rates. In 1857 it was reported that the chancellor of the exchequer had distanced the government from Overend's, anticipating problems.[42] *The Economist* also supported Overend's behaviour in the case of Paul, Strachan and Bates, where at a time money was available on call at 3–3.5%, they had charged Sir John Paul 5%, suspecting he was not a sound risk.[43]

Bagehot later argued that the directors of the Bank felt that their discount policy encouraged the bill brokers to behave rashly. In March 1858 the Bank issued a statement which announced it would shut down rediscounting facilities to bill brokers, except in exceptional circumstances 'to make them keep their own reserve, and not be dependent on the Bank of England'.[44] Yet in the Bank of England's rush to expand itself in the bill-broking market, it also began to run up bad debts. The Court of

Directors minutes for the Bank of England of 18 March 1858 show that defaults in bills discounted by them had risen from £7,083 in 1855 to £93,332 in 1857.[45] Overend's losses were almost certainly worse because their discount policy was laxer.

At the beginning of 1860 the Bank of England began to creep up its rates again. From 2.5% they rose to 3% on 19 January and 4% on 31 January. On 29 March the Bank of England rate jumped to 4.5% and to 5% on 12 April. These last rises caught the financial press by surprise. They went against a previous principle that the Bank would never raise interest rates during the period for tax payments and the peak dividend season for shares because liquidity would be tight. In view of the Bank's remarks about bill brokers the rises were seen as an attack on the bill market and were highly criticised. Even *The Times* of 30 March 1860 complained 'the Bank as banker to the government...accumulates in its hands the revenue payments made by the people at large and that it has not been deemed fair to take advantage of the scarcity thus created by charging an extra price for letting the commercial world have the use of its money back again'. It went on that there was no drain of bullion which could be used as an excuse.[46] This was incorrect; there had been a slow drain from £15.86m at the beginning of January 1860 to £14.51m in March, bottoming out at £13.89m on 18 April. The capital flows behind this were moderate but steady streams of bullion shipped to France and India. The Bank of England was probably anticipating a flight into gold because of the risk of war on the continent and in the United States. These fears started to be fulfilled later in the year.

Meanwhile, Overend's launched their retaliation over the variations in Bank Rate. This was reported by *The Economist* of 21 April and repeated word for word in *The Times*.

> They took advantage of the moment at which it seemed likely that the Bank reserve would be less than it had ever been since the end of the panic of 1857 and at which they themselves happened to have rather more spare money than usual and they withdrew the whole of it from the Bank.[47]

The amount quoted as being withdrawn was £1.65m, but the record in the Bank of England daily account books shows a withdrawal of £0.8m worth of £1,000 notes on 10 April 1860, noted as by Overend's.[48] This had no real effect on the Bank and, as Bagehot later described, the attempt failed and weakened the bill brokers' case by 'exciting a distrust of "Overend's"' while the 'credit of the Bank of England was not diminished' because Overend's had to return the money within a few days.[49]

There then was a continuing series of problems with Overend's customers. In July 1860 Messrs Streatfield, Laurence and Mortimore of the leather trade went bankrupt and Overend's were creditors.[50] In 1864 *The Times* of 26 September attacked the bill broker because the extensive fraud of one of its customers had brought down the Leeds Banking Company: 'one of the customers of the bank has passed through it no less than 1,000 forged bills of exchange representing £68,000'... 'the principle delinquent is John Woodhead Marsden'. Marsden was an iron founder whose business had failed, principally due to the sudden increase in interest rates to 9% that year, and he responded by sending a letter to the bank saying, 'all was up' and 'I'm off to New York', where he could not be pursued for his outstanding liabilities.[51]

7.3 The American Civil War and the Cotton Industry

On 7 November 1860 the Bank of England noted the 'election of President of US in favour of Lincoln (Republican candidate)' in its daily accounts book. The significance of this was that Abraham Lincoln had been elected with the support of mainly the northern states after the party representing southern states split. The result was 'panic in the United States' and the 'threatened dissolution of the Union between North and South' as the Bank put it, in its summary. Free-market short-term interest rates in the United States rose to over 12%, but, even so, investors moved sharply into gold. The Bank of England put up rates to 6% on 29 November 1860, in response to a decline in the Bank's bullion reserve from £15.60m on 19 September to £13.16m on 6 November. Despite this action, in the week ended 10 December 1860, £0.95m in bullion was shipped to the United States, but America still suspended payments nonetheless. In the New Year, the Bank's reserves continued to fall, dipping to £10.75m on 13 February and causing the Bank Rate to reach a peak of 8% from 14 February to 21 March 1861.

The Lincoln administration in America was trying to find ways of financing the civil war. American banks wanted to charge unsustainable rates of interest and so in July 1861 Congress authorised the issue of $30m worth of 'Demand' notes. These were redeemable in gold and so they remained at par against gold. Before this, specie coins, gold or silver were the only legal tender in the United States. Even so, in December 1861 the government suspended redemption of 'Demand' notes because of a shortage of bullion, which had started to leave the country.

In order to prevent an excessive drain, the notes were gradually withdrawn because customs duties could be paid with them, and the government wanted to be paid in gold instead. To replace them the government issued $150m worth of 'United States notes', also known as 'greenbacks' after their design. These were not backed with specie and thereafter the value of the dollar fluctuated according to the fortunes of the North in the war (Fig. 7.5). After the war, the United States gradually got itself into a position where the notes could be redeemed for specie and the greenback dollar resumed its former value against gold from 1879. The fluctuation in the exchange rate meant that the effectiveness of the interest rate in controlling the flows of bullion to and from the United States was reduced in the United Kingdom, where the pound was still attached to a fixed-exchange rate to gold.

The civil war also had a negative impact on the real economy in Britain. Supplies of raw cotton that America exported, and British factories needed, were cut off. Before the start of the conflict, pro-secessionists in the southern states (the future Confederacy), to justify the feasibility of independence and to prove there was no need to fear a war with the north, had pushed the notion of 'King Cotton'. The theory claimed that control over raw cotton exports would make an independent Confederacy prosperous and would force Great Britain and possibly France to come to the aid of the Confederacy militarily because their industrial economies

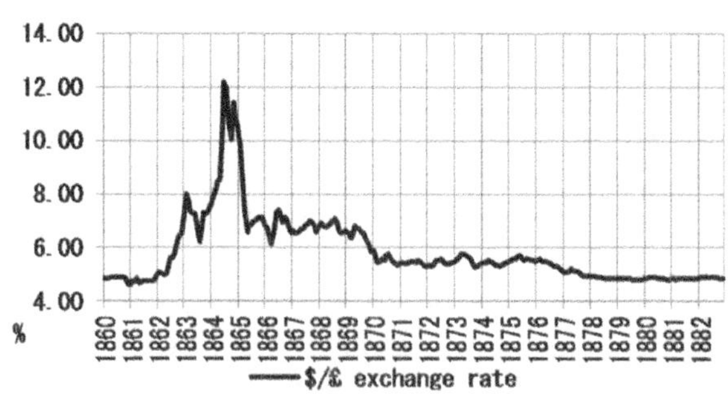

Fig. 7.5 $/£ exchange rate 1860–1882, showing the 'greenback period' (*Source* As Fig. 4.2)

depended on Southern cotton. By February 1861 the seven states whose economies were based on cotton plantations had all seceded and formed the Confederacy. Confederates bombarded Union soldiers at Fort Sumter, South Carolina on 12 April 1861 beginning the war.[52]

To demonstrate the power of 'King Cotton', southern cotton-merchants suspended cotton exports in early 1861, but in doing so demonstrated its lack of immediate power. By the summer of 1861, the Union Navy had blockaded every major Confederate port and shut down over 95% of exports. Since the British mills had large stockpiles of cotton, they suffered no immediate effect from the embargo; except that the value of their stockpiles soared. On 8 November 1861 the *USS San Jacinto*, commanded by Union Captain Charles Wilkes, intercepted the British mail packet *RMS Trent* and removed, as contraband of war, two Confederate diplomats, James Mason and John Slidell. The envoys were bound for Britain and France to argue the case for diplomatic recognition of the Confederacy and to lobby for financial and military support, trusting in the power of cotton diplomacy. It was this event that coincided with the low point of Bank of England's bullion reserves. In spite of this, by the end of 1861, the financial situation had stabilised, and the Bank Rate was back down to 3%. It remained low and reasonably stable and did not rise above 4% until November 1863. That reason was that the flow of newly-mined gold, payments in exchange for trade and investment income still flowed out of America to Britain, but new investment in the opposite direction ceased because of the uncertainty of war. As the *Daily News* of the time explained:

> Before the commencement of the war in America we had been in the habit of importing annually some thirty-five millions sterling worth of cotton from America alone. That supply suddenly having been stopped...the capital thrown out of the cotton trade accumulating rapidly, beating down the rates of interest through its competition for employment for short periods with the ordinary supply of money in the discount market. The glut was increased by the constant influx of gold from America, that country finding itself no longer able to discharge her indebtedness to Europe in commodities when the exportation of the chief staple had ceased. The next movement was the transfer to other countries of a portion of the cotton business hitherto almost monopolised by America.[53]

Thus, although when cotton stocks ran short in Britain there was much suffering among the millworkers who were laid off having nothing to spin in the 'Lancashire Cotton Famine', the Bank of England's bullion reserves did not suffer with them. The cessation of the American cotton exports caused a continuous flow of bullion from the 'United' States, most of which eventually found its way to India and the East via London (Table 7.1). However, the figures to and from India from 1866 do not tell the whole picture because bills of exchange were increasingly used instead of physical bars of bullion for transactions within India.

The bullion flows from the United States were also used to fund new loans to Latin America and other parts of the world. In 1862–1863, for instance, the following loans were offered in London:

International loans offered in London 1862–1863 (Table 7.2).

The returns on most of these investments contributed to increased bullion flows reaching the United Kingdom from the mid-1860s and some of this added to the Bank of England's reserves.[55] The investment flows to India and subsequent income resulted from a cotton industry set up to replace that from America which became unavailable during the civil war. The Government of India issued a waste lands order in October 1861, taking control of uncultivated lands and turning them over to individuals who were required to grow cotton and other crops. Soon capital flows to India were to become the subject of a tug-of-war with the United Kingdom.

A nervous Bank of England did not hesitate to put its rate up to 8% in late 1861 as the succession of the Confederate states took place and again in November and December 1863 because of demand for bullion from Europe. Interest rates in America, Britain and France converged in November and December at around 8% and international bullion flows stopped. Exports of gold to France from the United Kingdom halved between 1862 and 1863.[56] A banking panic occurred in Paris in January

Table 7.1 Bullion transfers to and from the UK, US and India[54]

£m	*From US*	*To US*	*From India, etc.*	*To India, etc.*
1862	10.428	n/a	0	n/a
1863	8.179	0.172	0	9.377
1864	7.749	0.377	0.103	8.530
1865	4.538	0.150	0.752	4.487
1866	10.471	1.215	1.595	3.837

Table 7.2 International loans offered in London 1862–1863

Date	*Loan to*	*Amount*	*Offer rate (%)*
19 February 1862	Italy	£1.782m	5
24 March	Turkey	£8m	6
5 April	Egypt	£2.195m	7
26 April	Russia	£15m	5
20 July	Portugal	£5m	3
30 July	Venezuela	£1m	6
1 August	Peru	£5.5m	4.5
1 August	Egypt (2nd loan)	£1.098m	7
27 February 1863	Holland	£0.5m	4
16 March	Italy	£3m of £28m	5
19 March	Confederates	£3m	7
28 September	Colombia	£0.2m	6
8 October	Brazil	£3.3m	4.5
8 October	Portugal	£2.5m	3

1864, as a consequence, and spread around Europe. This crisis was an important, but too often forgotten, prelude to the more famous events of 1866.

7.4 Europe and the Crisis of 1864

In 1864 the Bank of France's interest rates had shadowed British rates with just a few days' lag. Likewise, the Bank of England carefully monitored the Bank of France's rates.[57] This was the characteristic policy of the Bank of France's Governor, Count de Germiny. Before he was appointed as governor in 1857, the rate had been changed 20 times in 57 years. During his six-year period of office up to 1863, it changed 30 times.[58] By 1866, Governor Rouland had taken over. The mystery surrounding bullion flows to France under his direction is why France was able to maintain a low interest rate, in comparison with the United Kingdom, throughout 1866 and yet retain large quantities of bullion.

Figure 7.6 shows the disparity between the French and UK official interest rates in 1866 but *The Times* was complaining in June 1866 that the Bank of France stock of bullion had risen to £23.12m as opposed to the Bank of England which only had £11.43m.[59] The situation had changed from 1857 when the holdings were similar: £10.1m in England,

£9.2m in France. Flows of bullion from the United Kingdom to France were sustained through the years of the crisis and this explains to an extent, the push to a very high rate of 10% by the directors of the Bank in 1866. They were frustrated that flows of bullion to France could not be curtailed. In 1866, France received a gross flow of £10.56m of gold and silver from the United Kingdom, less exports this was a net flow of £5.23m.[60]

There were several reasons for this situation: France had bought gold in 1864, it was successful at trading with the United Kingdom, the use of hard cash was more traditional than in the United Kingdom and there is some evidence the export of bullion from France was obstructed. In 1864, by following the raised rates of the United Kingdom, France had found itself in a financial crisis and had therefore, as it had done in times past, followed the policy of amassing a large reserve of bullion to enable it to weather future storms. It purchased 229m francs in gold at a premium in 1864 in order to do this.[61] This tactic followed the method of Earl Grey and James Wilson in constructing the currency of Mauritius, a currency board run by commissioners. Their currency was partially secured on bullion which was owned by the Commissioners on behalf of the country. Unlike much of the bullion in the Bank of England reserve it could not be withdrawn by depositors, because the board was not a commercial bank. France also gained an advantage through trade.

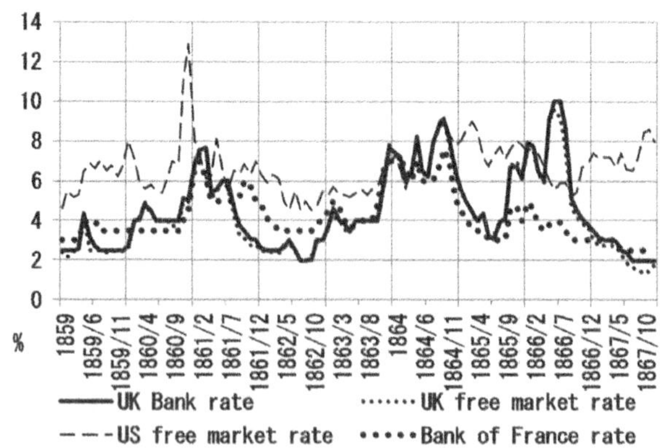

Fig. 7.6 Short-term interest rate in the UK, US and France 1859–1867 (*Sources* As Fig. 7.1)

After the 1860 Cobden–Chevalier trade agreement between the United Kingdom and France, France reaped the benefit more than the United Kingdom because it produced the goods that the United Kingdom wanted, particularly wine. The agreement was part of Napoleon III's plan to shadow the United Kingdom and achieve international power and financial success which rivalled it. It also served the United Kingdom's purpose of extending free trade. The 'most favoured nation' clause meant that any trade agreement negotiated by one of the parties applied to both. Up to 1866, this meant that trade agreements were finalised with Belgium, the *Zollverein*, Italy, Switzerland, Spain, Holland, Scandinavia and Austria.[62]

The knitting together of Europe and the United Kingdom through trade increased bullion flows between them. In 1862 total annual bullion flows between the two were £16.3m but by 1866 they had increased to £21.6m.[63] France was still demanding silver bullion because there was a bi-metallic currency and notes were not generally accepted. Instead, '*écus sonnants*', or money that rings on the counter was built into the French national psyche.[64] *Espèces sonnantes et trébuchantes* still means 'hard cash' today and shows the long-lasting nature of the attitude. Increased prosperity had strengthened the demand for money, and this translated directly into a demand for bullion. In addition, Alfred de Rothschild gave evidence to a government enquiry in 1888 that the French were loath to part with bullion and in crises printed lots of small notes to prevent the exportation of coin.[65]

There were numerous other international loans raised in London at the beginning of 1864, including to France, Denmark, Russia and Venezuela, which contributed to an accelerating bullion drain from the Bank of England. A Mexican loan of £8m that was issued in the London market in 1864 at 6% made the situation worse.[66] The Union gaining the upper hand in the American civil war as the year progressed also meant a resumption of investment flows westwards across the Atlantic. The flow of bullion imported from America averaged £0.162m per week during the first six months of 1864 but fell to £0.135m in the second. Meanwhile, silver exports that year to India tripled to £6.338m. As a result of all these demands, the Bank of England's bullion reserve began falling again from around £14.7m at the beginning of September 1863 to £11.8m at the start of May 1864.[67] The Bank responded with Bank Rate rises in stages to 9%, where it remained from 5 to 19 May 1864. The casualties of this round of rate rises included the East of England Bank which suspended payments in July 1864 with liabilities of £0.6m and, on 17 September, the Leeds Banking Company. The Bank Rate rose to 9% again from 8 September 1864 to 9 November, as drains to France and India continued.[68] This second rise almost bankrupted the original Overend, Gurney & Co., whose directors were pushed into looking into ways of rescuing the firm. This resulted in Overend's being re-establishing as a limited liability company, only for it to finally fail on 'Black Friday' in May 1866.

7.5 The Indian Connection to the Crisis of 1866

Before this chapter discusses the reasons for Overend's failure, it is necessary to explain why the Bank of England raised its interest rate so high again in 1866. The Bank Rate rose from a trough of 3% in June 1865 to 8% just days before Overend's collapse on 10 May 1866, 9% on 11 May and 10% on 12 May—the highest Bank Rate in the Bank of England's history. This has baffled commentators as this is the only time in the nineteenth century when the Bank of England raised its rate to a level substantially above those prevailing in America. Neither was the Bank's bullion reserves particularly low in 1866 or in danger of running out. Was the Bank guilty of overkill? The established view, shared by the Currency School, is no: the British economy was overheating and higher rates were needed to restrain excessive speculation, such as Overend's. Yet that does not explain everything; if anything the end of the American Civil War in 1865 had a deflationary impact on the world economy. This section reveals a new explanation for the Bank's tight policy in 1866: it was worried about the deteriorating fiscal position of the Indian government, whose bullion in London the Bank increasingly relied upon for its stability.

This story starts again with a boom. During the American Civil War, the Lancashire millowners demanded that the British government develop India's cotton-growing sector to provide an alternative source of raw material. Such was their impatience that Hugh Mason, chairman of the Manchester Cotton Company tried to impeach Charles Wood as Indian secretary for implementing this policy too slowly.[69] The Bombay area consequently experienced a boom in its cotton industry between 1863 and 1865.

In 1865 American supplies to Britain resumed when the Confederacy was defeated. By 1866 prices had fallen back to pre-war levels and the

Indian cotton industry was struck by a crisis. Many businesses, including the Bank of Bombay, the government's banker with some similar responsibilities as the Bank of England, subsequently collapsed. Increased cotton supplies from India competed with American growers for the same prewar level of demand from Britain. The resulting structural oversupply caused a long-term gradual decline in prices to between 4 and 6 d/lb in the 1880s (Fig. 7.7).

News of peace in America in May 1865 and a surprise announcement on 23 June 1865 revealing that India was running a fiscal deficit rather than a surplus triggered a persistent decline in Bank of England's bullion reserve from the week ending 5 July 1865.[70] It was in response to this news that the Bank began to sharply raise its rate over the next 12 months. The reason why this was a shock was that the City of London thought India would be self-financing after years of trying to set up the new colony (gained from the East India Company in 1858) with a new self-sufficient currency and financial system. Instead, in June 1865, the shocked British press was presented, without warning, with a restatement of the government of India's budget, which showed a deficit of nearly £0.7 million, rather than a surplus of around £0.48–1.8m as expected. As *The Times* of London put it:

> It is not to be concealed that the ex-Finance Minister of India has left the finances of the East in an embarrassed condition. The export duties have

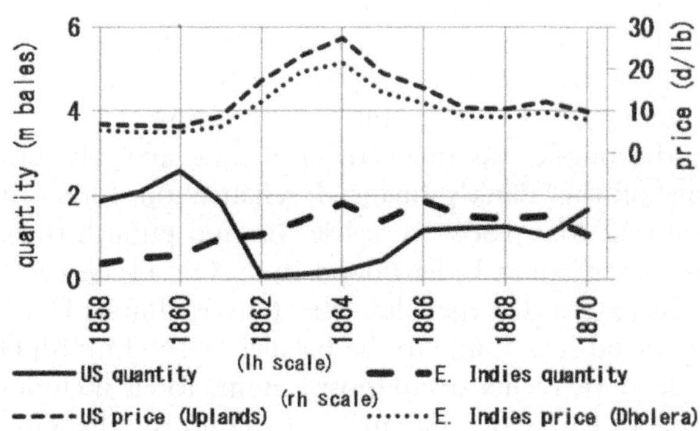

Fig. 7.7 Prices (rh scale) and quantities (lh scale) of raw cotton imported via Liverpool (d/lb) (*Source* T. Ellison, *The Cotton Trade of Great Britain* [London: Effingham Wilson, 1886] Table 1, rear fold out)

> been negatived by the SECRETARY OF STATE, the loan is not to be raised, but the Income-tax has lapsed. The consequence is that for the first time for some years the Estimates show a deficit.[71]

It was even more scathing the following year as the crises of 1866 came to a head: 'While high officials squabble from year to year our Indian subjects die of famine, and our Indian finance goes along limping in the old style'.[72] In view of the timing, there can be little doubt that the situation in India contributed to the exodus of bullion from the Bank. The boom in India's cotton production had been under threat as competition resumed from cotton-growers in the American South when the civil war ended, so bad news on its fiscal position was not encouraging. India came to be seen by the City of London as an expensive commitment requiring capital investment by Britain in railways and irrigation schemes to improve the movement of food and goods within the country to prevent famine.

The reaction of investors was slow but steady, yet the Governor and Directors of the Bank moved quickly. In the early 1860s, the Bank had hoped India, after it became a formal colony in 1858, would provide the bullion deposits in the future that they needed to build up their reserves, which, if they believed Tooke, were too small.[73] Today, it can be seen from the Bank's accounts books that since 1863, 'Council of India' deposits were recorded under their own heading. Between 8 and 15 April 1865 the percentage of 'Public Deposits' in the Bank's published accounts belonging to the Indian government, varied between 7.8% and 18.2%, meaning that the Bank had to watch Indian affairs carefully to preserve the stability of its reserves. The Indian government also became an increasingly important source of fees for the Bank, paying £10,313.0s.8d for the management of India's public debt in 1864/65.[74]

However, the public was unaware until long after the crisis of 1866 of the extent of the Bank's financial reliance on India. It took *The Economist* until 22 May 1869 to realise this and publish that the 'Public Deposits' contained some Indian deposits.[75] On 11 November 1871 it revealed the full extent that they did; 'the item of "Public Deposits" which it would be inferred refers only to the balance of the English Government with the Bank, is in reality a composite item, for it includes the home balance of the Indian Government'.[76] In contrast, the Governors and Directors of the Bank knew of its reliance on India as the source of the deposits that formed its reserves, with their inside knowledge and records of bullion flows to India and France in 1864. And so they reacted more strongly with rate hikes in 1865 and 1866 to the deteriorating financial situation in India than the public anticipated. This can be seen in the pages of *The Economist* in this period, which was only later to find out the real source of the public deposits in the Bank. It stated its surprise at the increase of Bank Rate to 7% on 3 May 1866 because there was 'no authentic evidence of the mode in which the bullion exported from this country is going to be used' and it was of 'limited magnitude'.[77] The differing extent of knowledge of Indian finances by the two groups explains this disparity of concern.

The deficit budget of June 1865 came as a disappointment to the City of London because the original aim was for the colony of India would be self-financing. The economy had been urged upon the Secretary of State for India since before administrative control of India had been passed to him.[78] As *The Economist* noted in 1857, 'up to this time India is the solitary foreign possession of the British Crown which can be said to have borne the whole of its own expenses'.[79] Although the East India Company and other Indian principalities had run up debts of some £58 million, this was 'independently of, and unaided by, the credit of the Imperial Government'.[80] Now the government of India was brought directly under the control of the Crown, its deficits needed to be curbed. The Earl of Ellenborough, who was drafting the new arrangements for the government of India, told the House of Lords in 1858:

> …it is the duty of the person, whoever he may be, who is placed at the head of Indian affairs in this country, to endeavour so to reduce expenditure in India as to make that expenditure, if possible, come within the revenue. That, undoubtedly, is his first duty; and, above all, I desire and trust that we shall effect the object of relieving this country from any burden on account of India.[81]

The Times commented in the same year that 'India must provide for her own pecuniary wants in the same manner as Canada, Australia, or any other possession'.[82]

An array of financial experts was sent out to India to achieve the required ideal of a balanced budget, the 'Peelite fiscal prudence' to which Miles Taylor has credited colonial stability.[83] However, it did not mean that they agreed on how to do this and conflict between them became the source of the restated accounts that shocked the City of London in

1865. Many of those in charge at home and in India had gained experience during the Irish famine. Peel, prime minister at the start of the Irish famine, had died in 1850.[84] His successor as prime minister during that crisis, Lord John Russell, was also prime minister at the start of the Orissa famine.[85] Wood, who controlled the finance for relief efforts during the Irish famine as chancellor of the exchequer between 1846 and 1852 was later Secretary of State for India from 1859 until early 1866.[86] Both Wilson, editor of *The Economist* and commentator during the famine, and Sir Charles Trevelyan, Assistant Secretary to the Treasury at the same time, were finance ministers of India in the 1860s.[87] The Earl of Derby, who replaced Russell as prime minister in June 1866, had been colonial secretary to Peel's government during the first months of the Irish famine in 1845, until he resigned over the decision to repeal the Corn Laws.[88]

Unfortunately for Indian finance, their differing experiences of the Irish famine and the crises of 1847 meant that they disagreed on what was the best set of policies for India. Wilson, the founder and first editor of *The Economist*, was appointed as the first financial member of the Council of India and set about raising revenue and cutting spending to reach a balanced budget. Having seen how the Bank Charter Act of 1844 prevented an Irish loan for relief, his currency plans included a low initial third backing by bullion and an expandable amount by securities, rather than what Wood, who was firmly Currency School, wanted.[89] The Currency School viewed Wilson's plan as a dangerous expansion of the money supply.[90] He also proposed taxes including an income tax to ensure sufficient revenue so that the accounts of the Indian government were balanced.[91] He set about slashing military expenses and replaced, on the grounds of cost, the sepoy soldiers with a civilian police force organised by Trevelyan, then president of Madras.[92]

Trevelyan, by contrast, had had to deal with the negative consequences in Ireland of high local taxes and so fought against an income tax for India.[93] He published the Madras government's objections to Wilson's proposals, known as the Madras Minute, in local newspapers. Bagehot—Wilson's son-in-law—came to his aid reminding *The Economist*'s readers that 'India belongs to us, and if the Indian Exchequer should permanently be in disorder we cannot hope to escape' and called the Madras Minute, an 'act of insubordination' in public opinion.[94] Trevelyan was recalled home by Lord Palmerston's government in early 1860, but his old friend Wood who was Secretary of State for India had him return in 1862 as Indian finance minister to replace Wilson, who had died.[95]

Trevelyan had been writing since the 1830s to *The Times* as 'Indophilus' arguing that Britain should do more to help the native population of India.[96] When he became India's finance minister, he put his ideas into practice, instituting extensive public works schemes, including irrigation and transport. However all this cost money and Trevelyan began to frame the Indian accounts to allow expenditure in India while using creative accounting to hide it from politicians and investors at home. He wrote to Wood reassuringly in 1862, 'The steady increase in the Indian cash balances is, I think, a more certain indication of an advancing state of finances than any result on the face of the accounts'.[97]

When Trevelyan left India in 1865, Wood had the accounts cleaned up. He moved items from the capital to current expenditure. His commitment to Peel's low tariff policy in the 1840s resurfaced when he cancelled Trevelyan's tariffs, cutting revenue. Debts for rent to the zamindars (landowners), and the accompanying tax to government, were enforced.[98] His fear of loans revived—the crises of 1847 were still on his mind—and caused him to cancel a proposed loan for India, just as he had cancelled further loans for Ireland in 1847.[99] The result was a deficit that was revealed by *The Times* announcement of 23 June 1865 reporting Trevelyan's 'financial freaks'.[100] Worse still, correspondence between Wood and Trevelyan was published showing that expenditure on public works in progress was a significant reason behind the proposed £1.25 million loan.[101] The triggering of the fall in the bullion reserve of the Bank from the beginning of July 1865 therefore had similarities to the first crisis of 1847 in which a bullion drain was caused by the prospect of a deficit budget and big loan being issued to pay for relief works.[102]

At a similar time to the announcement in *The Times*, came the news that the Civil War had ended in America.[103] India's cotton-growing industry was now threatened by competition from America for British trade. Moreover, from autumn, news began to filter through from India about droughts in Orissa, which increased worries about the health of the Indian economy as well as emphasising the need for public-works expenditure for irrigation projects and as famine relief. All these factors indicated a continuing deterioration in the Indian government's fiscal position—and added to a persistent drain in the Bank's bullion reserve due to the risk they posed by extension to the British government's finances.[104] The Bank reacted with a series of renewed Bank Rate rises.

On 2 June 1865 Wood had raised with the Bombay government reports he had received of inappropriate transactions by the Bank of

Bombay.[105] The Presidency banks were meant to only lend money to public companies in India that held 'a guarantee from the Government with regard to the dividends or interest', but this phrase was omitted from the legislation defining the Bombay Bank's charter, and the ideas which underlay the Companies Act 1862 could have been an influence, particularly as similar provisions were enacted in India.[106] On 23 June 1865 Wood announced the accounts for British India had a surprising deficit when a surplus had been expected and the bullion reserve fell sharply from that date at the rate of £0.4–0.5m a week for several weeks. In the middle of this period, Overend Gurney decided to reorganise their old firm into a new limited liability company, absorbing £5m in new share capital which the Bank noted in the margin of its account book along with events likely to reduce the bullion reserve. A general election took place in the United Kingdom on 11–24 July 1865 which distracted politicians 'in hurry and confusion' from other matters.[107] The Bank raised its Rate to 3.5% on 27 July and 4% on 3 August. In India the Bank of Bombay maintained its deposit rate at 9% to attract deposits which was successful for August and September but then faltered as the balance of flows subsided towards Britain, thanks to the Bank's rate hikes (Figs. 7.8 and 7.9).[108] Then in October, Lord Palmerston died, and Lord Russell became prime minister at which time the Bank Rate rose from 4% to 7% in just 10 days. Few people initially seemed to note that in Orissa it did not rain in October or November.[109] The Bank of England tried lowering its rate in November to 6% as the bullion reserve had recovered, but bullion soon started to drain away to India again and the rate went back up to 7% at the end of December.

Bullion was exported from India to Britain throughout the year from March onwards up to a total of £0.762 million whereas in previous years there had been virtually no exports. *The Economist* noted this was encouraged by a 'distrust of long-dated bills accepted in England' since 1864 which made countries such as India send bullion as payment for goods.[110] The result was that liquidity was reduced in India, just as the weakened Bank of Bombay needed it. The process of the Bank of Bombay raising rates for a limited effect on deposits repeated in December 1865. There were hopes that the Bank would be 'reinforced with Silver held at the Mint', but the government's Paper Currency Department instead sent its spare bullion to London to shore up the Bank of England's reserves.[111] Wadan Narsey has described how the Bank of England continued to rely

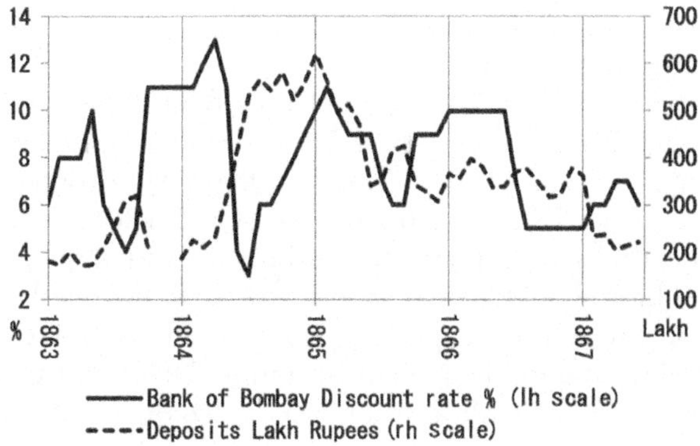

Fig. 7.8 Bank of Bombay Discount Rate for Private Bills (%) and Total Deposits (Lakh Rupees) (1 Lakh = 100,000 Rupees ≈ £10,000 in 1864) monthly figures (*Source* Accounts of Bank of Bombay BL. IOR/L/F/3/662–63)

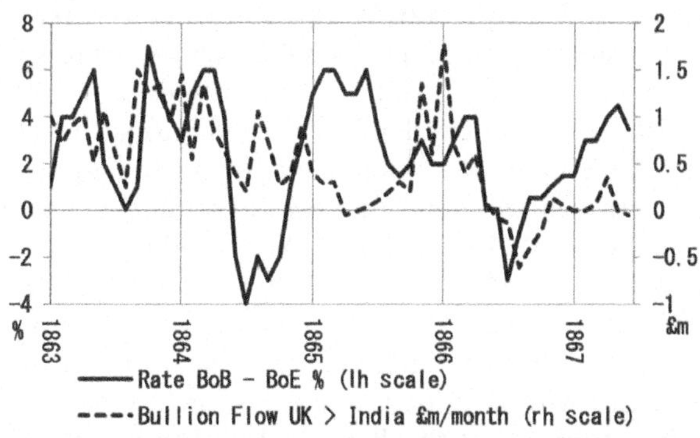

Fig. 7.9 Bank of Bombay Discount Rate for Govt. Bills—Bank of England Minimum Discount Rate (Bank rate) and Net Bullion Flows from the United Kingdom to India (£million/month). Exports to India may include onward transfers to China (*Sources* Bank of England, Daily Account Books 1863–1867; Accounts of Bank of Bombay BL. IOR/L/F/3/662–63)

on India's reserves to bolster its position in times of crisis throughout the rest of the nineteenth century.[112]

In 1866 the rise in the Bank of England's Bank Rate continued up to 8% on 4 January. Bullion flowed back into its reserve, which rose to about £13.5m by mid-March, by which time the Bank had dropped its Rate to 7% on 22 February 1866 and 6% on 15 March 1866. In India at this time the opportunity to import rice for the relief of famine passed, as the transport would now take too long for it to arrive in time.[113] In Britain, however, people were preoccupied. At the beginning of May, the Bank of England's bullion reserve had fallen by about £0.8m and the Bank Rate went back up to 7% on 3 May, 8% on 8 May, 9% on 11 May and 10% on 12 May.

On 10 May the new limited company Overend, Gurney & Co. stopped. Alexander Brown, a director of the Bank of Bombay, later blamed the failure of that bank directly on Overend's stoppage.[114] The high 10% Bank Rate in Britain had turned the flows of bullion positively towards Britain (Fig. 7.9). The Bank of Bombay had used a high rate to attract deposits from which it could earn an income to make up funds lost by some irresponsible lending. This strategy had worked in 1864 when deposits rose in the second half of the year in response to a rate rise in the first half. In 1866 the Bombay Bank had reputational problems and the reverse of flows to Britain took bullion away from India just as it required deposits. The desire of the Bank of England to get its hands on Indian bullion was shown by R. W. Crawford, MP for the City and director of the Bank, who in July 1866 demanded that instructions be sent out 'to India to send to this country the accumulations of gold which had taken place in the Indian Treasury' and £1.595m did arrive. But much more came from America with a sudden influx as shown in Fig. 7.4.[115]

Arguably, the stoppage of the Bank of Bombay was more astounding than Overend's collapse because it was partly owned by the government which had two board members representing its interests. It had performed many governmental functions that the Bank of England did in Britain although it had had the profitable business of note issue transferred away to the Government Paper Currency Department in 1862.[116] The series of events shows the powerful effect of bullion flows in transmitting crises, an effect ignored by the Currency School, as well as the unstable financial conditions in which Overend's finally failed.

7.6 Limited Companies or Interest Rates?

Most conventional accounts of the demise of Overend's, heavily influenced by commentary from the Currency School at the time, have tended to blame the 'rapid creation of companies, especially those with limited liability' for the failures of this time and have suggested that 'tightened supervision' alongside Bagehot's principles of providing credit at high rates ensured that after 1866 systemic crises disappeared until the next century.[117] The Limited Liability Acts of 1856, 1858 and 1862 extended the option of limited liability to all companies with seven or more members without any checks.[118] The number of such companies formed expanded rapidly. In 1862 500 were registered with the new limited status. For the next three years 746, 967 and 992 companies followed.[119] Many of the promotions for the new firms were misguided and some were fraudulent. New finance companies that took on risky debt at high rates, were vulnerable in a crisis, and combined with the disturbance in the cotton market, failures occurred frequently after 1862.

However, the Banking School also emphasised the consistent factor of high and varying discount rates which ran alongside the failures. Patterson claimed, 'the rate of interest is the most important practical point in the wide question of Monetary Science'.[120] To the Banking School, there was an obvious financial connection between higher interest rates and defaults on interest payments by firms. This was a prosaic but common factor in the failures. Even Marsden's fraud against the Leeds Banking Company was inspired by resentment against them for having raised their rates.

Overend's were led astray by their customers who pulled tricks such as discounting chains of bills. Short-term loans were intended to be repaid at the end of the loan to ensure the money was freely available. Banks generally would not issue another loan to cover an expiring short-term one. However, by obtaining loans from different banks and chaining them together long-term loans could be obtained at short-term rates. *The Economist* in 1861 quoted the example of a Mr. Laurence who traded on the good name of a firm even though it was insolvent to obtain a chain of discounts from twenty banks.[121] By the beginning of 1866, the journal was reporting that using short-term funds for long-term investment was a common practice 'everyone acquainted with Lombard Street has long known' there were 'investments in railways secured on railway shares' and not 'real bills' as the Banking School advised.[122]

Such practices made financial institutions very vulnerable to the rate changes made necessary by the Bank Charter Act of 1844.[123] The issue of limited liability was investigated by a select committee after 1866 and it was decided, basically, to support the principle. As *The Economist* summarised the outcome, the Committee 'was asked to confine limited liability; it has extended and completed it'.[124] This outcome was a tacit admission by the committee that it considered other forces, such as interest rates, were more important than a limited liability in the formation of crises.

The reasons for Overend's failure can be illuminated by the records from a legal dispute between shareholders and creditors concerning who would take the losses. The decision came down on the side of the creditors who received a full repayment, but shareholders had to pay further calls. As part of this dispute, John Gurney gave a detailed deposition about the last months of the firm. He was asked 'how is it that the limited company failed?' He answered that on 10 May the amount of deposits sought to be withdrawn was larger than the amount of cash in hand to meet them. It was acknowledged that this was why the firm had stopped—but why had it failed? Gurney answered, 'I consider the two things identical'. He claimed not to know whether the assets would meet liabilities but acknowledged that the sale of the partners' estates had been considered.[125] This exchange indicated that the firm was run on a very poor accounting basis of 'cash in hand'. Victorian bankruptcy laws meant that cash in hand had to be held to trade, but knowledge of assets and liabilities was essential to judge whether it was worth raising a loan to keep the organisation running. It may have been this incapacity to produce this information that really worried the Bank of England. Gurney admitted that the old firm had run at a loss from 1860. The discounting business had been profitable in general, but when loans went bad for fraud or other reasons David Chapman had been too forgiving and asked for more security rather than exposing the frauds. Acting in this way led to a fraud charge against the directors themselves, from which they were later acquitted in court.

The firm had to run on borrowed money in order to recover. If it had had access from then on to stable loan rates, then then it might well have recovered. However, the variability of interest rates took away this possibility. Fraud (not Overend's but their clients') was an issue, but the greater issue was high interest rates.

Some raised suspicions that the Bank of England had purposefully encouraged Overend's demise. There was the variation of interest rates, which could have been unintentional and more related to the tug-of-war over bullion between the Bank of England and the Bank of Bombay, but also the spreading of rumours. Patterson believed the Bank wanted to take over Overend's market share and make more profit on the back of crises.[126] Sir Edward Watkin, a Railway Company director and MP for Stockport, called for a Royal Commission on the panic, but this was then quietly dropped.[127] As a result there never was an enquiry into the 1866 crisis, even though there had been one each for the crises of 1847 and 1857.[128]

The Bank made significant preparations for an increase in discount and short-loans business in 1863. Their existing arrangements dated from 1844 and the Bank Charter Act; now they made changes for increased volume and efficiency. After a 'Special Committee' on the issue they split the Discount Office into two sections; one as a counting house and for bookkeeping and one to actually arrange the discounts and obtain information and keep a register as to 'the position and character of Houses of Business'.[129] The Chief of the Discount Office had discretion about whether to discount bills. The experienced clerks were transferred to other expanding business such as that for India and 15- to 16-year-old youths or 'Mechanics' were employed to do the work more efficiently.[130]

The Bank's income from discounts and short loans from August 1863 to August 1864 more than doubled from 1862 to 1863 and tripled from 1861 to 1862. All periods of crisis in 1847, 1857 and 1866 show high income for the Bank (Fig. 7.10). Mike Anson et al. have shown that profits follow a similar pattern.[131] The total value of bills discounted and short-term advances on bills 1861–1868 are shown in Table 7.3. The figures show that the amount of business did grow from 1862 to 1863 but fell sharply after the failure of Overend's brought credit into disrepute. They also show the 1864–1866 period as one in which there was a continuous heavy demand for credit. It was indeed the case that the Bank benefitted financially from crises while commerce faced uncertainty.

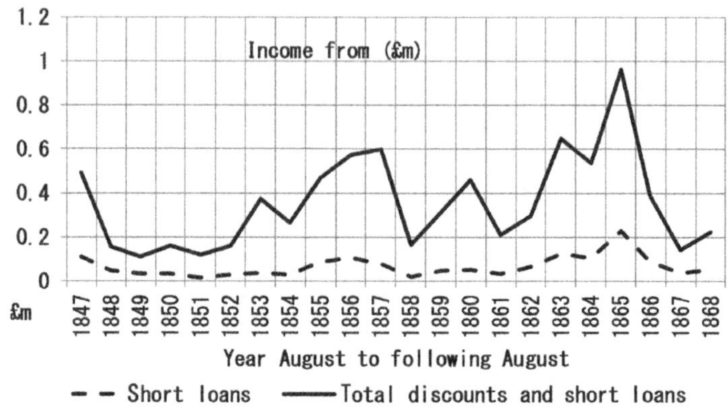

Fig. 7.10 Income of Bank of England from discounting and short loans August 1847 to August 1869 (*Source* J. Clapham, *The Bank of England*, II [Cambridge: Cambridge University Press, 1970] pp. 433, 435)

Table 7.3 Total value of discounts and advances for short periods from London and branches[132]

Total value of discounts and advances	
Year	*£m*
1861–62	79.083
1862–63	82.294
1863–64	102.358
1864–65	114.177
1865–66	123.966
1866–67	104.650
1867–68	68.922
1868–69	31.877

Gladstone, the chancellor of the exchequer at the time of Overend's failure, never mastered the complexity of the monetary debates ongoing in this period, but he had some sympathies with the Banking School, shown by his attempts to place downward pressure on the Bank's charges. His influence was limited because the government he was part of was about to resign over its unrelated failure to pass a bill to widen the voting franchise further. Gladstone went through the motions of writing the usual letter to the Governor of the Bank, after discussion with them:

Downing Street, 11 May 1866

To: The Governor and the Deputy Governor of the Bank of England

Gentlemen, We have the honour to acknowledge the receipt of your letter of this day to the Chancellor of the Exchequer, in which you state the course of action at the Bank of England under the circumstances of sudden anxiety which have arisen since the stoppages of Messrs Overend Gurney & Company (Limited) yesterday. We learn with regret that the Bank reserve, which stood, so recently as last night, at a sum of about five millions and three quarters, has been reduced in a single day, by the liberal answer of the Bank to the demands of commerce during the hours of business, and by its just anxiety to avert disaster, to little more than one half of that amount, or sum (actual for London and estimated for Branches) not greatly exceeding three millions. The accounts and representations, which have reached Her Majesty's Government during the day, exhibit the state of things in the City as one of extraordinary distress and apprehension. Indeed deputations composed of persons of the greatest weight and influence, and representing alike the private and the Joint Stock Banks of London, have presented themselves in Downing Street, and have urged with unanimity and with earnestness the necessity of some intervention on the part of the State, to allay the anxiety which prevails, and which appears to have amounted through great part of the day to absolute panic. There are some important points in which the present crisis differs from those of 1847 and 1857. Those periods were periods of mercantile distress, but the vital consideration of banking credit does not appear to have been involved in them, as it is in the present crisis. Again, the course of affairs was then comparatively slow and measured, whereas the shock has in this instance arrived with intense rapidity and the opportunity for deliberation is narrowed in proportion. Lastly, the Reserve of the Bank of England has suffered a diminution without precedent relatively to the time in which it has been brought about, and, in view especially of this circumstance, Her Majesty's Government cannot doubt that it is their duty to adopt without delay the measures which seem to them best calculated to compose the public mind, and to avert the calamities which may threaten trade and industry.

Of them, the Directors of the Bank of England, proceeding upon the prudent rules of action by which their administration is usually governed, shall find that, in order to meet the wants of legitimate commerce, it is requisite to extend their discounts and advances upon approved securities so as to require issues of Notes beyond the limit fixed by law, Her

Majesty's Government recommend that this necessity should be met immediately upon its occurrence, and in that event they will not fail to make application to Parliament for its sanction. No such discount or advance, however, should be granted at a rate of interest less than ten per cent, and Her Majesty's Government reserve it to themselves to recommend, if they should see fit, the imposition of a higher rate. After deduction by the Bank of whatever it may consider to be fair charge for its risk, influences and trouble, the profits of these advances will accrue to the public.

We have the honor to be, Gentlemen, your obedient servants.

(Signed) *Russell, Gladstone,* Chancellor of the Exchequer.[133]

This letter exempted the Bank from the note issue requirements of the 1844 Act from 11 May 1866, as the Bank put its Rate up to 9% on the same day and 10% on the following day. There it stayed, until 16 August, while the Russell government collapsed, and a minority Disraeli administration took over. The depth of the crisis, in terms of keeping banknotes available while complying with the Bank Charter Act, could be judged from the fall in the total value of notes kept in the note reserve ready to be issued: from around £8m in March 1866 to £0.304m on 29 May 1866.

The Economist explained 'it is alleged that the Bank Directors do not reduce the rate because 10 per cent was fixed in the Treasury letter and because they are still held to that letter'.[134] Gladstone had washed his hands of the Bank, saying they 'acted entirely on their own judgement'.[135] His practical energies were consumed by his attempt, as Leader of the House of Commons, to push through an expansion of the franchise against fierce Parliamentary opposition.[136] Within weeks of Overend's stopping payment, Gladstone had lost control in the House of Commons and his party split in two.[137] As a result, Russell and his entire government were forced to resign on 26 June 1866.[138] The minority Conservative government that succeeded it was slow to take power, and Benjamin Disraeli, the new chancellor of the exchequer, took until the middle of August to start dealing with the financial crisis.[139]

The tumult caused by the Russell government's collapse, and the deeply politically contentious proposals by both parties for electoral reform, meant that political interest in the crisis of 1866 quickly waned. Gladstone's letter had insisted that 'the profits of these advances [discounting of bills] will accrue to the public'.[140] In other words, the supernormal profits resulting from the 10% interest rate he specified would be transferred to the Treasury. Yet there is no record that this instruction was acted upon.

7.7 Consequences of the Crisis

For the moment, public approval by the Bank's directors for the idea of it taking on the role of a central bank was withheld. Its Governor struggled to serve its two masters: the government and the Bank's own private shareholders. *The Economist* reported that Henry Holland, the Bank's Governor during the crisis, had informed the Bank's Court on 15 March 1866 that a higher dividend would be paid 'in consequence of the higher rate of interest that had ruled, and he hoped that the proprietors would be satisfied that the directors had done the best for their interest'.[141] After the crisis, Holland protested the contrary: that the Bank had made every effort to provide sufficient discount facilities, but the fact remains that a rate of 10% for three months may have sent many sound businesses to the wall along with the unsound.[142] Other directors voiced their opposition to the Bank taking on the role of lender of last resort including J.G. Hubbard, Thomson Hankey and G.W. Norman.[143] In short, as Bagehot summed up in *Lombard Street*, published in 1873, the security of the nation's monetary system, in the form of the reserve, was 'in the hands of a single board of directors not particularly trained for the duty—who might be called "amateurs"… who have never been told by any great statesman or public authority that they are so to keep it…'.[144]

In the longer term, the Bank eventually accepted its role as a central bank and the 'lender of last resort' as the rest of the nineteenth century progressed, but it took time for all of its directors to be convinced of this. This change occurred much later, and less explicitly than commonly assumed. Initially there was not the pre-commitment that is a necessary prerequisite for Bagehot's dictum to operate. Something more than the Bank becoming a 'lender of last resort' is needed to fully explain the timing and nature of the disappearance of severe systemic crises in Britain after 1866.

The lesson from the Banking School that the Bank of England took on after 1866 was that it needed to increase its bullion reserve and control bullion flows gently, doing so by using small but prompt adjustments to the Bank Rate. The mistake of 1866, of suddenly raising the Bank Rate substantially above American rates, did not occur again until the panic at the start of the first world war in 1914, when the gold standard was suspended.

Such a prescription became clear to the Bank of England's directors as they could see the process of the Banking-School crisis cycle in real time for the crisis of 1864 and the crisis of 1866 from the Bank's daily account books (Fig. 7.11). Falls in the Bank Rate to a low level (1) gave rise to a search for better investments and therefore a bullion drain (2). The drain caused the Bank to raise its rate (3) which caused American and British interest rates to move together and investment flows to stop, causing a crisis or commercial disturbance (4). The first cycle is from March 1863 ending in early 1864. A second cycle is marked on the chart ending in 1866, triggered in this case by bullion flows to India, but this pattern re-runs continuously. The extent of the crises at position (4) in cycles that took place after 1866 depend on the exact circumstance, but what the Bank saw was the opportunity to calm the storms by moderating the cycle almost before it had begun, avoiding the harsh rate hikes and stoppages in investment flows that characterised events in 1847, 1857–1858 and 1866.

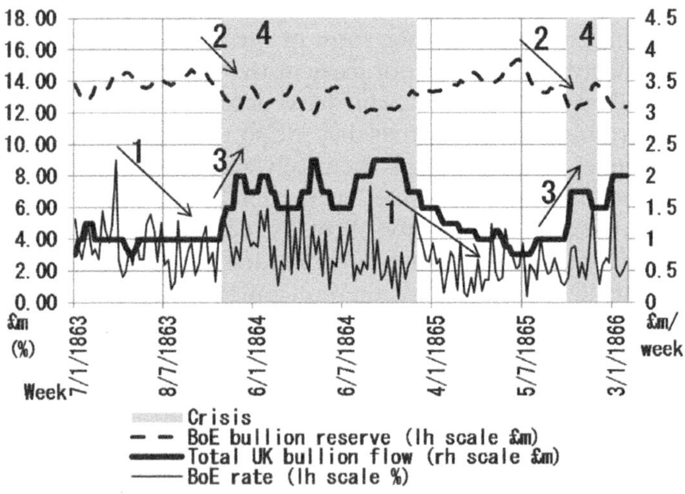

Fig. 7.11 Total bullion flows in and out, bullion reserves and Bank rate of the UK weekly, June 1864–March 1866 (*Source* Bank of England daily account books)

The crisis of 1866 was also followed by profound changes in the economic landscape that aided the Bank's hopes for greater financial stability in the future. In the United Kingdom food price fluctuations began to disengage from the timing of such crises and fall to consistently reduced levels. This was the result of falling food prices and also that flows of capital for investment became much greater than ones for trade in foodstuffs. Increasingly, credit transactions replaced the transportation of bullion in payment for the trade of merchandise and faster communication reduced the profits from interest-rate arbitrage on gold. The use of bills of exchange as a form of credit for transactions within Britain went into a slow decline. The Bank of England grew its bullion reserves gradually, meaning that it had the capacity to avoid sudden and sharp interest-rate hikes. Crises which threatened its stability became a thing of the past.

The crisis of 1866 was very much a policy failure that could have been avoided. The tug-of-war over bullion between Britain and India destabilised the Bank of England's Bank Rate, which intentionally or unintentionally drove Overend's to the wall. The Bank then shot itself in the foot by putting up its Bank Rate further, so bullion flooded in from the United States seeking the higher rate, with both those bullion depositors, as well as the Country Bankers seeking liquidity to survive higher rates, stripping it bare of notes, and triggering more failures in Britain and around the world as a credit crunch set in. As many as one in six multinational banks based in London collapsed and stopped all domestic and foreign activities. As Chenzu Xu has shown, the crisis in London in 1866 'disrupted short-term bank-intermediated financing in almost every country in the world', triggering a deep slump in world trade, as the world's financial infrastructure for the financing of exports became so damaged.[145]

Yet perhaps the most disturbing consequence of the economic crisis was the effect which it had on the financing of relief for the famine in Madras and Orissa (now Chennai and Odisha) which occurred in India in 1866. In many respects, the controversy over that event reflects that concerning the Irish Famine of 1847. Whereas, in Ireland, the immediate cause of the famine was the occurrence of potato blight, in India the famine was preceded by drought, but in both cases, the result can be considered as a demand problem rather than solely a food supply problem. In Ireland, the poorest grew their food supplies, hand to mouth, and did not have sufficient money to buy replacement food when that failed.

In India, contemporary observers suggest that the drought meant that agricultural workers were not employed and had no money even before the crops failed. *Laissez-faire* attitudes have been conveniently blamed in the case of the 'Indian' government for the delays in providing aid, just as they were in the case of the UK government in cutting direct aid in 1847.[146] However, in both cases, the aim was to constrain the cost of relief to the countries (India and Ireland) themselves and not be a burden on the credit of the British Treasury during a time of financial turmoil. The collapse of the world's export financing sector as a result of the crisis of 1866 also made it harder for the private sector to import food in Orissa for those that still had money. However, British officials on the ground did not realise the full implications of this for local food markets and the consequent need for government intervention until it was too late.

A report of the measures taken, issued in December 1866, emphasised in great detail the cost of them and whether they would fall upon the government.[147] A small fund within the Indian government accounts was used to buy rice. John Lawrence, the Governor General, had learnt some of the lessons of Ireland in 1847, when local taxes had soared, and insisted on 'light taxation' for India. 'Light taxation in my mind is the panacea for foreign rule in India'; whatever the miseries of people of Orissa, 'the present Govt. of India is not to blame for them'.[148] Combined with the general attitude expressed in the British House of Commons that the United Kingdom should be relieved 'from any burden on account of India' after the government took over from the East India Company, immediate financial concerns, including the crisis in the City of London, ruled the day and the response was too slow. Despite the assistance that was recorded as given in Orissa, 12,000 people in relief work for fifteen months, and free food to 31,000 people for sixteen months, it has been estimated that a third of the local population of the area died (as many as one million people) in the period 1866–1868.[149]

Back in Britain, there continued to be incidents of unpleasant financial disturbances after 1866. Although these were not as serious, they still coincided with short-term interest rates in the United States and United Kingdom moving together. Nevertheless, the Bank, by following the Banking School's prescriptions of moderation and subtlety in the use of the Bank Rate managed to avert systemic crises on the scale of 1847, 1857–1858 and 1866. Yet calm in the City of London did not solve all of the British economy's problems and this period became known as the start of 'the Long Depression'.

Notes

1. *Hansard*, 31 July 1866, CLXXXIV, c. 1716.
2. Ranald Michie has pointed out that there was a small run by savers on London and County Securities in December 1973 during the secondary banking crisis, but the episode was little reported upon the press and thus it does not count as a 'major' or 'high-profile' bank run in most British financial histories. See F. H. Capie, *The Bank of England: 1950s–1979* (Cambridge: CUP, 2010), pp. 525–585, cited in R. C. Michie, *British Banking: Continuity and Change from 1694 to the Present* (Oxford: OUP, 2016) p. 187.
3. Capie, *The Bank of England: 1950s to 1979*, p. 524.
4. F. H. Capie, M. Billings, 'Profitability in English Banking in the Twentieth Century', *European Review of Economic History* 5 (December 2001) 367–401.
5. W. Bagehot, *Lombard Street: A Description of the Money Market* [1873] (Westport: Hyperion Press, 1962) p. 85.
6. R. Sowerbutts, M. Schneebalg, F. Hubert, 'The Demise of Overend Gurney', *Bank of England Quarterly Bulletin 2016 Q2* (2016) p. 99.
7. S. Schneider, 'The Politics of Last Resort Lending and the Overend & Gurney Crisis of 1866', *Economic History Review* 75 (2022) p. 581.
8. A. Hotson, *Respectable Banking: The Search for Stability in London's Money and Credit Markets Since 1695* (Cambridge: CUP, 2017) p. 8.
9. See letters between Overstone and Norman in D. P. O'Brien, *The Correspondence of Lord Overstone* (Cambridge: Royal Economic Society, 1971) pp. 1100–1162.
10. Obituary, *The Times*, 1 October 1904, p. 13.
11. H. Chubb, 'The Bank Act and the Crisis of 1866', *Journal of the Statistical Society* 35 Pt. 2 (1872) pp. 175–77.
12. Sowerbutts et al., 'The Demise of Overend Gurney', pp. 94, 103.
13. F. W. Fetter, *Development of British Monetary Orthodoxy 1797–1875* (Cambridge, MA; Harvard, UP, 1965) pp. 257–283.
14. Bagehot, *Lombard Street*, p. 160.
15. J. Grant, *Bagehot: The Life and Times of the Greatest Victorian* (New York: Norton, 2019) p. 268.
16. G. J. Goschen, *Theory of the Foreign Exchanges* (London: Effingham Wilson, 1861) pp. 114, 117–124, 130.
17. W. Fowler, *The Crisis of 1866, a Financial Essay* (London: Longmans, 1866) pp. 7–9.
18. Bagehot to Gladstone, 11 May 1866, B.L., Add. MS. 44410 f. 154.
19. Bagehot to Gladstone, 24 May 1866, B.L., Add. MS. 44410 ff. 201–203.

20. J. Gurney Hoare to Gladstone, 11 May 1866, B.L., Add. MS. 44410 ff. 156–158.
21. Fowler, *The Crisis of 1866, a Financial Essay*, p. 42; *The Economist*, 29 September 1866, p. 1134.
22. *The Economist*, 19 May 1866, p. 582.
23. Bagehot, *Lombard Street*, p. 123.
24. W. S. Jevons, *A Serious Fall in the Value of gold Ascertained* (London: Stanford, 1863) frontispiece.
25. C. Juglar, *Les crises commercial et leur retour périodique en France, en Angleterre et aux Etats-Unis* (Paris: Guillaumin, 1889) pp. 387–389; see references to Banking-School ideas in D. Besomi, 'Clément Juglar (1819–1905) Les origines de la théorie des cycles', *Revue européenne des sciences sociales*, 47 (2009) 17–47, e.g. floating capital, p. 23, excess credit and capital p. 27.
26. R. H. Patterson, 'On Our Home Monetary Drains, and the Crisis of 1866', *Statistical Society of London* 33 (1870) pp. 226–228.
27. A. Rothschild to Chairman of the Commission, 30 January 1888, *Second Report of the Royal Commission appointed to enquire into the recent Changes in the relative Values of the precious metals…* PP 1888 (c. 5248) XLV.1, p. 285.
28. J. M. Robson (ed.), *Collected Works of John Stuart Mill* XXI (Toronto: University of Toronto Press, 1984) p. 433.
29. O'Brien, *The Correspondence of Lord Overstone*, p. 41; *The Times*, 23 May 1868, p. 12.
30. *The Economist*, 15 September 1866, p. 1080.
31. Overstone to Norman, 21 November 1862 in O'Brien, *The Correspondence of Lord Overstone*, p. 126; *The Economist*, 23 June 1866, p. 730.
32. *The Times*, 20 May 1859, p. 8.
33. *The Times*, 24 June 1859, p. 7.
34. Bank of England daily account book, 1859.
35. *The Economist*, 10 September 1859, p. 1019.
36. *The Times*, 18 September 1858, p. 5.
37. Sowerbutts et al., 'The Demise of Overend Gurney', pp. 96–97.
38. Idem., p. 97; there is no reference to the evidence of this note ever existing.
39. *The Economist*, 3 February 1866, p. 123; A. Liesse, *Evolution of Credit and Banks in France* (Washington: National Monetary Commission, 1909) p. 106.
40. *The Economist*, 19 May 1855, p. 544; 26 May 1855, pp. 572–574;
41. *The Economist*, 23 June 1855, p. 671.
42. *The Times*, 5 December 1857, p. 5.
43. *The Economist*, 14 July 1855, p. 756.

44. Bagehot, *Lombard Street*, p. 21.
45. Bank of England court of directors minutes, 18 March 1858.
46. *The Times*, 30 March 1860, p. 10.
47. *The Economist*, 21 April 1860, p. 417; *The Times*, 23 April 1860, p. 7.
48. Bank of England daily account book, 10 April 1860.
49. M. Flandreau, S. Ugolini, 'The Crisis of 1866', *The Graduate Institute, Geneva, Working paper* 10/2014, p. 6; W. Bagehot, *Lombard Street*, p. 299.
50. *The Times*, 21 July 1860, p. 10.
51. *The Times*, 26 September 1864, p. 5; 23 September 1864, p. 10.
52. *Fremont Journal Extra*, 13 April 1861, p. 1.
53. *Daily News*, 15 December 1862, p. 4.
54. *Source* Bank of England daily account books.
55. Bank of England daily account books, 1862, 1863.
56. Ibid.
57. Bank of England daily account books, 1864.
58. K. R. Bopp, 'Bank of France Policy: Brief Survey of Instruments, 1800–1914' *American Journal of Economics and Sociology* 11 (1952) pp. 237–238.
59. *The Times*, 21 March 1866, p. 10.
60. *Annual statement of Trade and Navigation...* PP 1866 LXVI-1 (3942), pp. 40, 43.
61. Bopp, 'Bank of France Policy: Brief Survey of Instruments, 1800–1914', p. 242.
62. A. Di Vittorio, *An Economic History of Europe* (Abingdon: Routledge, 2006) p. 226.
63. *Annual statement* ... PP 1866 LXVI-1 (3942), pp. 40, 43.
64. C. P. Kindleberger, *A Financial History of Western Europe* (Abingdon: Routledge, 2015) p. 108.
65. A. Rothschild to Chairman of the Commission, 30 January 1888, *Second Report of the Royal Commission appointed to enquire into the recent Changes in the relative Values of the precious metals...* PP 1888 (c. 5248) XLV.1, p. 285.
66. Bank of England daily account books, 1864; P. L. Cottrell, *Investment Banking in England 1856–1881* I (Abingdon: Routledge, 2012) p. 312.
67. Bank of England daily account books.
68. Ibid.
69. J. F. Riddick, *The History of British India* (Santa Barbara CA: Greenwood, 2006) p. 138.
70. Bank of England, daily account books, 29 June to 5 July 1865.
71. *The Times*, 23 June 1865, p. 10.
72. *The Times*, 5 May 1866, p. 5.

73. Wood negotiates fees: Bank of England court of treasury minutes June–November 1863, pp. 7, 33.
74. *London Gazette*, Bank of England published returns 8 April 1865 p. 406 (w/e 5 April), 15 April 1865 (w/e 12 April) p. 439, Indian Deposits Bank of England daily account books 5 April 1865, 12 April 1865; Indian Government Ledger B.L., L/AG/1/1/37 May 1864–1865, p. 93.
75. *The Economist*, 22 May 1869, p. 589.
76. *The Economist*, 11 November 1871, p. 1366.
77. *The Economist*, 5 May 1866, p. 525.
78. Government of India Act, 1858, 21 & 22 Vict. c. 106.
79. *The Economist*, 19 December 1857, p. 1397.
80. Ibid.
81. *Hansard*, 19 March 1858, CXLIX, c. 415.
82. *The Times*, 15 March 1858, p. 7.
83. M. Taylor, 'The 1848 Revolutions and the British Empire', *Past & Present*, 166 (2000) p. 178.
84. N. Gash, *Sir Robert Peel: The Life of Sir Robert Peel After 1830* (London: Longman, 1972) Epilogue.
85. P. Scherer, *Lord John Russell: A Biography* (London: Associated University Presses, 1999) pp. 152, 323–332.
86. C. Read, 'Laissez-Faire, the Irish Famine, and British Financial Crisis', *Economic History Review* 69 (2016) pp. 414–416; R. J. Moore, *Sir Charles Wood's Indian policy*, 1853–66 (Manchester: Manchester UP, 1966) pp. viii–ix.
87. C. Ó Gráda, *The Great Irish Famine* (Cambridge: CUP, 1997) pp. 43–45; M. McRae, 'Sir Charles Trevelyan's Indian letters', *English Historical Review* 77 (1962) p. 706.
88. A. Hawkins, *The Forgotten Prime Minister: the 14th Earl of Derby* I (Oxford: OUP, 2007) pp. 298–302; II, Chapter 6.
89. Moore, *Sir Charles Wood's Indian Policy*, pp. 234–235.
90. *Quarterly Review*, April 1861, p. 575.
91. Moore, *Sir Charles Wood's Indian Policy*, p. 234.
92. J. Wilson, *Speech of the Right Hon James Wilson* (London: Allen & Co., 1860) p. 40.
93. For Trevelyan's difficulties with raising funds for famine relief by taxation in Ireland, see C. Read, *The Great Famine in Ireland and Britain's Financial Crisis* (Woodbridge: The Boydell Press, 2022), Chapter 5.
94. *The Economist*, 7 April 1860, pp. 363–364; 15 December 1860, p. 1389.
95. *Hansard*, 11 May 1860, CLVIII, cc. 1130-61; C. E. Trevelyan, *Statement of Sir C. E. Trevelyan*; Trevelyan to Wood 12 March 1866, Wood papers microfilm, Cambridge University Library.

96. L. Trevelyan, *A Very British Family: The Trevelyans and Their World* (London: I.B. Tauris, 2012) p. 54. Indophilus = Friend of India.
97. Trevelyan to Wood, 8 August 1862, Wood Papers Microfilm, Cambridge University Library.
98. Bengal Rent Recovery (under-tenures) Act, 1865 (Bengal Act VIII of 1865).
99. Read, 'Laissez-faire', pp. 427–428; *The Times*, 20 January 1866, p. 9.
100. *The Times*, 1 July 1865, p. 9.
101. *The Times*, 23 June 1865, p. 10.
102. Read, 'Laissez-faire', p. 423.
103. *Hansard*, 4 July 1865, CLXXX, c. 1143.
104. G. Patnaik, *The Famine and Some Aspects of the British Economic Policy in Orissa 1866–1905* (Cuttack: Vidyapur, 1980) p. 20; B. B. Bhatta, *The Natural Calamities in Orissa in the Nineteenth Century* (New Delhi: Commonwealth Publishers, 1997) p. 116.
105. Wood to Bombay, 2 June 1865, B.L., IOR/L/F/3/271, p. 29.
106. *Report of the Bombay Bank Commission* PP 1868–69 (q. 4162) p. 2; Bombay Act X, 1863.
107. Wood to Lawrence, 3 July 1865, B.L., MS. Eur F909/26 no. 40.
108. *Times of India*, 2 August 1865, 6, 20 September 1865, *Report of the Bombay Bank Commission* PP 1868–69 (4162) p. 36.
109. *East India Famine Papers* PP 1867 (335) p. 356.
110. *The Economist*, 29 September 1866, p. 1134.
111. *Times of India*, 8 November 1865.
112. W. Narsey, *British Imperialism and the Making of Colonial Currency Systems* (Basingstoke: Palgrave Macmillan, 2016) pp. 74–75.
113. *East India (Bengal and Orissa famine). Papers and correspondence relative to the famine in Bengal and Orissa, including the report of the Famine Commission and the minutes of the Lieutenant Governor of Bengal and the Governor General of India*, Pt. II PP 1867 (335) LI.1, 403, 641, pp. 65, 73, 298.
114. *Report of the Bombay Bank Commission* PP 1868–1869 (4162-I) p. 55.
115. *Hansard*, 19 July 1866, CLXXXIV, c. 1114.
116. C. Weintraub, K. Schuler, 'India's Paper Currency Department 1862–1935 as a Quasi-Currency Board', *Studies in Applied Economics*, 9 (2013) p. 3.
117. Fowler, *The Crisis of 1866: A Financial Essay*, pp. 3–4; Flandreau, Ugolini, 'The Crisis of 1866', p. 3.
118. 19 & 20 Vict. c. 47; 21 & 22 Vict. c. 91; 25 & 26 Vict. c. 89.
119. H. A. Shannon, 'The First Five Thousand Limited Companies and their Duration', *Economic History* 3 (1932) p. 421.
120. R. H. Patterson, 'On the Rate of Interest', *Journal of the Statistical Society of London* 34 (1871) p. 334.

121. *The Economist*, 26 January 1861, p. 88.
122. *The Economist*, 8 February 1866, p. 123.
123. For more on this theme: R. C. Michie, 'Choice and Connections, 1825–1914', in R. C. Michie, *British Banking: Continuity and Change from 1694 to the Present* (Oxford: OUP, 2016).
124. *Select Committee on the Limited Liability Acts* PP 1867 (329) X.393; *The Economist*, 31 August 1867, p. 982.
125. Deposition of John Gurney, 8 January 1867, N.A. C16/445(01), pp. 33–35.
126. Patterson, 'On the Rate of Interest', p. 342.
127. *Hansard*, 31 July 1866, CLXXXIV, c. 718, c. 1706, c. 2125.
128. Gladstone reply to Mr. Watkin, *Hansard*, 31 July 1866, CLXXXIV, c. 1744.
129. Bank of England court of directors minutes, 1863, pp. 249–253.
130. Idem., p. 254.
131. M. Anson, D. Bholat, M. Kang, R. Thomas, 'The Bank of England as lender of Last Resort Historical Dataset 1847–1919', *Working paper* 691, 2017.
132. *Source* Bank of England court of directors minutes.
133. Bank of England court of directors minutes, 1866b; *The Economist*, 19 May 1866, p. 588.
134. *The Economist*, 30 June 1866.
135. *Hansard*, 2 July 1866, CLXXXIV, c. 718.
136. R. Shannon, *Gladstone: Heroic Minister 1865–1898* (London: Allen Lane, 1999) pp. 21–24.
137. Idem., p. 22.
138. J. R. Vincent (ed.), *Disraeli, Derby and the Conservative Party: The Political Journals of Edward Henry, Lord Stanley 1849–69* (Hassocks: Harvester Press, 1978) p. 255.
139. M Pharand, E. Hawman, M. Millar, S. Den Otter, M. Wiebe (eds.), *Benjamin Disraeli Letters, 1865–1867* IX (Toronto, 2013) p. 126 (letter 4127).
140. Gladstone to the Governor and the Deputy Governor of the Bank of England, 11 May 1866, quoted in Sowerbutts, et al., 'The Demise of Overend Gurney', pp. 104–105.
141. *The Economist*, 19 May 1866, p. 4.
142. *The Economist*, 20 October 1866, p. 1208.
143. J. G. Hubbard (Director of the Bank) to *The Times*, 12 May 1866, published 14 May 1866, p. 7; T. Hankey (Director of the Bank) *Principles of Banking, Its Utility and Economy: With Remarks on the Working and Management of the Bank of England* (London: Effingham Wilson, 1867) p. 25; *The Economist*, 22 December 1866, p. 1488.
144. Bagehot, *Lombard Street*, p. 21.

145. C. Xu, 'Reshaping Global Trade: The Immediate and Long-Run Effects of Bank Failures', *Stanford University Working paper* (March 2022). https://chenzi-xu.com/docs/reshaping_global_trade_Xu.pdf [accessed 27 May 2022].
146. Secretary Board of Revenue Calcutta to Commissioner of Cuttack, 1 February 1866, in *Papers and Correspondence relative to the famine in Bengal and Orissa*, II PP 1867 (335) LI.1, 403, 641, p. 234; C. E. Trevelyan, *The Irish Crisis* (London: Longmans, 1848).
147. *East India (Madras and Orissa) Famine* PP 1867 (490) LII.173, pp. 250–269.
148. Sir John Lawrence to Viscount Cranborne, 5 November 1866, B.L., Lawrence Collection, MSS Eur F90/31, no. 48.
149. R. C. Dutt, *Famines and Land Assessment in India* (London: Kegan Paul, 1900) p. 9; H. K. Mishra, *Famines and Poverty in India* (New Delhi: APH, 1991) p. 104; Patnaik, *The Famine and Some Aspects of the British Economic Policy in Orissa 1866–1905*, p. 52.

CHAPTER 8

The Fading Away of Crises After 1866

> I am sure, however, that everyone who is conversant with the subject will agree with me when I say that, Bank Act or no Bank Act, if the Bank of England wish to retain its business it must follow the market rate of interest. The Bank of England is often said to fix the rate of interest, just as Britannia is said to rule the waves, we cannot however prevent storms in the money market any more than we can level the waves of the ocean.
>
> —Sir John Lubbock, Lord Avebury, MP for Maidstone, banker, *Hansard*, 25 March 1873, CCXV, c. 130.[1]

> We have refined our methods of working until we are spinning a big top on a needle point.
>
> —George Pownall, Institute of Bankers, 'Bank Reserves', *The Economic Journal* 9 (1899) p. 400.[2]

An end to the systemic crises in which the Bank of England came near to running out of liquidity did not bring complete tranquillity, rather a new set of problems. *The Economist* introduced the year of 1873 as being in a 'Very Peculiar Position' with capital lying idle because 'for a very long period enterprise is so slack and credit so bad that there is no possibility of employing an increasing capital to advantage'.[3] Its diagnosis matched the circumstances that the Banking School recognised as a seeding ground for crises, as owners of that capital eventually go on a search for a better

C. Read, *Calming the Storms*, Palgrave Studies in Economic History,
https://doi.org/10.1007/978-3-031-11914-9_8

investment yield abroad. However, 1873 is notable in that these circumstances did not result in a severe systemic crisis of the sort that occurred in 1847, 1857–1858 and 1866.

This chapter argues that the application by the Bank of England of the Banking School's ideas about how to prevent financial crises was partly responsible for this. The Bank of England managed its bullion reserve by following Thomas Tooke and James Wilson's advice: that it should only make small adjustments in its Rate, but it should make them as soon as any movement in the bullion reserve is detected to prevent any speculative excess from getting out of hand. The bank also started to monitor its note reserve because, as the crises of 1847, 1857–1858 and 1866 had shown, this was becoming increasingly crucial for the Bank of England's stability. The chapter goes on to explain how other potential speculative bubbles and crises were headed off using similar tactics, in 1878, 1882, 1884–1885, 1888, 1890 and 1896–1899.

It was in this period that the Bank slowly assumed its role as the 'lender of last resort'. Yet even at the end of the nineteenth century it was far from accepting 'Bagehot's dictum' as its main strategy to prevent crises. In some ways it was more preventer of first resort and more mender than lender of last resort in these decades. Interest-rate hikes were used more promptly than before 1866 to head off speculative booms before they became a systemic risk. The Bank's accumulation of a bigger bullion reserve—thanks in part because it began to help itself to India's reserves—meant that it could raise rates more slowly in response to interest-rate shocks from abroad, preventing a repeat of the sharp rises that triggered banking panics at home in 1847, 1857–1858 and 1866. There were also rescues of banks before they collapsed. In particular, the rescue of Barings in 1890 was a 'lifeboat' operation, carried out before Barings actually sank, and was far from Walter Bagehot's suggested policy of a general supply of credit to other sound businesses at high interest rates after a collapse had occurred.

Bagehot himself would probably have been surprised that his suggestion of how to deal with an aftermath of a collapse in a second-best world would be interpreted by posterity as a prescription for preventing crises from forming in the first place. This chapter explores the other ideas of the Banking School on how to do this, which have been ignored by much of the recent literature. Nevertheless, they should merit much more consideration from economists and historians of modern Britain.

8.1 An Overview of the Period

Confirmation that the Bank had adopted the Banking School's policies was recorded by Bonamy Price, a professor at the University of Oxford. Price started out his working life as a schoolteacher but, through his interest in the currency question, was elected as the Drummond Professor of Political Economy at the University of Oxford in 1868. His economic views can be categorised as 'extreme' Banking-School harking back to early-nineteenth-century anti-bullionism and supporting free banking. His views moderated quickly, but his inquisitive nature enabled him to prise out of the Governor of the Bank of England, Henry Hucks Gibbs, information that showed the Banking School's ideas had achieved considerable influence over its policies, as the last three decades of the century ran their course. Price's early lectures, published as *Currency and Banking* in 1876, exposed the sleight of hand used to establish the currency system in 1844 with what was apparently, but not actually, sufficient bullion:

> The gold stored and kept in the Government Office, the Issue Department, in no sense whatever belongs to the Bank of England. It is no part of its reserve, and it is a great misfortune that the framers of the Act of 1844 should have made the exceedingly unintelligent blunder of mixing up together in the weekly reports of the bullion at the Bank, two absolutely dissimilar and distinct things—the gold stored away by one office to face the bank-notes, and the gold belonging to the Bank of England as a banker.[4]

Some bullion that the Act counted as part of the reserve against issued notes did not belong to the Bank and could be withdrawn by depositors in the banking department as well as by holders of banknotes issued by the issue department. Nevertheless, Price believed the Bank Charter Act of 1844 did have some merits, in that it had provided a currency secure in value. He suggested that its faults could be remedied by the use of cheques instead of cash and that the United States should copy the British currency system.[5] However, he did not credit the Act with any stabilising influence on the banking sector in the way that Sir Robert Peel, the bill's author, had originally hoped it would. In *Chapters on Practical Political Economy* in 1878, Price protested that:

> Overstone and all the City erected and preached up the Bank Charter Act as the controller of the circulation, and thereby the creator of steady interest and trade, and the averter of panics. I had to cry, Bosh! and was put away as an unpractical fellow, who knew nothing about it. The talk about the Bank Act has been for the most part nonsense. From the very first, I wrote that it had done two things: it had given a safe Bank of England note,—and, secondly, decreed the ultimate extinction in England of private notes. It did nothing more.[6]

At the end of the book, he published his correspondence with Gibbs and with Sir Stafford Northcote, the chancellor of the exchequer. He provoked Gibbs by accusing the Bank of damaging the economy with very hard and fast rules on changing the Bank Rate with fluctuations in the Bank's bullion reserve: 'the grand formula is this: "Gold has gone away, up with the rate: gold has come in, down with it."'[7] Price stated that he thought the consequences for commerce to be 'very mischievous'. The response from Gibbs was that this was a consideration, but it was taken into account with other factors including 'the mood of our depositors, the condition of our borrowers, their strength or weakness, the state of trade, of the harvest, of home and foreign politics, of the markets for produce, of the exchanges, everything, in short, which can affect the case'.[8] Price then revealed that he too had agreed with Gibbs' policy all along.

The admission that the state of the exchanges was an issue confirmed the influence of the Banking School's ideas on the Bank, but Gibbs went further. A timely, subtle approach was necessary.[9] The Bank had to consider 'the state of our Reserve, the amount which we have in our coffers wherewith to pay our debts and to meet demands upon us', but this 'Reserve' was the note reserve in the issue department, confirming the note reserve to total liabilities ratio was being monitored.[10] Gibbs confirmed that note reserves were counted as notes in circulation when assessing circulation against bullion reserves because 'Notes which we hold are as truly "Notes with the Public" as are those held by a man in Berwick-upon-Tweed; for the Bank, in its banking capacity, is one of the Public'.[11]

All these revelations demonstrated the influence of the Banking School's ideas. The consideration of the health of the note reserve not only as much as, but more than the bullion reserve in determining interest rates, had arisen from the circumstances recognised by Bagehot in 1866, when higher rates and influxes of bullion caused a raised demand for notes. Chapter 3 has shown how the 1847, 1857 and 1866 crises were serious when measured by the note reserve to total liabilities ratio, and how this measure was stable thereafter. That the Bank was prioritising the monitoring of this ratio from the 1870s onwards is consistent with this pattern.

While banking matters had been stabilised, and food prices had diminished, the economy did not inspire confidence in the period up to the end of the 1890s and it became commonly known as the 'Long Depression', particularly in the United States and on the European continent. The Repeal of the Corn Laws, when combined with falling transport costs for grain across the Atlantic in the 1870s, caused food prices to fall in the United Kingdom and a severe agricultural depression. The 'Great Depression' became a frequent topic of discussion in the newspapers of the time, with a Royal Commission established in 1885 to inquire on its causes. More than that, it reduced the value of returns on investment. Profit on agricultural land and industrial investment did not just reduce in proportion to the price level but fell lower, and sometimes turned to a loss.[12] The word 'depression' was a colloquial label and was not given on the basis of the current economic definition, but it indicated the dissatisfaction that was felt with the economic situation of the time. 'There is a certain gloom, an indefinable uneasiness and apprehension abroad in the world...and the spirits of most people are somewhat depressed', *The Times* noted in 1873.[13]

An attempt to legislate for the Banking School's idea of an automatic easing of the Currency School restrictions in times of difficulty was made in 1873. The Bank of England Note Bill was intended to allow an expanded note circulation if interest rates reached 12.5% and the exchanges were against the United Kingdom (i.e., a net flow out). It was introduced to Parliament on 12 June 1873 by the chancellor of the exchequer in Gladstone's administration, Robert Lowe (Viscount Sherbrooke after 1880).

It was soon the subject of intense hatred by Lord Overstone and the then Financial Secretary to the Treasury William Baxter, whose family were textile manufacturers.[14] Lowe had also been a leader writer for *The Times* and although Marmaduke Sampson had now gone, his replacement, Arthur Crump, still insisted on maintaining a line that supported the Bank of England. This policy was most likely so that *The Times* could not be accused of destabilising the market, as Sampson was reputed to have done by puffing up projects. But the result was that Currency

School theories of currency were rigorously protected against all opposition. Robert Giffen recorded that he 'was informed that my duty as City editor was, not to give news or information, but to keep stocks at their proper prices—that I was to be the providence of investors, and give them opinions to go by, and *not* give them data upon which to found their own'.[15] The same attitude appears to have applied to economic theories as to securities because *The Times* slated the thinking behind the Note Bill, saying the City thought any legislation should be called 'an Act for the discouragement of commercial prudence' and it was withdrawn on 7 July 1873.[16] Overstone was triumphant at this news, but found it strange that the City of London generally supported the bill, suggesting this viewpoint arose mainly from George Warde Norman and the Bank.[17] In the same letter Overstone referred to a potential future '4th crisis' since the passage of the Bank Charter Act—one that the Bank was eventually able to delay until 1914 or 1973 depending on how it is measured—showing his lack of interest in the issue of preventing future crises.[18]

So, without legislation for a formal change in direction, the Bank was left with three main informal policies: Bagehot's ideas of the Bank acting as a central bank and the reassurance it would bring, an increased bullion reserve, and the policy of adjusting interest rates carefully. As William Stanley Jevons put it: 'a careful observation…of the fluctuations of the money market is sufficient to enable us to avoid the inconveniences of the periodic pressures'. 'Allow for the normal', and only adjust interest rates in the face of international drains caused by investment flows by using small but prompt movements.[19] Normal trading flows should not provoke a reaction. This method was referred to by Pownall as 'spinning a big top on a needle point'.[20]

In the years up to the end of the century a variety of events and circumstances caused bullion flows, disturbed the Bank's bullion reserve and thus the Bank Rate. None of these was catastrophic from a systemic banking point of view in the United Kingdom, but the regular rhythm of it continued to cause problems for commerce. The trigger to the initial bullion flows was sometimes a search for better investments and sometimes other issues such as approaching war or currency upheavals, but each financial disturbance showed the same characteristics of interest rates equalising and a crisis ensuing as capital flows were disturbed or reversed. The Bank now kept sufficient information to see this process and moved quickly to defeat it, but the consequences abroad were often more serious (Fig. 8.1).

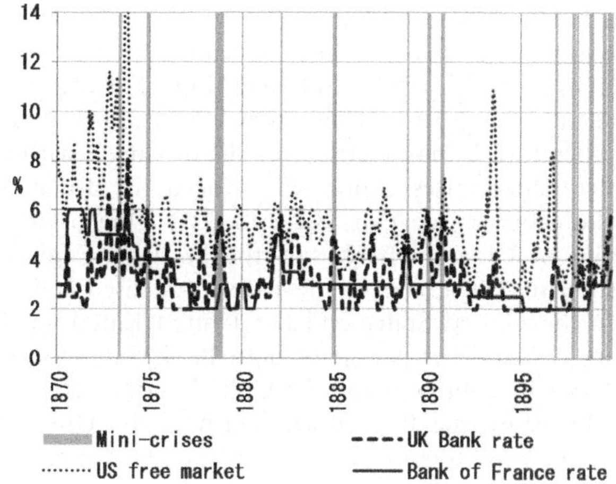

Fig. 8.1 Short-term interest rates 1870–1899 (*Source* as Fig. 7.1)

In 1873 another bullion drain began. Napoleon III lost a war with Prussia, and France suddenly required bullion as capital inflows. The opening of the Suez Canal reduced income from British sailing ships, which were unable physically to use it. The United States and Germany depressed silver prices by ceasing to use the metal as a basis for their currency. Investments in American railroads disappointed, not least thanks to city fires there that depressed economic activity. Once again there were high capital flows. After rates in America and Britain equalised from June 1873, gold returned to the United Kingdom and from September, many American banks and firms went bust. Sharp rises in short-term interest rates that autumn in the United States provoked the Bank of England to raise its rate in the United Kingdom to 9% in November 1873. The United Kingdom mainly escaped the immediate effects, but the next two decades nonetheless marked a slowdown in economic growth. There was continued downward pressure on fiscal expenditure and on interest rates. The Bank of England kept bringing the Bank Rate down to 2% or 2.5%, but then had to raise it for short periods to 5% or 6% to forestall a bullion drain. These events brought down its reserve of bullion in the Issue Department and of its reserve of notes and coins in the Banking

Department. However, its bullion reserve and note reserve nearly always stayed above £18m and £7.5m respectively, much higher levels than seen during the crises of 1847, 1857–1858 and 1866. For comparison, in the previous systemic crisis (that of 1866) they fell to £11.3m and £0.8m.[21]

This was therefore a minor crisis, or 'disturbance', without systemic failure. Similar minor crises continued to occur in Britain throughout the rest of the century (see Figs. 8.2 and 3.6). One occurred in 1878 when the City of Glasgow Bank and the West of England & South Wales District Bank failed, after interest rates equalised and gold did not flow between the United States and the United Kingdom. From 1882 to 1885 there was another period of high Bank Rates for a mixture of reasons. In 1882 the continent and the United States were again in financial trouble. Prices on the Paris *Bourse* crashed, the Union Générale, a French bank, failed and there was a considerable price and output depression in the United States. In 1884–1885 gold reserves in Europe ran low and in America bank loans were called in. This situation potentially could have caused a larger credit shortage than it did. Interest rates equalised between America and Britain at the beginning of 1885 and gold flows from Britain to America paused and then reversed, worsening financial problems in the United States. In America the New York Clearing House provided loans to American banks at risk of failure. The Munster Bank in Ireland fell victim to the resulting credit crunch and collapsed, although this did not trigger a domino effect on banks in the British mainland because the Bank promptly adjusted its Bank Rate down.[22] In 1890 Barings had to be propped up by a consortium of banks, organised by the Bank of England, over problems with its Argentinian loans. The Bank Rate had risen to equalise with returns available in Argentina, investment virtually ceased, projects collapsed, and Barings found both its balance sheet and its reputation in tatters. However, the 'lifeboat operation' orchestrated by the Bank prevented Barings from triggering a full-blown crisis across the City of London. The century ended with the Bank Rate at 6% and still fluctuating periodically. Nevertheless, the Bank had managed to avoid crises of the scale and systemic importance of 1847, 1857–1858 and1866 for just over three decades—a great achievement compared with its record in the middle of the nineteenth century.

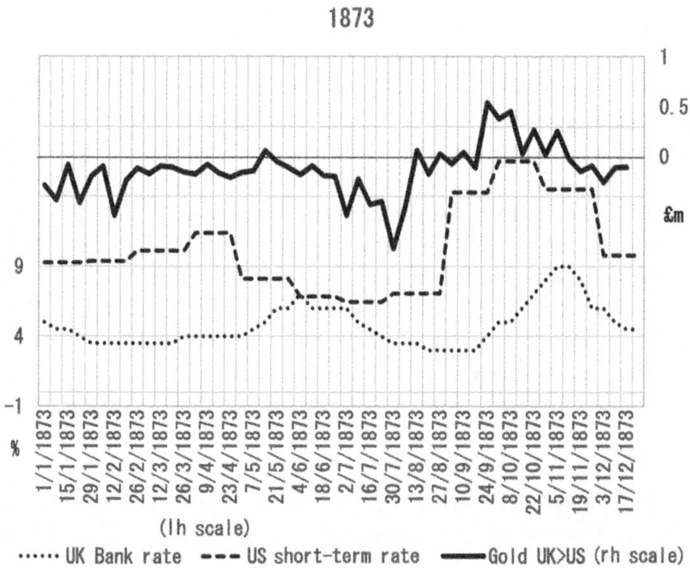

Fig. 8.2 UK Bank rate weekly, US short-term commercial-paper rate monthly, net gold exports UK > US, 1/1/1873 to 24/12/1873 (*Sources* Bank of England daily account books; F. R. Macauley, *Some Theoretical Problems Suggested by the Movements of Interest Rates, Bond Yields and Stock Prices in the United States since 1856* [NBER, 1938] A146 col. 3)

8.2 The Build-Up to Problems in 1873

The mini-crisis of 1873 has its origins in the aftermath of the Franco-Prussian War of 1870–1871. The war itself was short and decisive. Prussian and German victories in eastern France came quickly; Napoleon III was captured at the Battle of Sedan at the start of September 1870 and the army of the Second Empire was effectively defeated. The Government of the Third Republic was set up in Paris on 4 September 1870 and carried on the war for a further five months. The Germans eventually triumphed, however, and took Paris on 28 January 1871. A revolutionary government, the Paris Commune, seized power in the capital and held it for two months, until it was put down by the regular French army at the end of May 1871.

By the end of all this, the French had amassed a lot of state debt and were liable to pay the Germans reparations for the cost of the war. The loans made by the Bank of France to the various forms of the State during the war amounted to 1.470bn francs. In addition, there was the 210m francs loaned to the city of Paris and the 16.5m francs requisitioned by the Paris Commune. The convertibility of the franc was suspended, but France still needed to pay punitive war reparations of 5bn francs (about £200m) demanded by the Germans and agreed in the Treaty of Frankfurt, 10 May 1871, to be settled by March 1875.[23] As it turned out, it was paid by the end of 1873, as the result of the determination of Adolphe Thiers, the president of France, to be free of obligations to the German Empire. Most of the payments were not paid in bullion but in bonds, domestic loans (though about half were initially taken up by foreigners), and with assets. So the high bullion flows it caused were from the United Kingdom to Germany via France.

Despite the flows to Germany in 1871, the Bank of England was relatively unconcerned over economic events and noted nothing of interest relating to these flows in its daily account books. The Bank Rate started off the year at 2.5% but when the bank tried to lower this to 2.25% on 15 June 1871 and then to 2% on 13 July 1871, the Bank's bullion reserves once again started to slide. This was not surprising as an issue of French *rentes* had been launched on 15 June 1871 at 5% to pay towards the reparations. The Bank had to raise the rate up to 5% in three stages between 21 September and 7 October 1871 and it remained there for six weeks; again, a higher rate of interest was available in France. However, it had managed to bring it back down to 3% by the end of the year. In comparison to previous rate rises in crises, these variations were moderate, and the Bank did not see it as necessary to boost the note circulation in the country at the risk of its own liquidity. The lowest to which the bullion reserve sank was £18.395m at the beginning of October and this was not sufficient to constitute a systemic crisis. Nevertheless, note and coin reserves fell to £8.065m in the same month from their normal level of around £13–£15m.

Bullion flows generally reached high levels in 1871. Of the £38.026m in silver and gold bullion which was imported during the year, £13.531m came from the United States and £6.918m from Australia. £15.792m of silver was imported. In turn, £34.072m of bullion was exported, but only about £1m went to the United States. £19.641m went to Europe. Once again, the United Kingdom was the conduit through which bullion flows ran between America and Europe and the Bank of England was left riding the storm, adjusting its interest rate to hang on to a sufficient amount in its bullion reserve, but this time without causing quite so much of a crisis by running its note reserve very low.

Imports to the United Kingdom of bullion from the United States continued at a high level from 1871 to 1873: £13.531m in 1871, £13.216m in 1872 and £10.447m in 1873, but £2.458m of gold and £1.428m in silver in 1874. These flows would have been ever greater were it not for reparations the United Kingdom paid the United States in this period as a result of the Alabama Claims. These were damages sought by the United States for the attacks during the American Civil War upon Union merchant ships by Confederate commerce raiders built in British shipyards. The claims focussed chiefly on the most famous of these ships, the *CSS Alabama*, which captured over sixty US vessels before she was sunk off the coast of France in 1864. The British government had tried (and failed) to prevent the ship going into service in this way, and was hardly to blame directly, but after arbitration in Geneva announced on 14 September 1872, Britain settled, paying the United States $15.5m (about £3m), to keep the peace and repair relations between the two countries.

There was another bullion drain, starting immediately upon this news, and interest rates had to be raised to 7% on 9 November 1872 for over two weeks to reverse it. The note and coin reserve fell to £9.049m at its lowest, and the stock of bullion to £18.962m, but the drain of bullion from the United States continued as foreign bond holders withdrew their money fearing overexpansion generally and over-optimism in the railway sector. Considerable property losses arose from fires in Chicago and Boston in 1871 and 1872 respectively. There was also another reason for the drain of US bullion to the United Kingdom and that was the decreasing price of silver in the bimetal currency of the dollar.

8.3 The Peak of the 1873 Mini-Crisis

A confluence of unrelated events in both London and Central Europe was the short-term trigger for the mini-crisis of 1873 itself. On 28 February 1873 the Bank of England noted the discovery of forged bills in its daily account book, worth £102,217 19s 7d. Three American con men led by George Bidwell had forged bills of exchange on stolen Bank letterhead and cashed them with other banks. The deception was discovered when one of the fraudsters forgot to date a bill and a bank clerk contacted the supposed issuer (the Bank of England) for the date and found that, in reality, it had never been issued. The affair shook confidence in the Bank of England and was followed by a drain of bullion. Worse was to come in the form of the Vienna Stock Exchange crashing on 9 May 1873. A series of Viennese bank failures followed, causing money available for business lending to become scarce. The bills-of-exchange fraud, compounded by the Central European crisis, meant that the Bank needed to defend its bullion reserves, and so the Bank Rate rose to 7% on 4 June 1873. However, it started to fall again just eight days later, before a serious credit crunch had time to take place in the City of London.

This pattern of events produced the same set of conditions that the Banking School associated with the warning signs of a crisis ahead (Fig. 8.2). Thanks to Bank Rate hikes as a result of events in Europe, in May 1873 British and American interest rates converged. Investment that was liquid and remained in the United States had been held back by the higher American rates, but with convergence capital began to flow back to the United Kingdom at a rate of around £1m a week. Such an outflow was bound to have its effect and on 18 September 1873, the announcement of Jay Cooke and Company, an American bank, suspending payments sent Wall Street into a panic. The failure of Jay Cooke was followed by that of Henry Clews and a series of other bank failures, and the New York stock market temporarily closed. By November 1873, 55 of that nation's railroads had failed.

After the German financial problems became worse, and interest rates in the United States rose dramatically, the Bank of England's Rate also rose steeply, following the American rate. The Bank Rate rose from 3% on 24 September 1873 to 9% on 7 November, where it stayed until 20 November 1873, returning to 4.5% by the end of the year. The bullion reserve and note and coin reserve still only fell to £18.59 and £7.851m, though, again not constituting a threat to the Bank's legal responsibilities. This outcome showed the benefit of the Banking School's recommendation of higher bullion reserves, as the Bank was able to sustain more outflows while it raised rates slower and more gradually than it otherwise would have.

Bullion flows to Germany also followed the typical pattern recognised by the Banking School as a precursor to crises. The German Empire needed to import large amounts of bullion between 1871 and 1873 as a result of Otto von Bismarck's decision after the Franco-Prussian War to replace the German states' currencies, which were mainly based on silver, with a new German mark on a full gold standard. The Bank of England daily account books note that in 1871 just £2.018m of bullion was exported to Germany and the Netherlands from the United Kingdom. This rose to £8.15m in 1872 and £7.519m in 1873, but fell to just £1.743m in 1874 as the transition to the new currency was completed by 9 July 1873. The annual 1873 figure disguises the sudden change that just after the rise in American interest rates that spring the flow of bullion from the United Kingdom was suddenly diverted from Germany to the United States. Weekly exports to the United States rising from around £0.015m to £0.495m and those to Germany falling by the same amount. This was the result of the Bank of Prussia, Germany's central bank, keeping its rates too low after the introduction of the new mark: 4.5% in October 1873, while Britain and France set theirs at 7% and America's market rate was as high as 16%.[24]

The changeover of Germany and America to a gold standard and the consequent fall in price of silver affected India adversely, as, despite calls to combine the Indian and English currency systems, it still had a silver-based currency locally but had to pay its dues to London in gold. After 1874 an increased difference emerged between bonds issued in silver and gold. India's bullion, held by the Secretary of State, was stored at the Bank of England as gold. Trade with India was not paid for by bullion transfers but by setting debts off against each other while the bullion remained in the Bank of England's vaults. As A.K. Bagchi has inferred, India remained on a silver-based currency in the long term because of a lack of understanding about the amount of gold required to change systems and whether to do so would damage the Bank of England, rather than its being best for the Indian economy in the long run.[25]

The accounts of the Indian government for 1878–1879, for example, included an expenditure of £12m for famine relief in Bombay and Madras, but also an item of 'net loss by exchange' of £7.25m which could have considerably added to relief.[26] The deficit for the year was a comparatively small £1.355m which was covered by a £2m loan. The 'loss by exchange' was incurred because remittances to Britain were expected to be on the basis of the exchange rate before the decline in the value of silver, so that returns on investments made were not diminished by the fall in the value of silver. In short, India had to take the loss caused by the drop in the price of silver while paying for its own famine relief, severely depleting its available resources to offer the impoverished assistance.

8.4 Mini-Crises in the Remainder of the Nineteenth Century

8.4.1 1878

The next mini-crisis took place in 1878. In this year there was great nervousness about Russia's intentions towards expansion in central and southern Asia. The fear was that if they did expand, they might well threaten India and all the capital that the British had invested there. The fear was probably exaggerated, but it had a long pedigree and its own name: 'The Great Game', made famous in the Rudyard Kipling novel *Kim*.[27] Russia was worried about Britain extending commercial and military influence into the same area. Sher Ali Khan, the Amir of Afghanistan, a country sandwiched between the two empires, tried not to see missions from either country but the Russians turned up uninvited and so the British demanded an audience as well. A conflict was triggered when this was rebuffed at the Khyber Pass.

A bullion drain from the Bank of England took place as investors in Britain feared the worst as the crisis escalated. In response the Bank Rate was gradually raised from 2% in February and March to 6% from 14 October to 21 November 1878. This move was in response to a fairly minor reduction in the bullion reserve from around £23.7m to £20.65m. The rate gradually dropped to 2% in April 1879, but the Bank Rate had equalised with rates available in America between July and October 1878, and this had, in accordance with the Banking School's ideas, the outcome of bringing capital flows between the United Kingdom and United States (in both directions and therefore also as a net outcome) close to nil (Fig. 8.3).

This situation had a detrimental effect on those companies and banks which dealt with trade and investments in the United States. These included the City of Glasgow Bank, which collapsed in October 1878. It had invested heavily in American railroads but struggled to refinance these investments when tighter credit conditions struck. As the bank already had debt problems, higher interest rates triggered its demise.[28]

The directors of the bank had reported a rosy picture of its finances as recently as June 1878. However, by September rumours were circulating that the bank was in trouble. The end of cheap money and higher interest rates meant that it began to struggle to finance itself from wholesale lending markets. The bank tried to seek support from other Scottish

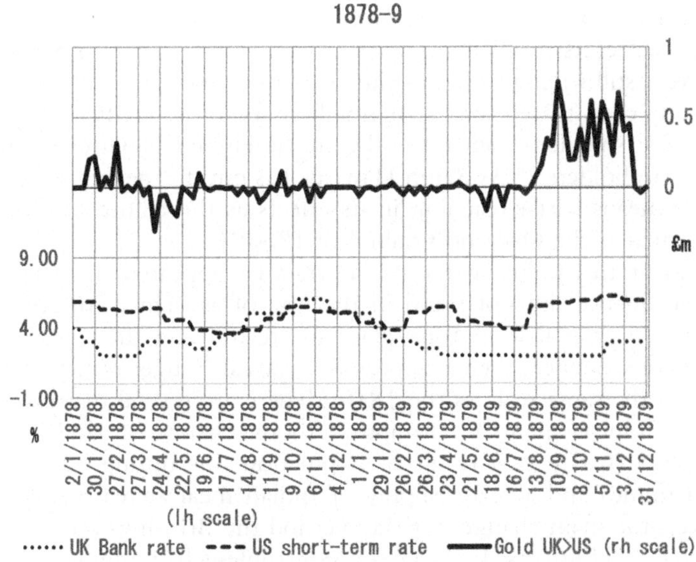

Fig. 8.3 UK Bank rate weekly, US short-term commercial-paper rate monthly, net gold exports UK > US, 2/1/1878 to 31/12/1879 (*Sources* Bank of England daily account books; F. R. Macauley, *Some Theoretical Problems Suggested by the Movements of Interest Rates, Bond Yields and Stock Prices in the United States since 1856* [NBER, 1938] A147 col. 3)

banks, but after an independent audit of its accounts, this was refused. It was then forced to cease trading.[29]

On 2 October the newspapers reported that it would stop payments.[30] The shareholders had unlimited liability for the bank's debts, and they were ultimately called upon to pay £2,750 of the bank's liabilities for every £100 in paid-up capital they possessed.[31] All but 254 of its 1200 or so shareholders were ruined. The West of England & South Wales District Bank also stopped in December, but this was said to be due to a sudden economic slump in its area of local operation in South Wales making many of its loans go bad, rather than because of the interest-rate rises or any contagion from Scotland.[32]

It was partly luck which meant that the City of Glasgow Bank failure was localised and did not spread to other banks. Also reputation played a part because it had relatively few depositors and borrowers for an institution of its size; its problems were perceived to be unique; other Scottish banks were still willing to honour its banknotes and service its customers; and in any case its depositors, its noteholders, other creditors and other banks were shielded from losses by the unlimited liability of the bust bank's shareholders.[33] As Ralph Hawtrey has put it: 'the failure of a bank is by no means so far-reaching in its effects as the failure of a discount house', such as the Overend's failure of 1866.[34]

It was at this point that food shortages reappeared in Ireland, but this time finance did not stand in the way of assistance. In contrast to 1847, when crop failures took place in Ireland and the Great Famine was the consequence, their reappearance caused hunger rather than mass deaths on the same scale as the 1840s. There are several reasons for this including improvements in farming methods, changes in landholding to larger plots (partly as a result of population loss during and after the Great Famine) and a ready supply of Indian meal at reasonable prices. However, the main change was the method the British government used to finance relief efforts. In 1847 the government had attempted to raise funds with a loan just as a commercial and financial crisis was erupting in the City of London. It had compounded a pre-existing bullion flow from the Bank of England and, instead of further loans being raised, the bill for relief ended up being thrown upon those who paid local land taxes.[35] This time, rather than loans being issued on the London money markets, grants were provided from already accumulated government funds, as well as an increase in income tax and various purchase and licencing taxes.[36]

8.4.2 1882

The next challenge for the Bank of England came in 1882, in which it displayed the quick action to combat a bullion drain that the Banking School had recommended. It began in January 1882, when the Paris *Bourse* crashed. The French stock market was already hit hard by the railroad boom bursting in 1881. However, panic did not set in until the refusal of the Austrian government to give the Banque de Lyon et de la Loire a concession for the creation of a maritime bank and the consequent collapse of l'Union Générale, a bank based in Lyon, in January 1882. Around a quarter of the brokers on the *Bourse* were about to fail. That catastrophic event, which would have closed the *Bourse*, was prevented by a loan worth 80m francs to the brokers from the Bank of France that provided them with sufficient liquidity to support settlement, a move inspired by the Banking School's idea that there needed to be sufficient liquidity during crises to meet the needs of commerce. With the approval of the government, the *Bourse* obtained credit from the Bank of France, using private bankers and financial institutions as intermediaries because the Bank could only provide a loan upon paper collateral that the brokers did not possess (in this way this move varied from Bagehot's dictum, in which lending had to be upon good security). The *chambre syndicale* thus created 160 ten-year bonds of 0.5m francs each carrying 5% interest. The Statistical Society of London commented at the end of the year on the success of the rescue in preventing further panic: 'the effect of the Paris collapse seems rather to have been sedative than otherwise', but that was mainly due to prompt action by the Bank of France.[37]

In the United Kingdom, the Bank of England, used to regular importations of gold from the United States, had received none in January 1882, with bullion exports picking up speed in the last week of that month. These were the ideal conditions for a bullion drain and although the bullion reserve seemed to vary little from day to day at first, on Saturday 28 January, the bullion reserve fell from £19.022m to £18.199m (4.3%) in one day. The next banking day, on Monday 30 January, the Bank Rate was increased from 5% to 6%. This illustrates how the reactions of the Bank were now lightning-quick, in the context of the time, and every indication of a drain was immediately acted upon according to the lessons learnt by the Banking School in terms of the effects of interest rates on bullion flows and note circulation. It also illustrates the extent to which the Bank of England had begun trying to manage bullion flows in times of crisis. The Bank purchased additional gold for shipping to France from that newly arrived from Spain and was said to be searching for more from the United States, but there they were competing with demand from Italy, which required a loan at that time.[38] After the panic in France passed, the Bank returned its Bank Rate to 3% in March 1882, at the earliest moment it could, showing that it had learnt a lesson from 1866 of not leaving rates too high for too long.

8.4.3 1884–1885

Financial summaries of the year 1884 tended to emphasise a steady 'depression', which had begun two years before. Prices continued to fall much lower than they were at the beginning of the year, and this in itself was taken as a sign of depression; the prospect of recovery seemed further off than ever.[39] Brokerage firms and banks backing them were vulnerable because of the falling prices. An undue increase in interest rates would have been seen as fatal in these circumstances by commercial interests, even if it lasted for a short time. Banking problems in the United States caused capital flows which set off a mini-crisis in the United Kingdom. This also brought down a large bank in Ireland, the Bank of Munster, in 1885, partly due to low agricultural prices.

The problems began in the United States with a small number of financial firms in New York City. In May 1884 the Marine National Bank and brokerage firm Grant and Ward failed when some speculative investments they made tumbled in value. Shortly afterwards, the Second National Bank suffered a run after it became known that its president had embezzled \$3m and fled the country. The Metropolitan National Bank was forced to temporarily close after a similar rumour concerning it (which proved to be untrue) was spread.[40] Just as the American banking system required increased liquidity, those holding greenback dollars in the United Kingdom and Europe started to redeem them for gold, fearful of the rumours and panic there. This combination of circumstances caused a sharp peak of flow of gold from the United States to the United Kingdom in the first half of 1884 (Fig. 8.4) and a rise in market interest rates in America.

The New York Clearing House stepped in and halted the chain reaction by pooling the reserves of its member banks and providing credit to institutions beset by runs, effectively acting as 'a central bank with reserve power greater than that of any European central bank', in the words of Elmus Wicker.[41] For instance, the Metropolitan National Bank was audited by the New York Clearing House and was advertised to be solvent. It was loaned \$3m so that it could withstand the run. These actions reassured the public and the panic subsided. After the banking crisis in the United States, part of the bullions flows returned westwards, drawing some of the Bank of England's reserve with it which dropped to a low of £18.357m in the week of 12 November 1884 from around £24m in July. The Bank of England reacted with its, now, accustomed promptness and the resulting high rate of 5% from 5 November 1884 to 19 January 1885 caused a number of failures in the City of London and wider British commercial world, but little special action was taken by the Bank.

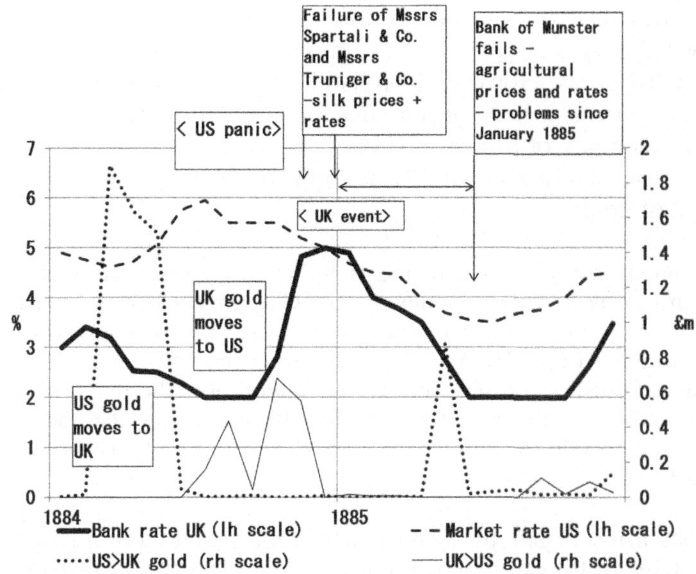

Fig. 8.4 Short-term interest rates and gold movements between the United Kingdom and the United States 1884–1885 (*Source* Bank of England daily account books)

On 16 November 1884 the Bank noted in the margin of its daily account book the failure of Mssrs. Spartali & Co. with liabilities of £1.1m and capital of around £0.75m. Everyone was surprised that this was allowed to fail. *The Times* of 17 November 1884 reported that 'the credit and standing of the firm have been so good…that general surprise has been expressed at the announcement'.[42] On 29 December 1884 Truninger & Co. Ltd. failed despite 'good reputation of the partners' according to *The Times*.[43] Searching for an explanation, newspaper reports later confirmed that both firms were involved in the silk trade and taking into account the 'severe losses sustained from the heavy decline in the value of silk' and the sudden rises in interest rates that made short-term loans so expensive that the firms effectively became illiquid because of a lack of cash in hand.[44] In Ireland the Bank of Munster failed in June 1885, among accusations of corruption, yet both on paper and after liquidation it turned out to have a surplus of assets over liabilities; in other words it collapsed because it was illiquid rather than insolvent.[45] In essence, the allegations of corruption were to cover up the same problems of falling prices and hikes in interest rates which had finished off their English rivals. However, in Ireland, the failure had a wider effect in the community as it had concentrated on agricultural loans, upon which the rural economy of Munster relied.

A financial summary of the year summed up the problem as a global shortage of gold:

> The amount of gold held in the [US] treasury against the greenbacks has, in fact, been about a minimum, the Government having been weakened as compared with its position some years ago. In other words, the large surplus in the New York banks has to some extent masked the real monetary situation of the country, where until now the real surplus has been smaller than this apparent one. The difficulty remains that the surplus all over the world, looking at what the dullness of trade has been, is so small.[46]

British firms began to wonder why they had to put up with such volatile Bank of England interest rates with all the damage that they did to business, when, in contrast, French and German interest rates were quite stable in spite of being on gold standards. For instance, in 1884 while the Bank of England rate varied between 2% and 5%, rates at both the Bank of France and Germany's central bank remained level throughout the year. Academic enquiry encouraged this questioning when R. H. I. Palgrave, a journalist and economist, collected data on the interest rates in various countries and published, analyses of the variation in each country.[47] British rates varied more than other European countries, a circumstance which he argued disadvantaged business in the United Kingdom, as it provided them with an unstable macroeconomic environment on which to base investment decisions. He went on to collect further data on this subject, publishing a more detailed book in 1903, *Bank Rate and the Money Market, 1844–1900*.[48]

Having been subjected to this criticism, the Bank began to be even more careful about imposing Bank Rate increases with every fluctuation in its bullion reserve. Yet for many influential bankers, it simply added to the case for the Banking School's policies. Most notably, Alfred de Rothschild gave his answer to the question of why other countries had more stable rates than Britain in a letter to the Chairman of the Gold and Silver Commission in 1888, in which he emphasised the need for the

Bank of England to accumulate and defend its bullion reserves against countries that were unofficially still using capital controls:

> ...the Bank of France in ordinary times does not give any really large amounts of gold in exchange for its notes, whilst in extraordinary times it adopts, very promptly, the necessary steps to protect its stock of bullion. What took place when the late war broke out between France and Germany? The Bank of France not only did not pay its notes in gold, but a quantity of five franc notes were immediately printed, in addition to which the Bank was authorised to issue more notes than it was legally entitled according to its charter...As regards Germany, that country has also certainly a gold standard, but it would be difficult, if not impossible, to obtain any large amount of gold from Berlin or from any of the branches of the Imperial State Bank...to sum up we have to be doubly careful to protect our stock of gold.[49]

8.4.4 1888

The mini-crises of 1888 provide another good example of the Banking School's theory of crises in action. It begins, as usual, with an attempt to lower interest rates that causes a speculative boom as investors go on a search for yield. In March 1888 George Goschen, Lord Salisbury's new chancellor of the exchequer, announced in Parliament the proposal that the 3% government bonds for the national debt were to be repaid and reissued at 2.75% for fifteen years and then 2.5% for twenty years. This conversion was expected to save £1m in the first year and around £1.3m per year thereafter. This balanced, to an extent, the one penny drop in income tax that he had announced in his budget of the previous year. That concession to popular demand was paid for by £2m deducted from the sinking fund the purpose of which was gradually to repay the national debt. Shortly after the conversion was announced, income tax was reduced by a further penny in another budget.[50]

The result of these changes was that bullion drained from the Bank of England's reserve from the week of Goschen's announcement. It fell steadily from £21.933m in March 1888 to £18.215m in mid-May and some went to Germany. From mid-May, it started rising again after the Bank Rate was increased from 2% to 3% on 10 May. The Bank of England was trying to limit and smooth out the variation in rates, but after a few fluctuations in the reserve and the rate, this proved ineffective and the rate went up to 5% on 4 October 1888.[51] American rates had been closely tracking British rates since 1874, while both countries had experienced falling prices and what was commonly called there, at the time, a 'depression'. The hike in rates in Britain brought them almost level with the rates in the United States, in spite of a similar small spike there, and therefore caused an initial 'disturbance in bullion flows', but the full consequences of this were not seen until 1890 when a similar but more pronounced event took place. The British government also had to borrow money to fund the Irish Land Purchase Acts, 'the Ashbourne Acts', while this high rate was current.[52]

Investment funds, seeing their rates of return repressed at home, once again sought out better returns in loans to Latin American countries. Some of the flows went into a wider spectrum of other opportunities, such as over 80 private breweries including Guinness, which floated on the London stock exchange in the 1880s, so some of the drain was internal.[53] In April and May £0.81m of gold departed for Argentina. Over the year £8.342m of gold and silver bullion was exported to Brazil, Mexico and the West Indies.

There was a continual drain of silver from the United States which then departed for India. In India the currency was still pegged to silver and its price against gold was slightly higher than the United States where it was no longer the basis of currency. £5.799m of silver left the United Kingdom for India over the year while £4.013m was received from the United States. An added attraction was the high rates of interest earned on loans; in December 1888 the rate of the Bank of Bengal and Bank of Bombay was 7%.[54] The price of silver against gold declined steadily, and the general level of prices kept pace with the silver price rather than that of gold. This situation created an impression in the popular consciousness that the price of metals was the root cause of changes in the price of commodities in spite of Alfred Marshall's comments that the price of commodities was more to do with trading conditions.

8.4.5 1890

In 1890 the United Kingdom received large imports of bullion, £23.642m in gold, while exports were only £14.435m and the excess represented a surplus looking for investments, a circumstance which the Banking School believed encouraged rash behaviour.[55] Baring Brothers bank made the classic mistake in these circumstances of using short-term loans to fund long-term investments abroad. Because of its loans to Argentina, Barings Brothers, a powerful force in British banking, got into difficulties in 1890 when the Bank of England was forced to raise its rate to 6%, equalling returns from investments in Argentina.[56] Since the beginning of 1889, the Bank of England's interest rates had been around 2.5% and US rates 5% and the increased rate was to prevent drains to the United States. As rates equalised in Argentina there was a disincentive to invest there and Barings' investment model did not work. Barry Eichengreen has pointed to the damage done to Argentina by the sudden stop to investment flows, as the Banking School's theories played out once again in reality.[57]

The trigger for Barings's near collapse in 1890 was bad fiscal news from Argentina. That year Miguel Juárez Celman, Argentine president, resigned after the Revolución del Parque, and Argentina came close to defaulting on its debt payments. Barings lacked sufficient reserves to support losses on the Argentine bonds until they were recapitalised. The Governor of the Bank of England, William Lidderdale, organised a consortium of banks, headed by a former Governor, Banking-School inclined Gibbs and his firm of Antony Gibbs & Sons, to provide loans to bail Barings out and support a bank restructuring.

The rescue was a 'lifeboat' operation, carried out before Barings actually sank and was not quite the same as Bagehot's suggested policy of a general supply of credit to sound businesses at high interest rates after a collapse had occurred.[58] However, it followed broadly the same principles as those suggested by the Banking School and by acting in a timely way, a number of advantages were gained. Firstly, it made the difference between Barings being solvent or not. It needed a £8–9m loan to help meet maturing loans of £15.2m and possible deposit withdrawals of £5.2m.[59] An immediate stoppage would have required Barings to liquidate assets at a loss or raise finance at an unpredictable high rate of interest, possibly pushing it into insolvency. The arrangement gave Barings time to rearrange its affairs. Secondly, it helped Argentina by avoiding an immediate fire-sale of investments with the consequent additional plunge in share prices to that caused by the ceasing of inflows.[60] Thirdly, it avoided a much larger financial crisis in Britain. *The Economist* approved but warned about the moral hazard of using the policy too often.[61]

When it appeared that the Bank of England might have difficulty in meeting its liquidity requirements, the Bank of France temporarily loaned the Bank of England 75m francs in gold. The loan was one example of the increasing tendency for bullion not to travel. Patron, writing on behalf of the National Monetary Commission, claimed 'It seems that these 75m francs were not only returned to the Bank of France with seals unbroken, but that they did not even cross the Channel. It was enough that the public was conscious of such moral and material support for the frenzy to disappear'.[62] The government also used India's bullion reserves to help boost the Bank's position through the crisis.[63]

Short-term American and British interest rates drifted apart, although long-term rates became closer. In 1893 the scene was set again for another cycle of crisis but the Bank of England was now an expert in adjusting interest rates just enough to discourage excessive flows to the United States, raising the Bank Rate to 5% as the American rates spiked to 10%. The Bank Rate rise in August choked off the export of bullion to America that had risen from nothing to £1–£1.5m per week that summer.[64] Thus the 1893 panic in the United States did not spread to the United Kingdom which had a relatively tranquil period. However, in the United States a crisis affected every sector of the economy, and produced a political reaction that led to the 1896 election and the presidency of William McKinley who sponsored more tariff rises.

8.4.6 The Late 1890s

Towards the end of the century the Bank became very short of gold in comparison with its liabilities. R. S. Sayers has vividly described its position as 'a powerful Bank Rate weapon' protecting 'a thin film of gold'.[65] Partly because of this shortage, the picture towards the end of the century was of nations globally engaged in a tug-of-war over gold and most of the ropes appear to have gone through London and the United Kingdom.

One tug-of-war was set off by a financial panic in America between 1896 and 1899. The Chicago Bank Panic started with the collapse of the National Bank of Illinois in late December 1896, with others following it soon afterwards. Two well-known bankers in the city, Otto Wasmandorf and William Hammond, committed suicide as a consequence, helping the crisis stick in popular American memory.[66] British rates had to rise along with American ones to prevent a bullion drain and in 1896 the Bank of England promptly boosted its rate to 4%, up from 2% at the start of the year. Bullion had been exported from the United Kingdom to the United States between 26 July and 18 November 1896 amounting to £8.349m. At the end of the year Germany and India began to outbid the United States for the gold. India was preparing to move from a silver currency to the gold standard from 1893 to 1899.[67] Germany's Reichbank pushed up their rate to 5% from 10 October 1896 and those of the Banks of Bengal and Bombay rose to 9% on 9 December 1896 and 10% on 23 December 1896.

Yet in spite of this tug-of-war over bullion—reminiscent of the events leading up to the crisis of 1866—there was no systemically important crisis in this period in Britain. The Bank of England had just about perfected its art of stabilising its reserve by varying interest rates, promptly but by the minimum necessary. In comparison, India, new to the game, made extravagant gestures with its rate-setting policy which destabilised other countries' bullion reserves (but not Britain's this time). As Andreas Andréadēs, an early historian of the Bank of England, wrote in 1909, 'London is the only free market for gold in the world…it leaves only one means of resisting a demand for gold, —that is an increase in the value of capital lent, or in other words a rise in the rate of discounts'.[68]

Notes

1. *Hansard*, 25 March 1873, CCXV, c. 130.
2. G. Pownall, 'Bank Reserves', *The Economic Journal* 9 (1899) p. 400.
3. *The Economist*, 4 January 1873, p. 2.
4. B. Price, *Currency and Banking* (New York: Appleton, 1876) p. 66.
5. Idem., pp. 70, 95.
6. Price to Gibbs, 19 July 1877 in B. Price, *Chapters on Practical Political Economy* (London: Kegan Paul, 1878) pp. 491–492.
7. Price to Gibbs, 27 November 1877, in idem., p. 505.
8. Gibbs to Price, 7 February 1878, in idem., p. 551.
9. Gibbs to Northcote, 25 March 1875, in idem., p. 558.
10. Gibbs to Price, 7 February 1878, in idem., p. 551.
11. Gibbs to Northcote, 25 March 1875, in idem., p. 559.
12. For example, *The Times*, 2 July 1879, p. 5.
13. *The Times*, 1 January 1873, p. 9.
14. D. P. O'Brien, *The Correspondence of Lord Overstone* I–III (Cambridge: CUP, 1971) pp. 40, 899, 1227.
15. R. Giffen, *Stock Exchange Securities* (London: George Bell & Sons, 1879) p. 162.
16. *The Times*, 4 June 1873, p. 7.
17. Overstone to Norman, 17 June 1873 in O'Brien, *The Correspondence of Lord Overstone*, pp. 1249–1250.
18. Idem., p. 1250.

19. W. S. Jevons, 'On the frequent autumnal pressure in the Money Market and the action of the Bank of England', *Journal of the Statistical Society of London* 29 (1866) p. 240.
20. Pownall, 'Bank Reserves', p. 400.
21. Bank of England daily account book 1866, 23–30 May 1866.
22. S. Kenny, J. Lennard, 'Monetary Aggregates for Ireland, 1840–1921', *Economic History Review* 71 (2018) pp. 1264–1265.
23. M. Patron, *The Bank of France in its Relation to National and International Credit* (Washington: Government Printing Office, 1910) p. 137; M. B. Devereux, G. W. Smith, 'Transfer Problem Dynamics: Macroeconomics of the Franco-Prussian War Indemnity', *Queen's University Working Paper* 1025, Appendix A.
24. Bank of England daily account book, 1873.
25. A. K. Bagchi, 'Contested Hegemonies and Laissez Faire: Controversies over the Monetary Standard in India at the High Noon of the British Empire', *Fernand Braudel Center Review* 20 (1997) pp. 33–34.
26. East Indian Finance. *Speech of the Hon. Edward Stanhope, M.P., (Under Secretary of State for India) on the financial statement (India) in the House of Commons, 22 May 1879* (London: Cornelius Buck, 1879) p. 11; A. Loveday, *The History & Economics of Indian Famines* (London: G. Bell and Sons, 1914) p. 56.
27. R. Kipling, *Kim* (London: Macmillan, 1901).
28. 'Glasgow Bank in Liquidation', Glasgow UL Archives, UGD 108/4.
29. R. Button, S. Knott, C. Macmanus, M. Willison, 'Desperate adventurers and men of straw: the failure of City of Glasgow Bank and its enduring impact on the UK banking system', *Bank of England Quarterly Bulletin 2015 Q1* (2015) pp. 23–24.
30. *The Times*, 2 October 1878, p. 5.
31. R. G. Hawtrey, *A Century of Bank Rate* (London: Frank Cass & Co., 1968) p. 99.
32. *The Times*, 9 December 1878, p. 10.
33. Button et al., 'Desperate adventurers and men of straw', pp. 24–29.
34. Hawtrey, *A Century of Bank Rate*, p. 100.
35. C. Read, *The Great Famine in Ireland and Britain's Financial Crisis* (Woodbridge: The Boydell Press, 2022) Chapters 4 and 5.
36. *Hansard*, 4 April 1878, CCXXXIX, cc. 555–556; Read, *The Great Famine in Ireland*, pp. 292–293.
37. 'Financial and Commercial History of 1882', *Journal of the Statistical Society of London* 46 (1883) 101–113.
38. *Northern Evening Mail*, 3rd edition, 31 January 1882.
39. 'Financial and Commercial History of 1884', *Journal of the Statistical Society of London* 48 (1885) p. 54.

40. G. Gorton, E. W. Tallman, 'Too big to fail before the Fed', *American Economic Review* 106 (2016) p. 530.
41. E. Wicker, *Banking Panics of the Gilded Age* (Cambridge: CUP, 2000) p. 16.
42. *The Times*, 17 November 1884, p. 11.
43. *The Times*, 30 December 1884, p. 9.
44. *The Times*, 12 January 1885, p. 3.
45. C. Ó Gráda, 'Should the Munster Bank have been saved?' *UCD Centre for Economic Research Working Paper Series*, WP01/15, 2001, 1–33, pp. 24–25.
46. 'Financial and Commercial History of 1884', p. 60.
47. R. H. I. Palgrave, *Bank Rate in England, France, and Germany, 1844–1878* (London: Effingham Wilson, 1880).
48. R. H. I. Palgrave, *Bank Rate and the Money Market, 1844–1900* (London: John Murray, 1903).
49. A. Rothschild to Chairman of the Commission, 30 January 1888, *Second Report of the Royal Commission appointed to enquire into the recent Changes in the relative Values of the precious metals...* PP 1888 (c. 5248) XLV.1, p. 285.
50. T. J. Spinner, *George Joachim Goschen* (Cambridge: CUP, 1973) p. 141.
51. Bank of England daily account book, 1866.
52. 1885 48 & 49 Vict. c. 73, 1888 51 & 52 Vict. c. 49; *The Times*, 24 November 1888, pp. 6, 8.
53. C. P. Kindleberger, *Keynesianism vs. Monetarism* (Abingdon: Taylor and Francis, 1985) p. 228.
54. Bank of England daily account book, 1888, vol. 2.
55. Bank of England daily account book, 1890.
56. J-H. Flores, 'A Microeconomic Analysis of the Baring Crisis 1880-90', *Berkeley University Working Paper* (2006) p. 51.
57. B. Eichengreen, 'The Baring Crisis in a Mexican Mirror', *International Political Science Review* 20 (1999) pp. 249–270, 254.
58. E. N. White, 'How to Prevent a Banking Panic', *Economic History Association Paper* (2016).
59. Baring Bros. & Co. liabilities and assets 31 October 1890 to 6 October 1894, Bank of England Archive, 9A240/5.
60. Baring Bros. & Co. valuation of assets 31 October 1890 to 6 September 1894, Bank of England Archive, 9A240/6.
61. *The Economist*, 22 November 1890, p. 1466.
62. Patron, *The Bank of France in its Relation to National and International Credit*, p. 142.
63. W. Narsey, *British Imperialism and the Making of Colonial Currency Systems* (Basingstoke: Palgrave Macmillan, 2016) pp. 74–75, 157.
64. Bank of England daily account book, 1893.

65. R. S. Sayers, 'The Development of Central Banking after Bagehot', *Economic History Review* 4 (1951) p. 116.
66. *Chicago Tribune*, 28 December 1896; 3 January 1897.
67. *(Fowler) Committee to enquire into Indian Currency* PP 1898 (c. 9037) LXI.469.
68. A. Andréadēs, tr. C. Meredith, *History of the Bank of England* (London: King & Son, 1909) p. 317.

CHAPTER 9

The Twentieth and Twenty-First Centuries: From the Banking School to the Carry Trade

> Very low rates over long periods can induce a reach for yield among investors who, for contractual or behavioural reasons, haven't fully adapted their desired or expected returns to the new low-rate environment. Low short-term rates and upward sloping yield curves encourage increased maturity mismatch—a borrowing short to lend long carry trade—with associated vulnerability to runs and other financial stability risks.
>
> —'Monetary policy and financial stability'; Speech given by Don Kohn, External Member of the Bank of England's Financial Policy Committee, at Tsinghua University, Beijing, 21 May 2016.[1]

As the previous chapters have shown, a range of hypotheses on the causes of crises has been put forward by various Banking-School commentators from Henry Thornton, Thomas Tooke and James Wilson through to Walter Bagehot and George Clare. They vary from person to person, but together their ideas shared common themes. This chapter summarises these common themes and compares their ideas about central banking, interest rates and crises to theory and practice in the twentieth and twenty-first centuries. The chapter explains the similarity between the subject of Banking-School apprehension from the nineteenth century and the practice of the Carry Trade in recent decades, both of which profited from international interest-rate differentials. It then goes on to explain how the Carry Trade was prevented—with the help of policies along the lines of the prescriptions suggested by the Banking School the previous

C. Read, *Calming the Storms*, Palgrave Studies in Economic History,
https://doi.org/10.1007/978-3-031-11914-9_9

century—from causing systemic crises in Britain during the interwar years and under the Bretton Woods System (1944–1971). Finally, it describes the policy decisions that contributed towards the return of the Carry Trade and, with it, the return of systemic crises in 1973–1975 and 2007–2009.

Britain managed to avoid major policy-induced systemic banking crises from the crisis of 1866 until the secondary banking crisis of 1973–1975.[2] The slight exception is the panic of 1914, which was caused by the outbreak of war rather than the credit cycle as were the other crises. No other major capitalist economy in the world can match that length of time without some sort of systemic banking panics. Initially, the secondary banking crisis of 1973–1975 was seen as a temporary blip from that trend. In the decades after that crisis, a number of individual banks and building societies failed or came close to doing so, including the Grays Building Society in 1978, the New Cross Building Society and the Johnson Matthey Bank in 1984, the Bank of Credit and Commerce International in 1991 and Barings Bank in 1995.[3] A mini-crisis developed in 1990–1991, which involved a number of smaller banks going out of business and being liquidated, triggered in part by the high interest rates necessary for Britain to stay in the European Exchange Rate Mechanism (better known as the ERM).[4] These events were then followed on a much larger scale by the global financial crisis of 2007–2009. Anthony Hotson and Nicholas Dimsdale have called that event the largest banking crisis in British history; in terms of its economic consequences, since at least 1825: 'This Time Really Was Different'.[5]

The period since the collapse of the Bretton Woods system in 1971 has also been notable for the rise in the influence of Monetarist ideas in policy-making circles. The Banking School's focus on monitoring investment flows and financial stability was overtaken by a focus on hitting a money-supply target and, later under the influence of New Keynesian ideas, an inflation target. Nevertheless, over the past decade, an increasing number of commentators, policymakers and academics have, perhaps unwittingly, begun to revive the Banking School's worries about the low interest-rate environment that inflation targeting has helped to bring about. The phenomenon they worry about is the Carry Trade, which occurs after the low-interest-rate policies of central banks cause the bond-yield curve to slope excessively upwards and encourage capital flows and asset bubbles to occur. It can help to destabilise the financial system, particularly if it results in economies overheating and a sharp tightening of monetary policy to combat rising inflation expectations. As the speech by Don Kohn at the start of this chapter shows, the Bank of England's policymakers have become very concerned about this. Moreover, thanks to the covid-19 pandemic of 2020 and the looser monetary policies that central banks across the world adopted in response to stave off deflation, their worries about the threat this poses for future financial stability should be growing greater still.

9.1 Lessons from the Banking School's Ideas

The critical starting point in the Banking School's theory of crises is low short-term interest rates, when compared with long-term rates and other available investments. When central banks set their rates too low and better returns are available elsewhere, the Banking School would have suggested, the situation encourages inexperienced investors, in particular, to go on a search for yield without fully appreciating the risks associated with this strategy. A prolonged spread between interest rates also incentivises professional investors to raise money at short-term rates for long-term investment, a form of maturity 'transformation' (or mismatch).[6]

Both these activities have been criticised by the Banking School as very unwise.[7] When short-term rates rose above long-term rates, schemes funded in this way would collapse. The real-bills doctrine emphasised the need to accept only collateral for short-term loans which had a secure, sustainable, and quickly realisable value. In other words, this is a situation where the maturity period of the loan and the investment matches. The opposite of matching is where short-term loans are used to fund long-term investment. One example of this was the use of short-term bills for financing railways, for instance where the short-term loans for building railways were secured on the shares of a company that may take years to construct any income-earning infrastructure.

In recent years, both financial commentators and academics have highlighted the problem posed by the behaviour of inexperienced investors in a period of low interest rates. The personification of these investors was the fictional character of Mrs. Watanabe, who represents the traditional Japanese matriarch in charge of domestic finance. From the early 2000s Mrs. Watanabe was credited with engaging in 'the Carry Trade' by buying investments in countries with higher interest rates than Japan and hedging against exchange-rate losses when the money was to be returned.[8] The trade collapsed in the crisis of 2008 when international interest rates drew together. The practice of borrowing short-term and lending long-term, which Mrs. Watanabe personified, became the cause of the banking boom of the 2000s, but far from being frowned upon, it gained the respectable name of 'maturity transformation', on the basis of the derivatives used to avoid interest-rate risks. As Ranald Michie has explained, these derivatives did not provide the protection expected and, in Britain, led to the collapse of Northern Rock, a bank specialising in mortgages, in 2007–2008.[9]

The Banking School also pointed to capital flows for investment, rather than trade, as a growing feature of the international money market and the root cause of crises. The flows would increase according to the difference between interest rates in various countries, it was suggested, and the interest rates would move together thanks to investment arbitrage. In periods of credit difficulty or crisis the interest rates in different countries equalised if there was a fixed exchange rate between the countries and capital was allowed to flow freely.[10] Exceptions to this were, for instance, France in 1866 when the export of gold was inhibited and the 'greenback period' in America when the exchange rate fluctuated and interest rates did not equalise for as long a period as expected. When interest rates drew together, there was no advantage in further investment and flows stopped, suddenly starving the target investment of funds.[11] The price of the targeted asset would then drop, damaging any banking system that had lent on the collateral of the asset class in question.

The Banking School argued that the particular reason why interest rates tended to draw together before crises in the nineteenth century was action by the Bank of England to stem a bullion drain by raising interest rates. The Banking School had accepted this need, but only reluctantly because of the damage to non-financial firms that the raised rates on their debts were likely to cause.[12] The Currency School had come to regard raised rates as essential on occasions when the problem of bullion drains emerged. In contrast, the emphasis of the Banking School was to link the problems caused by drains with the requirements of the Bank Charter Act of 1844 and the openness of the United Kingdom to capital flows without discretion.[13] They saw the policies of central banks and the government as fuelling a destructive credit cycle. When investment flows stopped suddenly, they argued, spare funds would build up as deposits in Britain, attracted by the high interest rates intended to stem a bullion drain. However, after the crisis, interest rates were eventually lowered, encouraged by a government that wished to reduce its cost of borrowing.

Although it borrowed mainly at the long-term rate there were opportunities for reissuing consols at a low rate when the short-term rate was low. Eventually, the surplus of funds with low returns would be pulled into higher yielding but riskier assets, creating asset bubbles. These bubbles would then burst, typically after the Bank raised its rates to stem a bullion drain, eliminating the interest-rate differential incentivising the flows. The sharp fall in asset prices and shortage of commercial credit due to high interest rates would cause a crisis. The cycle would then restart. In order to avoid the worst of a credit crunch, the Banking School persistently pressed for a higher bullion reserve in the Bank of England, to allow flexibility rather than a hard stop on the limits to the circulation and credit when a bullion drain began to occur.[14]

After the 2008 financial crisis, some researchers began to discuss mechanisms in modern times which were similar to those described by the Banking School. For instance, Swarnali Hannan, using a sample of 34 emerging markets and developing economies from 2009 Q3 to 2015 Q4, discovered that the gap between long-term and short-term government bond yields is a driver of capital flows during periods of high capital flows.[15] Her conclusions directly parallel Thornton's theories about how crises start from the beginning of the nineteenth century. It also confirms Thornton's observations that interest-rate differences have more effect in periods of high capital flow, which tend to be just before crises. In a more recent Bank of England working paper, Ambrogio Cesa-Bianchi, Fernando Eguren Martin and Gregory Thwaites also demonstrated the importance of capital flows by using a set of 38 advanced and emerging economies from 1970 to 2011 to show that credit growth in the rest of the world has the statistically significant effect of increasing the likelihood of a banking crisis at home, a conclusion that is close to the Banking School's theory that cross-border capital flows were a contributor to banking crises in Victorian Britain.[16]

At the height of the gold standard, from 1870 onwards, the Bank of England achieved reasonable stability in interest rates, according to Banking-School ideas, by timely small adjustments in the face of bullion drains, to keep the markets stable, distinguishing between seasonal trade flows and capital flows for investment purposes.[17] This prevented the type of problems seen in the crises of 1847, 1857–1858 and 1866, caused when the Bank of England kept its rates too low in the run-up to a crisis and then, to protect its bullion or note reserve, suddenly raised them too much and too fast, putting excessive strain on commerce and the banking system.

Subsequent analysis of the stability of the period from the 1870s to the first world war has come up with several differing reasons which might have been behind this. Those following the Currency School line of thought gave credit mainly to the operation of the price-specie flow mechanism.[18] Some economic historians have pushed back against this explanation. For instance, Knick Harley strenuously denied this interpretation, pointing to the management of capital flows and 'the Atlantic Economy' as the stabilising influence, in line with the Banking School's ideas.[19] He describes the 1880s railway-building boom in the United States and the potential strain this put on British financial markets, gold reserves and the balance of payments. While a potential balance of payments deficit was counteracted in part by increased exports, following the Currency School's theories, the main stabilising influence to the British monetary base was 'the London market's ability to attract short-term funds with small adjustments in short-term interest rates', in other words, through the application of the Banking School's theories.[20] Michael Bordo and Hugh Rockoff, together with Barry Eichengreen and Marc Flandreau, have also pointed out the credibility that accrued to the pound sterling through central-bank interventions, a policy which grew from the Banking-School ideas of how to prevent and mitigate crises, and the stability of its convertible status.[21] Tamin Bayoumi and Eichengreen have identified faster macroeconomic adjustments as the force behind financial stability, while Luis Catão and Solomos Solomou have highlighted the flexibility afforded by exchange-rate fluctuations which were speedy, but not unduly large, at the periphery of the geographical gold standard where trade took place with countries outside it.[22] Both these observations about how the stability of the classic gold standard was owed to its surprising flexibility and responsiveness are consistent with the notion that a subtle but reactive management of interest rates by the Bank of England helped to prevent serious financial instability in Britain after 1866.

9.2 The Carry Trade and Economic Theory

From the beginning of the twentieth century, attitudes to the Banking School's ideas divided into two streams: that of the practical traders who developed the 'Carry Trade' from them and the mainstream reactions to the theories by academics and commentators. The practical trader found in the Banking School's understanding of interest-rate movements and capital flows a way of making an easy profit. Long before the heyday of Mrs. Watanabe, the traders noted that a profit could be made without capital by borrowing in a country with low interest rates and lending or investing in a country with high interest rates. To mitigate the problem of whether changes in the exchange rate between when the money was exported and re-imported would eat into any profit, options to hedge against this could be arranged. Behaviour of this sort can be also seen in Victorian money markets. Jacob Viner has pointed out that the Bank forward traded in government stocks in 1847 to avoid a loss when it felt forced to sell them at a low price to contract the circulation.[23] These practices grew out of options to buy shares at a certain price in the future (a 'put') or have one bought at an agreed price (a 'call'). The development of 'put's and 'calls' or forward and back premiums in trading was explained by Charles Castelli in *The theory of 'options' in stocks and shares* in 1877 and Leonard Higgins in *The Put-and-Call* published in 1896.[24] The principles were promoted in America by Samuel Nelson in *The ABC of Options and Arbitrage* in 1904.[25] Foreign exchange options were commonly traded by the 1930s.[26] Thus, a profit could be made at low risk in the situation where the interest rates in the two countries were far enough apart.[27]

It was not until after the crisis of 2007–2009 that academics in economics and economic history really focussed on discussions of this trading strategy and the implications that it had for financial stability. These remained overlooked by central bankers and policymakers as the result of the growing influence since the 1970s of Monetarism, which owed much to the ideas of the Currency School. Interest rates were used to control the money supply and inflation without considering capital flows as an important metric to track. Many countries abandoned capital controls, such as Britain in 1979. This contributed to a lack of data being collected on capital flows by central banks, which inhibited academics from testing their theories about them. When Forrest Capie argued in a think-tank policy paper in 2002 that a policy of controlling capital flows would have a worse outcome than one of them being tolerated, he referred mainly to long-term investment flows and his argument preferred theoretical models to hard data.[28]

Yet back in the nineteenth century, the Banking School had placed capital flows and what is now called the Carry Trade at the centre of its theory of crises by observing the characteristics of interest-rate movements. Following the tradition of the Banking School, the understanding of the process had arisen from practical traders dating from the 1930s, rather than academics, who only began to pick up on it in the 1970s as an 'unexploited profit opportunity'.[29] Jeffrey Frankel has only more recently linked this practice with international capital movements.[30] This type of transaction relied on the economic theories of Uncovered Interest Rate Parity and Covered Interest Rate Parity failing to operate and therefore not bringing the relevant interest rates together for a period long enough to make the transactions.[31] To an investor seeking to make this kind of trade, the respective prices of commodities in the two countries are irrelevant; they are sending money out from and receiving it in one particular country and so relative prices in the other country do not matter directly. Therefore, nominal and not real interest rates are relevant for investment flows as opposed to trade flows.[32] Real interest rates and prices are important in Monetarist theory, but the Banking School had pointed to capital flows for investment being linked to the fluctuations in nominal interest rates in the nineteenth century. The 'Carry Trade' illustrates the process in action. In the nineteenth century exchange-rate swaps were not as common as they are today, but this did not matter as a gold standard guaranteed a steady exchange rate between countries (except in certain periods such as the Greenback era).

Two attitudes to exchange-rate variations emerged in the twentieth century, which as Jacob Frenkel has pointed out, relate to the controversies of the early 1880s. The Currency School's ideas developed into theories based on the supply of money (Monetarism) and Banking-School ideas contributed to theories based on circular flow, 'that gained popularity with the Keynesian revolution'.[33] Most balanced commentators agreed with Frenkel that the mechanism operating was an 'interaction of flow and stock' conditions.[34]

For example, Alfred Marshall in the 1920s described the mechanism of how a gold outflow that lowered the Bank of England's reserves would cause economic problems. The Bank would respond by raising its discount rate, and 'the result would be a check to speculative investments, a diminished demand for commodities, and a fall of prices'.[35] He saw flows of capital as caused both by disparities in interest rates and also by imbalances in trade.[36] John Maynard Keynes considered both price and interest rate mechanisms as behind capital flows.[37] Keynes explained his ideas on monetary theory to the Macmillan Committee in 1929–1931 as a mixture of Currency-School and Banking-School theories: 'the balance in our favour on income account depends, broadly speaking, on relative prices at home and abroad' but also 'the movement on short money is not governed by whether prices are higher here than elsewhere; it is governed by whether interest rates are higher here than elsewhere'. Keynes advised that 'the only method the Bank of England has of affecting either of these two factors, either the price factor or the interest factor is by means of the Bank Rate'.[38]

Keynes was an academic, but he was also the Bursar of King's College as well as an investor in his own right, and so he was aware of the short-term trading strategies that caused capital flows. His wider ideas inspired the Hicks-Hansen (or IS-LM) model and that, in turn, produced the Mundell-Fleming model which dealt with the possibility that an economy can be open to trade and capital flows. Conclusions from the model were presented as a 'fundamental macroeconomic policy trilemma' by Obstfield and Taylor in 1997.[39] The theory of 'the impossible trinity', communicates the policy implications of the Mundell-Fleming model and sets out the options available to countries in setting macroeconomic policy.[40] According to the theory, a country cannot achieve the free flow of capital, a fixed exchange rate and independent setting of interest rates simultaneously. By implementing any two of this list, it necessarily loses control of the third. Since exchange rates became uncontrolled and to an extent uncontrollable in recent decades, some economists such as Helene Rey have suggested the theory is now a 'dilemma' between control of interest rates and control of openness to capital flows.[41]

The trilemma theory links Sir Robert Peel's choice of policies to capital flows and therefore to crises. His policies were similar to the three trilemma policies. There were no restrictions on capital flows and the boosting of trade with low tariffs encouraged higher flows as trade increased and more payments for goods moved between countries. The linking of the pound to gold meant that a fixed exchange rate was achieved with other countries using or approximating to the same standard. Further, when payments were made in gold, for example in times of reduced credit, currencies were cut out of the picture and the only thing that mattered was the price of goods or investment in relation to gold. The constant pressure to reduce long-term interest rates and therefore cut the cost of repaying the national debt to balance the fiscal budget showed that monetary policy was being set, rather than being allowed to find its own level. The Mundell-Fleming theory states that one policy would have to be abandoned and, assuming the theory holds, that was interest rates, as the Bank of England was forced to move them sharply upwards to stem bullion drains during the crises of 1847, 1857–1858 and 1866.

Nonetheless, some economists have criticised the Mundell-Fleming model because it utilised the interest-rate parity theorem to explain international interest rates. Several analyses have shown both the covered and uncovered interest-rate parity theories not to hold, long term, calling the Mundell-Fleming model into question.[42] However, the experience of traders in the Carry Trade market suggests that the extent to which interest-rate parity holds depends on the quantity of the trade and the parity of nominal rates only tends to hold after a considerable period of trade. If correct, this assertion explains the result of enquiries into interest-rate parities and suggests that the conclusions from the Mundell-Fleming model are useful mainly in crisis situations when the parity is operating. As has been shown, since the usury laws were abandoned in the early to mid nineteenth century, control of interest rates was normally lost in a crisis. This accords with the recent research of Charles Engel, who has suggested that the failure of the interest-rate parity to apply in the long term may be because different circumstances apply during 'normal times' and 'rare disasters'.[43]

In support of the Currency School's ideas, Milton Friedman interpreted the price-specie flow mechanism in relation to the price of money (interest rates) and linked imports and exports to the demand for money. He came closer to the ideas of some Banking-School theorists when he distinguished between high-powered money, or the monetary base, and the stock of money, which had a more gradual and flexible effect.[44] Stephen Williamson and Randall Wright developed this view, incorporating the growth in real output as a factor in determining the demand for goods and money and therefore capital flows, a relationship that can be shown in the long-term, but not in the short-term.[45] In March 1982 at a National Bureau of Economic Research conference, Milton Friedman responded to a paper, 'the success of Purchasing-Power Parity'. In doing so, he stated a priced-based rather than interest-rate-based version of the Mundell-Fleming trilemma:

> There are three things of which a country can choose any two: stable internal prices, stable exchange rates, and free trade. You can't have all three; you can have only two. That proposition is critical.[46]

9.3 Carry Trades, Interest Rates, Capital Flows and Crises

The Carry Trade has highlighted problems with interest-rate-parity theories because it relies on them not occurring. Theories associated with the Banking School dating from the nineteenth century can offer a possible explanation for the mechanism behind these problems.

Uncovered interest-rate parity has no guaranteed forward rate. It assumes that interest rates in the two countries (i, i^*) will equalise. To the international investor, the spot exchange rate on money going out (S_1), and the spot exchange rate coming back (S_2), will be a factor. The situation of parity or nil profit is usually shown in an equation including a factor to adjust S_2 because it is being estimated in the future (E) thus:

$$\frac{1 + i}{S_1} = \left(1 + i^*\right) E\, S_2$$

The investor will only make the expected profit if parity does not occur and they have predicted the future exchange rate ($E\, S_2$) correctly and the interest rate (i^*) is beneficial. Various studies have shown that the uncovered interest-rate parity does not hold in the data and various reasons have been explored including asynchronous data, non-comparability of asset risk, transaction costs and taxes. Those associated with the Banking School would have pointed out that this theory relied on a continuous availability and flow of capital, which was not in reality the case.

The covered interest-rate parity replaces the estimated future exchange rate ($E\, S_2$) with the reciprocal guaranteed future option (F_2) in an otherwise similar equation. To the investor his profit on an initial sum of y is the return from abroad less the possible return at home:

$$\left[\frac{(1+i^*)}{S_1} F_2 - (1+i)\right] y$$

Economists are interested in what the actual spot exchange rate would turn out to be compared with the forward rate F_2. As the investors who have anticipated a profit will be buying up the currency with the higher interest rate (i^*), they would expect the value of the currency against others to rise to the expected rate. However, frequently it falters and a 'sudden stop' occurs with a large fall in the value of the currency and a financial crisis with all the accompanying problems.[47] Charles Engel confirmed the tendency of forward rates to be negatively related to the actual spot rate at the same time and called it the 'Forward Discount Anomaly'.[48] The Banking School's theory raises the possibility that long-term analysis of these relationships is hiding an initial rise followed by a crash. Not all trades are able to be covered because, as Robert Aliber has pointed out, when an option is issued, 'someone pays a higher price for foreign exchange in the forward market than in the spot market'.[49] Those who have carried out trades uncovered are likely to withdraw as soon as there is no advantage to them, exactly as was the case in the nineteenth century, but which in modern times since the end of the gold standard may lead to an exchange-rate crash. Capital flows into the high-interest-rate country cease or even reverse and a balance of payments deficit must be compensated for by boosting trade. Thus, the mechanism defies long-term analysis, but is very clear in short-term analyses of particular crises.[50]

Examples of exchange-rate crashes induced by interest-rate equalisation stopping or reversing capital flows can be observed from experience around the world in recent decades. Three examples will be given here. The first is Chile, which liberalised its policy towards capital flows in the early 1970s. It maintained an interest rate higher than the world rate and received increasing inward capital flows. In 1980 interest rates around the world began to increase, the American rate rose to 7% and then 8% and rates converged. By the end of 1981 capital flows had reversed, interest rates in Chile had soared to try and stop outward flows.[51] In 1982 the dollar-peso exchange rate fell by over 50%.[52]

The second good example is Argentina in the 1990s and 2000s. In Argentina the Argentine peso was pegged to the American dollar in 1991 so that the only major tool which could be used to attract and retain foreign funds was interest rates. Rates reached 15% in 1995 but lowered to 6% in 1997 to try and provide reasonable rates for domestic loans.[53] Russia's crisis in 1998 stopped capital flows from there and American rates rose to 6% in early 2001. And so, the nominal differential between American and Argentine rates evaporated. Capital flows changed from being positive (around 8% of GDP per quarter until the final quarter of 1999) to being severely negative (around minus 10% of GDP per quarter) from the third quarter of 2001 onwards.[54] Argentina's real effective exchange rate fell suddenly by five-eighths at the beginning of 2002 when the peg was abandoned.[55]

The third good example is Iceland. Low interest rates in America and Europe between 2001 and 2004 flooded Iceland with capital flows seeking better returns and enabled its newly privatised banks to expand at breakneck speed.[56] At the end of that period, Iceland had accumulated debts up to ten times its GDP, including a significant amount of mortgage debt denominated in euros, which was used to feed a property asset-price bubble.[57] Fearful of a capital outflow, Iceland imposed capital controls in 2008, but it was too late. Flows had already reversed, falling sharply in 2008 and resulting in net outflows in the second and third quarters of 2009. Iceland had effectively cut itself off from the international credit market and any significant inflows, and it should therefore be no surprise to anyone aware of the Banking School's ideas that all three of the country's main banks then failed. The krona-euro exchange rate depreciated by 45% between January 2008 and January 2009, another sudden exchange-rate crash.[58]

9.4 The Interwar and Post-War Years

Policymakers in Britain continued to prevent the Carry Trade from causing crises from the Victorian era until the start of the 1970s. However, after the adoption of Competition and Credit Control, a policy adopted in 1971 that was influenced by early Monetarism, the Carry Trade and the crises it can cause reappeared again. This section of the chapter surveys the interwar and post-war periods and suggests reasons for how policies that aligned with the Banking School's ideas continued to assist banking stability in those eras.

The interwar years were notable for the failure to return permanently to Peel's policy regime after the first world war. At the outbreak of the conflict, the gold standard was abandoned with the Currency and Bank Notes Act of 1914, after a brief panic caused by the uncertainty of the slide to war. There was an attempt to bring back the gold standard after the war on the pre-1914 exchange rate of $4.86 to the pound. This had a period of temporary success from 1925 to 1931. The aim was to maintain the international status of sterling as a reserve currency by preserving its pre-war value. The decision to return to the gold standard at $4.86 resulted in a well-known disagreement between the chancellor of the exchequer, Winston Churchill, and Keynes, who estimated that the value of the pound had been fixed 10% too high.[59] Scholars have ever since continued to argue over the extent to which the return to the gold standard overvalued British exports and by how much this damaged economic growth in the 1920s, as a result.[60]

Other old battles resumed too. Montagu Norman, the Governor of the Bank of England between 1920 and 1944, was a supporter of the gold standard on the basis that it helped to maintain confidence in the pound. He slugged it out with various chancellors of the exchequer who wanted to reduce interest rates and move away from fixed exchange rates to ease the fiscal burden of servicing Britain's huge national debt from the first world war.[61] However, Norman's views on this subject did not prevail over policy. The gold standard was abandoned in September 1931—albeit not entirely intentionally—to prevent yet another financial crisis as the Bank's reserves drained away.[62] Now, with the pound floating, or at least on a managed float, exchange rates as well as interest rates were a consideration for international speculators and investors. During the year after devaluation, the pound fell by 28% against the dollar.

A freer-floating currency also allowed the circulation of notes and money supply to increase dramatically in the 1930s, which enabled a swift economic recovery to take place. Interest rates fell from 5.5% in 1929 to just 2% between June 1932 and August 1939. Between 1932 and 1939 there was a strong upturn in the British economy, characterised by rising total-factor productivity growth and falling unemployment. Thus it appears that the United Kingdom benefited from the demise of the classic Currency School policies and the introduction of a Banking School or even Anti-bullionist stance.[63] The United States, by contrast, continued to restrict and decrease its money circulation between 1929 and 1933, despite healthy gold reserves. The result was a series of banking crises during the Great Depression that wiped out two-thirds of American financial institutions between 1929 and 1933—a period in which there were no systemic banking crises in Britain. American GDP fell much more sharply than in the United Kingdom, at least until President Franklin D. Roosevelt devalued the dollar against gold in 1933, and the recovery to pre-crisis output started later and took longer to complete.

Nevertheless, how did Britain both avoid a banking crisis during the interwar years and enjoy low interest rates after 1932 without fear of the Carry Trade? The answer partly lies in leaving the gold standard and devaluation, which re-inflated asset prices in sterling terms by reducing the deflationary pressures on the British economy that eventually caused widespread banking failures in other countries. However, this was also because, in spite of low interest rates, the conditions for Carry Traders to make money were very limited in the interwar period. Olivier Accominotti and David Chambers have shown that during the 1930s, the 'naïve' carry trade strategy did not bring good returns.[64] This is unsurprising, because American nominal short-term rates were at 1% and the United Kingdom's at 2% for most of the 1930s, and there were wide and unpredictable fluctuations in the exchange rate. In short, the potential Carry profit was not worth the risk. By 1934 the exchange rate with the American dollar had more than recovered from Britain's devaluation in 1931, a sign of the level of currency volatility at the time. In any case, any capital flows from the trade would have been in favour of the United Kingdom and, apparently, according to Accominotti and Chambers, Keynes did not use the method in his trades.[65]

Keynes was aware of a similar trading strategy, however, and explained how it worked to the Macmillan Committee in 1930.[66] He saw it as an example of trading which could cause troublesome capital flows but he claimed that it did not matter greatly at the time he spoke. The separation of interest rates was not sufficient to make gold move unduly because the 'the gold points' or interest rates at which transfer from one country to another became profitable, were held far apart by the high cost of transporting gold across borders in this period. At the time of the Committee, Keynes was preoccupied with the issue of how to reduce unemployment through increasing investment. His writings do not address the Banking-School theory of crisis at the point when nominal interest rates converge, despite many other theoretical similarities, as this was not the big policy problem of the 1930s. However, in modern times, the development of electronic money has reduced the cost of Carry Trade-type investment flows—effectively closing the gap between the equivalent of the 'gold points'—making them a much greater issue today than in Keynes's time.

After the end of the 'classical' gold standard in 1931, the Bank of England increasingly used 'Open Market Operations' to stifle capital flows. Anthony Hotson has described how this worked, based on an explanation given in 1931 to the Macmillan Committee.[67] If the Bank wished to raise its interest rate to stop drains, it might find that market rates remained low and the drains continued. If it sold increased government debt, this lowered the price of these assets, increasing the yields (equivalent to interest rates) and pushed the market rate of interest up to the Bank Rate. This action was equivalent to keeping the market short of credit. The reverse was to purchase government debt which increased the availability of credit and kept interest rates low. This procedure developed into 'Quantitative Easing' much later on, the difference being that the 'Easing' was carried out with fiat money (not backed by gold or foreign currency). After 1931 it was used to keep interest rates low, which decreased from around 6% in 1931 to 2% through most of the 1930s. Confusingly, in spite of being based on Thornton's and Palmer's ideas about how interest rates could and should be manipulated, these actions came to be called 'the classical system'. They had grown in popularity among bankers in the latter part of the nineteenth century, the Banking-School lamb in Currency-School wolf's clothing.

Capital mobility remained in place, in theory, in the 1930s, but the war called for heavy restrictions on cross-border flows to be introduced, to preserve bullion reserves for the war effort. The war gradually normalised capital controls and credit controls as policy tools for peacetime. Restrictions on capital flows out of Britain remained heavy until they were finally abolished by Margaret Thatcher's government in 1979.[68]

Capital controls were just one part of the post-war Bretton Woods system (1944–1971), under which Britain maintained a fixed exchange rate between the pound and the American dollar until 1971. The period is unique in having very few banking crises around the world.[69] Just as looser controls on exchange rates in the early 1930s coincided with better financial stability in Britain than the United States, the flexibility built in by Keynes into the Bretton Woods system—with its tolerance of exchange controls and occasional devaluations—underpinned a period of relative banking stability between 1944 and 1973. Although the Bretton Woods agreement reintroduced fixed exchange rates with the dollar, Keynes as the head of the British delegation, negotiated controls with some flexibility (a key idea associated with the Banking School), including those over the use of capital controls, tariffs and devaluations to help countries maintain economic stability internally. Yet it was the decision in the Bretton Woods era for most members to use credit controls and capital controls to preserve fixed exchange rates and independent monetary policies that really smothered the cross-border Carry Trade in this era, which relied on capital mobility.

Nonetheless, the Bank of England retained its instincts from the Banking School, even as the centenary of the crisis of 1866 passed. The observation of capital flows and interest-rate differentials between Britain and America remained an important factor behind decisions about Bank Rate. Most notably, Forrest Capie has described how from the February 1964 rise in Bank Rate the Bank attempted to coordinate any rate changes with the United States, so that changes in interest-rate differentials did not create adverse capital flows for the United Kingdom.[70] Nevertheless, there was a growing aversion by post-war politicians to raising the Bank Rate, not least thanks to growing levels of home ownership that meant more of the electorate would be affected by rising mortgage payments than in the past. This culminated in the devaluation of 1967 and threatened the traditional policy of raising interest rates promptly to stem a drain before it accelerated out of control and required more aggressive action.[71] Indeed, one Governor of the Bank in the 1960s, Rowland Baring, 3rd Earl of Cromer, decided in 1966 not to seek a second term because of disputes with the government of Harold Wilson over the setting of Bank Rate.[72]

That was the context in which the Bank attempted to find a policy that would depoliticise rises in Bank Rate, tackle rising levels of inflation and replace ceilings on bank lending that had damaged relations between it and the City of London, where the clearing banks had blamed the controls for their recent loss of market share.[73] The answer it came up with was Competition and Credit Control, in which ceiling controls would be replaced by tighter control of the money supply using higher interest rates.[74] In short, as Duncan Needham has put it, 'credit rationing by cost replaced rationing by control'.[75] The policy was sold to the incoming Conservative government of Edward Heath, which wanted to boost competition within British industry, as a way to make the banking sector more competitive.[76] Yet rather than make rate hikes easier, defeat inflation and control the money supply, the new policy unleashed the sort of monetary and banking chaos that had not been seen in Britain for more than a century.

9.5 The Secondary Banking Crisis of 1973–1975

The new policy provided the British government with a plan for monetary policy when President Richard Nixon formally brought the Bretton Woods era to an end by suspending the convertibility of the American dollar on 15 August 1971. The pound floated away from its peg on 23 August 1971. Britain's new monetary policy, Competition and Credit Control, was in full operation by September 1971.[77] In just over two years, just as the secondary banking crisis was getting into full swing in December 1973, the broad-money supply had risen by 72%, at what must have been its fastest rate thus far in British history.[78] Bank advances to the property sector rose from £362m in February 1971 to £2,584m in February 1974, with most of the funds lent out borrowed short term from the money markets.[79] By June 1973 nominal interest rates in America and Britain converged to a level of around 7%. The scene was set for Britain's first systemic banking crisis in over a century when this speculative splurge came to a shuddering end.

The secondary banks were small banks which had moved towards a business model of borrowing short-term on the wholesale market and lending long term in the property market to expand quickly.[80] The loosening of credit restrictions as part of Competition and Credit Control fuelled this growth, but the sharp tightening of monetary policy by Anthony Barber as chancellor of the exchequer in 1973 made the secondary banks illiquid and sent the property market into a tailspin.[81] A consequent pause in capital flows in the autumn of 1973 tightened short-term credit markets.

The first secondary bank to require assistance was London and County Securities in November 1973, which triggered deposits to flow out of its peers into the clearing banks and building societies, followed by Cedar Holdings a month later. The Bank of England came to the rescue, just as it had previously done in the crisis of 1890 for Barings. In 1974 it and the clearing banks launched a 'lifeboat' scheme under Deputy Governor Jasper Hollom.[82] Eighteen institutions were rescued, but eight were allowed to fail because they were insolvent or there was evidence of fraud. The lifeboat expended £1.3bn in financial assistance (about 1% of British GDP at the time) at an estimated final cost to the Bank (or to its owner, the British taxpayer) of £55m.[83]

There are two ways of interpreting what went wrong using the insights provided by the Banking School. The first is that it was a re-run of the crisis of 1847. In other words, that rates were held too low for too long, followed by an attempted fiscal stimulus by the government, and then rates being raised too late, too sharply and by too much, causing the banking sector to collapse. As *The Economist* put it in 1975, the cause was 'a super-tight squeeze' and the result was 'an old-fashioned banking crisis'.[84]

The end of credit controls, combined with Heath's refusal to allow the Bank to raise rates significantly until late 1972, fuelled a credit boom.[85] He, just as Wilson had, appeared to fear the impact on private industry and homeowners of making borrowing more expensive, a sign that Competition and Credit Control had failed in its aim of making interest-rate hikes politically easier.[86] The 1972 budget added more petrol to the fire by raising income-tax thresholds and by honouring the Conservatives' manifesto commitment to make interest payments deductible against tax, in effect producing a 30% subsidy on debt costs for basic-rate taxpayers and 90% for those paying the highest rate.[87] This, in effect, meant that interest rates had to be raised even higher to restrain inflation and the money supply.[88] However, with unemployment reaching close to the politically unacceptable level of one million, in late 1971 Heath and Barber decided to keep rates on hold and also engineer a fiscal stimulus called 'the dash for growth', which increased the public-sector borrowing requirement forecast for 1972/1973 to 5% of GDP, the highest level since the end of the second world war.[89] With the London stock market reaching a peak in May 1972 and then falling not least thanks to a profitability crisis in British industry, excess credit creation was redirected into a property bubble, much of it via lending by the secondary banks.[90]

By the summer of 1973 inflation was rising, helped by widespread industrial unrest in Britain and an OPEC embargo increasing oil prices by up to 300%. To cool the economy the government increased the minimum-lending rate to 11.5% in July 1973—a record high, exceeding the rates used during the crisis of 1866 and panic of 1914—and to 13% in November the same year. *The Economist* later argued that this was too much tightening too fast; Competition and Credit Control's focus on £M3, which was soaring, as a target distracted from £M1, a narrower definition of money supply, which had stabilised by the end of 1972 and was falling in the second half of 1973.[91] Whether *The Economist* was correct or not about £M1, it was these high rates that tipped the secondary banks into the first stage of the crisis, in which they were still solvent but illiquid, thanks to high rates freezing them out of the money market and worried depositors withdrawing their funds from them.[92]

The second way of interpreting what went wrong is that it was by encouraging the Carry Trade. Before the oil-price shock, American rates had been slightly lower than in the United Kingdom and there had been significant inward capital flows from there into Britain.[93] This had helped to feed the asset-price bubbles associated with the Barber boom of 1971–1973. Interest rates briefly converged between America and Britain in June 1973 (see Fig. 9.1). At the same time, the OPEC oil crisis hit. It was at this moment that the flows paused, as the incentives fuelling them had been extinguished. Just as the Banking School's theories would suggest, this was the moment the secondary banking crisis began.

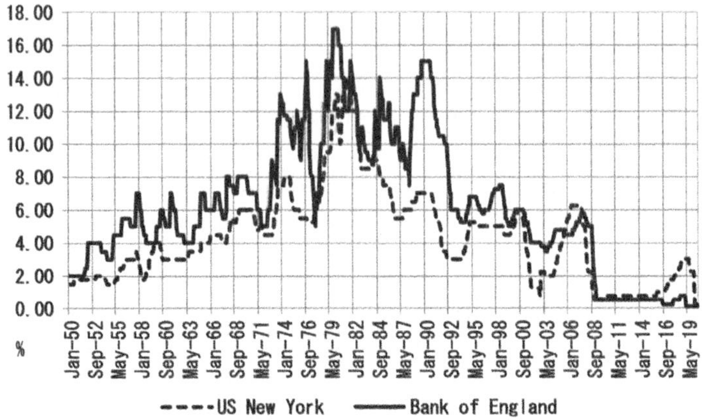

Fig. 9.1 Interest rates (short term) US (New York) and UK (Bank of England) 1950 to 2019 (*Sources* Bank of England; OECD database)

Later in the 1970s, American rates were much lower than in those in Britain, which rose beyond 15% (Fig. 9.1). In line with the Banking School's theories, inwards capital flows into Britain resumed as interest rates separated.[94] Government pressure on the clearing banks kept their rates a little lower than other banks and internal arbitrage developed with large corporate customers borrowing from the clearing banks at a low rate and investing in property at the higher rate. This diverted investment from industry to property, which created another housing boom at the end of the 1970s.[95]

It also showed that the lessons of the secondary banking crisis were not fully learnt by policymakers. By 1986 a book by John Grady and Martin Weale surveying British banking between 1960 and 1985 argued that the practice of borrowing money on the short to lend on long-term investment had returned.[96] As Michie has noted, the two economists were concerned that the conditions that had led to the banking crisis of 1974 were starting to re-emerge.[97] It thus might have been more luck than judgement that the bank failures of the 1980s and 1990s did not turn into full-blown banking crises, particularly given that the Bank's Banking Supervision Division was both understaffed and under-experienced in this era.[98]

9.6 The Crisis of 2007–2009

The Banking School's ideas about crises can be seen reflected again in the events of the global financial crisis of 2007–2009, which hit the British banking sector hard. Northern Rock, the first British bank to get into difficulty, had borrowed at low rates in the short-term wholesale market to lend long term with the risk inadequately covered, yet another example of this mistake. Once again, low interest rates of just 1% in the United States, between 2001 and 2004, had provoked the export of funds by European banks who borrowed low and lent out at higher rates, including in Britain. Once again, in general, short-term loans had been used to invest long-term, so when interest rates equalised in 2006–2008 and the capital flows dried up, banks such as Northern Rock that relied on wholesale markets for their funding got into trouble, and disaster followed.

Excessive faith in flawed statistical formulae also played a role. Both the Currency School and latter-day Monetarism have established themselves in academia by showing that their simple, long-term propositions, such as a connection between the money supply and prices, could be verified by statistical analysis of data. In contrast, the Banking School's theories, such as the connection between interest rates, capital flows and crises, was more difficult to demonstrate using these methods, as there were so many variables involved. Furthermore, many of the key concepts behind their ideas, such as interest-rate parity, appeared to operate in a crisis but not at other times, making them more difficult to observe using econometrics and long-run data. The move in the economics profession towards a greater reliance upon quantitative methods and models thus put their ideas in the shade.[99]

It was one of these models, the 'Black–Scholes' equation that claimed to enable the avoidance of risk, which turned out to have been used inappropriately after it had inspired the creation of a great number of defective securities.[100] The use of the equation assumed that money could always be borrowed with options in the future at a known, fixed, risk-free interest rate. However, the Banking School's ideas about cycles of crises had warned as long ago as the early nineteenth century that this was bound to eventually fail.

There is some evidence that a similar process to the Banking School's cycle of crises operated between America and Britain in the 2000s. Recent research by Christiane Kneer and Alexander Raabe published by the Bank of England has produced a measure of capital flows based on information from banks receiving international transfers.[101] The results offer an unusual opportunity to see the effect of American-British interest-rate differentials on capital flows, which is not normally possible, due to a lack of data. It can be seen from Fig. 9.2 that nominal short-term interest rates in the United States were lower than those in the United Kingdom from 2001 to 2006, six years in which the Carry Trade could earn a profit. During this period capital flows into the United Kingdom rose from around £100bn per quarter to around £300bn per quarter. In 2006 American and British interest rates converged and this was then followed by a crash in net inflows from 2007 onwards, resulting in outflows between 2008 and 2010. According to Kneer and Raabe, 'capital inflows into banks drive lending to the corporate sector and to other domestic financial institutions'; thus Northern Rock's problems as well as the depth of the resulting recession in Britain could be attributed to these capital inflows from America stopping.[102] In contrast, Friedman's alternative measure of the purchasing-power parity of the pound is virtually constant with the American dollar throughout the period and gives no clue as to an impending crisis, nor the passing of it.[103]

So, the reversal of the flows caused a significant credit crunch in the United Kingdom and would have adversely affected the balance of payments, causing the pound to depreciate 35% against the dollar over the course of the crisis. This situation tends to confirm Clare's assertion that it is mainly variations in credit linked with capital flows which provoke crises, and not principally variations in the international trade of goods.[104] The lagged reaction to the convergence of interest rates in 2006 has been linked to initial expectations that the large inwards flows earlier in the 2000s would soon resume.[105]

Moreover, there is some evidence that the Carry Trade also occurred internally within America because that country had widely different interest rates for different types of investments. As Tim Lee, Jamie Lee and Kevin Coldiron have noted, Carry Trades can take place between different financial instruments and sectors within an economy, the flows do not need to cross borders.[106] The low returns on safe investments such as Treasury bonds at home not only encouraged American funds to be attracted abroad to European banks, but into sub-prime mortgage lending at home in America. The repackaging of such mortgages with other investments into Collateralised Debt Obligations (CDOs)

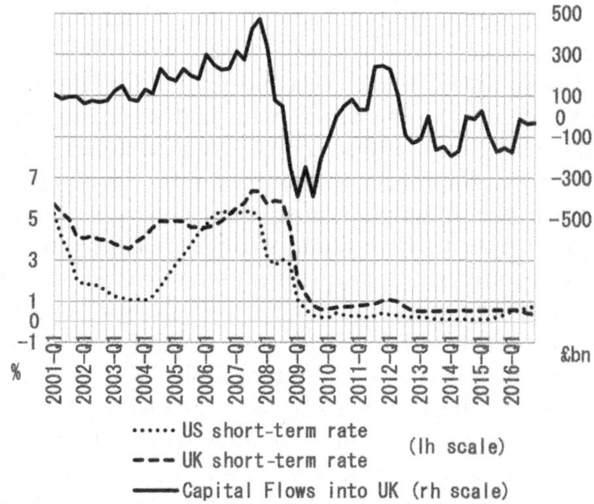

Fig. 9.2 Quarterly short-term US and UK interest rates and capital flows into the United Kingdom (£bn) 2001-Q1 to 2016-Q4 (*Sources* OECD database; C. Kneer, A. Raabe, 'Tracking foreign capital: the effect of capital inflows on bank lending in the UK', *Bank of England Staff Working Paper*, No. 804 [2019] p. 28)

supposedly produced securities that gave high returns from the mortgages granted to those who had self-certified their earnings and were deemed low risk thanks to the 'Black–Scholes' equation.

One explanation frequently given by commentators for the ensuing sub-prime mortgage crisis is that it arose from 'liar loans'; dishonest borrowers and brokers as well as overenthusiastic lenders and investors.[107] This argument aligns with the ideas of the Currency School, which emphasised these themes in their own descriptions of Victorian banking crises. Yet this explanation does not fully account for what was incentivising this excess to take place.

Here, the ideas of the Banking School can help fill the void. Once again low interest rates in America can be seen as fuelling a search for yield that encouraged investment in riskier areas with (nominally) higher returns. As the Federal Reserve hiked interest rates, they rose towards the returns from the CDOs—from just 1% in June 2004 to 5.25% in June 2006—and the pressure to produce an attractive return on new CDOs induced ever more risky loans to be included in them.[108] As the rates of return equalised between the CDOs and safer assets, the number of new ones sold dropped from 2006, as there was no reward for taking on the extra risk. At the same time, homeowners who had taken on the mortgages at lower rates (particularly introductory so-called teaser rates) found it impossible to service them now that interest rates were higher.[109]

So, once again, the underlying cause of the consequent boom and bust in CDOs can be seen to have some strong similarities to the Banking School's ideas of converging or equalising interest rates as a threat to the financial system. If the rates had not risen so sharply—again a common feature of Victorian crises that the Banking School criticised—some sub-prime mortgages may have still been affordable for the homeowners and there may have still been a market for refinancing. Moreover, if the Federal Reserve had not kept interest rates so low between 2000 and 2004, the financial sector would have never been so incentivised in the first place to lend to those who could never have afforded the repayments in normal times.

Such explanations of the 2008 crisis that involved interest-rate differentials, capital flows and financial trouble when returns converge—which unwittingly parallel the ideas of the Banking School—have gained increasing prominence in the press in more recent years.[110] The risk of the Carry Trade triggering a bout of financial instability had already been noted by some commentators even before the global financial crisis. In February 2007 *The Economist* predicted the collapse of the Carry Trade between the yen and dollar before its part in the credit crunch:

> The "carry trade"... involves investors borrowing a low-yielding asset (often the yen) and buying a higher-yielding one. Past financial-market wobbles have been associated with periods when the carry trade was unwound. No one knows precisely how much capital is involved. But Tim Lee, of Pi Economics, reckons as much as $1 trillion may be staked on the yen carry trade. Were the yen ever to rise sharply (making the trade unprofitable), there could be hell to pay in the markets.[111]

Research since that time by economists at the Bank for International Settlements has found that the withdrawal of yen funding from America by Carry Traders did coincide with the start of the credit crunch in August 2007, and that it also continued into the latter half of 2007 and into 2008 as the credit crisis developed.[112]

9.7 The Covid-19 Pandemic and Beyond

Even so, the lessons of the 2007–2009 crisis in this regard have still not been fully addressed by central banks. The slashing of interest rates to record low rates in the wake of that crisis fuelled another cycle of the boom, culminating in the 'taper tantrum', which is widely regarded as having done damage to emerging-market economies. After central banks cut interest rates to near the zero-lower bound in late 2008 in the wake of the collapse of Lehman Brothers, in an effort to stave off deflation, revive growth and meet their inflation targets, they used quantitative easing to lower market interest rates further. This situation attracted investment funds to developing countries that had higher interest rates or provided better returns on capital. However, the Federal Reserve began to talk about tapering off quantitative easing from 2013, which reduced these outflows, triggering a fall in prices and an increase in yields of emerging markets bonds. Furthermore, in order to keep inflationary pressures under control as the economy reached full employment, the Federal Reserve raised its interest-rate target from 0.25 to 2.25–2.5% between 2015 and 2019. The result was that GDP growth in emerging economies fell sharply, particularly affecting Argentina, India and Turkey, some of which ended up in renewed crisis. Recent research published by the Fed confirmed the effect on developing countries, although it partially missed the point because it examined absolute increases in American interest rates rather than the difference between rates in different countries.[113]

Some recent research on financial stability echoes the Banking School's idea that an important underlying condition for frenzied investment booms is low interest rates—i.e. that it is the result of central-bank monetary policy—rather than solely the result of inadequate banking regulation.[114] In 2018 Yueran Ma of Harvard University and Wilte Zijlstra of the Dutch Authority for the Financial Markets observed that when the risk-free yield falls below its historic average, investors' use of risky assets increases in a non-linear fashion.[115] This insight, similar to the Banking School's ideas, dates, as this book has stated many times, from Henry Thornton in the nineteenth century, although it was labelled in the research, understandably, as 'new'.[116] This research helps to confirm the scenario that when interest rates decline and investors start searching for higher yields, systemic financial risk increases.

Many financial commentators have noted that since interest rates declined after the 2007–2009 crisis, the opportunity for currency

Carry Trades has greatly increased, particularly since 2014. There is a burgeoning demand for forward foreign currency hedges and a widening spread between interest rates, both short-term and long-term.[117] Another parallel concern is that major banks and other financial institutions will use quantitative-easing funds from central banks to engage in Carry Trades in order to try and build their reserves.[118] This has been a particular danger since the covid-19 pandemic hit the world in 2020, when central banks yet again slashed interest rates to as low as possible to avoid mass credit defaults. The lesson from the monetary thought of the Banking School is that this situation, if not handled correctly, could provide the seeding ground for yet another financial crisis.[119]

In order to prevent the covid-19 lockdowns from causing a global economic implosion, central banks around the world have resorted again to quantitative-easing measures to try and push down short-term and long-term interest rates. The reasoning behind why such quantitative easing is increasingly seen by the central banks as a safe course of action, owes something to a growth in popularity of a newer heterodox group of economic theories called Modern Monetary Theory (MMT) as well as the emergency conditions created by the pandemic. MMT proposes that a country which issues its own currency can use quantitative easing to create money to buy government debt without causing inflation until a situation of very full employment arises. At first glance, the theory appears to have something in common with the Banking School's ideas, in that they both effectively vary the money supply according to commercial needs. However, the difference is that the Banking School provided a clearer scenario of how MMT will fail unless sufficient precautions are taken to maintain financial stability.

In 2020 central banks used quantitative easing beyond the wildest dreams of many MMT theorists. Between April and September 2020, £745bn was created by the Bank of England alone through quantitative easing. Most of this was used to buy government bonds (gilts) from banks and major investors; some direct monetary financing of government expenditure did occur during the first covid-19 lockdown. Although there was a pledge back in 2008 that quantitative easing would be reversed by selling back into private hands some of the purchased bonds, some, at least £100bn, has so far been allowed to run to maturity. This meant that the Treasury had to pay the Bank the face value of the bonds, but the Bank appears to have returned the money to the Treasury along with £57bn of interest it had received on the bonds. The effect of this exercise was to pay off a chunk of the British government's debt with no apparent costs on the national accounts.[120] The Federal Reserve proposed a similar exercise in March 2020, intending to spend an additional $500bn on Treasury securities and $750bn on corporate bonds, but the debt appears to remain with the Board of Governors of the Federal Reserve System.[121] Meanwhile, in June 2020 the European Central Bank (ECB) announced an expansion of its quantitative-easing programme to reach €1.35trn.[122] During the pandemic, the ECB also started to accept bonds of below investment grade status as collateral and to lend money to banks at rates as low as −1%—in other words paying them to borrow money from it.[123]

According to the warnings from the ideas of the Banking School, the ultra-loose monetary policy of the covid-19 era may end in the same way as the 'taper tantrum'. Investors in government bonds and domestic investments in developed countries will lose patience and move their investments abroad to developing countries where rates and returns are higher.[124] Eventually the developed countries will be forced to raise their rates in order to return inflation to its target level. As interest rates in the developed and developing worlds converge, investment flows will stop, causing asset prices to fall, possibly leading to the contagion spreading around the financial system of the investor and investee country. This is essentially the same mechanism that can be seen operating in financial markets since the early nineteenth century. Since the collapse of the Bretton Woods system in the early 1970s, cycles of monetary tightening by the Fed have always led to financial crises somewhere in the world (even if America itself escapes), including every major global crisis in recent decades.[125] Governments, regulators and the world of finance have been unable to moderate it in the twenty-first century, so far.

9.8 Policy Prescriptions

What can be done to control these adverse flows? One suggestion would be to return to the capital controls of the Bretton Woods era. However, technological change means that this is no longer possible. The recent development of cryptocurrencies such as bitcoin means that hot money can be transferred across borders, illegally if there are capital controls, more cheaply, easily and speedily than ever before. All that is needed is an internet connection. Removing access to the internet is not a realistic policy to stop cryptocurrencies. Such a step could harm productivity, be entirely inconsistent with liberal democratic values and may well cause a revolution, given most people's attachment to the online world.

Another approach, championed by Adair Turner and many others, is greater regulation. The advocates of this approach argue that excessive financialisation of the economy is harmful; taxation or regulation of the externalities caused by the financial sector is what is needed. So-called 'macro-prudential policies' have become the fashionable tool to use in recent years.[126] In Britain stricter salary caps on mortgage lending have been introduced to cool returns from the housing market, while Ireland has also used a similar regulatory toolkit to prevent yield-searching capital from central Europe causing yet another credit-fuelled boom and bust at home.

However, the problem here is that the regulators will always be one step behind the yield-searching investors. Limits on one asset class will simply divert the hot money into another. As Ruchir Sharma, Chairman of Rockefeller International, has noted, when financial regulators cracked down on the causes of the global financial crisis of 2007–2009—excessive leverage by big banks and high-risk mortgage lending—the flow of easy money, added to by two bouts of quantitative easing, was diverted into less heavily regulated sectors, particularly corporate lending by 'shadow banks'.[127] The issue with shadow banks—that together manage as much as $63trn in assets around the world at the time of writing—is that they are firms that are not banks but still provide financing for other firms in the same way as a bank would.[128] Many are based off-shore, meaning that they are beyond the reach of most big financial regulators.[129] The world's major stress-tested banks may emerge unscathed in the next downturn, but the shadow banks and the rest of the financial sector might not.

British financial history can also provide some further examples. As Anthony Hotson has pointed out, macro-prudential policies are rather like the selective credit controls that Britain tried in the 1960s.[130] Permanent ones resulted in the lending being diverted via newer and less regulated institutions (such as building societies in the 1930s and secondary banks in the 1960s and 1970s), while temporary ones simply triggered anticipatory behaviour by the banks to evade them.[131]

Rather like proverbial generals, financial regulators are often prepared to fight the last war, not the one which is about to break out. One example in Britain is that the monetary-policy shock caused by Kwasi Kwarteng's mini budget of September 2022 threatened the pension funds as their liability-driven investment strategies triggered them to fire-sale gilts in order to fund margin calls. That risk was not foreseen by regulators who had focussed their attention on the banking system, which therefore easily weathered Kwarteng's storm. A tendency to fight the last war could also be clearly seen when an economic crisis threatened in March 2020, triggered by the covid-19 lockdowns sweeping the world. Many of the macro-prudential limits on lending and capital-reserve requirements introduced since the previous global financial crisis were suspended or swept away to encourage banks to lend recklessly to households and firms facing cashflow problems.[132] These precautions had simply been the wrong policy for dealing with the next economic crisis. Government-backed loans under the CARES Act in America and under the bounce-back loans scheme in Britain encouraged further lending beyond what the risk-management practices of the private sector were otherwise willing to permit. The result of the pandemic's ultra-loose monetary policy and excessive lending has been an 'everything market bubble' that has seen virtually every asset class in the world reach giddy heights—one that, potentially, has sown the seeds of the world's next financial crisis.[133]

The real lesson from the Banking School for modern times is that interest rates, interest-rate differentials and capital flows still do matter for financial stability, particularly during times of crisis or turbulence internationally. It should be no surprise that the first two severe systemic financial crises induced by policy in Britain since 1866 occurred in the years since it adopted policies involving the use of interest rates as its main weapon against inflation in 1971. It should also be no surprise that the largest banking crisis to hit Britain over the past two centuries occurred in the period between 1998 and 2013 when the Bank of England's sole goal was to keep inflation as close to a target as possible, and when it was stripped of virtually all responsibility for the regulation of the financial sector. It is because the lessons learnt from the painful experience of regular crises between the 1820s and the 1860s, and then from a century of banking stability, have been forgotten since the 1970s.

The use of interest rates as a weapon against the Carry Trade and the crises they cause should be considered. This does not mean the role of central banks is to provide ever more 'Greenspan puts' or loosening monetary policy every time that there is a big stock market decline. It means that there should be the opposite in good times, slow but steady interest-rate rises as soon as market excess, the potential for adverse capital flows or a bout of inflation is spotted on the horizon. For instance, a sharp increase in interest rates (that risked recession and another crisis) to combat the great inflation of 2022 could have been avoided if the Bank of England had begun to raise rates earlier in 2021—perhaps in baby steps of just a few basis points if it was still worried about stuttering aggregate demand—as this would have helped inflation expectations remain anchored nearer the Bank's target. A prompter, but slower, increase in rates could both have prevented excessive lending before it had occurred and then have avoided a sharp increase in rates when problems (or exogenous shocks such as the war in Ukraine) were spotted too late. It was the failure of the Bank of England to do this previously that caused the severity of the crises of 1847, 1857–1858, 1866 and 1973–1975; for a century after 1866 it learnt its lesson, but then lost the plot in 1971 with Competition and Credit Control.

However, what if using monetary policy to aid financial stability, for instance by maintaining a steady interest-rate differential with other major central banks, resulted in rates being too tight or loose to maintain a desired inflation target or level of aggregate demand at home? In this situation, there could be a role for fiscal policy to play, although there would be the need for some institutional mechanism to prevent politicians wishing to boost their short-term popularity at the cost of higher medium-term inflation from printing too much money or from going on a spending spree such as in Kwarteng's mini budget of 2022. One idea (among many other possibilities) would be that in times of crisis an independent fiscal agency of experts, perhaps a fiscal-policy committee, with an inflation target or other objective, could set borrowing targets or authorise positive (when more demand is needed) or negative (when demand needs to be curbed) monetary financing for the government.[134] This would not necessarily be as radical as it sounds, seeing that the Bank of England has already been accused of engaging in covert monetary financing of the British government, for instance during the first covid-19 lockdowns in 2020.[135] Making the use of monetary financing overt would increase the public accountability of its use. Likewise, having it available as an officially sanctioned tool could help the Bank of England deal with situations in which the need of financial stability and of meeting its inflation targets are pulling it in opposite directions when setting interest rates.

An approach along these lines would help to avoid some of the unintended negative consequences of quantitative easing on interest rates and on equality in terms of the distribution of wealth. While it is virtually impossible for a central bank to control the precise redistributive consequences on incomes or wealth of quantitative easing or quantitative tightening (the reverse), it is much easier for a government to do this with tax and spending decisions as part of a positive or negative fiscal stimulus. Moreover, the other benefit of this is that fiscal policy is a weapon that can be instantaneously effective, whereas interest-rate changes and money-supply growth can take up to 18 months to have their full effect on demand, increasing the risk of interest-rate overshooting, such as that which *The Economist* suggested triggered the secondary banking crisis in Britain in 1973.[136]

From a historian's perspective, what is clear is that the unintended consequence of Britain's experiments with interest rates as the main tool for hitting money supply and then inflation targets since the 1970s has been an increase in banking instability. A central-bank mandate that incentivises financial stability would help (the Bank of England has made some steps towards adopting one since 2013[137]); as would targeting a much wider range of indicators when setting interest rates. More data needs to be gathered on capital flows to aid these judgements. Further research could also be carried out by economists and historians on the relationship between the Bank of England's policies and the yield curve over the period covered by this book, to assist the judgements of modern central bankers. Those setting interest rates need to ensure that their decisions do not set off asset bubbles or cause monetary-policy shocks that threaten financial stability.

In short, the unintended consequences for financial stability of excessive monetary stimulus needs to be better understood by policymakers. It should be realised that low interest rates play an important role in stimulating capital flows out of a country and in incentivising rash investment decisions, both of which are often followed by asset-price and banking crashes when international interest rates converge again. The supply of money should be flexible and sufficient for productive commercial needs both in a downturn and prosperous period. Nevertheless, just as Keynesian fiscal stimulus can be taken too far for its own and the general good, monetary stimulus can also be overdone, provoking its own concomitant problems.

Notes

1. https://www.bankofengland.co.uk/-/media/boe/files/speech/2016/monetary-policy-and-financial-stability.pdf [accessed 19 November 2020].
2. The seizing-up of financial markets in 1914 is usually excluded from this story by financial historians on the basis that the crisis was caused by panic resulting from the start of the first world war rather than by financial speculation. Prompt action by the Bank of England and the Treasury quickly restored confidence in the City of London. 1931, which was a balance-of-payment crisis that was resolved through devaluation without a banking panic, has been treated in a similar manner.
3. R. C. Michie, *British Banking: Continuity and Change from 1694 to the Present* (Oxford: OUP, 2016) p. 184.
4. Ibid.
5. N. Dimsdale, A. Hotson, *Financial Crises Since 1825* (Oxford: OUP, 2014) p. 32.
6. A. Hotson, *Respectable Banking: The Search for Stability in London's Money and Credit Markets Since 1695* (Cambridge: CUP, 2017) p. 7.
7. For example, H. Thornton, *An Enquiry into the Nature and Effects of the Paper Credit of Great Britain* [1802 edition] (New York: Kelley, 1965) pp. 253–256, 335–336.
8. J. Frankel, 'Getting Carried Away: How the Carry Trade and Its Potential Unwinding Can Explain Movements in International Financial Markets', *Milken Institute Review* 10 (2007) 1.
9. Michie, *British Banking*, pp. 249–250.
10. G. Clare, *The ABC of Foreign Exchanges* (London: Macmillan, 1911) pp. 93–103.
11. G. Clare, *A Money-Market Primer and Key to the Exchanges* (London: Effingham Wilson, 1900) p. 100.
12. R. H. I. Palgrave, *Bank Rate and the Money Market* (London: Murray, 1903) p. viii.
13. Clare, *A Money-Market Primer and Key to the Exchanges*, pp. 63–64, 67.
14. Palgrave, *Bank Rate and the Money Market*, p. 225; J. Viner, *Studies in the Theory of International Trade* (New York: Harper, 1937) Chapter V notes 135–136.
15. S. A. Hannan, 'The Drivers of Capital Flows in Emerging Markets Post Global Financial Crisis', *IMF Working Paper* WP/17/52 (2017).
16. A. Cesa-Bianchi, F. Eguren Martin, G. Thwaites, 'Foreign Booms, Domestic Busts: The Global Dimension of Banking Crises', *Bank of England Working Paper* 644 (2017).
17. W. S. Jevons, 'On the Frequent Autumnal Pressure in the Money Market and the Action of the Bank of England', *Journal of the Statistical Society of London* 29 (1866) p. 240.

18. M. D. Bordo, A. J. Schwartz (eds.), *A Retrospective on the Classical Gold Standard 1821-1931* (Chicago: University of Chicago Press, 1984) pp. 3–4.
19. C. K. Harley, 'The Classical Gold Standard's Adjustment to Shocks: American Railroads and British Investment in the 1880s', in J. Reis (ed.), *International Monetary Systems in Historical Perspective* (London: Palgrave Macmillan, 1995) pp. 23–46.
20. Idem., p. 24.
21. B. Eichengreen, M. Flandreau (eds.), *The Gold Standard in Theory and History* (London: Routledge, 1997) Introduction, p. 18.
22. T. Bayoumi, B. Eichengreen, 'The Stability of the Gold Standard and the Evolution of the International Monetary system', in T. Bayoumi, B. Eichengreen, M. Taylor (eds.), *Modern Perspectives on the Gold Standard* (Cambridge: CUP, 1996) pp. 165–188; L. A. Catão, S. N. Solomou, 'Effective Exchange Rates and the Classical Gold Standard Adjustment', *American Economic Review* 95 (2005) pp. 1259–1261, 1273.
23. Viner, *Studies in the Theory of International Trade*, Chapter V note 119.
24. C. Castelli, *The Theory of "Options" in Stocks and Shares* (London: Mathieson, 1877); L. Higgins, *The Put-and-Call* (London: Effingham Wilson, 1906).
25. S. A. Nelson, *The ABC of Options and Arbitrage* (New York: Nelson, 1904).
26. J. H. Auten, 'Monetary Policy and the Forward Exchange Market', *Journal of Finance* 16 (1961) p. 558.
27. T. Berge, Ò. Jordà, A. M. Taylor, 'Currency Carry Trades', *NBER International Seminar on Macroeconomics* 7 (2011) 358.
28. F. H. Capie, *Capital Controls* (London: IEA, 2002) pp. 41–45, 56–57.
29. R. Z. Aliber 'The Interest Rate Parity Theorem: A Reinterpretation', *Journal of Political Economy* 81 (1973) p. 1451.
30. Frankel, 'Getting Carried Away'; J. R. Lothian, L. Wu, 'Uncovered Interest Rate Parity Over the Past Two Centuries', *Journal of International Money and Finance* 30 (2011) 448–473.
31. C. Burnside, M. Eichenbaum, I. Kleshchelski, S. Rebelo, 'Do Peso Problems Explain the Carry Trade?', *The Review of Financial Studies* (2011) pp. 853–857.
32. *The Economist*, 'Carry on Trading', 10 August 2013.
33. J. A. Frenkel, 'A Monetary Approach to the Exchange Rate: Doctrinal Aspects and Empirical Evidence', *The Scandinavian Journal of Economics* 78 (1976) p. 201.
34. Idem., pp. 205–206.
35. A. Marshall, *Official Papers of Alfred Marshall*, J. M. Keynes (ed.), (London: Macmillan, 1926) p. 158.
36. A. Marshall, *Principles of Economics* (London: Macmillan, 1890) p. 624.

37. J. M. Keynes, *The Collected Writings*, V (Cambridge: CUP, 2013) pp. 293–294.
38. Keynes, *The Collected Writings*, XX, pp. 40–41.
39. M. Obstfield, A. M. Taylor, 'The Great Depression as a Watershed', *NBER Working Paper 5960* (1997).
40. R. A. Mundell, 'A Theory of Optimum Currency Areas', *American Economic Review* 5 (1961) 657–665; J. M. Fleming, 'Domestic Financial Policies Under Fixed and Under Floating Exchange Rates', *IMF Staff Papers* 9 (1962) 369–379; The Noble Prize in Economic Sciences *Press Release* (1999) contains a description of the high capital mobility, fixed exchange rate situation created by Peel's policies and how it defeats control of monetary policy and open market actions by central banks.
41. H. Rey, 'Dilemma Not Trilemma', *NBER Working Paper* 21162 (2018).
42. R. Dornbusch, 'Exchange Rate Expectations and Monetary Policy', *Journal of International Economics* 6 (1976) 232–234; B. T. McCallum, 'A Reconsideration of the Uncovered Interest Parity Relationship', *Journal of Monetary Economics* 33 (1994) 105–132.
43. C. Engel, 'Exchange Rates, Interest Rates, and the Risk Premium', *American Economic Review* 106 (2016) 436–474.
44. H. Rockoff, 'On the Origins of "A Monetary History"', *NBER Working Paper* 12666 (2006) 1–60.
45. S. Williamson, R. Wright, 'New Monetarist Economics: Models', *Federal Reserve Bank of Minneapolis Research Department Staff Report* 443 (2010).
46. Bordo and Schwartz, *A Retrospective on the Classical Gold Standard*, p. 157.
47. E. F. Fama, 'Forward and Spot Exchange Rates', *Journal of Monetary Economics* 14 (1984) 319–338.
48. Engel, 'The Forward Discount Anomaly and the Risk Premium', *Journal of Monetary Economics* 14 (1984) 123–191; a more modern exposition of the same theme is C. Burnside, M. Eichenbaum, I. Kleshchelski, S. Rebelo, *The Returns to Currency Speculation*, *NBER Working Paper* 12489 (2006).
49. Aliber 'The Interest Rate Parity Theorem: A Reinterpretation', p. 1452.
50. Engel, 'The Forward Discount Anomaly and the Risk Premium', p. 98.
51. J. M. Broughton, *The Silent Revolution: The IMF 1979-1989* (IMF, 2001) p. 350.
52. Idem., p. 349; S. Edwards, *The Behaviour of Interest Rates and Real Exchange Rates During a Liberalisation Episode: The Case of Chile 1973-83*, *NBER Working Paper* 1702 (1985) pp. 12–13.
53. A. Lahiri, C. A. Végh, 'Output Costs, Currency Crises and Interest Rate Defence of a Peg', *The Economic Journal* 117 (2007) p. 219.

54. IMF Policy development and Review Department, *Lessons from the Crisis in Argentina* (IMF, 2003) p. 41.
55. IMF database.
56. A Grønn, M. W. Fredholm, *Baltic and Icelandic Experiences of Capital Flows and Capital Flow Measures*, IMF Working Paper 13/242 (IMF: 2013) pp. 7–9; D. Carey, *The Financial and Economic Crisis, Working Paper* 725 (OECD Economics Department, 2009) p. 14.
57. Grønn, Fredholm, *Baltic and Icelandic Experiences of Capital Flows and Capital Flow Measures*, pp. 7–8.
58. S. Schmitt-Grohe, M. Uribe, M. Woodford, *International Macroeconomics* (Princetown UP, advance preliminary copy) p. 344.
59. Keynes, 'The Economic Consequences of Mr. Churchill', *The Collected Writings* IX [1925] (2010) 207–230.
60. See, for instance, S. N. Solomou, *Themes in Macroeconomic History: The UK Economy 1919–1939* (Cambridge: CUP, 1996) pp. 34–50.
61. Bank of England archive, The diaries of Montagu Norman.
62. M. Kitson, 'End of an Epoch: Britain's Withdrawal from the Gold Standard' (2012) https://michaelkitson.files.wordpress.com/2013/02/kitson-gold-standard-june-2012.pdf [last accessed 1 June 2022].
63. Bank of England, Three centuries of data v.3.
64. O. Accominotti, D. Chambers, 'If You're So Smart: John Maynard Keynes and Currency Speculation in the Interwar Years', *The Journal of Economic History* 76 (2016) 342–386.
65. Idem., pp. 369–370.
66. Keynes, *The Collected Writings* XX [1930] (2013) pp. 181–184.
67. Hotson, *Respectable banking*, pp. 4, 103–105.
68. Capie, *Capital Controls*, p. 45.
69. C. M. Reinhart, K. S. Rogoff, *This Time Is Different* (Princeton NJ, Princeton UP, 2009) Figure 10.1.
70. G1/253, Bank of England archives, cited in F. H. Capie, *The Bank of England: 1950s–1979* (Cambridge: CUP, 2010) pp. 193–194.
71. Idem., pp. 199, 201.
72. Idem., pp. 225–226.
73. D. Needham, *UK Monetary Policy from Devaluation to Thatcher 1967-82* (Basingstoke: Palgrave Macmillan, 2014) pp. 44–45.
74. Ibid.
75. Idem., p. 46.
76. Idem., p. 45.
77. Idem., p. 46.
78. Ibid.
79. P. Scott, *The Property Masters: A History of the British Commercial Property Sector* (London: E & FN Spon, 1996) p. 183, cited in Capie, *The Bank of England: 1950s–1979*, p. 527.

80. C. R. Schenk, 'Summer in the City', *English Historical Review* 129 (2014) p. 1132.
81. *The Economist*, 3 May 1975.
82. The first use of the term 'lifeboat' in this context was used by Margaret Reid in *The Financial Times* in January 1974 (*The Financial Times*, 29 January 1974). She later wrote a very useful history of the secondary banking crisis, see M. Reid, *The Secondary Banking Crisis, 1973-75: The Inside Story of Britain's Biggest Banking Upheaval* (London: Hindsight Books, 2003).
83. Capie, *The Bank of England*, p. 583; D. Needham, 'The Story of the Secondary Banking Crisis 1973-75', *The Property Chronicle*, 9 June 2020.
84. *The Economist*, 3 May 1975.
85. Needham, *UK Monetary Policy from Devaluation to Thatcher 1967-82*, pp. 50–52.
86. See the recollections of Christopher Dow in G. Hacche, C. Taylor (eds.), *Inside the Bank of England: Memoirs of Christopher Dow, Chief Economist 1973–84* (Basingstoke: Palgrave Macmillan, 2013) p. 36.
87. Needham, *UK Monetary Policy from Devaluation to Thatcher 1967-82*, p. 52.
88. Ibid.
89. Idem., pp. 50–52.
90. Capie, *The Bank of England*, pp. 526–27.
91. *The Economist*, 3 May 1975.
92. Capie, *The Bank of England: 1950s–1979*, p. 547.
93. Bank of England, 'Analysis of Financial Statistics 1971', *Bank of England Quarterly Bulletin 1972 Q2* (1972) pp. 182–84.
94. Bank of England, *Report and Accounts for the Year Ended 29 February 1980* (London: Bank of England, Court of Directors, 1980) p. 7.
95. Ibid.
96. J. Grady, M. Weale, *British Banking, 1960–85* (New York: St. Martin's Press, 1986).
97. Michie, *British Banking*, p. 191.
98. D. Chambers, 'Review: Harold James, Making a Modern Central Bank: The Bank of England 1979–2003 (Cambridge: CUP, 2020)', *Economic History Review* 74 (2021) p. 1122.
99. A. Cairncross, C. A. E. Goodhart, 'Richard Sidney Sayers (1908–1989)', in R. A. Cord (ed.), *The Palgrave Companion to LSE Economics* (London: Palgrave Macmillan, 2018) pp. 533–554.
100. I. Stewart, *In Pursuit of the Unknown* (New York: Basic Books, 2012); F. Black, M. Scholes, 'The Pricing of Options and Corporate Liabilities', *Journal of Political Economy* 81 (1974) 637–654.

101. C. Kneer, A. Raabe, 'Tracking Foreign Capital: The Effect of Capital Inflows on Bank Lending in the UK', *Bank of England Staff Working Paper* 804 (2019) p. 28.
102. Idem., p. 20.
103. Author's calculations from OECD database.
104. Clare, *A Money-Market Primer and Key to the Exchanges*, pp. 57–58; OECD database.
105. R. MacDonald, J. Nagayasu, 'Currency Forecast Errors and Carry Trades at Times of Low Interest Rates: Evidence from Survey Data on the Yen/Dollar Exchange Rate', *Journal of International Money and Finance* 53C (2015) 1–19.
106. T. Lee, J. Lee, K. Coldiron, *The Rise of Carry: The Dangerous Consequences of Volatility Suppression and the New Financial Order of Decaying Growth and Recurring Crisis* (New York: McGraw-Hill, 2020) pp. 128–129.
107. For an overview of the role that liar loans played in America during the financial crisis, see T. Herndon, 'Liar's Loans, Mortgage Fraud, and the Great Recession', *Review of Political Economy* 31 (2019) 479–508.
108. S. M. Turnbull, M. Crouhy, R. A. Jarrow, 'The Subprime Credit Crisis of 07', *SSRN* 1112467 (2008) 51.
109. Idem., pp. 51–52.
110. E. Chancellor, 'Breakingviews: The Carry Trade That Followed Lehman', *Reuters*, 14 September 2018.
111. 'What Keeps Bankers Awake at Night?', *The Economist*, 1 February 2007.
112. M. Hattori, H.-S. Shin, 'Yen Carry Trade and the Subprime Crisis', *IMF Staff Papers* 56 (2009) 407.
113. M. Iacoviello, G. Navarro, 'Foreign Effects of Higher Interest Rates', *Federal Reserve System International Finance Discussion Papers* 1227 (2018).
114. Ibid.
115. Y. Ma, W. Zijlstra, 'A New Take on Low Interest Rates and Risk Taking', *VOX, CEPR Policy Portal*, 7 March (2018).
116. Ibid.
117. D. John, 'The Return of Carry', *IPE Magazine*, January (2018).
118. T. Chuffart, C. Dell'Eva, 'Did Carry Trades Hamper Quantitative Easing Effectiveness in Japan?', *International Symposium on Money, Banking and Finance*, paper (France, 2018).
119. C. Borio, R. N. McCauley, P. McGuire, V. Sushko, 'Covered Interest Rate Parity Lost', *BIS Quarterly Review*, September (2016); N. Coffey, W. Hrung, H. Nguyen, A. Sakar, 'Capital Constraints, Counterparty Risk and Deviations from the Covered Interest Rate Parity', *Federal Reserve Bank of New York Staff Report* 393 (2009).

120. Bank of England, *Monetary Policy Report and Financial Stability Report* (August 2020).
121. Board of Governors of Federal Reserve System, *Implementation Note Press Release*, 15 March 2020; Idem, *Secondary Market Corporate Credit Facility* effective 9 April 2020.
122. *The Financial Times*, 4 June 2020.
123. *The Financial Times*, 18 June 2020.
124. R. Vergnhanini, B. di Conti, 'Modern Monetary Theory: A Criticism from the Periphery', *Brazilian Keynesian Review* 3 (2017) 16–31.
125. *The Financial Times*, 23 May 2022.
126. Hotson, *Respectable Banking*, p. 184.
127. Ibid.
128. Ibid.
129. *The Financial Times*, 10 October 2019.
130. Hotson, *Respectable Banking*, p. 184.
131. Ibid.
132. D. Aikman, 'Role of Macroprudential Policy in the Covid Crisis', https://www.kcl.ac.uk/news/qcgbf-role-macroprudential-policy-covid-crisis [last accessed 1 June 2022].
133. D. Lachman, 'Georgia and the Everything Market Bubble', *The Hill*, 7 January 2021.
134. For discussion in the academic literature of this concept, see X. Debrun, D. Hauner, M. Kumar, 'Independent Fiscal Agencies', *Journal of Economic Surveys* 23 (2009) 44–81.
135. *The Financial Times*, 13 September 2020.
136. *The Economist*, 3 May 1975.
137. 'Financial Policy Committee', Bank of England website, https://www.bankofengland.co.uk/about/people/financial-policy-committee [last accessed 1 June 2022].

CHAPTER 10

Conclusion: Calming the Storms

It's awful. Why did nobody notice it?

—Queen Elizabeth II asking professors at the London School of Economics why the economics profession had not predicted the global financial crisis, 5 November 2008.[1]

… in summary, Your Majesty, the failure to foresee the timing, extent and severity of the crisis and to head it off, while it had many causes, was principally a failure of the collective imagination of many bright people, both in this country and internationally, to understand the risks to the system as a whole.

—Professor Tim Besley and Professor Peter Hennessy's reply to Queen Elizabeth II, 22 July 2009.[2]

Those who cannot remember the past are condemned to repeat it.

—George Santayana, *The Life of Reason: Reason in Common Sense* 1 (Cambridge, MA: MIT Press, 2011) p. 172.[3]

In November 2008, a little over a month after the collapse of Lehman Brothers had plunged the world into the depths of the global financial crisis, Queen Elizabeth II was opening a new building at the London School of Economics. She asked a question about the crisis that stumped a group of assembled economics professors: 'Why did nobody notice it?'[4]

Her question and the immediate response it received provoked much soul searching among economists and influential commentators about

C. Read, *Calming the Storms*, Palgrave Studies in Economic History,
https://doi.org/10.1007/978-3-031-11914-9_10

why academic economics, for the most part, did not predict the crisis nor have much to say about it in its immediate aftermath. Even central banks were taken by surprise. In May 2012 Mervyn King, the Governor of the Bank of England during the crisis, admitted he should have 'shouted from the rooftops' about the risks building up in the banking system in the lead up to the global financial crisis, but he did not.[5] Nonetheless, even if modern economists had suffered 'a failure of the collective imagination... to understand the risks to the system as a whole', to quote from a letter sent from the British Academy to answer the Queen's question a year after it was asked, there existed a group of nineteenth-century economists that lived two centuries ago that would have had much that was relevant to say about the impending global financial crisis.[6]

As this book has shown, the Banking School's ideas can be used to interpret many of the financial crises and banking panics that have occurred in Britain since 1825. Their ideas, in the form of worries about what is now known as the Carry Trade, have contemporary relevance as one way of understanding why crises occur. In addition to this, they provide a compelling explanation for the series of severe financial crises in mid-nineteenth century Britain, for why they faded away after the 1860s and for why they reappeared a century later in 1973–1975.

The research presented in this book demonstrates the historical benefits of studying short-run processes (such as financial crises and the Carry Trade) over the long run. It has answered the call of Jo Guldi and Richard Armitage for historians to set past events in their '*longue-durée* contextual background', but it does so in a way that does not neglect the role that short-term phenomena, such as speculative bubbles, financial panics and carry crashes, played in shaping historical outcomes over the past 200 years of British history.[7] This book also reveals the importance of looking at British financial history from a more global and macroeconomic-policy perspective, rather than simply from a domestic-focused microeconomic, regulatory, or corporate-governance angle. A focus on these latter concerns may have been why the role that monetary policy has played in fuelling the cross-border Carry Trade, a situation in which investment flows are generated by external differentials in interest rates, has been omitted from previous studies. Likewise internal movements of funds caused by interest rate differentials have largely been ignored. This book exposes the major role these phenomena have actually played over the past 200 years. It thus stresses the importance of looking at the international causes and consequences of crises and provides new insights into how the process of globalisation has affected British financial stability over the long-run.

In contrast, ever since Neville Ward-Perkins was writing in the 1950s, a more inwards-looking historiography has tended to downplay the seriousness of the crises of 1837, 1847, 1857–1858 and 1866.[8] Fewer banks may have gone bust in each one of these crises than in 1825, but the later crises produced increasingly severe consequences for Ireland, the empire and abroad, as this book has revealed. Purely banking considerations should not nudge economists or historians into ignoring the role of monetary policy in financial crises and its commercial consequences in Britain and internationally. The academic community should remain open to explore new avenues of enquiry in this area. For instance, this book has revealed that Sir Robert Peel's economic-policy regime change towards freer trade, the classical gold standard and the monetary restrictions of the Bank Charter Act of 1844 not only failed to secure financial stability at home but also had negative consequences around the world. The latter subject would be a fruitful area for future research; only time and space meant that this book does not contain more detail concerning the consequences of British financial crises for the empire than it already does. Nevertheless, what is already clear is that, thanks to the size of London's capital markets and the nineteenth-century era of globalisation, this was a period in which the rest of the world economy would catch a cold whenever Britain sneezed. At that time British economic policy and the stability of its banking system mattered not only at home, but to most of the rest of the world too.

10.1 Going Back and Forth for Two Centuries

As Charles Goodhart and Meinhart Jensen have pointed out, the controversy between the Currency School and the Banking School is still very much relevant today. They have characterised the Currency School v Banking School-dispute as between 'rules v discretion', 'money v quasi-money' and an 'evolutionary v static structure'.[9] This study has added their 'attitude to crises' to the list of criteria by which to distinguish between the Schools. Although many different economists contributed to its development, by the late nineteenth century the Banking School had produced a relatively coherent understanding of the mechanism of financial crises.

The Currency School offers little in this respect except to note that occasionally crises will arise and therefore must be borne. Even so, because of the *de jure* victory of the Bank Charter Act in the 1840s, it is the Currency School version of British financial history that remains prevalent to this day. Its focus on the maintenance of price stability above all other considerations and committed attachment to the quantity theory of money have enjoyed renewed popularity in policy-making circles since the Great Inflation of the 1970s. Even New Keynesian central-bank policy has emphasised the same theme. By absorbing the whole attention of those in decision-making roles, and by being embedded into the remit of central banks through inflation targeting, it has distracted from the Banking School's contribution to the disappearance of severe and systemic financial crises in Britain in the late nineteenth century. The neglect of their insights has meant that the growing risks in the banking system were downplayed by policymakers, particularly in Britain, before 2008, preventing the storm-to-come from being smoothed out. It is important that meaningful insights from the Banking School's contribution to understanding financial crises in Britain are recognised and acted upon to ensure the mistakes of the decades leading up to 2008 in Britain are not repeated again around the world.

The legislative victory of the Currency School in the 1840s should not distract economists and historians from the need to challenge and revise received wisdoms about the histories of British economic policy and British banking. As Chapter 2 suggested, the hagiography of Sir Robert Peel as the 'chief architect of the mid-Victorian age of stability' needs to be revised, as his policies may well have exacerbated an era of financial instability in Britain.[10] The chapter argues that his economic-policy regime change was aimed at ensuring food prices were stable and remained at a reasonably low level to both satisfy the labouring classes and preserve social stability for the benefit of the aristocracy. In summary, they were (i) free capital movement and low tariffs (ii) a currency tied to gold at a fixed rate with banknote circulation limited according to bullion reserves according to the Bank Charter Act of 1844 (iii) tight fiscal control, including low interest rates to make the servicing of the national debt affordable.

The problem, acknowledged by economists in the 1960s as the Mundell–Fleming trilemma, is that it was not always possible to achieve the first two policies together with low interest rates at all times. When global interest rates rose in the nineteenth century, Britain often lost its freedom of manoeuvre over monetary policy, such in the crises of 1847, 1857–1858 and 1866. Although the nineteenth century in Britain was characterised by stable prices over the long term, periodic financial crises during the period counteracted some of the benefits, particularly for Ireland and some of Britain's colonies.

Chapter 3 outlined, explored and analysed some of the Banking School's ideas about monetary policy and financial crises. The Banking School developed a theory about how these crises developed, which was at odds with the ideas of the Currency School that lay behind the Bank Charter Act. The theory is that a search for better returns on investments is prompted by a period of low short-term rates. As opportunities are taken up within a country, rates gradually move up, either because of arbitrage or for other reasons such as a natural catastrophe. As they rise above long-term interest rates, investors who used short-term funds in long-term investment schemes fail. The schemes suffer as the flow of funds is cut off. International investment also stops as nominal short-term interest rates of different countries move together and a no-arbitrage position is reached. Asset prices may fall; investment, investor and lender may be damaged, along with the banks that lent on their security. The investments will have caused bullion drains (or capital outflows) and interest rates will be pushed still higher by central banks. After a period, during which flows of capital have decreased, low interest rates return, encouraged by governments looking to fund their debt cheaply or seeking to correct a deflationary undershoot, and the process restarts.

An analysis of financial data collected from the Bank of England's records, as well as American and British newspapers, given in Chapter 3, showed that nominal interest rates of countries (and within countries) do tend to equalise in a crisis and that low interest rates precede a crisis, in line with the Banking School's ideas. Other parts of the process can also be identified. There appears to be a relationship between the Bank Rate and the bullion reserve in the nineteenth century. The short-term interest rate spread between countries is only correlated with capital flows in brief periods around crises, whereas the long-term rates spread is correlated with overall size of flows adjusted by GDP and prices. This possibly explains why the Banking School thought that short-term flows were connected with crises, while the Currency School insisted that they were connected with trade flows. Tim Lee, Jamie Lee and Kevin Coldiron suggest that in the modern era there are variations of the Carry Trade that differ from the mechanism recognised by the Banking School. As well as the danger of investing long term using short-term borrowing, seeking short-term earnings on the basis of long-term debt is equally unwise; they also bring the volatility of financial markets into their thesis, arguing that when daily volatility of the S&P 500 index exceeds monthly volatility, a reversal of direction of investment flows will soon take place that will trigger a carry crash. Yet the warning indications of nominal interest rates moving together, as noted in this book, provided an indication that a carry crash and reversal of capital flows would soon occur in 2007–09 exactly as they did in the mid-nineteenth century; the slightly different warning signs provided by the Banking School era are therefore worth taking seriously.[11]

10.2 The Disappearance and Reappearance of British Banking Crises

The detailed examinations of financial crises in Chapters 4, 5, 6, 7, 8, 9 suggest that the Banking School's insights about crises in the short run do tell a compelling narrative of British financial history over the past two centuries. The Banking School's worries about the consequences of interest-rate arbitrage between Britain and other countries for British financial stability appear to be vindicated.

Chapter 4 showed how the Banking School's ideas about crises developed as a result of the crises of 1825 and 1837–1839 and provides new narratives about the causes and consequences of these events. The bullion drain and subsequent crisis in 1825 was to an extent caused by commodity trading, but, as the Banking School identified, investment flows were also influential and increasingly so through the next decades. The origins of the 1825 crisis were British, not Latin American, in origin. It was a consequence of the overexpansion of credit at home, a search for yield abroad and eventually interest rates between Britain and elsewhere converging, leading to investment flows to Latin America ceasing, triggering a credit crunch at home and a chain of defaults on debts abroad. The chapter also shows that the development of the 1837 and 1839 crises were contributed to by the distribution of a large amount of capital paid out as compensation to former slave owners in the empire in exchange for emancipation, which soon became inter-country investment flows.

Chapter 5 exposed the role that Peel's Bank Charter Act of 1844, interest rates and capital flows played in the two crises of 1847. The April crisis is shown to have been contributed to by the raising of an 'Irish loan' to provide relief in the Irish Famine in the circumstances created by the Bank Charter Act of 1844. At the same time there were demands for capital to construct railways and to import additional food, which meant that the Bank of England was forced to squeeze credit under the Act, and the Irish loan made matters worse. Capital was also attracted abroad by high interest rates in America, but the flows suddenly ceased as interest rates converged in the two countries. This triggered a second crisis, in October, that led to the suspension of the Bank Charter Act. Many Banking-School adherents subsequently blamed the legislation for the two crises.

Chapter 6 describes how, in the aftermath of the crises of 1847, a culture war developed between the Bank of England and the newer joint-stock banks, in addition to competition between them for discounting business. The same moral divide extended to the attitudes of some adherents of the Currency School and the Banking School. The chapter also showed how the 1857–1858 crisis arose from interest-rate movements and a sudden halt in capital flows, once again caused by interest rates in Britain and other countries converging. In the crisis of 1857–1858 the initial increased demand for credit came from the Crimean War, but the same scenario of capital flows and British and American interest rates converging played out again. American bank shares dropped as British investment stopped and some funds returned to the United Kingdom. This triggered a much larger banking crisis in the United States, which then spread across the world.

Chapter 7 demonstrated how the crisis of 1866, which saw the demise of Overend, Gurney & Co., resulted in the Bank of England changing its use of monetary policy under the influence of the Banking School. Usually, the crisis of 1866 is seen as the event in which the Bank of England first adopted its role as 'lender of last resort' under what later came to be known as 'Bagehot's dictum'. Instead, this chapter suggested a new narrative of the events surrounding the crisis of 1866 that emphasises the problems to Britain's financial sector caused by the Bank's sharp rises in interest rates to protect its bullion reserves and, then as the main panic began, its note reserves as well. In its aftermath the Bank used smaller, prompt changes in interest rates to quell speculative bubbles and bullion drains before they got out of hand, a policy that prevented another crisis of the size of 1847, 1857–1858 and 1866 occurring for the rest of the century. Yet this was a precarious process referred to at the time as 'spinning a big top on a needle point', with the Bank Rate reviewed on a weekly if not daily basis.

When the crisis of 1866 occurred the Bank of England thought it had mastered halting bullion flows by increasing the Bank Rate. Nevertheless in 1866 it managed to raise it so much above the rates in the United States that capital flooded back into the United Kingdom. The general tide even drew back funds from India, as an important government bank, the Bank of Bombay, failed there. The circumstances were not altogether advantageous as the inward flows of bullion to the Bank of England's vaults created an additional demand for notes at a time of shortage, putting its note reserve under further pressure. Unlike after the 1847 and 1857–1858 panics, there was no inquiry into the 1866 crisis, as if the Bank of England and its advisers did not wish to admit their incompetence.

The raising of the Bank of England's rate so much above American rates in 1866 was a unique circumstance in the second half of the nineteenth century. After 1866 the Bank seemed to have learnt its lesson and used smaller adjustments, made more promptly, to avoid upsetting the financial system. Disturbances still occurred but they did not become major systemic crises in the fashion 1847, 1857–1858 and 1866 were.

As Chapter 8 showed, the main mitigation to avoid crises after 1866, due to pressure from the Banking School, was the Bank of England's more subtle use of Bank Rate adjustments, taking into account international flows, as Jevons suggested, as well as having a much greater store of bullion to smooth the impact of interest-rate shocks from abroad.[12] The crisis of 1866 marked the end of a period in which the Bank attempted to keep its interest rate as low as possible in the run-up to a crisis, only then to make it worse by raising it very sharply at the last moment to defend its bullion or note reserves. The Bank also gradually adopted Bagehot's dictum concerning its role as the 'lender of last resort' in terms of lending to institutions freely at a high rate of interest on good security to prevent a liquidity crunch in the money markets from turning in a full-blown banking panic. However, this process was much slower than some scholars have suggested, and there was no consensus within the Bank of England's management in the aftermath of 1866 that it should immediately adopt this role.[13] In the event of 1890, when Barings was saved from collapse, and the crisis of 1973–1975, when the secondary banks were rescued, the Bank's instinct was as much to act as 'mender of last resort' as lender of last resort in the 141 years in which Britain suffered virtually no high-profile bank runs at all.[14]

Chapter 9 found that periods in the twentieth century in which capital flows were inhibited and that saw policies pursued with similarities to those advocated by the Banking School did not have major systemic crises. However, when the Banking School's lessons were forgotten in favour of a 'mono-maniacal'—to quote Harold James—targeting of the money supply from the 1970s and then, from the 1990s, of a certain level of inflation, systemic crises made a comeback in British history.[15] Similar policy errors and crisis cycles to those made and played out in the nineteenth century reoccurred in the secondary banking crisis of 1973–1975 and in the global financial crisis of 2007–2009, when the Bank was found to be particularly unprepared for the Carry Trade's consequences. The role of monetary policy in preserving financial stability was forgotten. Cycles reappeared in which monetary policy was kept too loose for too long, triggering the start of a Carry Trade, followed by too much tightening too quickly, which led to 'carry crashes' when rates converged or when banks did not anticipate such a sudden change in macroeconomic conditions. Changes in the regulation and corporate governance of the financial sector in Britain may have exacerbated these problems, but it should be recognised that monetary policy played a role too.

It should be noted that although the period between the 1860s and the early 1970s was mostly a success in terms of avoiding systemic crises, many economic historians do not view the period as a success for the British economy. In fact, many view it as a 100-year period of 'failure' or 'decline', when long-run British economic growth started to fall behind its main rivals in relative (but not always absolute) terms.[16] Some factors unrelated to financial stability are partly responsible for that, including but not limited to the exhaustion of domestic natural-resource endowments and the rise of protectionism abroad in the late Victorian period, the cost of the first and second world wars, the collapse in economic cooperation and world trade in the interwar years, and the economic lethargy caused by the lack of competition after 1945.

However, some of the factors at work may have borne some relation to concerns about financial stability. The City of London's expertise at exporting British savings to fund foreign industry is one popular target in declinist historiography. Likewise, it is no contradiction in terms that a fast-growing economy in the mid-nineteenth century could have also been one prone to macroeconomic instability. It is possible that the more conservative lending practices and reserves policies adopted after the mid-century series of crises reduced the appetite of lenders for risk in late Victorian Britain, starving the most innovative entrepreneurs of capital.

Nevertheless, while financial crises at home in the mid-nineteenth century may or may not have been all bad for long-run economic growth within Britain, this book has gone some way towards showing that they were not good news for many people in Ireland and in the British empire. The first crisis of 1847 resulted in the cancellation of further loans for Irish-famine relief, resulting in an inadequately funded humanitarian effort there that cost hundreds of thousands of lives, entirely unnecessarily. The contagion from the second crisis of 1847 spread around the financial system of the wider empire, helping to crush the wages of ordinary labourers in British sugar colonies around the world by as much as half.[17] It also collapsed many banks that intended to loan money to former slaves to buy their own land so they could become part of the petty bourgeoisie.[18] The disappearance of these banks almost certainly retarded the reduction of inequality between former masters and former slaves in these places, as well as hindering long-run economic growth. The Bank of England's tussle with India for gold in the run-up to the crisis of 1866 collapsed the Bank of Bombay, the government bank there, distracting the attention of officials from the outbreak of famine in Orissa that ended up killing more than a million.[19] In short, the banking crises of mid-Victorian Britain may not matter in the long run if you are only interested in British economic growth. But if you are a famine victim in India or Ireland, they really do. For in the short run, they were both dead, never mind the long run.

10.3 The Carry Trade in British History

It is clear from the research outlined in this book that elements of what is now called the Carry Trade date right back to 1825 and that the same cyclical process behind financial crises has repeated many times. The nature of the trade may be venerable, but even so, it has been often presented as a novelty by many academics and commentators in recent years. However, many of the ideas describing it and fearing its consequences are not new and were developed by the Banking School in the nineteenth century.

Evidence of the trade in recent decades can also be seen in the 'sudden stops' and exchange-rate crashes in developing countries as flows from developed countries were curtailed. The 'Carry Trade', developed by traders as a profit-maximisation strategy, brought to notice the investment mechanism behind capital flows and crises which those associated with the Banking School had long before pointed out in Victorian times. The trade explains why it is nominal rates (not real rates) which equalise: the investment returns are compared from the viewpoint of an investor within a single country. The Carry Trade makes use of the disparity between rates before they draw together (by interest-rate parity if that theory applies or by influence of other major events). However, knowledgeable traders recognise that the period of disparity will end, and they will have to unwind their investments at some time. From the 1980s as the documentation and usage of the Carry Trade increased, an interest in capital flows and interest-rate differentials revived, at least among traders in financial markets. A trade similar to the Carry Trade must have existed in the nineteenth century. It was certainly referred to by Keynes, although not by that name.[20] A complication is that in the twentieth-century exchange rates varied as well as interest rates, yet nominal interest rates of different countries still drew together in crises. A sudden slowdown of capital flows into the higher interest-rate country can, however, cause a 'carry correction' or 'carry crash' in which the exchange rate of the recipient country for the exported currency suddenly and catastrophically plummets.[21]

The modern overlooking of an important part of nineteenth-century British financial history provides a good reason why policymakers and regulators in recent decades have not been quick to moderate the Carry Trade's undesirable consequences before a full-blown crisis hits. Central-bank independence and inflation targeting, in Britain and elsewhere, have played an important role in defeating the great inflation of the 1970s, restraining inflation expectations and ensuring price stability in recent decades (at least up to the great inflation of 2022).[22] Yet the tunnel-vision focus on the quantity theory of money and on consumer prices—an idea originally pushed by the Currency School of the nineteenth century—among modern central bankers has blinded many to the threat posed to financial stability from investment flows. The mandates of central banks, such as the Bank of England, should not be focussed solely on the achievement of an arbitrary inflation or money-supply target. In addition to these, they also need to include financial stability in their remits, with a wider range of indicators, including levels of relative interest rates, investment flows and an ever vigilant watch for the emergence of speculative bubbles, used in their policy deliberations. Further research about how exactly to do this would likely be fruitful. A nominal GDP target may provide more stability than a consumer-price inflation goal during downturns. The higher inflation a central bank would create in a recession to reach a nominal GDP target would partly offset the deflationary pressure placed on banks and the financial system. However the reaction of the financial community to fiscal and economic policy must also be a consideration; decisions based on pure ideology should be avoided.

This critique is similar to that made of the Currency School by the Banking School in the nineteenth century. Yet, while many economists today view such a position as heterodox, the work of theorists such as Adam Smith, Henry Thornton and Thomas Tooke on currency and banking still sits firmly within mainstream classical economics. It is time for both economists and historians to recognise the intellectual diversity that used to exist in classical economics on currency and banking, and the lessons that the Banking School's ideas may still have for preventing financial crises in the modern age.

Notes

1. D. N. Chorafas, *The Changing Role of Central Banks* (New York: Palgrave Macmillan, 2013) p. 15.
2. Letter, T. Besley, P. Hennessy to Queen Elizabeth II, 22 July 2009 http://wwwf.imperial.ac.uk/~bin06/M3A22/queen-lse.pdf [last accessed 31 December 2020].
3. G. Santayana, *The Life of Reason: Reason in Common Sense* 1 (Cambridge, MA: MIT Press, 2011) p. 172.
4. Chorafas, *The Changing Role of Central Banks*, p. 15.
5. Idem., p. 16.
6. Letter, T. Besley, P. Hennessy to Queen Elizabeth II, 22 July 2009.
7. J. Guldi, D. Armitage, *The History Manifesto* (Cambridge: CUP, 2014) pp. 117–8, 153
8. C. N. Ward-Perkins, 'The Commercial Crisis 1847', *Oxford Economic Papers* 2 (1950) 75–94.
9. C. Goodhart, M. Jensen, 'Currency School versus Banking School: An Ongoing Confrontation', *Economic Thought* 4 (2015) 20–31.
10. N. Gash, *Sir Robert Peel: The Life of Sir Robert Peel after 1830* (London: Longman, 1972) p. 714.
11. T. Lee, J. Lee, K. Coldiron, *The Rise of Carry: The Dangerous Consequences of Volatility Suppression and the New Financial Order of Decaying Growth and Recurring Crisis* (New York: McGraw-Hill, 2020) pp. 139–153.

12. W. S. Jevons, 'On the frequent autumnal pressure in the Money Market and the action of the Bank of England', *Journal of the Statistical Society of London* 29 (1866) p. 240.
13. W. Bagehot, *Lombard Street: A Description of the Money Market* [1873] (Westport: Hyperion Press, 1962) p. 21.
14. *The Economist*, 6 August 1977; Ranald Michie has pointed out that there was a small run by savers on London and County Securities in December 1973 during the secondary banking crisis, but the episode was little reported upon by the press and thus it does not count as a "major" or "high-profile" bank run in most British financial histories. See F. H. Capie, *The Bank of England: 1950s–1979* (Cambridge: CUP, 2010) pp. 525–585, cited in R. C. Michie, *British Banking: Continuity and Change from 1694 to the Present* (Oxford: OUP, 2016) p. 187.
15. H. James, *Making a Modern Central Bank: The Bank of England 1979–2003* (Cambridge: CUP, 2020) p. 2.
16. See, for instance, N. F. R. Crafts, 'Victorian Britain Did Fail', *Economic History Review* 32 (1979) 533–537; N. F. R. Crafts, *Forging Ahead, Falling Behind and Fighting Back. British Economic Growth from the Industrial Revolution to the Financial Crisis* (Cambridge: CUP, 2018).
17. For instance, in Barbados, *Past and Present State...* PP 1847–48 (1005) XLVI.1, pp. 65–66.
18. For instance, in Trinidad, idem., p. 171.
19. W. S. Meyer et al., *Imperial Gazetteer of India* III (Oxford: Clarendon Press, 1908) pp. 486–487.
20. Keynes, *The Collected Writings* XX [1930] (Cambridge: CUP, 2013) pp. 181–184.
21. Idem., p. 4.
22. S. Eijffinger, E. Schaling, 'Central Bank Independence in Twelve Industrial Countries', *Banca Nazionale del Lavoro Quarterly Review* 184 (March 1993) 49–89; S. Eijffinger, J. de Haan, 'The Political Economy of Central-Bank Independence', *Princeton Studies in International Economics* 19 (1996), cited in James, *Making a Modern Central Bank*, p. 4.

Appendix: Details of Econometric Analysis in Chapter 2

Table 2.1

y = Bullion Reserve	
x_1 = BoE Bank Rate	
x_2 = BoE Public Deposits	
x_3 = BoE Bank Deposits	
x_4 = BoE Other Deposits	
k = constant	

Equation estimated:

$$y = ax_1 + bx_2 + cx_3 + dx_4 + k$$

Test:
OLS test, confidence indicated by p-value. The series must be stationary, and the regression must be free from heteroskedasticity and autocorrelation and the residuals (or errors) must be normally distributed.

C. Read, *Calming the Storms*, Palgrave Studies in Economic History,
https://doi.org/10.1007/978-3-031-11914-9

Table 2.2

y = BoE Bank Rate
x_1 = Bullion Reserve
x_2 = BoE Public Deposits
x_3 = BoE Bank Deposits
x_4 = BoE Other Deposits
k = constant

Equation estimated:

$$y = ax_1 + bx_2 + cx_3 + dx_4 + k$$

Test: as Table 2.1.

Table 2.3

X_t = Bank Rate at time t
Y_t = Bullion Reserve at time t
p = period

Equations estimated:

$$Y_t = a_0 + a_1 Y_{t-1} + \cdots + a_p Y_{t-p} + b_1 X_{t-1} + \cdots + b_p X_{t-p} + u_t$$

$$X_t = c_0 + c_1 X_{t-1} + \cdots + c_p X_{t-p} + d_1 Y_{t-1} + \cdots + d_p Y_{t-p} + v_t$$

Test:
Granger causality test, causality indicated by f value and p-value of F test of VAR model. Null hypothesis is no causality (when $b_1 = b_2 = \cdots = b_p = 0$ or $d_1 = d_2 = \cdots = d_p = 0$). When this is rejected it implies that Y, X Granger cause Y (or X) more accurately than Y (or X) alone.

Table 2.4

X_t = Bank Rate at time t
Y_t = Bullion Reserve at time t
p denotes period

Equations estimated:

$$Y_t = a_0 + a_1 Y_{t-1} + \cdots + a_p Y_{t-p} + b_1 X_{t-1} + \cdots + b_p X_{t-p} + u_t$$

$$X_t = c_0 + c_1 X_{t-1} + \cdots + c_p X_{t-p} + d_1 Y_{t-1} + \cdots + d_p Y_{t-p} + v_t$$

Test: as Table 2.3.
Probit Model, Table 2.5

Y = Crisis indicator (1 or 0)
X_1 = UK Free Market Rate
X_2 = US Free Market Rate
X_3 = BoE Bank Deposits
p = denotes probability and Φ denotes the cumulative standard normal distribution function

Equation estimated:

$$P(Y = 1 | X_1, X_2, X_3) = \Phi(b_0 + b_1 X_1 + b_2 X_2 + b_3 X_3)$$

Test
Limited dependant variable Probit.

Table 2.6

y = Δ Gross Bullion exports UK > US
x_1 = Δ £/$ Exchange Rate
x_2 = Δ US-UK Short-term Interest Rates
k = constant

Equation estimated:

$$y = ax_1 + bx_2 + cx_3 + dx_4 + k$$

Test: as Table 2.1.

Table 2.7

y = Gross Bullion exports UK > US
x_1 = £/$ Exchange Rate
x_2 = US-UK Short-term Interest Rates
k = constant

Equation estimated:

$$y = ax_1 + bx_2 + cx_3 + dx_4 + k$$

Test as Table 2.1.

Table 2.8

X_t = Δ Gross Bullion exports UK > US at time t
Y_t = Δ £/$ Exchange Rate at time t
p = denotes period

Equations estimated:

$$Y_t = a_0 + a_1 Y_{t-1} + \cdots + a_p Y_{t-p} + b_1 X_{t-1} + \cdots + b_p X_{t-p} + u_t$$

$$X_t = c_0 + c_1 X_{t-1} + \cdots + c_p X_{t-p} + d_1 Y_{t-1} + \cdots + d_p Y_{t-p} + v_t$$

Test:
Granger causality test as Table 2.3

Table 2.9

y	= log Total bullion flows in and out of UK
x_1	= log US-UK Long-Term Interest Rate
x_2	= log GDP per capita
x_3	= log CPI price index
k	= constant

Equation estimated:

$$y = ax_1 + bx_2 + cx_3 + k$$

Test as Table 2.1.

Table 2.10

Y	= Total bullion flows in and out of UK
X_1	= US-UK Long-Term Interest Rate
X_2	= GDP per capita
X_3	= CPI price index
k	= constant

Equations estimated:

$$Y_t = \hat{a}_0 + \hat{a}_{1t} + \hat{a}_{2t} + \hat{a}_{3t} + \hat{u}_t$$

Extract $\hat{u}_t$ and carry out an Augmented Dickey–Fuller test.
Test:
An Augmented Engle-Granger Test is used as only one relation exists. An Augmented Dickey–Fuller test is used to test the series for stationarity.

Lags are chosen using the Akaike's Information Criterion. A cointegrating OLS regression is carried out and the residuals are tested using the Dickey–Fuller test.

Bibliography

Manuscript Primary Sources

Bank of England archive and digital resources

Baring Bros. liabilities and assets 1890–1894; daily account books 1851–1899; diaries of Bonamy Dobree 1857–1861; diaries of Montagu Norman; minutes of committee of treasury 1825–1899; minutes of court of directors 1825–1866; monetary policy and financial stability report 2019–2020; report and accounts 1970–1980; Three centuries of data, database, v.2–v.3.

Bedfordshire and Luton Archives and Records Service, Bedford

Lucas Archive collection (L30).

'Irish Diary of the Earl de Grey' [1844] (L31/114/17–21).

Transcript of 'Memoirs of the Earl de Grey' [1859] (CRT/190/45/2).

Bodleian Library, Oxford

Clarendon papers; Trevelyan papers (as microfilm).

British Library, St Pancras

Peel papers; Graham papers; Ripon papers; Gladstone papers; Liverpool papers; India Office records and private papers; Indian Government ledgers; Lawrence collection.

Cambridge University Library

Hickleton (Wood) papers (as microfilm).

Durham University Archives

Third Earl Grey papers.

C. Read, *Calming the Storms*, Palgrave Studies in Economic History,
https://doi.org/10.1007/978-3-031-11914-9

Glasgow University Library Archives
Records of the City of Glasgow Bank.

ING Baring Archive
Irish loan papers 1847 [HC3]; Reid, Irving, and Co. [HC3.62, HC17.30, HC3.75]; Argentina papers [HC4].

The National Archives, Kew
Chatham papers; Russell papers [PRO 30]; Treasury papers, Trevelyan [T64]; Mauritius Gazette and Blue Books; Colonial Office papers; Overend, Gurney & Co., liquidation and deposition papers.

The National Archives, Mauritius
Government records (HA/66).

Royal Archives, Windsor Castle
Microfilm 95709/5.

The Rothschild Archive, London
Records of N. M. Rothschild & Sons.

Southampton University Library
Wellington papers; Broadlands Archives, Palmerston papers.

Surrey History Centre
Goulburn papers.

Official Documents and Parliamentary Papers (PP)

PP 1814–1815 (87,88,89) X.469 *Account of quantity of grain, meal and flour imported and exported 1792–1814.*

PP 1819 (202) III.3 *Secret Committee on State of Bank of England with reference to expediency of resumption of Cash Payments report I.*

PP 1819 (282) III.3 *Idem, report II.*

PP 1819 (291) III.363 *Secret Committee of the House of Lords on State of Bank of England, reports I and II.*

PP 1825 (204) XX.215 *Account of Quantity of Gold and Silver Bullion, Coin and Plate imported and exported*, 1815–1824.

PP 1826 (94) XXII.5 *Country Banks.*

PP 1831–1832 (722) VI.1 *Report from the Committee of Secrecy on the Bank of England Charter.*

PP 1833 (489) XXXI.201 *Private Banks.*

PP 1837–1838 (215) XLVIII.331 *Slave owner's Compensation.*

PP 1840 (602) IV.1 *Report from Select Committee on Banks of Issue; with the minutes of evidence, appendix, and index.*

PP 1841 (I) (366) V.1 *Committee of Secrecy on Banks of Issue: First Report*

PP 1842 (104) XXVI.251 *Memoranda respecting the proceedings of government as to the unfunded debt from the year 1815.*
PP 1845 (12) XXVIII.197 *National debt funded and unfunded 1817–1844.*
PP 1847 (834) XVII.589, 603 *Report of Commissioners of Public Works (Ireland).*
PP 1847–1848 (395) VIII Pt.1.1, VIII Pt.II.1, 379 *First Report from the Secret Committee on Commercial Distress.*
PP 1847–1848 (565, 565-II) VIII Pt. III.1, 537 *Report from the Secret Committee of the House of Lords on the causes of distress.*
PP 1847–1848 (584) fiche no. 52.51–2 *Second Report from the Secret Committee on Commercial Distress with minutes of evidence.*
PP 1847–1848 (1005) XLVI.1 *Past and Present State of the Colonies.*
PP 1849 (588) L.403 *Grain, flour, &c. Returns of the quantity of grain and flour.*
PP 1850 (460) LII.287 *Price of wheat.*
PP 1851 (62) XXXI.159 *Public income and expenditure.*
PP 1854 (516) XXXIX.439 *Gold and Silver bullion.*
PP 1857 Session 2 (220 220–1) X Pt. I.1 *Report from Select Committee on Bank Acts.*
PP 1857–1858 (381) V.1 *Select Committee on Operation of Bank Acts, and Causes of recent Commercial Distress.*
PP 1860 (2669) LII.635 *Report to the Secretary of State for India in Council on Railways in India.*
PP 1861 (402) XXXIV.139 *Public income and expenditure.*
PP 1866 (3942) LXVI.1 *Annual statement of Trade and Navigation ....*
PP 1867 (329) X.33 *Select Committee on the Limited Liability Acts.*
PP 1867 (335) LI.1 *East India (Bengal and Orissa famine). Papers and correspondence relative to the famine in Bengal and Orissa, including the report of the Famine Commission and the minutes of the Lieutenant Governor of Bengal and the Governor General of India*, Pt. II.
PP 1867 (490) LII.173 *East India (Madras and Orissa) Famine.*
PP 1868–1869 (4162, I, II, III) XV.1, 51, 175, 423 *Report of the Bombay bank commission.*
PP 1888 (c. 5248) XLV.1 *Second Report of the Royal Commission appointed to enquire into the recent Changes in the relative Values of the precious metals....*
PP 1888 (c. 5512) XLV.285 *Royal Commission on Gold and Silver.*
PP 1888 (c. 5512-I) XLV.455 *Minutes of Evidence taken before the Royal Commission on Gold and Silver.*
PP 1890–1891 (c. 6475) XCII.73 *Report on Trade Unions.*
PP 1898 (c. 9037) LXI.469 *(Fowler) Committee to enquire into Indian Currency.*
Hansard records of debates in the House of Commons and House of Lords.

Periodicals and Newspapers

Athlone Sentinel, Chicago Tribune, Circular to Bankers, Daily News, Glasgow Herald, Herapath's Railway and Commercial Journal, Hunt's Merchants' Magazine and Commercial Review, Lloyd's Illustrated Newspaper, Mining Journal, Mississippi Free Trader, Morning Chronicle, Morning Post, New York Daily Tribune, New York Herald, Northern Evening Mail, Reynold's Newspaper, The Bankers' Magazine and State Financial Register, The Bankers' Magazine, The Economist, The Engineer, The Era, The Merchants' Magazine and Commercial Review, The Money Bag, The Spectator, The Times, Times of India, Yorkshire Advertiser.

Printed Material

Accominotti, O., Chambers, D., 'If You're So Smart: John Maynard Keynes and Currency Speculation in the Interwar Years', *Journal of Economic History*, 76 (2016) 342–386.

Alborn, T. L., *Conceiving Companies* (Hove: Psychology Press, 1998).

Aliber R. Z., 'The Interest Rate Parity Theorem: A Reinterpretation' *Journal of Political Economy*, 81 (1973) 1451–1459.

Allan, V., 'The Prince of Poyais', *History Today*, 2 (1952) 53–58.

Andréadēs, A., tr. Meredith, C., *History of the Bank of England* (London: King & Son, 1909).

Anon., 'Financial and Commercial History of 1882', *Journal of the Statistical Society of London*, 46 (1883) 101–113.

Anon., 'Financial and Commercial History of 1883', *Journal of the Statistical Society of London*, 47 (1884) 142–150.

Anon., 'Financial and Commercial History of 1884', *Journal of the Statistical Society of London*, 48 (1885) 54–63.

Attwood, T., *Distressed State of the Country* (Birmingham: Beilby, Knott and Beilby, 1829).

Austin, P. E., *Baring Brothers and the Birth of Modern Finance* (Hoboken: Taylor and Francis, 2015).

Auten, J. H., 'Forward Exchange Rates and Interest-Rate Differentials', *The Journal of Finance*, 18 (1963) 11–19.

Auten, J. H., 'Monetary Policy and the Forward Exchange Market', *The Journal of Finance*, 16 (1961) 546–558.

Bagchi, A. K., 'Contested Hegemonies and Laissez Faire: Controversies over the Monetary Standard in India at the High Noon of the British Empire', *Fernand Braudel Center Review*, 20 (1997) 19–76.

Bagehot, W., *Lombard Street: A Description of the Money Market* [1873] (Westport: Hyperion Press, 1962).

Bank of England, 'Analysis of Financial Statistics 1971', *Bank of England Quarterly Bulletin 1972 Q2* (1972) 180–204.

Barnes, D. G., *A History of the English Corn Laws: From 1660–1846* (London: Routledge, 2013).

Bayoumi, T., 'Saving-Investment Correlations', *IMF Staff Papers*, 37 (1990) 360–387.

Bayoumi, T., Eichengreen, B., 'The Stability of the Gold Standard and the Evolution of the International Monetary System', in Bayoumi, T., Eichengreen, B., Taylor M. (eds.), *Modern Perspectives on the Gold Standard* (Cambridge: CUP, 1996) 165–188.

Beach, W. E., *British International Gold Movements* (Cambridge, MA: Harvard University Press, 1935).

Benson, A. C., Viscount Esher, *Letters of Queen Victoria, 1861*, II (London: John Murray, 1908).

Berge, T., Jordà, Ò., Taylor, A. M., 'Currency Carry Trades', *NBER International Seminar on Macroeconomics*, 7 (2011) 357–388.

Bernanke, B. N., 'Non-Monetary Effects of the Financial Crisis in the Propagation of the Great Depression', *NBER Working Paper* 1054 (1983).

Besomi, D., 'Clément Juglar (1819-1905) Les origines de la théorie des cycles', *Revue européenne des sciences sociales*, 47 (2009) 17–47.

Besomi, D., 'Graphical Representations of Overstone's Cycle of Trade', in Salvadori, N. et al. (eds.), *Classical Political Economy and Modern Theory* (Abingdon: Routledge, 2013).

Bhatta, B. B., *The Natural Calamities in Orissa in the Nineteenth Century* (New Delhi: Commonwealth Publishers, 1997).

Bhattacharya, S., *The Financial Foundations of the British Raj* (New Delhi: Orient Longman, 2005).

Biagini, E. F., *Gladstone* (London: St. Martin's Press, 2000).

Black, F., Scholes, M., 'The Pricing of Options and Corporate Liabilities', *Journal of Political Economy*, 81 (1974) 637–654.

Bloomfield, A. L., *Patterns of Fluctuations in International Investment Before 1914* (Princeton: Princeton University, 1968).

Bloomfield, A. L., *Short-Term Capital Movements Under the Pre-1914 Gold Standard* (Princeton: Princeton University, 1963).

Bodenhorn, H., Rockoff, H., 'Regional Interest Rates in Antebellum America', in Goldin, C., Rockoff, H. (eds.), *Strategic Factors in Nineteenth Century American Economic History: A Volume to Honour Robert W. Fogel* (Chicago: University of Chicago Press, 1992) 159–187.

Bond, I., 'The British Banking Population 1790–82', in Hollow, M., Akinbami, F., Michie, R. (eds.), *Complexity and Crisis in the Financial System* (Cheltenham: Edward Elgar, 2016) 85–118.

Booth, P. (ed.), *Were 364 Economists All Wrong?* (London: IEA, 2006).

Bopp, K. R., 'Bank of France Policy, 1800–1914', *The American Journal of Economics and Sociology*, 11 (1952) 229–244.

Bordo, M. D., Schwartz, A. J. (eds.), *A Retrospective on the Classical Gold Standard 1821–1931* (Chicago: University of Chicago Press, 1984).

Borio, C., McCauley, R. N., McGuire, P., Sushko, V., 'Covered Interest Rate Parity Lost', *BIS Quarterly Review* (September 2016).

Bright, J., Rogers, J. E. T. (eds.), *Speeches on Questions of Public Policy by Richard Cobden, M.P.*, II (London: T. Fisher Unwin, 1908).

Broadberry, S., Chadha, J., Lennard, J., Thomas, R., 'Dating Business Cycles in the United Kingdom, 1700–2010' *Working paper ESCoE DP*, 16 (2022).

Broadberry, S., Wallis J., 'Growing, Shrinking and Long Run Economic Performance: Historical Perspectives on Economic Development', *CAGE Working Paper Series*, 323 (CAGE, 2017).

Broughton, J. M., *The Silent Revolution: The IMF 1979–1989* (IMF, 2001).

Brown, L., *The Board of Trade and the Free-Trade Movement 1830–42* (Oxford: OUP, 1958).

Burnside, C., Eichenbaum, M., Kleshchelski, I., Rebelo, S., 'Do Peso Problems Explain the Carry Trade?', *The Review of Financial Studies* (2011) 853–891.

Burnside, C., Eichenbaum, M., Kleshchelski, I., Rebelo, S., 'The Returns to Currency Speculation', *NBER Working Paper* 12489 (2006).

Button, R., Knott, S., Macmanus, C., Willison, M., 'Desperate Adventurers and Men of Straw: The Failure of City of Glasgow Bank and its Enduring Impact on the UK Banking System', *Bank of England Quarterly Bulletin 2015 Q1* (2015) 23–35.

Calomiris, C. W., Schweickart, L., 'The Panic of 1857: Origins, Transmission, and Containment', *Journal of Economic History*, 51 (1991) 807–834.

Capie, F. H., *Capital Controls* (London: IEA, 2002).

Capie, F. H., Billings, M., 'Profitability in English Banking in the Twentieth Century', *European Review of Economic History*, 5 (December 2001) 367–401.

Capie, F. H., *The Bank of England: 1950s to 1979* (Cambridge: CUP, 2010).

Castelli, C., *The Theory of "Options" in Stocks and Shares* (London: Mathieson, 1877).

Catão, L. A., Solomou, S. N., 'Effective Exchange Rates and the Classical Gold Standard Adjustment', *American Economic Review*, 95 (2005) 1259–1275.

Cesa-Bianchi, A., Eguren Martin, F., Thwaites, G., 'Foreign Booms, Domestic Busts: The Global Dimension of Banking Crises', *Bank of England Working Paper*, 644 (2017).

Chalmers, R., *A History of Currency in the British Colonies* (Colchester: John Drury, 1972).

Chambers, D., 'Review: Harold James, *Making a Modern Central Bank: The Bank of England 1979–2003* (Cambridge: Cambridge University Press, 2020)', *Economic History Review*, 74 (2021) 1122–1123.

Chodes, J., 'Richard Cobden: Creator of the Free Market', in Folsom, B. W. (ed.), *The Industrial Revolution and Free Trade* (Irvington-on-Hudson, NY: Foundation for Economic Education, 1996) 34–42.

Chorafas, D. N., *The Changing Role of Central Banks* (New York: Palgrave Macmillan, 2013).

Chubb, H., 'The Bank Act and the Crisis of 1866', *Journal of the Statistical Society*, 35 Pt. 2 (1872) 171–195.

Chuffart, T., Dell'Eva, C., 'Did Carry Trades Hamper Quantitative Easing Effectiveness in Japan?' *International Symposium on Money, Banking and Finance*, Paper (France, 2018).

Clapham, J., *The Bank of England*, II (Cambridge: CUP, 1970).

Clare, G., *A Money-Market Primer and Key to the Exchanges* (London: Effingham Wilson, 1900).

Clare, G., *The ABC of the Foreign Exchanges* (London: Macmillan, 1911).

Coffey, N., Hrung, W., Nguyen, H., Sakar, A., 'Capital Constraints, Counterparty Risk and Deviations from the Covered Interest Rate Parity', *Federal Reserve Bank of New York Staff Report* no. 393 (2009).

Cohen, J., et al. (eds.), *Karl Marx, Frederick Engels: Collected Works*, 10 (London: Lawrence & Wishart, 2010).

Cookson, J. E., *Lord Liverpool's Administration: The Crucial Years 1815–1822* (Edinburgh: Scottish Academic Press, 1975).

Cord, R. A. (ed.), *The Palgrave Companion to LSE Economics* (London: Palgrave Macmillan, 2018).

Cottrell, P. L., *Investment Banking in England 1856–1881*, I (Abingdon: Routledge, 2012).

Crafts, N. F. R., *Forging Ahead, Falling Behind and Fighting Back: British Economic Growth from the Industrial Revolution to the Financial Crisis* (Cambridge: CUP, 2018).

Crafts, N. F. R., 'Victorian Britain Did Fail', *Economic History Review*, 32 (1979) 533–537.

Craig, R., *Canada's National Policy 1883–1900: A Study in Canadian-American Relations* (Princeton, NJ: Princeton University Press, 1964).

Cramp, A. B., 'Horsley Palmer on Bank Rate', *Economica*, 26 ns (1959) 341–349.

Daugherty, M. R., 'The Currency-Banking Controversy: Pt. 1', *Southern Economic Journal*, 9 (1942).

Daunton, M., *Trusting Leviathan, The Politics of Taxation in Britain, 1799–1914* (Cambridge: CUP, 2001).

Dawes, M., Ward-Perkins, C. N., *Country Banks of England and Wales* (Canterbury: Chartered Institute of Bankers, 2000).

Dawson, F. G., *The First Latin American Debt Crisis: The City of London and the 1822–25 Loan Bubble* (New Haven: Yale University Press, 1990).

Deane, M., Pringle, R., *The Central Banks* (London: Hamish Hamilton, 1994).

de Bromhead, A., Eichengreen, B., O'Rourke, K. H., 'Political Extremism in the 1920s and 1930s: Do German Lessons Generalize?', *Journal of Economic History*, 73 (2012) 371–406.

Debrun, X., Hauner, D., and Kumar, M., 'Independent Fiscal Agencies', *Journal of Economic Surveys*, 23 (2009) 44–81.

Devereux, M. B., Smith, G. W., 'Transfer Problem Dynamics: Macroeconomics of the Franco-Prussian War Indemnity', *Queen's University Working Paper*, 1025 (2005).

Dimsdale N., Hotson, A., *British Financial Crises Since 1825* (Oxford: OUP, 2014).

Di Vittorio, A., *An Economic History of Europe* (Abingdon: Routledge, 2006).

Dornbusch, R., 'Exchange Rate Expectations and Monetary Policy', *Journal of International Economics*, 6 (1976) 231–244.

Dornbusch, R., Frenkel, J. A., 'The Gold Standard and the Bank of England in the Crisis of 1847', in Bordo, M. D., Schwartz, A. J. (eds.), *A Retrospective on the Classical Gold Standard 1821–1931* (Chicago: University of Chicago Press, 1984) 233–276.

Dutt, R. C., *Famines and Land Assessment in India* (London: Kegan Paul, 1900).

Earl Grey (Third), (Anon.), *Thoughts on the Currency* (London: Ridgeway, 1842).

Eastwood, D., '"Recasting Our Lot": Peel the Nation and the Politics of Interest', in Brockliss, L., Eastwood, D. (eds.), *A Union of Multiple Identities: The British Isles c.1750–c.1850* (Manchester: Manchester University Press, 1977) 29–44.

Edwards, S., *The Behaviour of Interest Rates and Real Exchange Rates During a Liberalisation Episode: The Case of Chile 1973–83, NBER Working Paper*, 1702 (1985).

Eichengreen, B., 'The Baring Crisis in a Mexican Mirror', *International Political Science Review*, 20 (1999) 249–270.

Eichengreen, B., Flandreau, M. (eds.), *The Gold Standard in Theory and History* (London: Routledge, 1997).

Engel, C., 'Exchange Rates, Interest Rates, and the Risk Premium', *American Economic Review*, 106 (2016) 436–74.

Engel, C. 'The Forward Discount Anomaly and the Risk Premium', *Journal of Monetary Economics*, 14 (1984) 123–191.

Erickson, A. B., 'Edward T. Cardwell: Peelite', *Transactions of the American Philosophical Society*, 49 (1959) 1–107.

Evans, D. M., *Facts, Failures and Frauds* (London: Groombridge & Sons., 1854).

Evans, D. M., *The City or the Physiology of London Business* (London: Baily Bros., 1845).

Evans, D. M., *The Commercial Crisis 1847–48* (London: Letts, 1849).

Fama, E. F., 'Forward and Spot Exchange Rates', *Journal of Monetary Economics*, 14 (1984) 319–338.

Ferguson, N., Kornejew, M., Schmelzing, P., Schularick, M., 'Central Bank Balance Sheets and the Macroeconomy 1587–2020' (2022) https://scholar.harvard.edu/pfschmelzing/bio [last accessed 4 July 2022].

Ferguson, N., *The House of Rothschild*, I, *Money's Prophets, 1798–1848* (Harmondsworth: Penguin, 1999).

Fetter, F. W., *Development of British Monetary Orthodoxy 1797–1875* (Cambridge, MA: Harvard University Press, 1965).

Flandreau, M., Ugolini, S., 'The Crisis of 1866', *The Graduate Institute, Geneva, Working Paper* 10/2014 (2014).

Fleming, J. M., 'Domestic Financial Policies Under Fixed and Under Floating Exchange Rates', *IMF Staff Papers*, 9 (1962) 369–379.

Flores, J-H., 'A Microeconomic Analysis of the Baring Crisis 1880–90', *Berkeley University Working Paper* (2006).

Fowler, W., *The Crisis of 1866, a Financial Essay* (London: Longman, 1866).

Frankel, J., 'Getting Carried Away: How the Carry Trade and Its Potential Unwinding Can Explain Movements in International Financial Markets', *Milken Institute Review*, 10 (2007).

Frenkel, J. A., 'A Monetary Approach to the Exchange Rate: Doctrinal Aspects and Empirical Evidence', *The Scandinavian Journal of Economics*, 78 (1976) 200–224.

Fullarton, J., *On the Regulation of Currencies* (London: John Murray, 1844).

Funke, M., Schularick, M., Trebesch C., 'Going to Extremes: Politics after Financial Crises, 1870–2014', *CEPR Discussion Paper* no. DP10884 (2015).

Garrison R. W., 'The Austrian Theory of the business cycle', in Glasner, D., *Business Depressions* (New York, Garland, 1997) 23–27.

Gash, N., *Aristocracy and People: Britain 1815–1865* (Cambridge, MA: Harvard University Press, 1979).

Gash, N., *Lord Liverpool* (Cambridge, MA: Harvard University Press, 1984).

Gash, N., *Sir Robert Peel: The Life of Sir Robert Peel after 1830* (London: Longman, 1972).

Gaunt, R. A., *Sir Robert Peel: The Life and Legacy* (London: I. B. Tauris & Co., 2010).

Gayer, A. D., Rostow, W. W., Schwartz, A. J., *The Growth and Fluctuation of the British Economy 1790–1850* (Sussex: Harvester Press, 1975).

Geoghegan, P. M., *Liberator: The Life and Death of Daniel O'Connell 1830–1847* (Dublin: Gill & Macmillan, 2010).

Ghosh, P., 'Gladstone and Peel', in Ghosh, P., Goldman, L. (eds.), *Politics and Culture in Victorian Britain: Essays in Memory of Colin Matthew* (Oxford: OUP, 2006).

Giffen, R., *Stock Exchange Securities* (London: George Bell & Sons, 1879).

Gilbart, J. W., 'On the Laws of the Currency in Ireland', *Journal of the Statistical Society of London*, 15 (1852) 307–326.

Gilbart, J. W., *History and Principles of Banking* (London: George Bell and Sons, 1905).

Gilbart, J., *An Inquiry into the Causes of the Pressure on the Money Market During the Year 1839* (London: Longman, 1830).

Gille, B., *La banque et le crédit en France de 1815 à 1848* (Paris: Presses Universitaires de France, 1959).

Goodhart, C., Jensen, M., 'Currency School Versus Banking School: An Ongoing Confrontation', *Economic Thought*, 4 (2015) 20–31.

Gorton, G., Tallman, E. W., 'Too Big to Fail Before the Fed', *American Economic Review*, 106 (2016) 528–532.

Goschen, G. J., *The Theory of the Foreign Exchanges* (London: Effingham Wilson, 1861).

Grant, J., *Bagehot: The Life and Times of the Greatest Victorian* (New York: Norton, 2019).

Gray, P., *The Making of the Irish Poor Law 1815–43* (Manchester: Manchester University Press, 2009).

Grønn, A., Fredholm, M. W., 'Baltic and Icelandic Experiences of Capital Flows and Capital Flow Measures', *IMF Working Paper*, 13/242 (IMF, 2013).

Guinnane, T. W., Ó Gráda, C., 'The Workhouses', in Dyson, T., Ó Gráda, C. (eds.), *Famine Demography* (Oxford: OUP, 2002).

Hacche, G., Taylor, C. (eds.), *Inside the Bank of England: Memoirs of Christopher Dow, Chief Economist 1973–84* (Basingstoke: Palgrave Macmillan, 2013).

Hall, F. G., *History of the Bank of Ireland* (Dublin: Hodges, Figgis & Co., 1949).

Hankey, T., *Principles of Banking, Its Utility and Economy: With Remarks on the Working and Management of the Bank of England* (London: Effingham Wilson, 1867).

Hannan, S. A., 'The Drivers of Capital Flows in Emerging Markets Post Global Financial Crisis', *IMF Working Paper* WP/17/52 (2017).

Harley, C. K., 'The Classical Gold Standard's Adjustment to Shocks: American Railroads and British Investment in the 1880s', in Reis, J. (ed.), *International Monetary Systems in Historical Perspective* (London: Palgrave Macmillan, 1995) 23–46.

Hattori, M., Shin, H.-S., 'Yen Carry Trade and the Subprime Crisis', *IMF Staff Papers* 56 (2009) 384–409.
Hawkins, A., *The Forgotten Prime Minister: The 14th Earl of Derby*, I (Oxford: OUP, 2007).
Hawtrey, R. G., *A Century of Bank Rate* (London: Frank Cass & Co., 1968).
Hawtrey, R. G., *The Art of Central Banking* (London: Frank Cass & Co., 1962).
Herger, N., 'Interest-rate Parity Conditions During the Era of the Classical Gold Standard', *Swiss Journal of Economics and Statistics*, 154 (2018).
Herndon, T., 'Liar's Loans, Mortgage Fraud, and the Great Recession', *Review of Political Economy*, 31 (2019) 479–508.
Higgins, L., *The Put-and-Call* (London: Effingham Wilson, 1906).
Hilt, E., 'Wall Street's First Corporate Governance Crisis: The Panic of 1826', *NBER Working Paper*, 14892.
Hilton, B., *Corn, Cash, Commerce: The Economics Policies of the Tory Governments 1815–1830* (Oxford: OUP, 1977).
Hilton, B., *Mad, Bad and Dangerous People?* (Oxford: OUP, 2008).
Hilton, B., 'Peel: A Reappraisal', *Historical Journal*, 22 (1979) 585–614.
Hilton, B., 'The Ripening of Robert Peel', in Bentley, M. (ed.), *Public and Private Doctrine: Essays in British History presented to Maurice Cowling* (Cambridge: CUP, 1993) 63–84.
Hobsbawm, E. J., Wrigley, C., *Industry and Empire: From 1750 to the Present Day* (New York: The New Press, 1999).
Homer, S., Sylla, R., *A History of Interest Rates* (Hoboken, NJ: Wiley, 2005).
Hotson, A., *Respectable Banking: The Search for Stability in London's Money and Credit Markets Since 1695* (Cambridge: CUP, 2017).
Howe, A., *Free Trade and Liberal England 1846–1946* (Oxford: OUP).
Huffman, W. E., Lothian, J. R., 'The Transmission of Business Cycles', in Bordo, M., D. Schwartz, A. J. (eds.), *A Retrospective on the Classical Gold Standard 1821–1931* (Chicago: University of Chicago Press, 1984) 455–512.
Hughes, J. R. T., 'The Commercial Crisis of 1857', *Oxford Economic Papers*, 8:2 (1956) 194–222.
Huskisson, W., *Speeches of the Right Honourable William Huskisson* (London: John Murray, 1831).
Hyndman, H. M., *Commercial Crises* (London: Swan & Co., 1908).
Iacoviello, M., Navarro, G., 'Foreign Effects of Higher Interest Rates', *Federal Reserve System International Finance Discussion Papers* no. 1227 (2018).
IMF Policy Development and Review Department, *Lessons from the Crisis in Argentina* (IMF, 2003).
Imlah, A., *Economic Elements in the Pax Britannica* (Cambridge, MA: Harvard University Press, 1958).
Irwin, D., 'Political Economy and Peel's repeal of the Corn Laws', *Economics and Politics*, I (1989).

James, H., *International Monetary Cooperation Since Bretton Woods* (Washington, DC: International Monetary Fund, and New York: OUP, 1996).

James, H., *Making a Modern Central Bank: The Bank of England 1979–2003* (Cambridge: CUP, 2020).

James, H., *The Creation and Destruction of Value: The Globalization Cycle* (London: Harvard University Press, 2009).

Jenkinson, R. B., Earl of Liverpool, *A Few Observations for the Consideration of the Farmers of Great Britain ... By an Agriculturist* (High Wycombe: J. W. Burnham, 1826).

Jevons, W. S., *A Serious Fall in the Value of Gold Ascertained* (London: Stanford, 1863).

Jevons, W. S., 'On the Frequent Autumnal Pressure in the Money Market and the Action of the Bank of England', *Journal of the Statistical Society of London*, 29 (1866).

John, D., 'The Return of Carry', *IPE Magazine*, January (2018).

Jones, W. D., *Prosperity Robinson: The Life of Viscount Goderich 1782–1859* (London: Macmillan, 1967).

Joplin, T., *An Analysis and History of the Currency Question* (London: Ridgway, 1832).

Joplin, T., 'Mr. Joplin's Circular to the Joint Stock Banks', *Hume Tracts*, 1840.

Jourdan, F., 'The Effect of the Gold Supplies on the Foreign Exchanges Between the United Kingdom and Foreign Countries, and on the Price of Silver', *Journal of the Statistical Society of London*, 24 (1861).

Juglar, C., *Les crises commercial et leur retour périodique en France, en Angleterre et aux Etats-Unis* (Paris: Guillaumin, 1889).

Kaminsky, G. L., 'The Centre and the Periphery: Two Hundred Years of International Borrowing Cycles', *Banco de España seminas* (2018).

Keynes, J. M., *The Collected Writings of John Maynard Keynes* [1930] (Cambridge: CUP, 2013).

Kindleberger, C. P., *A Financial History of Western Europe* (Abingdon: Routledge, 2015).

Kindleberger, C. P., *Keynesianism vs. Monetarism* (Abingdon: Taylor and Francis, 1985).

Kipling, R., *Kim* (London: Macmillan, 1901).

Kitson, M., 'End of an Epoch: Britain's Withdrawal from the Gold Standard' (2012) https://michaelkitson.files.wordpress.com/2013/02/kitson-gold-standard-june-2012.pdf [last accessed 1 June 2022].

Kneer, C., Raabe, A., 'Tracking Foreign Capital: The Effect of Capital Inflows on Bank Lending in the UK', *Bank of England Staff Working Paper* no. 804 (2019).

Kuznets, S., 'Review of Shumpeter's Business Cycles', *American Economic Review*, 30 (1940) 257–271.

Kynaston, D., *The City of London* (London: Pimlico, 1994–95).

Kynaston, D., *Till Time's Last Stand: A History of the Bank of England 1694–2013* (London: Bloomsbury, 2013).

Lahiri A., Végh, C. A., 'Output Costs, Currency Crises and Interest Rate Defence of a Peg', *The Economic Journal*, 117 (2007) 216–239.

Laidler, D., 'Two Views of the Lender of Last Resort: Thornton and Bagehot', *Papers in Political Economy*, 45 (2003) 61–78.

Lee, T., Lee, J., Coldiron, K., *The Rise of Carry: The Dangerous Consequences of Volatility Suppression and the New Financial Order of Decaying Growth and Recurring Crisis* (New York: McGraw-Hill, 2020).

Liesse, A., *Evolution of Credit and Banks in France* (Washington: National Monetary Commission, 1909).

Lindley, D. N., *The Collected Works of John Stuart Mill*, XV–Part II (London: Routledge and Kegan Paul, 1972).

Lothian, J. R., Wu, L., 'Uncovered Interest Rate Parity Over the Past Two Centuries', *Journal of International Money and Finance*, 30 (2011) 448–473.

Loveday, A., *The History & Economics of Indian Famines* (London: G. Bell and Sons, 1914).

Loyd S. J., (Lord Overstone) *Remarks on the Management of the Circulation* (London: P. Richardson, 1840).

Loyd, S. J., (Lord Overstone) *Tracts and Other Publications* (London: Longman, 1858).

Lyons, J. S., Cain, L.P., Williamson, S. H. (eds.), *Reflections on the Cliometrics Revolution* (Abingdon: Routledge, 2008).

Ma, Y., Zijlstra, W., 'A New Take on Low Interest Rates and Risk Taking' *VOX, CEPR Policy Portal*, 7 March (2018).

MacDonald, R., Nagayasu, J., 'Currency Forecast Errors and Carry Trades at Times of Low Interest Rates: Evidence From Survey Data on the Yen/Dollar Exchange Rate', *Journal of International Money and Finance*, 53C (2015) 1–19.

Madeleine, M. G., *Monetary and Banking Theories of Jacksonian Democracy* (Philadelphia: Immaculata College, 1943).

Mandler, P., *Aristocratic Government in the Age of Reform: Whig and Liberal 1830–52* (Oxford: OUP, 1990).

Marshall, A., *Official Papers of Alfred Marshall*, Keynes, J. M. (ed.), (London: Macmillan, 1926).

Marshall, A., *Principles of Economics* (London: Macmillan, 1890).

Marx, K., Engels, F., Isaac, J. C. (eds.), *The Communist Manifesto* (New Haven: Yale University Press, 2012).

Matthew, H. C. G., 'Disraeli, Gladstone, and the Politics of Mid-Victorian Budgets', *Historical Journal*, 22 (1979) 615–643.

Matthew, H. C. G., *Gladstone, 1809–1874* (Oxford: Clarendon Press, 1988).

Matthews, R. C. O., *A Study in Trade Cycle History: Economic Fluctuations in Great Britain 1833–42* (Cambridge: CUP, 1954).
McCallum, B. T., 'A Reconsideration of the Uncovered Interest Parity Relationship', *Journal of Monetary Economics*, 33 (1994) 105–132.
McGrane, R. C., *The Panic of 1837* (Chicago: Chicago University Press, 1924).
Metrick, A., Schmelzing, P., 'Banking-Crisis Interventions, 1257–2019', *NBER Working Paper* 29281 (2021).
Meyer, W. S. et al., *Imperial Gazetteer of India* III (Oxford: Clarendon Press, 1908).
Michie, R. C., *British Banking: Continuity and Change from 1694 to the Present* (Oxford: OUP, 2016).
Mishra, H. K., *Famines and Poverty in India* (New Delhi: APH, 1991).
Mitchell, B. R., *British Historical Statistics* (Cambridge: CUP, 1988).
Moore, R. J., *Sir Charles Wood's Indian Policy, 1853–66* (Manchester: Manchester University Press, 1966).
Morley, J., *The Life of William Ewart Gladstone* (Cambridge: CUP, 2011).
Moss, D. J., 'Circular to Bankers', *Victorian Periodicals Review*, 25 (1992).
Mullineux, A. W., *Business Cycles and Financial Crises* (Ann Arbor, MI: University of Michigan Press, 1990).
Mundell, R. A., 'A Theory of Optimum Currency Areas', *American Economic Review*, 5 (1961) 657–665.
Narsey, W., *British Imperialism and the Making of Colonial Currency Systems* (Basingstoke: Palgrave Macmillan, 2016).
Neal, L., 'The Financial Crisis of 1825 and the Restructuring of the British Financial System', *Federal Reserve Bank of St. Louis Review*, 80 (1998) 53–76.
Neal, L., *The Rise of Financial Capitalism* (Cambridge: CUP, 1990).
Needham, D., 'The Story of the Secondary Banking Crisis 1973–75', *The Property Chronicle*, 9 June 2020.
Needham, D., *UK Monetary Policy from Devaluation to Thatcher 1967–82*, (Basingstoke: Palgrave Macmillan, 2014).
Nelson, S. A., *The ABC of Options and Arbitrage* (New York: Nelson, 1904).
North, D., 'The United States Balance of Payments' in *The Conference on Research in Income and Wealth* (Princeton: Princeton University Press, 1960) 573–628.
Northcote, S. H., *Twenty Years of Financial Policy* (London: Saunders, Otley & Co., 1862).
O'Brien, D. P. (ed.), *The Correspondence of Lord Overstone*, I–III (Cambridge, CUP, 1971).
Ó Gráda, C., 'Should the Munster Bank Have Been Saved?' *UCD Centre for Economic Research Working Paper Series* WP01/15, 2001, 1–33.
Ó Gráda, C., *The Great Irish Famine* (Cambridge: CUP, 1997).
O'Neill Daunt, W. J., *Ireland and her Agitators* (Dublin: J. Browne, 1845).

O'Rourke, K. H., 'Did the Great Irish Famine Matter?', *Journal of Economic History*, 51 (1991) 1–22.

Obstfield, M., Taylor, A. M., 'The Great Depression as a Watershed', *NBER Working Paper*, 5960 (1997).

Odlyzk, A., 'Collective Hallucinations and Inefficient Markets: The British Railway Mania of the 1840s', *SSRN* (2010).

Olson, J. S., *Historical Dictionary of the Great Depression, 1929–1940* (United Kingdom: Greenwood Press, 2001).

Palgrave, R. H. I., *Bank Rate and the Money Market in England, France, Germany, Holland, and Belgium, 1844–1900* (London: John Murray, 1903 and New York: Dutton & Co., 1903).

Palmer, J. H., *The Causes and Consequences of the Pressure upon the Money Market* (London: Pelham Richardson, 1837).

Patnaik, G., *The Famine and Some Aspects of the British Economic Policy in Orissa 1866–1905* (Cuttack: Vidyapur, 1980).

Patron, M., *The Bank of France in Its Relation to National and International Credit* (Washington: Government Printing Office, 1910).

Patterson, R. H., 'On Our Home Monetary Drains, and the Crisis of 1866', *Journal of the Statistical Society of London*, 33 (1870) 216–242.

Patterson, R. H., 'On the Rate of Interest', *Journal of the Statistical Society of London*, 34 (1871).

Peel, R., *Memoirs by the Right Honourable Sir Robert Peel*, II/III, Earl Stanhope, Cardwell, E. (eds.), (London: John Murray, 1856–7).

Peel, R., *Speeches of the late Sir Robert Peel, Bart.*, IV 1842–50 (London: Routledge, 1853).

Peel, R., *Tamworth Election: Speech of Sir Robert Peel, June 28, 1841* (London: John Ollivier, 1841).

Phillips, C. A., *Bank Credit: A Study of the Principles and Factors Underlying Advances Made by Banks to Borrowers* (New York: Macmillan, 1924).

Pilbeam, P., 'The Economic Crisis of 1827–32 and the 1830 Revolution in Provincial France', *Historical Journal*, 32 (1989) 319–338.

Pownall, G. H., 'Bank Reserves', *The Economic Journal*, 9 (1899) 394–410.

Price, B., *Chapters on Practical Political Economy* (London: Kegan Paul, 1878).

Price, B., *Currency and Banking* (New York: Appleton, 1876).

Quinn, W., Turner, J. D., *Boom and Bust: A Global History of Financial Bubbles* (Cambridge: CUP, 2020).

Read, C., 'British Economic Policy and Ireland, c.1841–53', University of Cambridge, unpublished PhD thesis (2016).

Read, C., 'Laissez-faire, the Irish Famine, and British Financial Crisis', *Economic History Review*, 69 (2016) 411–434.

Read, C., 'Peel, De Grey and Irish Policy 1841–44', *History*, 99 (2014) 1–18.

Read, C., 'Taxes, Tariffs and the Economics of Nationalism in 1840s Ireland', in Kanter, D., Walsh, P. (eds.), *Taxation, Politics, and Protest in Ireland, 1692–2016* (London: Palgrave Macmillan, 2019).

Read, C., *The Great Famine in Ireland and Britain's Financial Crisis* (Woodbridge: The Boydell Press, 2022).

Read, C., 'The Irish Famine and Unusual Market Behaviour in Cork', *Irish Economic and Social History*, 44:1 (2017) 3–18.

Read, C., 'The Political Economy of Sir Robert Peel', in Hoppit, J., Leonard, A. B., Needham, D. J. (eds.), *Money and Markets: Essays in Honour of Martin Daunton* (Woodbridge: The Boydell Press, 2019).

Read, C., 'The Repeal Year in Ireland: An Economic Reassessment', *Historical Journal*, 58:1 (2015) 111–135.

Reed, M., 'Loyd, Samuel Jones, Baron Overstone (1796–1883)', *Oxford Dictionary of National Biography*, OUP, 2004; online edn.

Reeves, J., *The Rothschilds* (Chicago: McClueg & Co, 1887).

Reid, M., *The Secondary Banking Crisis, 1973–75: The Inside Story of Britain's Biggest Banking Upheaval* (London: Hindsight Books, 2003).

Reinhart, C. M., Rogoff, K. S., *This Time is Different* (Princeton, NJ: Princeton University Press, 2009).

Reisman, D., *Alfred Marshall's Mission* (London: Palgrave Macmillan, 1990).

Rey, H., 'Dilemma not Trilemma', *NBER Working Paper*, 21162 (2018).

Ricardo, D., *Plan for the Establishment of a National Bank* (London: John Murray, 1834).

Ricardo, D., *The Works and Correspondence of David Ricardo*, I, [1817 edition] (Cambridge: CUP, 1951).

Riddick, J. F., *The History of British India* (Santa Barbara CA: Greenwood, 2006).

Robson, J. M. (ed.), *Collected Works of John Stuart Mill*, XXI (Toronto: University of Toronto Press, 1984).

Rockoff, H., 'On the Origins of "A Monetary History"' *NBER Working Paper* 12666 (2006) 1–60.

Santayana, G., *The Life of Reason: Reason in Common Sense*, 1 (Cambridge, MA: MIT Press, 2011).

Sampson, M. B., *Slavery in the United States* (London: S. Highley, 1845).

Sampson, M. B., *The Currency under the Act of 1844... from the "City" Articles of The Times* (London: John Van Noorst, 1858).

Sayers, R. S., *Modern Banking* (Oxford: OUP, 1938).

Sayers, R. S., 'The Development of Central Banking after Bagehot', *Economic History Review*, 4 (1951) 109–116.

Schenk, C. R., 'Summer in the City', *English Historical Review*, 129 (2014) 1129–1156.

Scherer, P., *Lord John Russell: A Biography* (London: Associated University Presses, 1999).
Schmelzing, P., 'Eight Centuries of Global Real Rates, R-G, and the "Suprasecular" Decline, 1311–2018', *Bank of England Staff Working Paper* no. 845 (2020).
Schneider, S., 'The Politics of Last Resort Lending and the Overend & Gurney Crisis of 1866', *Economic History Review*, 75 (2022) 579–600.
Schumpeter, J. A., *Business Cycles*, I (London: McGraw-Hill, 1939).
Scribe, A. E., Delavigne, G., *Robert-le-Diable, an Opera in Five Acts: With an Easy Translation, Line for Line with the French* (London: H.N. Millar, 1847).
Shannon, H. A., 'The First Five Thousand Limited Companies and their Duration', *Economic History*, 3 (1932).
Shannon, R., *Gladstone: Heroic Minister 1865–1898* (London: Allen Lane, 1999).
Sharp, P., '1846 and All That', *University of Copenhagen Department of Economics Discussion Paper*, 06–16 (2010).
Sinclair, D., *The Land That Never Was: Sir Gregor MacGregor and the Most Audacious Fraud in History* (Cambridge, MA: Da Capo Press, 2004).
Smith, A., 'Wealth of Nations', in Glasgow Edition of the *Works of Adam Smith* (Oxford: OUP, 1976).
Smith, A., *Wealth of Nations* (Oxford: OUP, 1993).
Smith, M., *Thomas Tooke and the Monetary Thought of Classical Economics* (Abingdon: Routledge, 2011).
Solomou, S. N., *Economic Cycles: Long Cycles and Business Cycles Since 1870* (Manchester: Manchester University Press, 1998).
Solomou, S. N., *Themes in Macroeconomic History: The UK Economy 1919–1939* (Cambridge: CUP, 1996).
Sowerbutts, R., Schneebalg, M., Hubert, F., 'The Demise of Overend Gurney', *Bank of England Quarterly Bulletin 2016 Q2* (2016) 94–106.
Spinner, T. J., *George Joachim Goschen* (Cambridge: CUP, 1973).
Stanhope, E., *East Indian Finance, Speech of the Hon. Edward Stanhope, M.P., (Under Secretary of State for India) on the Financial Statement (India) in the House of Commons, 22 May 1879* (London: Cornelius Buck, 1879).
Steele, D., 'Baring, Francis Thornhill, first Baron Northbrook (1796–1866)', *Oxford Dictionary of National Biography*, OUP, 2004, online edn., Jan 2008.
Stewart, I., *In Pursuit of the unknown* (New York: Basic Books, 2012).
Stewart, R., *The Politics of Protectionism: Lord Derby and the Protectionist Party 1841–52* (Cambridge: CUP, 1971).
Strangeways, T., 'The Poyais Bubble', *Quarterly Review*, XXVIII (London: John Murray, 1823) 158–61.
Stukenbrock, K., *The Stability of Currency Boards* (Peter Lang, AG, 2004).

Taylor, J., 'Financial Crises and the Birth of the Financial Press 1825-80', in Schifferes, S., Roberts, R. (eds.), *The Media and Financial Crises* (Abingdon: Routledge, 2015) 203–214.

Taylor, J., 'Watchdogs or Apologists? Financial Journalism and Company Fraud in Early Victorian Britain', *Historical Research*, 85 (2012) 632–650.

Taylor, M., 'The 1848 Revolutions and the British Empire', *Past & Present*, 166 (2000) 146–180.

Thornton, H., *An Enquiry into the Nature and Effects of the Paper Credit of Great Britain* [1802 edition] (New York: Kelley, 1965).

Tomlinson, J., *Problems of British Economic Policy, 1870–1945* (Abingdon: Routledge, 2006).

Tooke, T., *A History of Prices and of the State of the Circulation* (London: Longman, 1838).

Tooke, T., Newmarch, W., *History of Prices*, VI (London: Longman, 1857).

Tooke, T., *On the Bank Charter Act of 1844* (London: Longman, 1856).

Torrens, R., *A Letter to Thomas Tooke* (London: Longman, 1840).

Trevelyan, C. E., *The Irish Crisis* (London: Longman, 1848).

Trevelyan, L., *A Very British Family: The Trevelyans and their World* (London: I.B. Tauris, 2012).

Turnbull, S. M., Crouhy, M., Jarrow, R. A., 'The Subprime Credit Crisis of 07', *SSRN*, 1112467 (2008).

Turner, J. D., *Banking in Crisis* (Cambridge: CUP, 2014).

Ugolini, S., 'The Origins of Foreign Exchange Policy: The National Bank of Belgium', *European Review of Economic History*, 16 (2012).

Van Oss, S. F., *American Railroads and British Investors* (London: Effingham Wilson, 1893).

Vergnhanini, R., di Conti, B., 'Modern Monetary Theory: A Criticism from the Periphery', *Brazilian Keynesian Review*, 3 (2017) 16–31.

Vincent, J. R. (ed.), *Disraeli, Derby and the Conservative Party: The Political Journals of Edward Henry, Lord Stanley 1849–69* (Hassocks: Harvester Press, 1978).

Viner, J., *Studies in the Theory of International Trade* [1937] (New York: Harper, 1965).

Wade, J., *The Black Book, or Corruption Unmasked!* (London: Effingham Wilson, 1820–1823).

Wallis, J. J., 'What Caused the Crisis of 1839?' *NBER Historical Paper* 133 (2001).

Ward-Perkins, C. N., 'Review', *Economica*, 16 (1949) 386.

Ward-Perkins, C. N., 'The Commercial Crisis 1847', *Oxford Economic Papers*, 2 (1950) 75–94.

Weintraub, C., Schuler, K., 'India's Paper Currency Department 1862–1935 as a quasi-Currency Board', *John Hopkins Institute: Studies in Applied Economics*, 9 (2013).

White, E. N., 'How to Prevent a Banking Panic', *Economic History Association Paper* (2016).

White, E. N., 'The Crash of 1882 and the Bailout of the Paris Bourse', *Cliometrica*, 1 (2007) 115–144.

Wicker, E., *Banking Panics of the Gilded Age* (Cambridge: CUP, 2000).

Williams, D., *The Rebecca Riots: A Study in Agrarian Discontent* (Cardiff: University of Wales Press, 1955).

Williams, F., *Ernest Bevin* (London: Hutchinson, 1952).

Williams, T. H., 'Observations on Money Credit and Panics', [1858] in Ashton, T. H. (ed.) , *Economic and Social Investigations in Manchester, 1833–1933* (London: King and Son, 1932).

Williamson, S., Wright, R., 'New Monetarist Economics: Models', *Federal Reserve Bank of Minneapolis Research Department Staff Report*, 443 (2010).

Wilson, J., *Capital, Currency and Banking* (London: The Economist, 1847).

Wilson, J., *Speech of the Right Hon James Wilson* (London: Allen & Co., 1860).

Wood, G. H., *History of Wages in the Cotton Trade* (London: Sherratt & Hughes, 1910).

Woodland, J., *Money Pits: British Mining Companies in the Californian Gold Rushes of the 1850s* (Farnham: Ashgate, 2014).

Xu, C., 'Reshaping Global Trade: The Immediate and Long-run Effects of Bank Failures', *Harvard University Working Paper* (2019).

Xu, C., 'Reshaping Global Trade: The Immediate and Long-run Effects of Bank Failures' *Stanford University Working Paper* (March 2022). https://chenzi-xu.com/docs/reshaping_global_trade_Xu.pdf [accessed 27 May 2022].

Index

C. Read, *Calming the Storms*, Palgrave Studies in Economic History,
https://doi.org/10.1007/978-3-031-11914-9

G

J

K

L

M

The manufacturer's authorised representative in the EU is Springer Nature Customer Service Centre GmbH, Europaplatz 3, 69115 Heidelberg, Germany. If you have any concerns regarding our products, please contact ProductSafety@springernature.com

Printed and bound by CPI Group (UK) Ltd, Croydon, CR0 4YY
28/09/2026
02224060-0002